W9-AUV-485

A 21ST CENTURY

ETHICAL TOOLBOX

Anthony Weston

New York   Oxford
OXFORD UNIVERSITY PRESS
2001

Oxford University Press

Oxford   New York
Athens   Auckland   Bangkok   Bogotá   Buenos Aires   Calcutta
Cape Town   Chennai   Dar es Salaam   Delhi   Florence   Hong Kong   Istanbul
Karachi   Kuala Lumpur   Madrid   Melbourne   Mexico City   Mumbai
Nairobi   Paris   São Paulo   Shanghai   Singapore   Taipei   Tokyo   Toronto   Warsaw

and associated companies in
Berlin   Ibadan

Copyright © 2001 by Oxford University Press, Inc.

Published by Oxford University Press, Inc.
198 Madison Avenue, New York, New York, 10016
http://www.oup-usa.org

Oxford is a registered trademark of Oxford University Press

All rights reserved. No part of this publication may be reproduced,
stored in a retrieval system, or transmitted, in any form or by any means,
electronic, mechanical, photocopying, recording, or otherwise,
without the prior permission of Oxford University Press.

Library of Congress Cataloging-in-Publication Data

Weston, Anthony, 1954–
    A 21st century ethical toolbox / Anthony Weston.
        p.   cm.
    Includes bibliographical references and index.
    ISBN 0-19-513040-5 (pbk. : alk. paper)
    1. Ethics.   2. Applied ethics.   I. Title: Twenty-first century ethical toolbox.   II. Title.
BJ1012.W447   2000
170—dc21   00-036327

Printing (last digit): 9 8 7 6 5 4 3 2 1

Printed in the United States of America
on acid-free paper

CONTENTS

◇

PREFACE

◇

A 21st Century Ethical Toolbox is a textbook for a first college ethics or applied ethics class, with applications in any class that ventures into practical ethical issues. Like many other texts for the same purpose, this book offers an entire course between its covers, including both a general set of ethical tools and a representative range of contemporary issues. It differs from other available texts, however, in four fundamental ways.

1. Practical skills are its consistent focus. The aim of this book is to enable its users to make a constructive difference, in both word and deed, in problematic ethical situations. Every tool introduced is directly and explicitly in service of that goal. Other skills often thought vital in philosophical ethics, such as theory-building and exegetical skills, also come up, but only in the way that music theory might come up in a singing course. In my view, the first, general-curriculum ethics course is not the best place for them.

2. A much wider range of skills is offered than in the traditional ethics text. Problem-solving creativity, for example, is as crucial to "making a constructive difference" as responsiveness to values and the analytical and critical skills usually featured in ethics texts. Finding the facts, defining key terms, making sure that we judge like cases alike, learning how to "break out of the box" that reduces so many ethical problems to dilemmas between two sharply opposed and supposedly exhaustive options—*all* have their place here. Just learning to talk constructively—knowing how to keep a dialogue from degenerating into a mere debate—is a way of putting ethics in practice in our very talking about ethical issues. A good toolbox needs all of these tools, and more besides.

3. Practical issues are likwise approached with a reconstructive intent. Familiar matters of ethical contention are here, of course: abortion, poverty and welfare, business ethics, animals, the environment, and others. But the reader will find that the familiar arguments pro and con are not the main focus—certainly not the *only* focus—of attention. Often, for instance, it is more helpful to explore practical changes that will give ethical concerns more force in the future, or make a space for better options—to make the hard cases less hard next time around. Even about the various contending arguments we can subtly but profoundly shift the question we ask. Suppose that instead of

trying to figure out which side is right, we ask what *each* side is right *about*. Then we may be able to find some common ground, or at least some creative ways to shift the problem toward matters that we can do something about—together.

4. This text is thoroughly and consistently optimistic. Its working hypothesis is that it is actually possible to make progress on the contentious ethical issues of the day—though we may need to rethink what counts as "progress" along the way. Surely, one side "winning" is not the only possible kind of progress. In fact one side "winning" might be no progress at all. It is one measure of the poverty of our current ethical tools that we have no other real idea of progress. You will find others here.

Teaching with This Book

Ethics so conceived readily lends itself to interactive teaching. Indeed, ethics conceived as a collection of practical skills *requires* interactive teaching. It requires constant in-class practice. There is no other way to learn it.

This book is therefore designed to enable an active and engaged classroom. It had its start in ever-growing sets of readings designed to free up my own classes' time for practice. My aim was, and is, to put most of the necessary discussions in material that can be assigned prior to class and for the most part can be understood by students on their own. Many suggestions for class practice and out-of-class projects are included here also, in the "Exercises and Notes" sections that close each chapter and in the Notes for Teachers that close the book.

Looking to a wide range of practical skills opens up a wide range of experiential and "applied" activities for an ethics class. Just to name a few, my class runs numerous in-class simulations, sponsors workshops on conflict mediation and creativity, helps staff local shelters for the homeless, and conducts a "Council of All Beings" for the college community to conclude our discussion of environmental ethics. These projects and many more are spelled out in the Notes for Teachers. All of them flow naturally from the Toolbox: they carry the essential skills into action. For teachers used to interactive classrooms, I hope that at least some of these suggestions are useful, and of course I would be delighted to hear of others that work for you. For those less familiar with such methods or less confident using them, I hope that this book eases the transition. Indeed, much more than that, I hope that this book helps to make the transition both philosophically and pedagogically *inviting*!

Acknowledgments

More than twenty years of teaching ethics in three different institutions leave me with many debts both large and small. First among these is my debt to my students, who have always taught me much and who have had in return, lately, to suffer through a variety of drafts of this material. I hope it is some compensation that some of their words are here as well. Certainly their feedback has greatly improved (also greatly shortened!) the text.

Among colleagues, I am especially grateful to my collaborators in the Elon College Department of Philosophy—Nim Batchelor, Ann Cahill, Yoram Lubling, and John Sullivan—where for some years we have been moving, each in our own interlacing ways, toward a practical ethics in something like the sense laid out here. Other colleagues far and near have inspired various commissions and omissions: Tom Birch, Amy Halberstadt, Patrick Hill, Bob Jickling, Eva Feder Kittay, Richard MacBride, Betty Morgan, Joey Santorum, Mike Simon, Peter Williams, and J. Christian Wilson, as well as a host of others. Thanks to you all!

At Oxford University Press, Robert B. Miller patiently nurtured this project through a variety of incarnations and allowed it to come to completion in its own good time. I could not ask for a more appreciative and politic editor. Jan Davis prepared the illustrations. Publisher's reviewers for this book include David Boersema, Jack Green Musselman, Richard L. Lipke, Patricia Murphy, and Verna Gehring. Some of these reviewers went far beyond the call of duty to offer suggestions and critical feedback and point me toward useful resources. All were helpful and encouraging in one way or another. Of course, the commissions and omissions that remain are to be laid to me alone.

I also want to thank my children, Anna Ruth and Molly, whose various struggles coming to ethical consciousness are cited here, from time to time, in fondness and in love. I hope in later years they will forgive my speaking of examples that are so cherished and close to home.

Finally, I am grateful to the many users of my little book *A Practical Companion to Ethics* (Oxford University Press, 1997), whose enthusiasm and encouragement have emboldened me to undertake a full-scale textbook in the same spirit.

A.W.
Durham, NC
August, 2000

Welcome to
the Ethical Toolbox

Ethical thinking today seems to be seriously "stuck." Abortion, capital punishment, animal rights—on issue after issue we hear only the extremes. Some people feel that their values are so obviously right that they doubt the other side even *has* any values. Certainly there is little interest in understanding the other side—as if there have to be two and only two views on such questions in the first place.

Yet we are not so stuck in other areas of life. Every public library has rack after rack of books about how to make intelligent choices when it comes to jobs or health or family finance or home decorating. We know how to compromise when necessary and find our ways around practical roadblocks. Product designers are trained in creative problem-solving. Elementary schools even teach peer conflict resolution.

The premise of this book is that we do not need to be so stuck in ethics either. *Especially* not in ethics, where the effects on our own lives and on the lives of others may be profound and permanent.

The aim of this book is therefore to offer you the skills—the tools—to make more creative and constructive thinking possible in ethics as well. You should leave this book better able to understand what is at stake with moral issues, quicker to seek out the factual or conceptual or imaginative resources you need to make progress on them, and better able to contribute constructively, in both word and deed, to the ongoing debate about them. In a word, this book is meant as a contribution to your ethical *intelligence*—recognizing, as psychologists are now telling us, that "intelligence" takes many forms besides the mere recall of facts. A well-rounded and effective person needs them all.

It takes some work—skills usually do. But the rewards are great as well. Besides, it will turn out that we have many of the necessary skills already, though we can improve all of them too. Most of them apply in other areas of life as well. The key thing is to put them to work *in ethics*.

The Ethics of Ethics

Another remarkable thing about our ethical debates today is that they are seldom carried on in an ethical way.

We know that we really ought to listen to other people. We know that we ought not to act out of impatience or anger or indifference or prejudice. We know that we ought to take special care when making decisions that deeply affect not only our own lives but the lives of many others too. This is what ethics itself requires.

Yet nowhere do we fail to do this so flagrantly as in debates about ethical issues. It's a melancholy but familiar story. We *don't* listen; we let prejudice take the place of thinking—so it goes. This is one reason ethical debates are often "stuck" in the first place.

So there are two good reasons to improve our ethical toolbox. One is that we may be able to get certain issues "unstuck." The other is that using these tools is an ethical act itself. Learning to listen, thinking creatively about problems, seeking common ground when we can—putting these and the other tools to use is both practical and *right*.

The Toolbox

The first part of the book—Parts I through V, Chapters 1 through 15—make up the Toolbox proper.

In Part I we are *Getting Started*. Ethics can be, in the first place, a learning experience—the theme of Chapter 1. We need to start by seriously acknowledging that we alone are not likely to have the whole and only truth. We need to be willing to take some time and care to think about moral issues that come up, rather than sticking to our first reaction come what may. And we need to think critically about our own views too, even though we might rather just "agree to disagree" any time difficult issues come up.

Chapter 2 explores the relation between ethics and religion. Religion plays a major role in shaping and sustaining moral values, but we also need to clarify its limits. We need to think for ourselves—indeed we can't avoid it. This turns out to be a biblical lesson too. The patriarch Abraham actually took it upon himself to argue with God—and God not only listened but approved!

Part II turns to *Values*. Chapter 3 offers some guidelines for unpacking moral issues. Chapter 4 gets one step more formal by classifying moral values into three different basic families, which also allows us to identify a variety of different ways that moral values come into conflict.

Traditional ethical theories systematize and extend each of the three families of moral values. In Chapter 5 we examine the three major theoretical traditions in turn, considered more or less by themselves. Each gives us a way of articulating certain kinds of values more deeply; each has its own history and appeal.

But moral values conflict—what then? Chapter 6 offers an overview of theoretical approaches. Some theories propose a common measure by which all moral values can be weighed against each other. Other theories propose to prioritize moral values according to various standards. Each theoretical approach also has its limits, and they tend to be fierce critics of each other too.

We can also approach conflict more practically. When moral values conflict we are often tempted to think that only one side can be right. Usually, though, *both* (all) sides are right about *something*. Instead of trying to decide who's right and who's wrong, then, it is often wiser to ask what *each* side is right *about*. From there we can ask what kind of common ground or (at least) common understanding we might be able to reach. Chapter 7 offers some tools along these lines—tools for "integrating values."

Part III offers some *Tools for Critical Thinking in Ethics*. Many moral disagreements turn on disagreements about the facts. How do we find out the facts? How do we make valid inferences? Chapter 8 offers some guidelines.

Chapter 9 concerns language: how to keep our terms neutral enough that we can see the issue without being swayed by half-conscious overtones; how to specify definitions when terms are unclear; and how to (try to) define a term whose meaning is contested.

Chapter 10's challenge is to "judge like cases alike." Our moral reasons in one case usually bear on many other cases. But if they really are good and sufficient reasons in the one case, they should be equally good and sufficient in any other relevantly similar case. Are they? What if we're not willing to go quite that far? We may need to do some adjusting all around. That is part of what ongoing ethical thinking is all about.

Part IV offers some *Tools for Creativity in Ethics*. Moral debates often get stuck because we can't think of any good options. But are there really no good options? More often than we think, I suggest, the limits really lie in our own imaginations. So we need the tools to imagine other options (Chapter 11). More radically, we can also ask how the whole problem might be *shifted* (Chapter 12) so that we can prevent it from coming up at all in the future, or at least from coming up so often and in so difficult a form. You may discover that ethical creativity can take us a lot farther than we usually think!

In Part V we are *Putting Ethics into Action*. Chapter 13 outlines a way to use the toolbox as a whole when approaching ethical issues. Much depends on our goals in coming to ethics in the first place—for our goals determine the appropriate tools in turn. Exploring an issue calls for one set of tools, making a constructive contribution to an ethical debate calls for another, and actually deciding a question calls for still others. There is specific advice here on writing a paper in ethics as well.

Chapter 14 specifically discusses ethics and/as *dialogue*. This may be puzzling. We all know how to talk already, don't we? Just open your mouth! But we are *not* so good at having a constructive discussion—identifying shared values, brainstorming better possibilities together. Once again, these more collaborative and constructive skills are not so unfamiliar, at least in theory, but we still need a lot of practice putting them to work.

Chapter 15 concerns ethics as *service*. Many schools are just beginning to recognize service as itself a form of learning—as when we speak of "service-learning" not as a combination of two different things but as *one* kind of activity. Ethics does ask us to be of service to others and to our communities and the world, yes, but what we may discover is that service is not just a way of changing the world but also a way in which the world changes us.

Applications

Part VI—Chapters 16 through 19—discusses some *Contemporary Debates*: sexuality; abortion; business and professional ethics; and poverty and welfare.

As you'd expect, each chapter explores the issue at hand, laying out a bit of its background and history and some of the relevant values. These chapters serve in part as introductions to the debates as they stand. But these chapters have another aim as well. Standard texts at this point explore a range of contending points of views between which students are invited to choose. In this book, however, although some contending views are usually introduced, I proceed in quite a different way. The aim is not so much to enter the controversy but to make some *progress* on it. The aim is to *illustrate* the toolbox in action—to show you how to use it in real-life practice, in useful and perhaps unexpected ways, and thereby to show you how just how powerful it can actually be.

It turns out that even the most painful and "stuck" moral debates—even the abortion debate, for the most notable example—are open to the constructive use of our tools. In fact, no moral debate is really so stuck that a little creativity or integrative thinking can't open it up again. There are ways that you—yes, *you*—can make a real contribution.

Finally, Part VII considers what some philosophers call *The Expanding Circle*: the possible extension or expansion of ethics to include other animals (Chapter 20) and nature itself (Chapter 21).

We may be living in a time of genuine moral revolution. The traditional restriction of ethical attention to human relations with other humans is under fire. Activists and philosophers are arguing that we have obligations not just to each other, but to the other-than-human beings who share our lives and with whom we co-inhabit this world. We may even have obligations to that world itself, quite apart from what good it does us. But how shall we understand these obligations? Where do they come from? Do they represent a new kind of value, for example ? And how far do they go?

Serious questions—quite probably the key moral questions of the first part of the twenty-first century. It's fitting that they close this book.

The chapters in parts VI and VII are somewhat longer than those in the preceding parts of the book. There is more to cover, and even these chapters offer just the barest outlines. All of these chapters also offer readings, short essays or stories by others. Don't overlook the exercises and notes too, which often contain additional substantive points or suggestions as well.

Bon Voyage

This is a thick book, and much of it may well be challenging. Many of the tools it offers will be familiar, but they are not often put to use in ethics. Even the familiar ones may need improvement. The mere possibility of *hope*, meanwhile, when a question is hotly debated and maybe painful, is sometimes hard to sustain. Analyzing arguments may seem too daunting, or too cold-blooded. And listening—actually listening—when others seem only to rant and rave takes a major leap of faith.

So it may take a while to discover the value of some of these tools. On the other hand, most of them are familiar, at least in some areas. Some of them also have immediate and obvious attractions. Take that as at least a place to start. Just don't forget that all of these tools really go together. At least sometimes, take the leap. Use the whole toolbox. Once you discover how many possibilities there are even in the most stuck debate, I hope you'll use it all the time!

I

GETTING STARTED

CHAPTER 1

○

Ethics as a Learning Experience

THE NEED FOR OPEN MINDS

It takes an open mind to learn and to grow. The world is seldom as simple as it seems at first—there's always more to find out.

This is no news, I'm sure. Yet when it comes to moral values we sometimes hear a different story. Here, all too often, we're supposed to know what we think already, and we're supposed to stick to it come what may. To talk about moral complexity or compromise, or to be curious about other moral views, makes you sound (to some people) spineless, "wishy-washy," practically immoral already.

It's not. Ethics concerns some of the hardest and most complex of our choices. Here, surely, most of the time at least, we need to listen, to keep at least a *somewhat* open mind. Otherwise doggedness is likely to blind us, to make us insensitive and unresponsive. Even a few new facts might change everything. We do not want to end up like the person Mark Twain once described as "so full of what's right that he can't see what's *good*." Open the door a crack or two.

Besides, even the firmest conviction in no way guarantees rightness. Every bad cause has firm convictions behind it too. Slavery, exclusion, the savage exploitation of other people and animals and the land—every one of the evils that calls forth such memorable courage in its opponents was and often still is defended, firmly and courageously too, by others. Ethics must ask more than that. Some sense of openness, some willingness to learn and change, is necessary too.

The Role of Feelings

Feeling right does not guarantee rightness either. Feeling is part of the story, yes. Care, concern, passion—these are what make ethics so engaging and so compelling. Feelings may also alert us to moral problems that we might otherwise paper over with excuses. Often it's feelings that really start moral revolutions—the arguments come later.

Still, we must also examine and temper our feelings too, even the strongest feelings. Take prejudice. To be prejudiced is to have a strong negative feeling about someone who is of a different ethnicity or gender or age or social class (or . . .) from yourself. If ethics were just a matter of feelings, there would be nothing to say against such prejudices. It would be perfectly ethical to discriminate against people you don't like.

Ethics asks us to challenge those feelings instead. "Prejudice" literally means "pre-judgment": it is one way of not really paying attention. But we *need* to pay attention. We need to ask why we feel as we do, whether our beliefs and feelings are true or fair, how we would feel in the other person's shoes, and so on. Only by working these feelings through, carefully, can we begin to recognize their limits, and then if necessary change them.

It's not that we can't ever trust our instincts—it's that we can't *only* trust our instincts. There must be some give and take between ethics and feelings. We need a more open-ended attitude, more critical and analytical at times too, tolerant of ambiguity, not so quick to judge or to jump.

It is in this spirit that ethics approaches controversial issues of the day. We care for other animals, for instance. But we also use many of them for food, shoes, chemical tests, even as objects of sport. Should all of this stop? No? Well, should *any* of it stop? Probably. So what kinds of use of other animals should stop and what kinds should not? Why? How do you decide?

Questions like these cannot be adequately answered by consulting your preexisting feelings. There are too many different possibilities, too many different "uses," too many different opinions and prejudices (on all sides) that need to be carefully sorted out. Again, it takes some time and care. Ethics is the space for precisely that.

Ethical Learning

I ask my students what they've learned about moral values in the last few years. A few say that very little has changed for them. More say that not so much has changed yet, but they're looking forward to it. Most say that they *have* changed, ethically, sometimes in ways they could never have predicted. Students who were strongly pro-life find themselves in an abortion clinic with a best friend, date-rape victim, supporting her decision all the way. Others, strongly pro-choice, can't go through with it.

Some learn the hard way to see people beyond the labels and categories: race categories, sexual orientation, criminals. The phrase, "They're people just like me," keeps coming up—something we know (we know the words, anyway) and yet, often, don't quite "know" well enough. This too must actually be learned, perhaps again and again.

The history of ethics itself is a story of struggle over values, and the appearance of new values in a culture that at first resisted them. The very idea of rights, for example, which most modern Americans take for granted, is a piece of ethical theory that was literally revolutionary in the eighteenth century. On the Fourth of July we shoot off fireworks and celebrate the Declaration of

Independence as if it were the most natural and obvious thing. But it was a radical document in its time, and could easily have earned its signers death.

And now instead of Declarations of Independence we are beginning to see Declarations of *Inter*dependence: the insistence that humans are deeply dependent on the rest of the biosphere for our health, wealth, and very survival, and that it would therefore be a good idea to treat nature with more respect. So we continue to learn and change. Thirty years ago whales were being slaughtered all over the high seas and no one recycled anything. Now we listen to whale songs on CD, whale hunting is banned (though some still goes on), and recycling bins are everywhere.

Not all change is good, of course. Having an open mind does not mean simply accepting whatever change happens to come along. But we also cannot just stick to whatever we happen to think at the moment or what others around us tell us is right. For better or worse, we are part of a larger dialogue, thinking things through *together*—and no one can guarantee where we will end up going.

THREE EASY ROUTES TO A CLOSED MIND (AND HOW TO AVOID THEM)

The routes to a closed mind are wide and inviting. We need to recognize what those routes are—and why they may sometimes be so tempting—if we are to find another way.

Dogmatism

Dogmatists are people who are unshakably committed to one answer to an ethical question, or perhaps to all ethical questions. They may appear to listen (or not), but they *will not* change their minds. Name "their" issue (or perhaps *any* issue), and they know the answer already.

Dogmatists don't necessarily agree—which is a bit ironic. One dogmatist is sure that capital punishment is ordained by God and deters thousands of would-be murderers from pulling the trigger. The next dogmatist may be equally sure that capital punishment is detested by God and useless or worse as a deterrent. And so it goes. Dogmatists on one side do not seem to give pause to dogmatists on the other. If anything they become even more entrenched in their own views.

If dogmatists agree about anything, it's that careful and open-ended thinking about ethical issues is not necessary. After all, if you already know the answer, there is no need to think about it. If you need to argue for your position, you admit that it needs defending, which is to say that people can legitimately have doubts. But that can't be true: you already know that your position is the only right one. Therefore, any reasoned argument for your

∞

A Few Key Terms

Here are a few brief definitions of key terms in this book. We return to them in more detail in Chapter 3.

When we speak of *values* in this book we will mean *those things we care about; those things that matter to us; those goals or ideals to which we aspire and by which we measure ourselves or others or our society.*

"Value" so understood is a very broad category. It includes all sorts of things, from personal desires like health or a sense of humor to social ideals like wealth or liberty. Artists value beauty; pirates value their loot; soccer teams value their goals.

When we speak of *moral* values, we are concerned with one specific *kind* of values in general. Moral values are a subset of values generally. Let us define *moral values* as *those values that give voice to the needs and legitimate expectations of others as well as ourselves.*

The term "others" includes other people, for sure, and maybe (some?) other animals and the natural world too. (Who or what else it may include is one question we take up near the end of this book.) "Legitimate expectations" may be of many sorts. For example, we have legitimate expectations to be treated with respect, as an equal, and to have our rights honored. We also legitimately expect ourselves and each other to act responsibly, keep promises, and so on.

Finally, the term *ethics* in this book will mean *the study of moral values; reflection on how best to think about moral values and clarify, prioritize, and/or integrate them.*

We don't always distinguish the "moral" and the "ethical" with such precision. In popular talk the terms are mostly interchangeable. Still, it is useful to make some distinction between the moral values we happen to hold and the deliberate process of thinking them through, criticizing them, and revising them. "Ethics" (or, sometimes, "moral philosophy") has more of a critical, self-conscious edge.

position is unnecessary. And any reasoned argument *against* your position is obviously absurd. So, why listen?

This much is right about dogmatism: being committed to a certain set of values—living up to them, or trying to, and sticking up for them when we can—is a fine thing. Stubbornness can sometimes be a virtue. It is *not* a fine thing, however, to be *so* committed to your views or values that you cannot see any other side, and cannot even defend them beyond simply asserting and reasserting them—more and more loudly, probably. This is a pitfall, a trap.

Ethics paints a different picture. Despite the popular stereotypes, the point of ethics is not to moralize or to simply dictate what is to be done. The point is to offer some tools, and some possible directions, for thinking about difficult matters, recognizing from the start—almost as the very *reason* for ethics, in fact—that the world is seldom so simple or clear-cut.

So we need to think carefully if we are to act morally. In fact, thinking carefully about moral issues—avoiding dogmatism—is *itself* a moral act. Thinking carefully *is* (part of) acting morally. Philosopher Joshua Halberstam puts it well:

> We need an "ethics of belief" that places value on the way we arrive at our opinions. A healthy ethics of belief requires that our judgments be based on sound evidence. Opinionated people have a weak ethics of belief. They make no distinction between a legitimate opinion and an arbitrary opinion; all that matters is that they have an opinion. The problem with opinionated people is that they don't take their own views seriously enough! When we do take our opinions seriously, humility follows. . . .

Avoiding Dogmatism

Here are some strategies for avoiding dogmatism.

Whenever you find yourself insisting too strongly on some view of your own, try to stop yourself and really listen to the "other side." You do not *always* have to be stating your own views front and center.

Imagine that you're an anthropologist or psychologist studying other people's views. Just consider what they're saying without immediately thinking of your responses to it. What sort of world do these people live in? How does it hang together? How can their views seem so simple and obvious to them (just as yours do to you)? Later on you can kick in your own views and compare them. First just give yourself a little space to listen.

Another useful strategy is to seek out *arguments* for the other side(s). One way that dogmatic views ensure themselves long lives is by systematically avoiding the other side's arguments. Only the other side's *conclusions* are registered. This person is for (or against) capital punishment, let's say, and that's all a dogmatist needs to know. He doesn't ask *why*; he's not interested. . . .

To look at the *reasons* for other and opposed positions both helps you understand the positions better, and may begin to introduce some more complex thinking. Very often I hear people say, in amazement, something like

There really are reasons *for* _____!
[fill in the blank with whatever position they previously despised]

Amazing but true: people don't just hold views that differ from our own out of sheer perversity or ignorance. I guess it's to our credit that when we discover this we tend to be surprised and intrigued. The world seems a little bigger than it did before. Again this is an "obvious" thing that we don't really "know" quite well enough.

It pays to adjust your language as well. Instead of categorical statements of opinion, especially bumpersticker-style slogans ("Meat is murder"; "It's Adam and Eve not Adam and Steve"; etc., etc.), try to speak in a way that is less categorical and final. Very few reasonable moral positions can be shoe-horned into a bumpersticker, clever as the slogan might be—and besides, this way of putting things polarizes views and makes the other side seem stupid and misled. Don't call names either ("You animal-rights fanatics . . ."; "You Bible-thumpers . . ."). Avoid the easy labels ("liberal," "right-wing," . . .).

Language leads the mind. Speaking in an open-ended way will help you begin to *think* in an open-ended way as well. Certainly it will create quite different conversations. Typically one dogmatic statement just provokes an equal and opposite dogmatic statement. Speak differently and not only your mind but your discussions may open up differently, and more constructively too!

Halberstam again:

> Don't elevate your every whim into a conviction. Having an opinion is one thing, delivering the Ten Commandments is something else. Intellectual honesty demands that unless you're a bona fide expert in the field, a hint of tentativeness should accompany all your views and decisions. Indeed, a hint of uncertainty is appropriate even if you *are* an authority. Here's a simple device to ensure that you have the proper humility when offering your opinion: When you speak, imagine that an expert is sitting right across from you. Now offer that opinion.

Offhand Self-Justification

I offer a view in an ethical discussion. Someone challenges me. My natural first reaction is to defend whatever it was I just said, even if the challenge is exactly on target.

This is *offhand self-justification*: a kind of automatic excuse-making or defensiveness, or what we sometimes call "rationalizing." I may not even get to the point of asking if the challenge actually is on target or not. Indeed, that's the idea. I'd rather not. Self-defense is all that counts. I try to paper over my uncertainties (or insecurities, or half-knowledge, or wishful thinking) by grabbing for some excuse, and any excuse will do. "It's OK to cheat the phone company, because . . . because, well, everyone else does it too . . . because the phone company cheats *you* . . . because. . . ."

Asked for your reasons, you should give them. There is nothing wrong with trying to defend yourself. The problem lies with the offhand or automatic spirit (or, more accurately, spiritlessness) of the defense. Once again, it's an excuse for not really *thinking*.

S: Of course the death penalty deters murders. It's a proven fact that murder rates are lower in states with the death penalty.

A: I'm not so sure about that. My understanding is that most states with the death penalty have *higher* murder rates.

S: Well, you can prove anything with numbers.

S initially appeals to "numbers," comparative murder rates, to support her position. Challenged, though, she does not reconsider her position or explore other possibilities. She just dismisses any studies that disagree with what she believes—and in the process manages to dismiss the very numbers she herself just cited. But she doesn't even notice. You can tell that nothing will change for her. In the next discussion she'll be right back citing the same "proven fact" again.

Resisting Offhand Self-justification

There are no surefire ways to avoid rationalizing. It takes a kind of self-confidence, honesty, and maturity that develop slowly, and even then we seldom escape the temptation entirely. Sometimes it's hard to recognize an offhand self-justification when it is right in front of our eyes. Yet there are some useful strategies for overcoming the urge.

Remind yourself how self-defeating it is. Making excuses only allows us to go on with some questionable behavior until we get into worse trouble. It may even be worse than merely hanging on to one unintelligent opinion. When we rationalize, we saddle ourselves with *more and more* unintelligent opinions—new ones invented, off the top of the head, to patch up the holes in the old ones. But the new ones are likely to be full of holes too. It's not a winning game.

Watch yourself. Step a little more slowly the next time you find yourself casting about for some excuse to put questions to rest. You may stop a little sooner to ask whether you really are justified in the first place.

Watch for that telltale anger or irritation at being challenged. We often find ourselves becoming irritated or angry when our especially precious excuses are too persistently or effectively challenged by someone else. But of course, we get angry at the person challenging us, rather than considering that we might be at fault for making an offhand excuse in the first place. Anger at someone else keeps us from having to be angry at ourselves. Better take the irritation as a warning sign.

Avoid the automatic counterattack. Again, watch yourself. Listening to someone else, are you trying to understand, or just waiting to give your comeback? Are you trying to "win," or to learn? Watch your voice tone: are you conveying ridicule, irritation? Take a time-out if you need it. Give yourself some space to think.

Relativism

"It's all relative," we sometimes say. What's right for you may not be right for me. Mind your own business. Don't criticize. Any moral opinion is as good as the next.

This attitude is a form of *relativism* (though this is a broad and tricky term—see the discussion in the box to follow). It begins with the simple observation that different individuals and societies sometimes have different moral values. Some societies tolerate homeless populations running into the millions, for example, while in other societies the very idea of allowing even one person to be homeless, whatever the cause, is shameful, unthinkable. Some societies condemn sex between unmarried young people; others approve and encourage it.

Relativists go on to conclude that no one single standard is "right." There's something to this. At least, it's mind opening to look at other points of view, and moral matters are complex enough that no one point of view is likely to have a monopoly on the truth. Besides, sometimes we need to assert our right to do as we please, even if others think we are making a big mistake. This is one of relativism's chief uses in practice: making a space for us to figure things out for ourselves.

But relativists go much farther. From our differences about moral values they conclude that there is no legitimate basis for arguing about them at all. It's all just opinion, and one opinion is as good as another. And here, though relativism may appear to be the very model of open-mindedness, it actually has just the opposite effect. It begins to close our minds instead.

U: I support the death penalty. I believe that it saves lives because it makes murderers think twice before killing someone. As the Bible says, "An eye for an eye, a tooth for a tooth."

V: I don't agree.

U: Why?

V: I just don't. That's my opinion and it's as good as yours!

Maybe that's a little blatant, but you get the idea. Here relativism slides right into offhand self-justification. V treats it like a magic key to escape any kind of thinking whatsoever. She cannot be bothered to offer any reasons, let alone engage U's.

☙

RELATIVISM: PHILOSOPHICAL QUESTIONS

The main text concentrates on practical objections to moral relativism. Even if most of relativism's claims are true, I argue, we can and must actually *think*, long and hard, about moral issues. The tools in this toolbox are no less vital.

Relativism is also much argued over among philosophers. Many would *not* grant most of its claims. In this box I want to explore some of these further objections and arguments over moral relativism, briefly, both to give you a sense of how philosophers argue and of how difficult some seemingly obvious things really are. Here are a number of loosely linked questions and challenges to think about.

A

Moral relativism is based upon the claim that moral values differ in fundamental ways between different people and cultures. This is called *descriptive* relativism. But how much *real* disagreement is there about moral values? That is, do we really disagree "all the way down," so to speak, or might apparently different moral values flow instead from different factual beliefs about the world?

Eskimo (Inuit) bands were discovered by early European explorers to sometimes leave their old people out in the cold of winter to die. This was contrasted to the European attitude, which was supposed to be one of respect and care for the old. The explorers were scandalized. It looked like a clear difference of values.

Later explorers, however, discovered several more facts. One was that these bands often lived at the margin between survival and starvation during the winter, and had to move quickly in the spring to find food. Very old people could not keep up. Leaving them behind was a matter of social survival—a choice that we too might make in the same circumstances.

Another discovery was that the Eskimo believe in an afterlife, and believe that people enter the afterlife in the same condition they leave this one. Thus, allowing or even encouraging the old to die once their usefulness was past was not evidence of heartlessness or disrespect for life—quite the opposite. Again, if we (really, truly) shared their belief, we presumably would do the same.

In this case, then, what seemed to be a disagreement about moral values turned out to be a disagreement about certain facts. So how real are other alleged disagreements about moral values? Do we really differ that much? Is descriptive relativism true? Can you think of contemporary moral disagreements that might dissolve under scrutiny, like the Eskimo case might? Can you think of some that wouldn't?

B

No doubt there are at least *some* serious disagreements about moral values themselves. But what exactly does this prove? Is disagreement the last word? After all, we could take our disagreements as starting points—something to think about and learn from—rather than as end points. The fact that some people are racists, for example, doesn't prove that racism is wrong only for us. It simply proves that people have some learning to do.

You might ask: how much disagreement about moral values would remain after all of this thinking and learning? Is it so obvious that we would still disagree in such fundamental ways? (And how could we settle this question?)

C

Now suppose that descriptive relativism *is* true. That is, suppose we really do differ, differ sharply, and would continue to differ even after careful criticism and argument. What then? What follows, if anything, about moral values or moral arguments? That is, what follows about relativism in what philosophers call the *prescriptive* sense?

Does it follow, for example, that there is no single "right" answer to moral questions? Not necessarily. Sheer difference, by itself, does not prove that no one single standard is right. Maybe all sides but one are *wrong*. People disagree about all kinds of facts (Is the Earth flat? Does vitamin C prevent colds?), but we don't suppose there is no truth of the matter in those cases. Is there something special about value judgments that makes them different from "facts" in this way? Maybe, but if you think so, see if you can explain what it is. Spell out the argument.

One note of caution. It may actually be true that there is no one single "right" answer to (many) moral questions—but not for relativistic reasons. Maybe it is true just because most moral situations are so complex that a variety of different but equally good responses are possible. This would not mean that any answer is as good as the next (there are still plenty of wrong answers) or that critical thinking is somehow pointless in ethics. Quite the opposite: wouldn't it call for more flexible and subtle thinking still?

D

Now suppose that prescriptive moral relativism *is* true. That is, suppose there is no provable right answer to moral questions, and maybe even that any answer is in some sense as good as the next. What exactly would this imply?

Does it imply tolerance, for example—that we should just live and let live? Many people have thought so. But does it really? Relativism is compatible with tolerance, no doubt, but it is just as compatible with *intolerance*. Remember, there is no "right" answer to moral questions. And the question of tolerance is a moral question. It seems to follow that tolerance is as good as intolerance— and vice versa.

Do you think moral relativism implies tolerance? If so, how could you make the argument without falling afoul of relativism itself? If not, how *would* you defend tolerance? Might it turn out that tolerance needs a nonrelativistic argument?

E

Where exactly would prescriptive moral relativism apply? What practical difference would it make? Suppose the "cultural" relativist is right that you and I cannot argue with, say, cannibals about cannibalism. How often do you argue with cannibals? Mostly we argue with people who share our terms. I have never argued with a cannibal, not even once, but I argue constantly with my own children (whose eating habits also leave something to be desired). And I *can* argue with them—they are growing into *our* culture, and have some learning to do.

On the other hand, sometimes we are asked to make moral judgments across cultural lines, as when American corporations were pressured to (and mostly did) pull out of South Africa to protest apartheid. Was that a valid action, in your view? What would the relativist say about it? What do you think of the relativist's response?

F

Doesn't relativism itself vary between people and cultures? Does the fact that some people disagree about the truth of relativism mean that the truth of relativism is itself relative? If you say no—that relativism could be true or serious anyway, despite disagreement—then why can't moral values? If you say yes—that the truth of relativism is itself relative—then what's the point? (This is tricky!)

G

Finally, for those who reject relativism, what do you think relativism is nonetheless right about? The complexity of many situations, for example, making it hard to say that there is one single right answer? The need for some moral space, even to make our own mistakes? A freer spirit, more flexibility in ethics, a reminder that the truth is not so easy to come by? The need to look at things from others' points of view?

In fact, all opinions on this and most moral subjects require further thinking. Are U's arguments good ones? What values stand on the other side? What are V's reasons against the death penalty? Is the death penalty really a deterrent? Doesn't the Bible also tell us not to kill? Whether values are "relative" or not, there is no way out of some good hard thinking.

Minding Our Own Business

There is another practical problem with relativism—again, even if values really do differ, maybe even fundamentally.

Ethics often concerns matters that affect us all. Take pollution. If the air is polluted, it doesn't merely affect the polluters. If we spend money on pollution clean-up and prevention, on the other hand, we can't spend that money on other things, perhaps better things, maybe again for all of us. For some people it could be a life-or-death matter however we decide. The same goes for issues like professional ethics, abortion and assisted suicide, other animals, and many others.

None of these is just our "own" business. Other people's lives and health and possibilities are at stake too. These matters—basic moral issues—are *everyone's* business.

The relativist's stock phrase "Mind your own business" is therefore an antisocial response. It not only avoids thinking on the relativist's part: it also refuses to acknowledge that on issues like these, however much we differ, we still need to work out some way of going on together.

> **D:** I oppose legal abortion.

> **E:** Why don't you just mind your own business? Like the slogan says, if you're against abortion, then don't have one!

But there is more to it than this. If some of us practice abortion and some do not, the result is a society in which abortion is practiced. The rest of us have to stand for it, at least insofar as we have to stand aside. Likewise, if some of us pollute and some don't, the result is pollution for everyone. In such matters, we cannot act as though everyone can simply do as they please without anyone else being affected.

Some philosophers argue that this is the very point of ethics: to help us arrive at certain standards that we all are to live by when all of us are affected by each other's behavior. Some philosophers even depart from this point to build a theory of ethics. On this view, ethics is precisely for those cases where "Mind your own business!" doesn't work as an approach to a problem. Instead, we need to work things out together. Keep an open mind: stay in touch and keep talking. *That* is nothing less than ethics itself in practice.

C. P. Ellis

STUDS TERKEL

Here is a striking example of moral change and learning—the odyssey of one man, C. P. Ellis, former head of the Ku Klux Klan in Durham, North Carolina, out of the Klan and into a very different attitude toward the people he formerly despised. Ellis speaks here with Studs Terkel, the radio host who has published many books of interviews like these, on innumerable topics with people from all walks of life. This is surely one of his most remarkable.

Ask yourself, as you read, how it was that Ellis managed to change so much. How does he find his way around the endless temptations and pressures to stay where and what he is? What does he have to fight in order to keep on opening his mind? And what has happened by the time he comes to the point of saying "It was almost like being born again. It was a new life . . ."?

MY FATHER WORKED in a textile mill in Durham. He died at forty-eight years old. It was probably from cotton dust. Back then, we never heard of brown lung. I was about seventeen years old and had a mother and sister depending on somebody to make a livin'. It was just barely enough insurance to cover his burial. I had to quit school and go to work. I was about eighth grade when I quit.

My father worked hard but never had enough money to buy decent clothes. When I went to school, I never seemed to have adequate clothes to wear. I always left school late afternoon with a sense of inferiority. The other kids had nice clothes, and I just had what Daddy could buy. I still got some of those inferiority feelin's now that I have to overcome once in a while.

I loved my father. He would go with me to ball games. We'd go fishin' together. I was really ashamed of the way he'd dress. He would take this money and give it to me instead of putting it on himself. I always had the feeling about somebody looking at him and makin' fun of him and makin' fun of me. I think it had to do somethin' with my life.

My father and I were very close, but we didn't talk about too many intimate things. He did have a drinking problem. During the week, he would work every day, but weekend he was ready to get plastered. I can understand when a guy looks at his paycheck and looks at his bills, and he's worried hard all the week, and his bills are larger than his paycheck. He'd done the best he could the entire week, and there seemed to be no

Reprinted by permission of Donadio & Olson, Inc. Copyright © 1980 by Studs Terkel.

hope. It's an illness thing. Finally you just say: "The heck with it. I'll just get drunk and forget it."

My father was out of work during the depression, and I remember going with him to the finance company uptown, and he was turned down. That's something that's always stuck.

My father never seemed to be happy. It was a constant struggle with him just like it was for me. It's very seldom I'd see him laugh. He was just tryin' to figure out what he could do from one day to the next.

After several years pumping gas at a service station, I got married. We had to have children. Four. One child was born blind and retarded, which was a real additional expense to us. He's never spoken a word. He doesn't know me when I go to see him. But I see him, I hug his neck, I talk to him, tell him I love him. I don't know whether he knows me or not, but I know he's well taken care of. All my life, I had work, never a day without work, worked all the overtime I could get and still could not survive financially. I began to say there's somethin' wrong with this country. I worked my butt off and just never seemed to break even.

I had some real great ideas about this great nation. (Laughs.) They say to abide by the law, go to church, do right and live for the Lord, and everything'll work out. But it didn't work out. It just kept gettin' worse and worse.

I was workin' a bread route. The highest I made one week was seventy-five dollars. The rent on our house was about twelve dollars a week. I will never forget: outside of this house was a 265-gallon oil drum, and I never did get enough money to fill up that oil drum. What I would do every night, I would run up to the store and buy five gallons of oil and climb up the ladder and pour it in that 265-gallon drum. I could hear that five gallons when it hits the bottom of that oil drum, splatters, and it sounds like it's nothin' in there. But it would keep the house warm for the night. Next day you'd have to do the same thing.

I left the bread route with fifty dollars in my pocket. I went to the bank and I borrowed four thousand dollars to buy the service station. I worked seven days a week, open and close, and finally had a heart attack. Just about two months before the last payments of that loan. My wife had done the best she could to keep it runnin'. Tryin' to come out of that hole, I just couldn't do it.

I really began to get bitter. I didn't know who to blame. I tried to find somebody. I began to blame it on black people. I had to hate somebody. Hatin' America is hard to do because you can't see it to hate it. You gotta have somethin' to look at to hate. (Laughs.) The natural person for me to hate would be black people, because my father before me was a member of the Klan. As far as he was concerned, it was the savior of the white people. It was the only organization in the world that would take care of the white people. So I began to admire the Klan.

I got active in the Klan while I was at the service station. Every Monday night, a group of men would come by and buy a Coca-Cola, go back to the car, take a few drinks, and come back and stand around talkin'. I couldn't help but wonder: Why are these dudes comin' out every Monday? They said they were with the Klan and have meetings close-by. Would I be interested? Boy, that was an opportunity I really looked forward to! To be part of somethin'. I joined the Klan, went from member to chaplain, from chaplain to vice-president, from vice-president to president. The title is exalted cyclops.

The first night I went with the fellas, they knocked on the door and gave the signal. They sent some robed Klansmen to talk to me and give me some instructions. I was led into a large meeting room, and this was the time of my life! It was thrilling. Here's a guy who's worked all his life and struggled all his life to be something, and here's the moment to be something. I will never forget it. Four robed Klansmen led me into the hall. The lights were dim, and the only thing you could see was an illuminated cross. I knelt before the cross. I had to make certain vows and promises. We promised to uphold the purity of the white race, fight communism, and protect white womanhood. After I had taken my oath, there was loud applause goin' throughout the buildin', musta been at least four hundred people. For this one little ol' person. It was a thrilling moment for C. P. Ellis.

It disturbs me when people who do not really know what it's all about are so very critical of individual Klansmen. The majority of 'em are low-income whites, people who really don't have a part in something. They have been shut out as well as the blacks. Some are not very well educated either. Just like myself. We had a lot of support from doctors and lawyers and police officers.

Maybe they've had bitter experiences in this life and they had to hate somebody. So the natural person to hate would be the black person. He's beginnin' to come up, he's beginnin' to learn to read and start votin' and run for political office. Here are white people who are supposed to be superior to them, and we're shut out.

I can understand why people join extreme right-wing or left-wing groups. They're in the same boat I was. Shut out. Deep down inside, we want to be part of this great society. Nobody listens, so we join these groups. . . .

This was the time when the civil rights movement was really beginnin' to peak. The blacks were beginnin' to demonstrate and picket downtown stores. I never will forget some black lady I hated with a purple passion. Ann Atwater. Every time I'd go downtown, she'd be leadin' a boycott. How I hated—pardon the expression, I don't use it much now—how I just hated that black nigger. (Laughs.) Big, fat, heavy woman. She'd pull about eight demonstrations, and first thing you know they had two, three blacks at the checkout counter. Her and I have had some pretty close confrontations.

I felt very big, yeah. (Laughs.) We're more or less a secret organization. We didn't want anybody to know who we were, and I began to do some thinkin'. What am I hidin' for? I've never been convicted of anything in my life. I don't have any court record. What am I, C.P. Ellis, as a citizen and a member of the United Klansmen of America? Why can't I go to the city council meeting and say: "This is the way we feel about the matter? We don't want you to purchase mobile units to set in our schoolyards. We don't want niggers in our schools."

We began to come out in the open. We would go to the meetings, and the blacks would be there and we'd be there. It was a confrontation every time. I didn't hold back anything. We began to make some inroads with the city councilmen and county commissioners. They began to call us friend. Call us at night on the telephone: "C. P., glad you came to that meeting last night." They didn't want integration either, but they did it secretively, in order to get elected. They couldn't stand up openly and say it, but they were glad somebody was sayin' it. We visited some of the city leaders in their home and talk to 'em privately. It wasn't long before councilmen would call me up: "The blacks are comin' up tonight and makin' outrageous demands. How about some of you people showin' up and have a little balance?" I'd get on the telephone: "The niggers is comin' to the council meeting tonight. Persons in the city's called me and asked us to be there."

We'd load up our cars and we'd fill up half the council chambers, and the blacks the other half. During these times, I carried weapons to the meetings, outside my belt. We'd go there armed. We would wind up just hollerin' and fussin' at each other. What happened? As a result of our fightin' one another, the city council still had their way. They didn't want to give up control to the blacks nor the Klan. They were usin' us.

I began to realize this later down the road. One day I was walkin' downtown and a certain city council member saw me comin'. I expected him to shake my hand because he was talkin' to me at night on the telephone. I had been in his home and visited with him. He crossed the street. Oh shit, I began to think, somethin's wrong here. Most of 'em are merchants or maybe an attorney, an insurance agent, people like that. As long as they kept low-income whites and low-income blacks fightin', they're gonna maintain control.

I began to get that feeling after I was ignored in public. I thought: Bullshit, you're not gonna use me any more. That's when I began to do some real serious thinkin'.

The same thing is happening in this country today. People are being used by those in control, those who have all the wealth. I'm not espousing communism. We got the greatest system of government in the world. But those who have it simply don't want those who don't have it to have any part of it. Black and white. When it comes to money, the green, the other colors make no difference. (Laughs.)

I spent a lot of sleepless nights. I still didn't like blacks. I didn't want to associate with 'em. Blacks, Jews, or Catholics. My father said: "Don't have anything to do with 'em." I didn't until I met a black person and talked with him, eyeball to eyeball, and met a Jewish person and talked to him, eyeball to eyeball. I found out they're people just like me. They cried, they cussed, they prayed, they had desires. Just like myself. Thank God, I got to the point where I can look past labels. But at that time, my mind was closed.

I remember one Monday night Klan meeting. I said something was wrong. Our city fathers were using us. And I didn't like to be used. The reactions of the others was not too pleasant: "Let's just keep fightin' them niggers."

I'd go home at night and I'd have to wrestle with myself. I'd look at a black person walkin' down the street, and the guy'd have ragged shoes or his clothes would be worn. That began to do somethin' to me inside. I went through this for about six months. I felt I just had to get out of the Klan. But I wouldn't get out.

Then something happened. The state AFL-CIO received a grant from the Department of HEW, a $78,000 grant: how to solve racial problems in the school system. I got a telephone call from the president of the state AFL-CIO. "We'd like to get some people together from all walks of life." I said: "All walks of life? Who you talkin' about?" He said: "Blacks, whites, liberals, conservatives, Klansmen, NAACP people."

I said: "No way am I comin' with all those niggers. I'm not gonna be associated with those type of people." A White Citizens Council guy said: "Let's go up there and see what's goin' on. It's tax money bein' spent." I walk in the door, and there was a large number of blacks and white liberals. I knew most of 'em by face 'cause I seen 'em demonstratin' around town. Ann Atwater was there. (Laughs.) I just forced myself to go in and sit down.

The meeting was moderated by a great big black guy who was bushy-headed. (Laughs.) That turned me off. He acted very nice. He said: "I want you all to feel free to say anything you want to say." Some of the blacks stand up and say it's white racism. I took all I could take. I asked for the floor and I cut loose. I said: "No, sir, it's black racism. If we didn't have niggers in the schools, we wouldn't have the problems we got today."

I will never forget. Howard Clements, a black guy, stood up. He said: "I'm certainly glad C. P. Ellis come because he's the most honest man here tonight." I said: "What's that nigger tryin' to do?" (Laughs.) At the end of that meeting, some blacks tried to come up shake my hand, but I wouldn't do it. I walked off.

Second night, same group was there. I felt a little more easy because I got some things off my chest. The third night, after they elected all the committees, they want to elect a chairman. Howard Clements stood up and said: "I suggest we elect two co-chairpersons." Joe Beckton, executive director of the Human Relations Commission, just as black as he can be, he nominated me. There was a reaction from some blacks. Nooo. And, of all things, they nominated Ann Atwater, that big old fat black gal that I had just hated with a purple passion, as co-chairman. I thought to myself: Hey, ain't no way I can work with that gal. Finally, I agreed to accept it, "cause at this point, I was tired of fightin', either for survival or against black people or against Jews or against Catholics.

A Klansman and a militant black woman, co-chairmen of the school committee. It was impossible. How could I work with her? But after about two or three days, it was in our hands. We had to make it a success. This give me another sense of belongin', a sense of pride. This helped this inferiority feelin' I had. A man who has stood up publicly and said he despised black people, all of a sudden he was willin' to work with 'em. Here's a chance for a low-income white man to be somethin'. In spite of all my hatred for blacks and Jews and liberals, I accepted the job. Her and I began to reluctantly work together. (Laughs.) She had as many problems workin' with me as I had workin' with her.

One night, I called her: "Ann, you and I should have a lot of differences and we got 'em now. But there's somethin' laid out here before us, and if it's gonna be a success, you and I are gonna have to make it one. Can we lay aside some of these feelin's?" She said: "I'm willing if you are." I said: "Let's do it."

My old friends would call me at night: "C. P., what the hell is wrong with you? You're sellin' out the white race." This begin to make me have guilt feelin's. Am I doin' right? Am I doin' wrong? Here I am all of a sudden makin' an about-face and tryin' to deal with my feelin's, my heart. My mind was beginnin' to open up. I was beginnin' to see what was right and what was wrong. I don't want the kids to fight forever.

We were gonna go ten nights. By this time, I had went to work at Duke University, in maintenance. Makin' very little money. Terry Sanford give me this ten days off with pay. He was president of Duke at the time. He knew I was a Klansman and realized the importance of blacks and whites getting along.

I said: "If we're gonna make this thing a success, I've got to get to my kind of people." The low-income whites. We walked the streets of Durham, and we knocked on doors and invited people. Ann was goin' into the black community. They just wasn't respondin' to us when we made these house calls. Some of 'em were cussin' us out. "You're sellin' us out, Ellis, get out of my door. I don't want to talk to you." Ann was gettin' the same response from blacks: "What are you doin' messin' with that Klansman?"

One day, Ann and I went back to the school and we sat down. We began to talk and just reflect. Ann said: "My daughter came home cryin' every day. She said her teacher was makin' fun of me in front of the other kids." I said: "Boy, the same thing happened to my kid. White liberal teacher was makin' fun of Tim Ellis's father, the Klansman. In front of other peoples. He came home cryin'." At this point—(he pauses, swallows hard, stifles a sob)—I begin to see, here we are, two people from the far ends of the fence, havin' identical problems, except hers bein' black and me bein' white. From that moment on, I tell ya, that gal and I worked together good. I began to love the girl, really. (He weeps.)

The amazing thing about it, her and I, up to that point, had cussed each other, bawled each other, we hated each other. Up to that point, we didn't know each other. We didn't know we had things in common.

We worked at it, with the people who came to these meetings. They talked about racism, sex education, about teachers not bein' qualified. After seven, eight nights of real intense discussion, these people, who'd never talked to each other before, all of a sudden came up with resolutions. It was really somethin', you had to be there to get the tone and feelin' of it.

At that point, I didn't like integration, but the law says you do this and I've got to do what the law says, okay? We said: "Let's take these resolutions to the school board." The most disheartening thing I've ever faced was the school system refused to implement any one of these resolutions. These were recommendations from the people who pay taxes and pay their salaries. (Laughs.)

I thought they were good answers. Some of 'em I didn't agree with, but I been in this thing from the beginning, and whatever comes of it, I'm gonna support it. Okay, since the school board refused, I decided I'd just run for the school board.

I spent eighty-five dollars on the campaign. The guy runnin' against me spent several thousand. I really had nobody on my side. The Klan turned against me. The low-income whites turned against me. The liberals didn't particularly like me. The blacks were suspicious of me. The blacks wanted to support me, but they couldn't muster up enough to support a Klansman on the school board. (Laughs.) But I made up my mind that what I was doin' was right, and I was gonna do it regardless what anybody said.

It bothered me when people would call and worry my wife. She's always supported me in anything I wanted to do. She was changing, and my boys were too.

I was invited to the Democratic women's social hour as a candidate. Didn't have but one suit to my name. Had it six, seven, eight years. I had it cleaned, put on the best shirt I had and a tie. Here were all this high-class wealthy candidates shakin' hands. I walked up to the mayor and stuck out my hand. He give me that handshake with that rag type of hand. He said: "C. P., I'm glad to see you." But I could tell by his handshake he was lyin' to me. This was botherin' me. I know I'm a low-income person. I know I'm not wealthy. I know they were sayin': "What's this little ol' dude runnin' for school board?" Yet they had to smile and make like they're glad to see me. I begin to spot some black people in that room. I automatically went to 'em and that was a firm handshake. They said: "I'm glad to see you, C. P." I knew they meant it—you can tell about a handshake.

Every place I appeared, I said I will listen to the voice of the people. I will not make a major decision until I first contacted all the organizations in the city. I got 4,640 votes. The guy beat me by two thousand. Not bad for eighty-five bucks and no constituency.

The whole world was openin' up, and I was learnin' new truths that I had never learned before. I was beginnin' to look at a black person, shake hands with him, and see him as a human bein'. I hadn't got rid of all this stuff. I've still got a little bit of it. But somethin' was happenin' to me.

It was almost like bein' born again. It was a new life. I didn't have these sleepless nights I used to have when I was active in the Klan and slippin' around at night. I could sleep at night and feel good about it. I'd rather live now than at any other time in history. It's a challenge.

Back at Duke, doin' maintenance, I'd pick up my tools, fix the commode, unstop the drains. But this got in my blood. Things weren't right in this country, and what we done in Durham needs to be told. I was so miserable at Duke, I could hardly stand it. I'd go to work every morning just hatin' to go.

My whole life had changed. I got an eighth-grade education, and I wanted to complete high school. Went to high school in the afternoons on a program called PEP—Past Employment Progress. I was about the only white in class, and the oldest. I begin to read about biology. I'd take my books home at night, 'cause I was determined to get through. Sure enough, I graduated. I got the diploma at home. . . .

Last year, I ran for business manager of the union. He's elected by the workers. The guy that ran against me was black, and our membership is seventy-five percent black. I thought: Claiborne, there's no way you can beat that black guy. People know your background. Even though you've made tremendous strides, those black people are not gonna vote for you. You know how much I beat him? Four to one. (Laughs.)

The company used my past against me. They put out letters with a picture of a robe and a cap: Would you vote for a Klansman? They wouldn't deal with the issues. I immediately called for a mass meeting. I met with the ladies at an electric component plant. I said: "Okay, this is Claiborne Ellis. This is where I come from. I want you to know right now, you black ladies here, I was at one time a member of the Klan. I want you to know, because they'll tell you about it."

I invited some of my old black friends. I said: "Brother Joe, Brother Howard, be honest now and tell these people how you feel about me." They done it. (Laughs.) Howard Clements kidded me a little bit. He said: "I don't know what I'm doin' here, supportin' an ex-Klansman." (Laughs.) He said: I know what C. P. Ellis come from. I knew him when he was. I knew him as he grew, and growed with him. I'm tellin' you now: follow, follow this Klansman." (He pauses, swallows hard.) "Any questions?" "No," the black ladies said. "Let's get on with the meeting, we need Ellis." (He laughs and weeps.) Boy, black people sayin' that about me. I won one thirty-four to forty-one. Four to one.

It makes you feel good to go into a plant and butt heads with professional union busters. You see black people and white people join hands to defeat the racist issues they use against people. They're tryin' the same things with the Klan. It's still happenin' today. Can you imagine a guy who's got an adult high school diploma runnin' into professional college graduates who are union busters? I gotta compete with 'em. I work seven days a week, nights and on Saturday and Sunday. The salary's not that great, and if I didn't care, I'd quit. But I care and I can't quit. I got a taste of it. (Laughs.)

I tell people there's a tremendous possibility in this country to stop wars, the battles, the struggles, the fights between people. People say: "That's an impossible dream. You sound like Martin Luther King." An ex-Klansman who sounds like Martin Luther King. (Laughs.) I don't think it's an impossible dream. It's happened in my life. It's happened in other people's lives in America.

I don't know what's ahead of me. I have no desire to be a big union official. I want to be right out here in the field with the workers. I want to walk through their factory and shake hands with that man whose hands are dirty. I'm gonna do all that one little ol' man can do. I'm fifty-two years old, and I ain't got many years left, but I want to make the best of 'em.

When the news came over the radio that Martin Luther King was assassinated, I got on the telephone and begin to call other Klansmen. We just had a real party at the service station. Really rejoicin' 'cause that son of a bitch was dead. Our troubles are over with. They say the older you get, the harder it is for you to change. That's not necessarily true. Since I changed, I've set down and listened to tapes of Martin Luther King. I listen to it and tears come to my eyes 'cause I know what he's sayin' now. I know what's happenin'.

Exercises and Notes

SELF-REFLECTION

What events in *your* life were occasions for ethical learning? What did you learn? What made that learning possible?

We have noted some of the ways in which people close their minds on some topic, often without even noticing or admitting that that is what is happening. So now consider yourself. About what do you get dogmatic? About what do you rationalize? About what do you get defensive? What do you have trouble hearing? Why? (Explore that *why* question—understanding yourself better is often the key to change.)

Give yourself some credit too. What are you *good* at hearing? On what topics are you truly open-minded? And why is this?

Admitting to a degree of closed-mindedness does not mean that you instantly have to change. Perhaps you will never be able to change completely. Even C. P. Ellis admits to remaining pockets of racism. The point is only to mark out the areas that need special attention—places where you need to watch yourself, and others need both to be more sensitive and maybe more insistent.

A variation on this project is to look for biographies or autobiographies of people you admire (and some of people you don't!) and pay attention to the ways in which *they* learned and changed—to what made learning and change possible for them. Or interview some people you know or can contact, asking the same questions: What have been major ethical changes in your life? Why did those changes happen? Were they hard? Why? How do you feel about them now that you look back at them? What advice do you have for younger people looking ahead to such changes in their own lives?

Hearing the "Other Side"

Name an ethical position that you find especially hard to take seriously. Do this before reading on.

Now, as an exercise in open-mindedness, your task is to write or state this position in as neutral a way as possible. You don't have to be effusive, and don't try to be extremely positive—usually it is easier to be overpositive than to state a view carefully. Just try to state the position in a reasonable way, not loaded or satirical but simply straight. You may have to do a little research to get it right. In class, ask a classmate who holds that position to help you out.

Consider also the *reasons* that are typically used to support this view. What are those reasons? What are the best reasons according to *you*—the reasons that would persuade you if any reasons could?

Again, don't argue with the position. Just look for the strongest defense of that position you can find.

You don't have to *agree* with this position, of course—after all, you picked it because you not only disagree with it but find it hard to take seriously. The point is to try to understand it, and in general to try to get a little distance from your own reactions: to create a little more space for open-mindedness.

This exercise works best if you avoid the hottest issues that we have all heard debated too many times already, such as abortion. People seem to have heard the two main positions on abortion enough that it is fairly easy to rattle them off. On other issues, it takes more care and work—and that is really the point.

A Dialogue

Dogmatism, relativism, and various kinds of offhand self-justification are partly conversational or argumentative moves: that is, they occur in dialogue, in the back-and-forth of conversation or argument. Sometimes they are also subtle!

Carefully consider the following classroom dialogue and consider where (and why) you think minds are closed or closing. Then try rewriting the dialogue (or writing your own) to illustrate more open-minded exchanges.

F: I admire C. P. Ellis, but you have to admit that it's pretty easy to look back and see that the Klan's racism was hateful and wrong. It's not so easy with our race issues now. Like affirmative action—it's just not so clear an answer.

G: I think it's clear. If Martin Luther King, Jr. were alive today, he'd be against affirmative action!

H: Why do you think that? He was *for* it when he was alive, wasn't he?

G: He always spoke up against what was wrong. I believe affirmative action is wrong, and . . .

J: No, it makes sense. This society is still racist and sexist, you know. And if you know someone is going to discount you because you're black or female, a little extra nudge just makes things equal again.

M: Well, you must be the exception that proves the rule. Everybody *I* know is against all those quotas!

L: I don't think they use quotas. They just check for biased patterns of hiring or school admissions over time.

M: And then what? Besides, how do you "check"? You have to use quotas!

L: Computers or something, I don't know.

P: It's discrimination either way. Either the racism or sexism J talked about, or reverse discrimination to correct past discrimination. Who's to say which is worse?

J: Oh give me a break! Colleges and universities already give preferential treatment to the children of alumni, and athletes, and even students from other parts of the country. What's so different about giving some preference on the basis of race or sex?

P: Right! It's all in your head. You're only discriminated against if that's how it feels to you.

Notes and Further Readings

Joshua Halberstam's book *Everyday Ethics* (Penguin, 1993) is an interesting and opinionated complement to this one. He is cited here from pages 155 and 156.

On the virtues of an open mind in an often fanatical and dogmatic world, there is no better source than some of the essays of Bertrand Russell, for example his *Skeptical Essays* (Barnes and Noble, 1961) and *Unpopular Essays* (Simon and Schuster, 1951). For some practical help getting there, see Zachary Seech, *Open Minds and Everyday Reasoning* (Wadsworth, 1993) and Robert Bramson, *Coping With Difficult People* (Dell, 1988).

Rationalizing may be one of the deepest of all pitfalls in ethics (and probably in life generally). For some psychological background, including some fascinating and unsettling experiments, see David Myers, *Social Psychology* (McGraw-Hill, 1993, 4th ed.), chapters 2 through 4. For a useful overview of self-deception, see Chapter 6 of Mike Martin's *Everyday Morality* (Wadsworth Publishing Company, 1995).

For more traditional discussions of relativism, see Joseph Ellin, *Morality and the Meaning of Life* (Harcourt Brace, 1995), Chapter 2; and James Rachels, *The Elements of Moral Philosophy* (McGraw-Hill, 1993), Chapter 2. I deal with relativism from a different angle in my *Toward Better Problems* (Temple University Press, 1992), Chapter 7. Ethical thinkers who have tried to derive a substantive ethics precisely from the need to go on together in the face of diverse values include John Rawls, *A Theory of Justice* (Harvard University Press, 1971), sections 3 and 20 through 26, and David Gauthier, in *Morals by Agreement* (Clarendon Press, 1986).

For Web-based ethics resources, including a discussion of pluralism and relativism and a glossary of key terms in ethics, an excellent site is Lawrence Hinman's "Ethics Updates" at <www.ethics.acusd.edu>.

CHAPTER 2

○

Ethics and Religion

For many people, religion is essential to ethics. Others find religious ethics controversial, or worse. Before we go farther, then, we need to take our bearings with respect to religion. What does religion contribute to ethics? And what are its limits?

RELIGION'S CONTRIBUTIONS TO ETHICS

For one thing, religion contributes moral training. For many of us the only formal moral training we will ever receive is in a religious institution (church, synagogue, mosque, . . .). Many of us fall back on that training, whether we remain religious or not, when the going gets tough. The words that come to mind come from the Ten Commandments or the Sermon on the Mount. "Thou shalt not kill." "Turn the other cheek." The stories that come to mind are parables—stories with a "moral"—like the "Good Samaritan," the "Widow's Offering," "I am my brother's keeper."

Religious leaders are not afraid to speak up for values, in a serious way that goes far beyond the rhetoric of politicians and graduation speakers. Paying attention to the needs of others; sustaining or rekindling hope in the face of despair; caring for all of creation—these are the stuff of sermons every week. Fundamentalism is much in the news, for example, and much of its concern is with values, especially with the need to return to certain traditional loyalties and limits that fundamentalists think we have let slide. Moderate and mainstream religions are just as concerned: they're just less likely to show up in the papers. "Liberal" ideas emerge as well. The American Catholic bishops crusade against abortion and contraception but also question multi-national capitalism for its effects on local communities and "good livelihood," and challenge a nuclear defense strategy premised on the threat of mutual annihiliation.

Religious leaders may speak for us even when they come from a religion different than our own. Some proclamations of Pope John Paul II, for example, are controversial even among Catholics, but he is still in certain ways "the world's conscience" (as he has been called)—not just for Catholics. He criticizes repressive regimes from their own podiums; he challenges wealthy countries to remember that wealth is not an end in itself.

Finally, religious leaders also stand in their own persons for a more ethical life. They are (among) the ones to whom the community turns for moral leadership at times of uncertainty or tragedy. They may not always step up to that leadership, but it is still part of their job. And surely it is a good thing that there are such jobs!

Are Religious Values Unique?

Are religious values somehow unique to religion, or unique to one specific religion as opposed to others?

In general: no. Take Pope John Paul II again, for example. In authoritarian countries he speaks for freedom and individual dignity—hardly just Catholic ideas, or just Christian ideas, or just religious ideas. In capitalist countries he speaks of respect for life and against our obsessions with material things: again, *common* values, even if we don't always live up to them.

Take the Ten Commandments. No one is in favor of killing or bearing false witness or dishonoring one's parents or lusting for what one's neighbor has—even though we may sometimes do all these things anyway. Who wants to squelch hope, leave children in pain, or trash the earth? None of us. We can put it many ways, tell many stories, worship in a hundred different ways, but in the end, as to values like these, we are mostly on the same page.

Take the Golden Rule—"Do unto others as you would have them do unto you." That's how we learn it in kindergarten, the secular version. Jesus asks of us the same thing. Love your neighbor, he says, as yourself (*Mark* 12:31). Jesus in turn was quoting the Torah, specifically *Leviticus* 19:17–18:

> You shall not hate your brother in your heart, but you shall reason with your neighbor, lest you bear sin because of him. You shall not take vengeance or bear any grudge against the sons of your own people, but you shall love your neighbor as yourself.

The same "rule" shows up in teachings of Confucius—"What is hateful to you, do not do to your fellow"—and in Buddhism; *and* it is very similar to a principle we will discover in a few chapters in the secular German philosopher Kant.

Shared values like these should come as no surprise. Religions don't develop in isolation from each other or from the culture, and the culture doesn't develop in isolation from them. It would be better to picture *all* of us, together, seeking better and fuller ways to understand and express values that mostly arise out of common experience. Religions offer one way—indeed, a whole set of ways: poetic, ancient, highly developed, compelling for many of us, though still not the only ways. Of course there are disagreements too, including very major ones. But, again, the broad moral thrust is a common one.

RELIGION'S LIMITS IN ETHICS

On the other hand, religions also differ, especially when questions get more specific. Can we find common moral ground *then?* Some religious leaders make very specific moral pronouncements in the name of their religions. Others make opposite pronouncements. What weight do these pronouncements carry, especially in a pluralistic society? When and how far is it necessary to think for ourselves?

When Religions Differ

Conflicting pronouncements imply right away that appealing to specific religious authorities can't carry much weight in a diverse society like ours. Their way of *putting* things may be helpful, and sometimes they may suggest useful arguments for others outside a particular faith, but the sheer claim to authority meets too many counterclaims to the same authority for any of them to carry much weight in the larger debate.

In that larger debate we speak not as Catholics or Jews, agnostics or atheists, but simply as *people*, united by certain values we are aiming to understand and put into practice together. While many non-Catholics admire the pope, for example, we are unlikely to take his word on family planning or the economy just because it is his word. (Many Catholics don't either.) Therefore we must talk and argue about what our shared values mean, and find ways to go beyond a particular religion's or religious spokesperson's interpretation of those values to some more general reasons that will appeal to others whose religious background is different.

So: look for shareable, general terms. Frame your arguments using common values—and be ready to accept the fact that the "right" answer will often be ambiguous.

Some ethical questions really do have right and wrong answers within a specific religious tradition. On the most controversial questions, though, even the experts within one religion disagree, and you can only conclude that the question is still open. Pay attention to the experts (on both or all sides) to understand the issue and the arguments better. But they cannot decide for you.

Of course, you can pick which experts you choose to believe—but then *you* are doing the picking, really, and can no longer claim that you're just submitting yourself to authority. The honest thing is to start with your view—keeping an open mind, of course—and examine and explain why you hold it, without claiming to be an expert yourself. Don't hide behind someone else's pronouncements as if they leave you no room to think for yourself.

The Problem of Ambiguity

Those who claim to be experts in religious ethics do have a backup: they quote the Bible (or Torah, or Koran, etc.). And religious texts, of course, claim to come with the authority of God. So perhaps no human can claim to be an "expert" in ethics, but surely we have the revealed Truth before us all the same!

Religious texts may well be among humanity's most precious possessions. However, arguably, they are precious because they are so very rich, poetic, and complex. Precisely because they are so rich, poetic, and complex, they are also *ambiguous*. They seldom yield clear, specific guidance in specific situations—certainly not in the problematic situations that really concern us. Once again, there is no escape from thinking for ourselves.

Consider this parable from the Sufi (Islamic mystic) master Yusuf of Andalusia:

> Nuri Bey was a respected and reflective Albanian, who had married a wife much younger than himself.
>
> One evening when he had returned home earlier than usual, a faithful servant came to him and said: "Your wife, our mistress, is acting suspiciously. She is in her apartments with a huge chest, large enough to hold a man, which belonged to your grandmother. It should contain only a few ancient embroideries. I believe that there may now be much more in it. She will not allow me, your oldest retainer, to look inside."
>
> Nuri went to his wife's room, and found her sitting disconsolately beside the massive wooden box. "Will you show me what is in the chest?" he asked.
>
> "Because of the suspicion of a servant, or because you do not trust me?"
>
> "Would it not be easier just to open it, without thinking about the undertones?" asked Nuri.
>
> "I do not think it possible."
>
> "Where is the key?"
>
> She held it up. "Dismiss the servant and I will give it to you."
>
> The servant was dismissed. The woman handed over the key and herself withdrew, obviously troubled in mind.
>
> Nuri Bey thought for a long time. Then he called four gardeners from his estate. Together they carried the chest by night unopened to a distant part of the grounds, and buried it. The matter was never referred to again.

Sufis have been teaching with this story for eight hundred years. But exactly what lesson does it teach? Take some time to figure out how *you* would interpret it, and see how your interpretation compares with others.

Is Nuri Bey's act a wise one? Does the story mean to suggest that it is? He doesn't push the point—he doesn't open the chest—but apparently he doesn't entirely trust his wife either. Or in burying the chest is his idea to also bury mistrust? Is he still trying to avoid the "undertones"? Would his wife agreed that he succeeded at this? Is the "moral" therefore that certain matters between husband and wife shouldn't be pushed?

And, after all, what was in the box? Is it obvious that his wife is hiding a lover? Could it be something else—a present, maybe, that she is not prepared to give him yet? Some other kind of magical possibility that his jealousy "buries" for him? After all, the story is an allegory—but the question is: an allegory for *what*?

The Sufis themselves, by the way, value such stories precisely because they *are* complex and unclear in this way. To insist that they mean one and only one thing misses the very point, so they would say. How many other stories are like that?

Reading the Bible

Here's another religious story, this one a little closer to home. When some Christians insist that the Bible condemns homosexuality, a common scriptural reference is to the story of the destruction of Sodom.

> The two angels came to Sodom in the evening; and Lot was sitting in the gate of Sodom. When Lot saw them, he rose to meet them . . . and said, "My lords, turn aside, I pray you, to your servant's house, and spend the night, and wash your feet; then you may rise up early and go on your way." . . . He urged them strongly; so they turned aside to him and entered his house; and he made them a feast, and baked unleavened bread, and they ate. But before they lay down, the men of the city, the men of Sodom, both young and old, all the people to the last man, surrounded the house, and they called to Lot, "Where are the men who came to you tonight? Bring them out to us, that we may know [i.e. rape] them." Lot went out of the door to the men, shut the door after him, and said, "I beg you, my brothers, do not act so wickedly. . . . Do nothing to these men, for they have come under the shelter of my roof. Behold, I have two daughters who have not known man; let me bring them out to you, and do to them as you please; only do nothing to these men, for they have come under the shelter of my roof." But [the crowd] said, "Stand back!" . . . Then they pressed hard against Lot, and drew near to break the door. But [the angels] put forth their hands and drew Lot into the house to them, and shut the door. And they struck with blindness the men who were at the door of the house, so that they wearied themselves groping for the door. (*Genesis* 19:1–11)

God destroys the city the next day, after helping Lot and his family to flee.

Since God destroys Sodom, there does seem to be something that God means to condemn. But what? The text does not say. The traditional reading is that the true crimes of Sodom are its shocking level of violence and its extreme disrespect for strangers. "Behold, this was the guilt of your sister Sodom: she and her daughters had pride, surfeit of food, and prosperous ease, but did not aid the poor and needy" (*Ezekiel* 16:49). On this view, homosexuality has nothing to do with it.

We might suppose that if anything is specifically condemned in this story, it is rape. After all, rape is what the crowd intended, and the crowd, along with the city it stands for, is quickly punished. But here too things are confusing. Lot, who is presented as the only decent man in Sodom, actually offers the crowd his own daughters in the place of his guests. The angels prevent these rapes too from happening. But God still saves Lot from the destruction of the rest of the city. Does not Lot's treatment of his own daughters offend God? Is the shelter of his roof for strangers more important than the shelter of his home for his own children?

We are reminded that this story was written at a time when some values were very different from those of today; when, for one thing, women were regarded only as a father's or husband's property, for him to dispose of as he saw fit. Regardless of what the story does or does not condemn, then, we might have doubts about its true moral authority.

In any case, again, we are left unclear about just what it is that God condemns about Sodom. That it is homosexuality is a major leap—added, we might suspect, by people who *already* oppose homosexuality and are looking to scripture for support. But in that case we need to hear and evaluate their actual reasons, not a forced reading of scripture to make it yield the desired conclusion. The actual story is richer and more ambiguous than that.

Commandments

But sometimes God explicitly commands certain acts and condemns others, right? And surely those commands, at least, are not ambiguous and open to multiple interpretations and all the rest. *Here* at least it seems that we can act with assurance. Here at least we have the word direct from ultimate authority with no uncertainty or question.

Actually, though, it turns out that even here things are complicated— fortunately or unfortunately, as the case may be. Even here there is a large element of interpretation and choice.

"Thou shalt not kill" is surely the clearest of the Ten Commandments. But almost all Christians and Jews eat other animals, which requires killing on a massive scale. Many Christians and Jews support capital punishment. Most fight in wars. Some also believe that suicide (self-killing) may be permissible too.

The Torah (Jewish) version reads "Thou shalt not murder." This seems a little more reasonable: it is at least arguable that killing in war or in the electric chair is not murder, and that the notion of murder is implicitly limited to other humans. Once we get into alternative translations, however, we return quickly to the question of alternative interpretations. After all, the word in the Christian Bible is "kill," so if you take it literally, in English, that should be the end of the matter.

Also, to say "Thou shalt not murder" is not helpful as a practical guide. In effect it says: "Don't kill unjustly." But when is killing unjust? Is capital punishment, for example, murder? You may have views about the answers to these questions, but they aren't given in the commandment "Thou shalt not murder." One way or the other we are back to a lot of interpretation.

Another commandment tells us to honor the Sabbath. But when is the Sabbath? Even this simplest of questions is unclear. Jews celebrate Sabbath from Friday sundown until Saturday sundown. Early Christians followed Jewish practice, eventually shifting the observance to Sundays to honor Easter and to distinguish themselves from the Jews. Some Christians celebrate Sabbath on Saturdays (the Seventh-Day Adventists). Is there a "right" answer? Not, it seems, in the text.

THINKING FOR YOURSELF

If interpretation is always necessary; if even the most explicit commandments cannot be simply obeyed but first have to be figured out and applied; if religions are diverse and even within a single faith there are diverse and even opposed interpretations and commands—what then?

The answer is certainly not that religious ethics are useless. They still have much to offer. Indeed the ambiguity and complexity of the stories and the diversity of interpretations make them even more fascinating. No: the implication is just that there is no such thing as simple obedience, as if no thinking and evaluation on our parts were required at all. Thinking for ourselves *is* required. All of us do it, and must do it, all of the time.

We Still Decide

For example, there are a large number of absolutely explicit commandments that almost no one takes seriously and almost all of us feel free to ignore (and that religious leaders, for their part, seldom even mention). Not too many people even "Honor the Sabbath" any more, for one thing, whenever we think it is. Here are a few more dramatic examples from *Leviticus*:

> 11:7: You shall not eat the swine; it is unclean to you.
> 11:11–12: Everything in the waters that has not fins and scales is an abomination to you. Of their flesh you shall not eat, and their carcasses you shall have in abomination.
> 19:9–10: When you reap the harvest of your land, you shall not reap your field to its very border . . . and you shall not strip your vineland bare, neither shall you gather the fallen grapes of your vineyard; you shall leave them for the poor and the sojourner.
> 19:19: There shall not come upon you a garment of cloth made of two kinds of stuff.
> 19:27: You shall not round off the hair on your temples or mar the edges of your beard.

A few people actually do follow (some of) these commandments: some Orthodox Jews, some Amish orders. But almost all other Christians and Jews feel free to disregard them entirely. Even confronted with explicit commandments, then, and commandments put in the strongest terms (*Leviticus*'s punishment for "abomination" is usually execution), we still feel entirely free to go our own way. Many people say that these commands are just "historical relics," like dietary restrictions that once made sense but no longer are necessary.

The point is not that we are hypocritical. The point is that *we can and must decide for ourselves*—understanding, for example, that regardless of what the text literally says, it comes from a historical place very unlike our own and therefore may apply differently to our time, or not apply at all. Even if we decide to follow its commands, that is still a *decision*—our decision.

This is not just an abstract point. Here is another passage from the same part of *Leviticus*:

> 20:13: If a man lies with a man as with a woman, it is an abomination.

This commandment is regularly cited by people who claim (as they put it) that "God hates homosexuality." However, these very same people, like most of the rest of us, disregard most of the rest of *Leviticus*. Down where I live, certain churches even hold pig roasts at rallies where speakers rail against homosexuality and other modern sins. But God hates pig eating just as much as God hates (male) homosexuality, if you take the text literally. And if you *don't* take the text literally, as seems plausible enough in the case of pig eating, you can hardly claim that you have no choice but to take it literally in cases where it happens to accord with your preexisting convictions. This does seem hypocritical. In neither case, really, is even an explicit commandment the end of the story.

People who continue reading *Exodus* after the Ten Commandments are often disturbed to discover that in the very next chapter the Bible seems to condone slavery:

> When you buy a Hebrew slave, he shall serve six years, and in the seventh he shall go out free, for nothing. If he comes in single, he shall go out single; if he comes in married, his wife shall go out with him. . . . [But] when a man sells his daughter as a slave, she shall not go out as the male slaves do. . . . When a man strikes his slave, male or female, with a rod and the slave dies under his hand, he shall be punished. But if the slave survives a day or two, he is not to be punished; for the slave is his money. (*Exodus* 21: 2–3, 7, 20–21)

These passages were used by American slaveholders during the struggle over abolition to show that God approved of slavery! Now, with slavery gone and its evil recognized, the rationalization is transparent. Yet the words are there. Literally, the text does not say slavery is wrong. It allows slavery under certain pretty broad conditions.

We can appreciate the writers of *Exodus* for what they tried to do: adapt a living ethical tradition to the needs of the moment. No doubt these rules promised at least some small improvement over slavery as it had been practiced. They began to give (some) slaves (some) rights. But now of course times have changed, drastically. We still have a living tradition (*many* living traditions) but the needs of three thousand years ago are no longer ours. We need to rethink and adapt the tradition just as the prophets and lawgivers of biblical times did. And that may mean—as clearly it does mean in the case of these words about slavery—that we need to go beyond their words to the *spirit* of their acts and of our shared tradition, as full of ambiguity and uncertainty as that is too! Again there is no refuge in the text. There is no alternative but to decide for ourselves.

A Biblical Ideal

There is a revealing part of the Sodom story never cited in appeals to God's authority, but a part nonetheless, and in fact right next to the episode cited above. Just before the angels visit Sodom, they visit the patriarch Abraham in his desert tent. As they leave, they declare God's intention to destroy Sodom if the rumors about it are true. Abraham is troubled by this. He cannot see the justice of killing the innocent along with the wicked. So Abraham, says the Bible, "went before the Lord." He actually took it upon himself to question God!

> Abraham drew near and said: "Wilt thou indeed destroy the righteous with the wicked? Suppose there are fifty righteous within the city; wilt thou then destroy the place and not spare it for the fifty righteous who are in it? Far be it from thee to do such a thing, to slay the righteous with the wicked, so that the righteous fare as the wicked! Far be that from thee! Shall not the Judge of all the Earth do right?"
>
> And the Lord said, "If I find at Sodom fifty righteous in the city, I will spare the whole place for their sake." Abraham answered, "Behold, I have taken upon myself to speak to the Lord, I who am but dust and ashes. Suppose five of the fifty righteous are lacking. Wilt thou destroy the whole city for lack of five?" And He said, "I will not destroy it if I find forty-five there." Again he spoke to him, and said, "Suppose forty are found there." He answered, "For the sake of forty I will not do it." Then he said, "Oh let not the Lord be angry, and I will speak. Suppose thirty are found there." He answered, "I will not do it, if I find thirty there." He said, "Behold, I have taken upon myself to speak to the Lord. Suppose twenty are found there." He answered, "For the sake of twenty I will not destroy it."
>
> Then [Abraham] said, "Oh let not the Lord be angry, and I will speak again but this once. Suppose ten are found there." The Lord answered, "For the sake of ten I will not destroy it". And the Lord went his way, when he had finished speaking to Abraham; and Abraham returned to his place.

CAN GOD DEFINE THE GOOD?

Here's a philosophical question for you. Are good things good because God says they are, or does God say they are good because they are good?

One view is: what's good is good because God says so. God's commanding something *defines* it as good. This view is called the "Divine Command Theory."

The Divine Command Theory seems simple, straightforward and, if you believe in God, pretty natural. That it doesn't work for atheists may be a problem—after all, atheists have values too—and there certainly will be problems when the commands of God are unclear or the commands of one religion's God conflict with those of another's. But there is also an intriguing problem with this theory first pointed out nearly 2500 years ago by the Greek philosopher Socrates.

If God's commands alone define the good, then God's commands begin to seem arbitrary. Suppose that instead of commanding us not to kill, God had commanded us to kill. *Thou shalt kill.* According to the Divine Command Theory, then, killing would be good and refraining from killing would be bad.

But this can't be right. Killing really is wrong whether God says so or not. And in fact we do have reservations and second thoughts at some of the points in the Bible where God's own ethics seem a little questionable—as in some of the examples just mentioned in the text. If the Divine Command Theory were true, the very idea of questioning God's own ethics—Abraham's question, "Shall not the Judge of all the Earth do right?"—would be completely senseless.

There's a related problem too. If the Divine Command Theory is true, it makes no sense to say "God is good." Whatever God commands is, well, whatever God commands. If God's commands *define* the good, then there is no point admiring God for goodness. (This is also why we can't respond by arguing that God never *would* command killing. Why not? *Whatever* God commanded, whatever God did, would be good, by definition.) But this seems, in a sense, to cheapen God. It ought to mean something (and God ought to want it to mean something) to say, "God is good."

We could conclude that God says certain things are good because they *are* good. Then, however, we consider the good to be independent of God. To say "God is good" *is* in a certain sense to judge God. God's commands are not the end of the story: we must still decide whether God (or rather, God's many and varied interpreters) is right. In the abstract this may sound like some kind of heresy, but as the last section has pointed out, we actually do it all the time, for example when we disregard commandments that we consider outdated. Once again, it appears that there is no alternative to thinking for ourselves!

What is the Bible telling us here? Surely not that we should simply do what we're told, and accept whatever authority, even the highest religious authority of all, decides to do. Quite the contrary. Abraham, the revered forefather, did not simply obey. He would not accept injustice even when God Himself proposed to do it. Abraham went to God—Abraham who is "but dust and ashes"—and complained. He questioned, he challenged. "Shall not the Judge of all the Earth do right?"

Abraham thought for himself. Moreover, he was honored for doing so. God listened and answered. Indeed Lot himself was saved, the Bible says later, because God was "mindful of Abraham."

Mustn't we do the same? Once again, I don't mean that we must never listen to others. Listening to good advice and thinking about new perspectives are crucial. Religious texts too have long been sources of great inspiration and stimulation: use them. Speak the shared language; retell the stories. Still, in the end, it is up to *us* to interpret, ponder, and decide what they mean. So the next time someone acts as though it is yours only to obey the commands of God (according to them), or yours only to obey some other authority—remember Abraham!

Exercises and Notes

EXPLORATIONS

Is there a distinctive way *you* approach moral questions that traces back to your religious background? If so, what is it? Consider the role that religion plays, or does not play, in ethics for *you*. If you are religious, you might explore the ethics of your religion more fully. Ask your priest, minister, rabbi, or other leader for some good readings. For Christian ethics, a weighty tome, both systematic and historical, is Servais Pinckaers, *The Sources of Christian Ethics* (Catholic University of America Press, 1995). For a vigorous and contemporary liberal Catholicism, see the works of Daniel MacGuire, for example *The Moral Choice* (Doubelday, 1978). For an equally vigorous traditional Catholicism, see the works of Pope John Paul II. For Jewish ethics, see Jacob Agus, *The Vision and the Way* (Frederick Ungar, 1968). For an atheist's view, see Kai Nielsen, *Ethics Without God* (Prometheus Publishers, 1973).

The natural next step is to explore the ethics of some religions other than your own. Talk to people from other traditions. Is there a distinctive way *they* approach moral questions that traces back to *their* religious background? If so, what is it? Take a course or look at some books that compare different religious traditions. One good place to start is Peggy Morgan and Clive Lawton, *Ethical Issues in Six Religious Traditions* (Edinburgh University Press, 1996).

Look carefully at the ethical arguments of religious leaders. For example, why do the popes oppose birth control? Read Pope Paul's "Humanae Vitae" and other relevant papal encyclicals ("Humanae Vitae" is widely reprinted in ethics collections, such as Robert Baker and Frederick Elliston, *Philosophy and Sex* [Prometheus Books, 1975]; most papal encyclicals are available directly from the United States Catholic Conference Publishing Service, 3211 4th Street NE, Washington DC 20017, 1–800-235–8722, <www.nccbuscc.org>) and find out. It's not because the embryo or fetus is a human being—in many cases, there's no fertilization at all. So why *is* it? Once you figure out the argument (it *is* an argument, not a mere pronouncement) ask yourself whether the values to which Pope Paul appeals are specific to Catholicism or more general. You may not necessarily agree, but there's often a lot to be learned anyway.

Another remarkable encyclical is Pope John Paul II's "Laborem Exercens" (1981). John Paul's marriage of Christian humanism and Marxist influences here produces a widely applicable and eloquent plea for work and work places that befit human beings, and therefore a sharp critique of what John Paul calls the "economism" of both capitalism and communism. John Paul II is now crusading for Third World debt relief and income redistribution. Here too a pope enters the contemporary discussion in a way that is far broader and more powerful than a merely sectarian pronouncement.

READ THE BIBLE!

Try reading the old Bible stories in a new light—not looking for a single and unambiguous "moral," but appreciating the complexity and depth of the stories as part of their appeal and their value, for that is what life itself is like.

All of the great figures of the Old Testament (Torah), for example, are morally complex. Abraham, the chosen forefather of the forefathers, raises the knife over his own son. He and Sarah (and in the next generation Isaac and Rebekah) consistently misrepresent their relationship to others, enriching themselves in the process but repeatedly imperiling others on the way. Jacob cheats his brother out of his birthright, and is in turned cheated, misled, manipulated, and exploited by his family for the rest of his life. Yet it is from his struggle with an angel that the name "Israel" is derived. Rachel steals her father's household idols and lies about it all around. Yet she is the beloved wife and matriarch.

Ask some questions. Does Jacob reap what he sowed? Would you sacrifice your child (or *any* child) as Abraham almost did? Why would God ask such a thing? (And don't just say: to put Abraham to the test. There is more depth in the story. Why would God need or *want* to put Abraham to the test?) Were these (and others) good acts? Did God think so? How could we tell?

Consider the Cain and Abel story in *Genesis* 4:1–16: the story of the first murder in history, mythologically speaking. Why does God reject Cain's offering and accept Abel's, thus setting off Cain's anger and the murder, a not entirely unforeseeable result? What does Cain mean when he asks, "Am I my brother's keeper?" Is the moral of the story that he *is* (that we *are*) his/our brothers' (each others') keepers? If so, or in any case, why doesn't God say so—why doesn't God answer him? Isn't Cain partly suggesting that *God* ought to be Abel's "keeper"—that God also bears some responsibility for what happened?

In the New Testament, Jesus's disciples constantly complain that his parables are confusing and ambiguous. (And don't you think it's interesting that the Bible reports this?) Each has been interpreted in many ways, put to many uses. Might they be more than a little like the story of Nuri Bey?

Jesus certainly had his reasons. Maybe he spoke in parables because it wasn't safe to speak more directly. Then again, maybe there is a deeper wisdom here. Could it be—could it just possibly be—that, as with the Sufis' stories, this is their very point? That what Jesus meant to teach us with these stories is not an exact moral lesson or rule, but something more like a sense for the subtlety of things, maybe even the mysterious ways of God?

Some intriguing parables and sayings of Jesus can be found in *Matthew* 6:25–33; *Matthew* 20:1–16; *Luke* 19:12–26; and *Luke* 9:23–27—a few of many examples.

ABORTION AND THE BIBLE

Does the Bible take a stand on abortion? Nowhere does the Bible actually discuss abortion explicitly, but related themes do come up, and Christian pro-life advocates regularly cite certain passages that suggest that a fetus has human standing in the eyes of God. For example, there is a stirring passage in *Psalms* 139:

> For thou didst form my inward parts; thou didst knit me together in my mother's womb. . . . My frame was not hidden from Thee, when I was being made in secret, intricately wrought in the depths of the earth. Thy eyes beheld my unformed substance, in thy book were written, every one of them, the days that were formed for me. . . .

If God cares for us even in the womb, then, pro-life advocates conclude, here must be an "us" to care for: we must already exist as persons in God's eyes.

However, others have questioned this reading of the passage, pointing out that it is more poetic than anything else (the *Psalms* are hardly meant literally), and is more concerned with creation in general than with the point at which life begins (indeed, the last two lines seem to suggest that God knows and cares for us even *before* we are in the womb, which by the pro-life logic would imply the unlikely view that we are fully human even *before* conception).

Christian pro-choice advocates, meanwhile, cite other passages that seem to suggest that abortion might be acceptable. One is in *Exodus* 21:

> When men strive together, and hurt a woman with child, so that there is a miscarriage, and yet no harm follows, the one who hurt her shall be fined,

according as the woman's husband lays upon him; and he shall pay as the judges determine.

The penalty for murder is death (e.g. in verse 12 of the same chapter: "Who strikes a man so that he dies shall be put to death") so pro-choice Christians argue that the Bible can hardly consider causing the death of a fetus (miscarriage) to be murder if only a fine is specified as punishment.

On the other hand, the phrase "and no harm follows" is puzzling. Isn't there necessarily harm to the fetus? From this pro-life advocates have taken heart, arguing that the passage is, well, ambiguous. The Hebrew phrase translated above as "so that there is a miscarriage" *might* also be translated as "so that her child comes out" (apparently there is no ancient Hebrew word specifically for miscarriage), which *might* be read as meaning that birth occurs prematurely but with no (other?) harm to the baby—in which case the passage could have just the opposite meaning. The Greek version has still other ambiguities.

It seems that neither passage is really very clear!

The following are some other places where the Christian Bible touches (or has been interpreted as touching) on the question of the status of fetal human life: *Job* 3 and 10; *Ecclesiastes* 4 and 6; *Jeremiah* 1; *Luke* 1. Read them (all), and read them in context (that is, read the whole chapters, even when only a few verses are relevant; also, read all of *Psalm* 139 and *Exodus* 21, cited above). Then ask what you can conclude about what the Bible thinks of the status of fetal human life. Does a clear picture emerge from these chapters taken together? Does a clear picture emerge from any of them taken separately? Explain your answers.

CITATIONS

"The Ancient Coffer of Nuri Bey" comes from Idries Shah, *Tales of the Dervishes* (Penguin, 1970). Citations from the Christian Bible (Revised Standard Version) are given in the text. For the original of the argument cited in the box "Can God Define the Good?", see Plato's *Euthyphro,* available in many editions, in complete editions of Plato's work, and in collections such as Penguin's *The Last Days of Socrates.*

On the *Genesis* passage cited in the text, remember that in biblical Hebrew, "to know" means to have sexual intercourse. Compare *Genesis* 4:1: "And Adam knew Eve his wife, and she conceived and bore Cain. . . ." A short but pointed treatment of the ambiguities and complexities of the Lot story and the biblical treatment of homosexuality (in the Torah and Koran as well) is Arthur Ide, *The City of Sodom* (Monument Press, 1985). On arguing with God, see also *Exodus* 32:1–15, where Moses dissuades God from destroying Israel after the incident of the Golden Calf. Here Moses argues with God almost as with an equal. And the Bible explicitly says that, as a result, God "repented of the evil which He thought to do to His people."

II

VALUES

CHAPTER 3

◯

Paying Attention to Values

Many moral issues arise from conflicting or unclear moral *values*. To understand moral issues, let alone to have any hope of making any progress on them, we therefore need to begin by looking at those values. What do we mean when we say something is a value? What do we mean when we say something is a *moral* value? And how do we begin spelling out the contending moral values in a particular issue?

DEFINITIONS: VALUES AND MORAL VALUES

What Are Values?

We hold many values. We value fairness, trustworthiness, the well-being of others and the world, and many other things too. These we consider moral values. We also value good neighbors, good music, daily exercise, our kids' laughter, meeting new people, and again many other things, which are *not* moral values (not *im*moral values either, simply *non*moral values). Truth, equality, cleanliness; "life, liberty, and the pursuit of happiness"; faith, hope, and charity; "random kindness and senseless acts of beauty"; peace and quiet, enthusiasm, good sportsmanship—all of these are "values" in the broad sense.

Or rather: all of these are *examples* of values in a broad sense. But they do not tell us what values themselves *are*. A philosopher will ask: what do they all have in common that makes them all examples of "values"?

Let us say this. Our values are *those things we care about, that matter to us; those goals and ideals we aspire to and measure ourselves or others or our society by.* When I say that I value playing fair or staying healthy, I mean (at least) that I am interested in these things, that I care about them, and probably that I do specific things to promote or safeguard them. I want to hear my kids laugh, so I tell them jokes.

Notice that this definition does not say anything about where values ultimately come from or how they might be prioritized or justified. That comes later. Right now we just need a standard for classification. "Bad" or questionable values count too. We also value having a lot of stuff, driving fast, lording it over others, and so on. Maybe we shouldn't, but we (sometimes?) do. Pirates value their loot; addicts value their drugs.

Values may also conflict. Certainly we value incompatible things, at least in certain situations. I value peace and quiet, and I also value my children's freedom. I can't always have both. On the other hand, if values didn't conflict, life would be a lot less interesting!

What Are Moral Values?

Values come in types. *Aesthetic* values have to do with art, beauty, and attractiveness. *Scientific* values and others have to do with knowledge, truth, experiment, and so on. *Economic* values have to do with production, efficiency, and market prices. *Instrumental* values have to do with the means to our ends: the effectiveness of technologies, the usefulness of our tools. There are other types too.

And: there are *moral* values—a kind of value distinct from those just listed, and crucial to our study here. Moral values are a subset, in other words, of values generally. Moral values include fairness, trustworthiness, the well-being of others and the world, as just mentioned, and many others too, such as equality, respect, and responsibility; reducing pain and suffering; "life, liberty, and the pursuit of happiness"; humility, benevolence, and keeping your promises.

Once again, though, these examples do not tell us what moral values themselves *are*. What do they all have in common that makes them all examples of "moral" values?

Let us say this. Moral values are *those values that give voice to the needs and legitimate expectations of others as well as ourselves*. Moral values connect us to a larger world ("the needs of others as well as ourselves") and introduce the question of what others are entitled to ask from us and what we are entitled to ask from them and from ourselves ("legitimate expectations").

These terms may need some explaining.

By "others" we usually understand other people. However, the term may also include (some?) other animals and the natural world too. Chapters 20 and 21 return to this question.

Note that our own selves are included. Morality on our definition is not opposed to the self: rather, it puts the self into context. We come to see ourselves as one among others. You can see already why values like equality and fairness come up. Highlighting the needs of others, you can also see why reducing suffering and promoting well-being are vital moral values too.

We have "legitimate expectations" to be treated with respect and as equals. Some legitimate expectations we regard as *rights*: rights to "life, liberty, and the pursuit of happiness"; rights to free speech or to hold property; and so on. We also legitimately expect each other to act responsibly, keep promises, and so on. Another way of saying this is: we have legitimate expectations both

Morality and Self-Interest

Moral values as defined here do not exclude your own needs and expectations. Quite the contrary: your own needs and expectations are built into the definition. Others' needs get a voice as well as your own. The essential thing, though, is that your own needs cannot be the whole story. Moral values connect us to a larger world. We come to see the self as one among others. The self doesn't vanish—its gets company.

On the other hand, pure egoism is excluded as a "moral" possibility. Taking no account of the needs and expectations of others leaves you with values, yes, but not moral ones. Is this a problem?

A

Some people think that we all just are, and cannot help being, pure egoists. Everything we do or value, they say, is purely for our own sakes. Really we only pay attention to the needs and expectations of others for our own sakes, for what we can gain from it.

This view is called "psychological egoism." If true, it *would* be a problem. It would imply that moral values—caring for the needs of others and responding to their expectations for their own sakes—are simply impossible.

But psychological egoism is false. In fact it makes nonsense of 99 percent of our lives. Very few people past infancy are *that* wrapped up in themselves. We're social animals, and in almost any life with others there's also awareness and responsiveness to others. It does not have to go anywhere near so far as self-sacrifice. It's enough that others' needs register, at least to some extent, without our always referring back to our own. An athlete sets a new record and all of us, watching, whatever our allegiances, are thrilled too. A kid gets lost in the airport and two dozen strangers are ready to help.

"Well," says the egoist, "that's because I couldn't sleep at night if I didn't help. I'm really doing it for myself."

"No—that's backwards!" I say. "Why couldn't you sleep at night if you didn't help? *Because you care about the kid!* If you really *were* a pure egoist the kid wouldn't matter to you at all."

"But what if I *want* to help?" asks the egoist. "Doing what I want is certainly following my self-interest."

"That depends on what you want," I reply. "If you want someone else's good for his or her own sake, then it's not an egoistic want, even if it happens to be your want. A desire for someone else's good is a desire for that person's good—it does not necessarily bear on your own. . . ."

B

Some people think that we *ought* to be pure egoists, even though we often aren't. This view is not committed to psychological egoism; it is called "ethical egoism."

Ethical egoism is not the claim that we ought to do whatever we want to do—for what we want to do might not be in our (carefully considered) self-interest. For example, we might want to do something harmful to ourselves in the long run (but fun now—you fill in the examples), or we might even want to put someone else's needs ahead of our own.

Ethical egoists are more calculating. Often they will be sociable enough. It's in their interests to maintain others' good will, after all, and besides sometimes their desires may coincide with others'. Still, they say, the bottom line ought to be their own good, and nothing but.

If it is to be *moral* on our definition, though, this sort of egoism must defend itself by reference to standards that go beyond the self. It must make reference to the needs and legitimate expectations of others as well as the self. Oddly enough, this is exactly what happens. Ethical egoists argue that everyone will be better off if we all act to further our own self-interests. Many argue on economic grounds, for example, that a system of universal self-seeking, like capitalism, produces the greatest social well-being in the long run.

These are arguable points, to be sure. What's really remarkable, though, is that they are not egoistic arguments. The whole aim is to show that *everyone* will be better off if everyone adopts ethical egoism. These are arguments that *do* give voice to the needs and legitimate expectations of others, because others' interests or rights are counted too. The ethical egoists I know (I do know some) are absolutely scrupulous in this regard. They *do* see themselves as one among others; their egoism *is* moral—just maybe unusual!

C

Self-centeredness sometimes has its uses. At times of transition in our lives, we may find ourselves with fairly few attachments and unsure of our direction. A turn inward—a preoccupation for a while with our selves—is natural and healthy. It's dramatically limited (I would argue) as a fulltime way of life, but sometimes sensible in the short run. Morality isn't the whole story either.

Besides, selves often are fragile. Sometimes we need to give ourselves the support and attention we need to recover a sense of who we are and what we want. This is probably much more common than the opposite—the self that claims too much and needs to be put in its place.

Still more common than both, though, are many other reasons why we fail to take account of the needs and expectations of others. I think that the real concern of moralists should not be egoism but *inattention*. Habit, for one thing, and the inability to listen. Or the unwillingness to listen, as in offhand self-justification. Or the unwillingness to acknowledge sheer *difference*—this would be "self-centeredness" not in the sense of pursuing only one's own interests but in the sense of taking one's self to be the only kind of self there can be. You can't even begin to cross the gap between self and other if you don't think there is a gap in the first place.

So morality sometimes does have an uphill fight. There are parts of ourselves that resist. It just may not be so useful to think of those parts as "egoistic." We're more complex and interesting than that!

about other people's *acts* (and our own) and *character* (and our own). Chapter 4 will make more of these distinctions.

Moral values "give voice" to needs and expectations. This means: moral values include those needs and expectations, maybe even insist upon them. They serve as a reminder of those needs and expectations, and give us a way to speak for those needs and expectations when or if they begin to slip out of focus.

GUIDELINES

When you turn to specific moral debates, keep our definition in mind. To spell out the moral values involved, ask: what needs and legitimate expectations, both your own and others', are at stake here? What needs and legitimate expectations are the parties to this debate trying to speak for?

Some moral debates will be new to you, and answering these questions will take some research or exploration—listening carefully to the different sides, asking around. For other moral debates you can fill in the blanks much more easily. You've heard the contending positions already, or can easily figure them out. The point of our definition of moral values, in any case, is to give you the right blanks to fill in. It gives you the right questions to ask. Here are some guidelines as you begin to answer them.

Expect Diversity

In the first place, expect *diversity*. We hold a lot of moral values, and they aren't shy about showing up all the time.

Here, for example, is a survey of some moral issues from just one weekend's newspapers. Notice how many different values quickly come up. I will underline them as we go.

The president is proposing to raise the minimum wage. It's a matter of fairness, he says. The underlying plea is that people who are working hard, supporting themselves and their families and contributing to society, should be able at least to get by. "If people are going to show up for work," he says, "they ought to be able to raise their children in <u>dignity</u>."

He also notes that many of the people struggling to get by on minimum-wage jobs are single mothers whose only fallback is welfare or homelessness. Meeting even their basic needs—<u>survival</u> and some degree of <u>independence</u>—requires action.

Meanwhile, opponents worry about losing the <u>social benefits</u> of lower wages, such as more jobs, and about <u>fairness</u> (again) to employers at the margins. Would raising the minimum wage push some of them out of business? Might it therefore actually reduce the number of jobs available?

The next page: The tobacco industry is back in court, fighting liability claims from individuals and from many of the states. Issues of <u>truthfulness</u> and <u>responsibility</u> come up. How dangerous did the manufacturers know cigarette smoking to be, and when did they know it? On the other hand, what are the responsibilities of smokers who "should have known better"?

A related article reports that small American tobacco farmers have now made common cause with antismoking forces against the big tobacco companies, who appear ready to cut them loose. The antismoking forces are unwilling to cut the farmers off completely. Probably they also need the farmers' political support. But the arguments are moral too: it's just not <u>fair</u> to cut them off, not after both the tobacco companies and the government led them on for most of the century. Besides, we care about saving small family farms and the values we associate with them: a more <u>family-focused life</u>, <u>self-reliance</u>, <u>stewardship</u> of the land.

A photo shows a line of Amish buggies stretching along a country road. A funeral procession for a buggy driver killed by a drunk driver in a car. An all too familiar story, made more poignant still because the accident we imagine is also a collision (literally) of two radically different cultures. A life of <u>simplicity</u> and <u>sobriety</u>, cut short too soon by a culture that is the opposite of both.

We learn from a related article, meanwhile, that the Texas state Senate is about to approve a bill that "would make people under age 21 who climb behind a wheel after drinking subject to losing their licenses for four to six months—even if there is only a trace of alcohol on their breaths." "Zero tolerance," the sponsor calls it. If we expect <u>responsible driving</u>, he says, we have to get (very) tough.

So: here are three issues and fourteen values, including some overlaps (fairness comes up more than once, but in different senses). That's diversity for you. And that's just a start, as you'll see in the next section. Each debate also has its own context—from social and political issues to personal responsibility and the nature of the "simple life"—or sometimes several at once. Other values lie in the background, a little less explicit. Doing the best by the most people, for instance (as in: what are the overall social effects of raising the minimum wage?). Old ways versus new ways, for instance (the unsettling question raised by the Amish way of life for mainstream culture). And others as well.

Look in Depth

Many different values also come up within each issue, quite apart from the others. Call this *depth*.

Take the Amish funeral. Most obviously, what's at stake is drunk driving: once again, a severe form of social irresponsibility. Think of what it means to take the wheel of a machine that can maim and kill when you are not fully aware and capable. Even worse is when you are just a beginning driver: hence the Texas response.

The Texas response, however, raises questions too. Other concerns come up. If a "trace of alcohol" is enough to revoke someone's license, how small is a "trace"? If an officer smells anything, is that enough? Is a blip on a Breathalyzer enough? What about people whose prescription drugs might have a trace of alcohol? My students, barely 21 themselves, tend to worry that the proposed law gives police officers an unsettling amount of discretion.

Fairness comes up. Is it fair to target only minors in this way? Isn't drunk driving an irresponsible act regardless of the driver's age? Is the idea that minors are more dangerous at the wheel with *any* alcohol because they are inexperienced drivers? Or is the idea that if minors have been drinking at all, they've already violated the law, and therefore deserve even stricter strict punishment? (The article doesn't say.) In that case, is a four- to six-month revocation strict enough?

There is still more. This photo would not even have appeared in the paper had the victim not been Amish. So we return to the clash of cultures the Amish symbolize for us. The Amish won the legal right to drive buggies on the roads only after a hard-fought struggle in many states and over many years. Why? They don't care to share many of the conveniences that the rest of us take for granted. Why not? The Amish say: modern "conveniences" corrupt the simplicity of our relation to each other, the earth, and God. Without them, the Amish have created and sustained tight-knit, mutually supportive communities that are the envy of many of the rest of us. Lately some environmentalists have also begun to champion Amish methods on ecological grounds. Using horses rather than tractors is much better for the land itself. It's no accident that the Amish have created and sustained the finest farms in their areas.

So there is much to think about here. Can we reclaim some of the virtues the Amish represent without simply giving up on modern life? If not, what does that say about how things are with us? If so, why aren't we doing it?

Notice again: all of this complexity arises from thinking about just one photograph, and even so we have just scratched the surface. Moral issues like these have *histories*, and represent the intersection or manifestation of many different concerns and struggles. When you are exploring a moral issue, then, don't just mention one or two main concerns and move on. Take some time with them—and give yourself some time to take. Look in depth.

Be Fair

Spelling out some of the moral values at stake in these cases may be hard, especially when you disagree with them. Amish buggy drivers may just make you impatient. Drunk drivers may make you impatient too, and you may not want to consider the dangers of "zero tolerance." People who always complain about helping the poor, or tobacco company lawyers who still won't admit that smoking may cause cancer, may just annoy you.

But: we've already spoken about keeping an open mind. Here is another place that we often turn more dogmatic than we should. It's wiser to remind ourselves again that we don't know everything there is to know. In particular, if we dismiss some moral values without any kind of exploration or careful attention, we might never know what kinds of depth we missed. To look at a buggy driver as a mere curiosity, or as a hazard that ought to be banned from the road, misses a lot that is intriguing and maybe even enriching. *Be fair* to them: ask what these people are about instead. What are their goals and ideals? What matters to them? What are their needs and expectations?

At least try to see matters from others' points of view. You're not being asked, at this point, to decide who is "right" and who is "wrong," or which way we ought finally to choose (if we must). No: the task here is just to figure out the values involved. And that means: on all sides. Not just filtered through a moral position you've already taken. Put your own position aside for a moment. Listen first; decide later.

Explain and Clarify

Moral values often show up in forms that are not fully spelled out or clear. Part of our job in unpacking moral issues, then, is to do some of the explaining and clarifying ourselves.

Make some distinctions.

MOLLY (four years old): Ruthie got to use the big markers and I only got to use the plain ones!

ME: Yup. [To myself: Uh oh]

MOLLY: That's not fair!

ME: Why not?

MOLLY: Because I should get to use the big ones if Ruthie does!

ME: But the big markers are not washable and you're not quite old enough to remember to keep them off your clothes and the table. As soon as you can keep them just on the paper, you can use them too.

MOLLY: I can! I can!

ME: Oh, Molly, that's what you said yesterday, and I let you use them, but you ended up with a big orange splot on your shirt. A nonwashable splot!

[Molly sniffles.]

Is it fair that Molly cannot use the big markers? If so, it is because fairness is not as simple as it looks on its face—because fairness cannot necessarily be measured by immediate equality of results. It's complicated. Fairness asks us to allow each child all that he or she is capable of, consistent with other needs and limits, including fairness to parents who have to try to wash markers off clothes or tables.

It's not so easy to spell out in a way that a 4-year-old can understand. In fact, just for that reason, some other approach to the problem sometimes may be needed. Getting bigger washable markers, for example. The point is that this is how it goes, in real-life practice. Pay attention and take seriously the demand for clarification and distinctions.

In fact, fairness is a passion with all of us. Is it fair, for example, to set up a system of preferences for one group over another, even if it only comes into play when qualifications are otherwise equal and/or does not compel any particular choice? Some people argue that it is; others argue that it cannot be. It's the same sort of issue. Would some distinctions help? Can you know until you've tried?

Don't Downgrade Emotion

One last clip from the newspaper. Developers and environmentalists clash over new building along a river that serves as many downstream communities' water supply and feeds major shellfish banks off the coast. The river is already polluted by runoff from farms and lawn fertilizers, sewage treatment plants, and so on, though for just that reason the impact of any single new development by itself is not that great.

The civil engineer who works for the developer and presented the case to the City Planning Commission has this to say about his environmentalist counterparts: "We're doing this from a fact standpoint and they [the environmentalists] are doing this from an emotional standpoint." *We* have facts, he says; *they're* just "emotional." His suggestion, of course, is that they should not be taken seriously. Emotion is supposed to be inappropriate when ethical or political matters come up. Is it?

No. Being emotional can be entirely appropriate. Indeed, it's necessary. Remember: values themselves are things we *care* about. "Care" is an emotion. It's not only an emotion—it rests on "facts," perspectives on the world, histories and personal choices, and many other things—but the emotional side, the caring side, is essential as well.

The developers "care" too, of course. They too have values. They want to build houses and roads and malls and make money. They're a little annoyed in this case too, if you read between the lines, because they have to work under many more restrictions than they used to, and still are being criticized for not doing enough. The suggestion is that this isn't quite fair—and that is a feeling, in part, too.

What *would* be inappropriate is "pure" emotion: having no facts at all, just a "feeling." But clearly this is not true of either side in this debate. The environmentalists in this case have facts just like the developers. They have facts about the overall state of the river, about alternative uses of the site in question, and so on. Perhaps the developers, sensing they have the Planning Commission on their side, can afford to speak with the appearance of dispassion, while the environmentalists sound more upset or desperate. But this has nothing to do with who has facts and who doesn't—it has to do with who is being listened to.

In short: moral values are partly emotional, just as they are partly fact based. All moral values, on both (all) sides. So don't avoid emotion in expressing them. Do not therefore become maudlin or hysterical; but also do not pretend to be dispassionate and accuse the other side of being uninformed. *Both* are unhelpful extremes. Just speak carefully, listen sympathetically, and try to give all of the relevant values a voice that is measured but strong.

"The Great American Desert" (selections)

EDWARD ABBEY

Edward Abbey was an American nature writer, backcountry hiker, and militant defender of wilderness whose writings include the classic *Desert Solitaire* as well as the controversial novel *The Monkeywrench Gang*, which allegedly inspired some infamous environmental actions in the eighties and nineties.

In this essay Abbey is trying to explain why he loves the desert—why he values it and why we should too. So you might expect a nice poetic rhapsody to the loveliness of the desert, making us think of cactus-and-sunset pictures in Sierra Club calendars or travel magazines. But this is not what Abbey says— just the opposite. First he details the desert's horrors; then he tells you how to prepare to hike there if you're crazy enough to go in the first place (not that *he* ever prepares at all); then he reminds you to disrupt any mining or hunting or road-building activites you happen to run across; and finally he tells a story about an ancient arrow pointing at nothingness.

Yet he *is*, after all, explaining why he loves the desert. He is calling on certain values. See if you can figure out what they are. What *is* he saying about the arrow pointing at nothingness, for example? What kinds of values is he so proudly appealing to here?

Don't overlook the irony in this piece either. The long list of desert horrors comes right after Abbey tells us that he loved the desert "at first sight." Somehow the horrors make the desert *loveable*. How? And why does he tell us to pull up survey stakes, take out billboards, and so on, and so on? Isn't that illegal?

IN MY CASE it was love at first sight. This desert, all deserts, any desert. No matter where my head and feet may go, my heart and my entrails stay behind, here on the clean, true, comfortable rock, under the black sun of God's forsaken country. When I take on my next incarnation, my bones will remain bleaching nicely in a stone gulch under the rim of some faraway plateau, way out there in the back of beyond. An unrequited and excessive love, inhuman no doubt but painful anyhow, especially when I see my desert under attack. "The one death I cannot bear," said the Sonoran-Arizonan poet Richard Shelton. The kind of love that makes a man selfish, possessive, irritable. If you're thinking of a visit, my natural reaction is like a rattlesnake's—to warn you off. What I want to say goes something like this.

Survival Hint #1: Stay out of there. Don't go. Stay home and read a good book, this one for example. The Great American Desert is an awful place. People get hurt, get sick, get lost out there. Even if you survive, which is not certain, you will have a miserable time. The desert is for movies and God-intoxicated mystics, not for family recreation.

Let me enumerate the hazards. First the Walapai tiger, also known as conenose kissing bug. *Triatoma protracta* is a true bug, black as sin, and it flies through the night quiet as an assassin. It does not attack directly like a mosquito or deerfly, but alights at a discreet distance, undetected, and creeps upon you, its hairy little feet making not the slightest noise. The kissing bug is fond of warmth and like Dracula requires mammalian blood for sustenance. When it reaches you the bug crawls onto your skin so gently, so softly that unless your senses are hyperacute you feel nothing. Selecting a tender point, the bug slips its conical proboscis into your flesh, injecting a poisonous anesthetic. If you are asleep you will feel nothing. If you happen to be awake you may notice the faintest of pinpricks, hardly more than a brief ticklish sensation, which you will probably disregard. But the bug is already at work. Having numbed the nerves near the point of entry the bug proceeds (with a sigh of satisfaction, no doubt) to withdraw blood. When its belly is filled, it pulls out, backs off, and waddles away, so drunk and gorged it cannot fly.

At about this time the victim awakes, scratching at a furious itch. If you recognize the symptoms at once, you can sometimes find the bug in your vicinity and destroy it. But revenge will be your only satisfaction. Your night is ruined. If you are of average sensitivity to a kissing bug's poison, your entire body breaks out in hives, skin aflame from head to toe. Some people

---

"The Great American Desert," from *The Journey Home* by Edward Abbey, copyright © 1977 by Edward Abbey. Used by permission of Dutton, a division of Penguin Putnam, Inc.

become seriously ill, in many cases requring hospitalization. Others recover fully after five or six hours except for a hard and itchy swelling, which may endure for a week.

After the kissing bug, you should beware of rattlesnakes; we have half a dozen species, all offensive and dangerous, plus centipedes, millipedes, tarantulas, black widows, brown recluses, Gila monsters, the deadly poisonous coral snakes, and giant hairy desert scorpions. Plus an immense variety and near-infinite number of ants, midges, gnats, blood-sucking flies, and blood-guzzling mosquitoes. (You might think the desert would be spared at least mosquitoes? Not so. Peer in any water hole by day: swarming with mosquito larvae. Venture out on a summer's eve: The air vibrates with their mournful keening.) Finally, where the desert meets the sea, as on the coasts of Sonora and Baja California, we have the usual assortment of obnoxious marine life: sandflies, ghost crabs, stingrays, electric jellyfish, spiny sea urchins, man-eating sharks, and other creatures so distasteful one prefers not even to name them.

It has been said, and truly, that everything in the desert either stings, stabs, stinks, or sticks. You will find the flora here as venomous, hooked, barbed, thorny, prickly, needled, saw-toothed, hairy, stickered, mean, bitter, sharp, wiry, and fierce as the animals. Something about the desert inclines all living things to harshness and acerbity. The soft evolve out. Except for sleek and oily growths like the poison ivy—oh yes, indeed—that flourish in sinister profusion on the dank walls about the quicksand down in those corridors of gloom and labyrinthine monotony that men call canyons.

We come now to the third major hazard, which is sunshine. Too much of a good thing can be fatal. Sunstroke, heatstroke, and dehydration are common misfortunes in the bright American Southwest. If you can avoid the insects, reptiles, and arachnids, the cactus and the ivy, the smog of the southwestern cities, and the lung fungus of the desert valleys (carried by dust in the air), you cannot escape the desert sun. Too much exposure to it eventually causes, quite literally, not merely sunburn but skin cancer.

Much sun, little rain also means an arid climate. Compared with the high humidity of more hospitable regions, the dry heat of the desert seems at first not terribly uncomfortable—sometimes even pleasant. But that sensation of comfort is false, a deception, and therefore all the more dangerous, for it induces overexertion and an insufficient consumption of water, even when water is available. This leads to various internal complications, some immediate—sunstroke, for example—and some not apparent until much later. Mild but prolonged dehydration, continued over a span of months or years, leads to the crystallization of mineral solutions in the urinary tract, that is, to what urologists call urinary calculi or kidney stones. A disability common in all the world's arid regions. . . .

Up north in the Great Basin Desert, on the Plateau Province, in the canyon country, your heart will break, seeing the strip mines open up and the power plants rise where only cowboys and Indians and J. Wesley Powell ever roamed before.

Nevertheless, all is not lost; much remains, and I welcome the prospect of an army of lug-soled hiker's boots on the desert trails. To save what wilderness is left in the American Southwest—and in the American Southwest only the wilderness is worth saving—we are going to need all the recruits we can get. All the hands, heads, bodies, time, money, effort we can find. Presumably—and the Sierra Club, the Wilderness Society, the Friends of the Earth, the Audubon Society, the Defenders of Wildlife operate on this theory—those who learn to love what is spare, rough, wild, undeveloped, and unbroken will be willing to fight for it, will help resist the strip miners, highway builders, land developers, weapons testers, power producers, tree chainers, clear cutters, oil drillers, dam beavers, subdividers—the list goes on and on—before that zinc-hearted, termite-brained, squint-eyed, near-sighted, greedy crew succeeds in completely californicating what still survives of the Great American Desert.

So much for the Good Cause. Now what about desert hiking itself, you may ask. I'm glad you asked that question. I firmly believe that one should never—I repeat *never*—go out into that formidable wasteland of cactus, heat, serpents, rock, scrub, and thorn without careful planning, thorough and cautious preparation, and complete—never mind the expense!— *complete* equipment. My motto is: Be Prepared.

That is my belief and that is my motto. My practice, however, is a little different. I tend to go off in a more or less random direction myself, half-baked, half-assed, half-cocked, and half-ripped. Why? Well, because I have an idolent and melancholy nature and don't care to be bothered getting all those *things* together—all that bloody *gear*—maps, light, inspirational poetry, water, food—and because anyhow I approach nature with a certain surly ill-will, daring Her to make trouble Later . . . I may wish I had packed that something extra: matches perhaps, to mention one useful item, or maybe a spoon to eat my gruel with.

If I hike with another person it's usually the same; most of my friends have indolent and melancholy natures too. A cursed lot, all of them. I think of my comrade John De Puy, for example, sloping along for mile after mile like a god-damned camel—indefatigable—with those J. C. Penny hightops on his feet and that plastic pack on his back he got with five books of Green Stamps and nothing inside it but a sketchbook, some homemade jerky and a few cans of green chiles. Or Douglas Peacock, ex-Green Beret, just the opposite. Built like a buffalo, he loads a ninety-pound canvas pannier on his back at trailhead, loaded with guns, ammunition, bayonet, pitons and carabiners, cameras, field books, a 150-foot rope, geologist's sledge, rock samples, assay kit, field glasses, two gallons of water in steel canteens, jingle books, a case of C-rations, rope hammock, pharmaceuticals in a pig-iron box, raincoat, overcoat, two-man mountain tent, Dutch oven, hibachi, shovel, ax, inflatable boat, and near the top of the load and distributed through side and back pockets, easily accessible, a case of beer. Not because he enjoys or needs all that weight—he may never get to the bottom of that cargo on a ten-day outing—but simply because Douglas uses his packbag for general storage both at home and on the trail and prefers not to have to rearrange everything from time to time merely for the purposes of a hike. Thus my friends De Puy and Peacock; you may wish to avoid such extremes.

A few tips on desert etiquette:

1. Carry a cooking stove, if you must cook. Do not burn desert wood, which is rare and beautiful and required ages for its creation (an ironwood tree lives for over 1,000 years and juniper almost as long).

2. If you must, out of need, build a fire, then for God's sake allow it to burn itself out before you leave—do not bury it, as Boy Scouts and Campfire Girls do, under a heap of mud or sand. Scatter the ashes; replace any rocks you may have used in constructing a fireplace; do all you can to obliterate the evidence that you camped here. (The Search & Rescue Team may be looking for you.)

3. Do not bury garbage—the wildlife will only dig it up again. Burn what will burn and pack out the rest. The same goes for toilet paper. Don't bury it, *burn it*.

4. Do not bathe in desert pools, natural tanks, *tinajas*, potholes. Drink what water you need, take what you need, and leave the rest for the next hiker and more important for the bees, birds, and animals—bighorn sheep, coyotes, lions, foxes, badgers, deer, wild pigs, wild horses—whose *lives* depend on that water.

5. Always remove and destroy survey stakes, flagging, advertising sign-boards, mining claim markers, animal traps, poisoned bait, seismic exploration geophones, and other such artifacts of industrialism. The men who put those things there are up to no good and it is our duty to confound them. Keep America Beautiful. Grow a Beard. Take a Bath. Burn a Billboard.

Anyway—why go into the desert? Really, why do it? That sun, roaring at you all day long. The fetid, tepid, vapid little water holes slowly evaporating under a scum of grease, full of cannibal beetles, spotted toads, horsehair worms, liver flukes, and down at the bottom, inevitably, the pale cadaver of a ten-inch centipede. Those pink rattlesnakes down in The Canyon, those diamondback monsters thick as a truck driver's wrist that lurk in shady places along the trail, those unpleasant solpugids and unnecessary Jersualem crickets that scurry on dirty claws across your face at night. Why? The rain that comes down like lead shot and wrecks the trail, those sudden rockfalls of obscure origin that crash like thunder ten feet behind you in the heart of a dead-still afternoon. The ubiquitous buzzard, so patient—but only so patient. . . . The ragweed, the tumbleweed, the Jimson weed, the snakeweed. The scorpion in your shoe at dawn. The dreary wind that blows all spring, the psychedelic Joshua trees waving their arms at you on moonlight nights. Sand in the soup de jour. Halazone tablets in your canteen. The barren hills that always go up, which is bad, or down, which is worse. Those canyons like catacombs with quicksand lapping at your crotch. Hollow, mummified horses with forelegs casually crossed, dead for ten years, leaning against the corner of a barbed-wire fence. Packhorses at night, iron-shod, clattering over the slickrock through your camp. The last tin of tuna, two flat tires, not enough water and a forty-mile trek to Tule Well. An osprey on a cardón cactus, snatching the head off a living fish—always the best part first. The hawk sailing by at 200 feet, a squirming snake in its talons. Salt in the drinking water. Salt, selenium, arsenic, radon and radium in the water, in the gravel, in your bones. Water so hard it bends light, drills holes in rock and chokes up your radiator. Why go there? Those places with the hardcase names: Starvation Creek, Poverty Knoll, Hungry Valley, Bitter Springs, Last Chance Canyon, Dungeon Canyon, Whipsaw Flat, Dead Horse Point, Scorpion Flat, Dead Man Draw, Stinking Spring, Camino del Diablo, Jornado del Muerto . . . Death Valley.

Well then, why indeed go walking into the desert, that grim ground, that bleak and lonesome land where, as Genghis Khan said of India, "the heat is bad and the water makes men sick"?

Why the desert, when you could be strolling along the golden beaches of California? Camping by a stream of pure Rocky Mountain spring water in colorful Colorado? Loafing through a laurel slick in the misty hills of North Carolina? Or geting your head mashed in the greasy alley behind the Elysium Bar and Grill in Hoboken, New Jersey? Why the desert, given a world of such splendor and variety?

A friend and I took a walk around the base of a mountain up beyond Coconino County, Arizona. This was a mountain we'd been planning to circumambulate for years. Finally we put on our walking shoes and did it. About halfway around this mountain, on the third or fourth day, we paused for a while—two days—by the side of a stream, which the Navajos call Nasja because of the amber color of the water. (Caused perhaps by juniper roots—the water seems safe enough to drink.) On our second day there I walked down the stream, alone, to look at the canyon beyond. I entered the canyon and followed it for half the afternoon, for three or four miles, maybe, until it became a gorge so deep, narrow and dark, full of water and the inevitable quagmires of quicksand, that I turned around and looked for a way out. A route other than the way I'd come, which was crooked and uncomfortable and buried—I wanted to see what was up on top of this world. I found a sort of chimney flue on the east wall, which looked plausible, and sweated and cursed my way up through that until I reached a point where I could walk upright, like a human being. Another 300 feet of scrambling brought me to the rim of the canyon. No one, I felt certain, had ever before departed Nasja Canyon by that route.

But someone had. Near the summit I found an arrow sign, three feet long, formed of stones and pointing off into the north toward those same old purple vistas, so grand, immense, and mysterious, of more canyons, more mesas and plateaus, more mountains, more cloud-dappled sun-spangled leagues of desert sand and desert rock, under the same old wide and aching sky.

The arrow pointed into the north. But what was it pointing *at*? I looked at the sign closely and saw that those dark, desert-varnished stones had been in place for a long, long time; they rested in compacted dust. They must have been there for a century at least. I followed the direction indicated and came promptly to the rim of another canyon and a drop-off straight down of a good 500 feet. Not that way, surely. Across this canyon was nothing of any unusual interest that I could see—only the familiar sun-blasted sandstone, a few scrubby clumps of blackbrush and prickly pear, a few acres of nothing where only a lizard could graze, surrounded by a few square miles of more nothingness interesting chiefly to horned toads. I returned to the arrow and checked again, this time with field glasses, looking away for as far as my aided eyes could see toward the north, for ten, twenty, forty miles into the distance. I studied the scene with care, looking for an ancient Indian ruin, a significant cairn, perhaps an abandonded mine, a hidden treasure of some inconceivable wealth, the mother of all mother lodes. . . .

But there was nothing out there. Nothing at all. Nothing but the desert. Nothing but the silent world.

That's why.

Exercises and Notes

PROVOCATIONS

Here are some questions to consider about values.

What values are most important to you? Not just moral values, first of all, but *any* values. What is it that you most deeply care about? Love? Money? Satisfying and productive work? One or two things, or a great many? Things easily described in a few words, or things that take a long story to explain?

Spell some of this out. If stories are required, tell them. Are there people whose lives you'd like your own to be like? Who—and why?

Now turn to *moral* values. What moral values are most important to you? Respect? Well-being? Fairness? Keeping your word? Are there one or two things, or a great many? Things easily described in a few words, or things that take a long story to explain?

Think of a time when you felt proud of yourself. What were you proud of having done (or not done) or of being (or not being)? Then think of some time when you felt angry at yourself. What were you angry about? Why? What values are called upon when you make these judgments? How many of these are moral values?

What moral values (if any) are involved in driving (besides not driving drunk)? Does ethics have anything to say about following speed limits, keeping your insurance up to date, keeping the car well maintained, and so on? (Clearly there *are* values involved; the question is whether you consider them *moral* values, and why or why not.) What about radar detectors? Moral, nonmoral, immoral? (And why?)

Speaking of driving, why do we find it morally annoying when people jump ahead and push their way into lineups on freeways? And why are most people reluctant to honk or block the way, even if they are annoyed? How about you?

What moral obligations do you have toward your parents? Why? Are these obligations different from the moral obligations your parents have toward you? If there is a difference, is the difference fair? Or does the value of fairness just not apply here?

What moral values would using illegal hallucinogens offend? On the other hand, are there any positive moral values to using illegal hallucinogens? If so, what are they?

Many businesses now have "codes of ethics." What kinds of moral values would, or should, such a code include? Could there be a debate about this? That is, might it be that a business code of ethics should concern only certain moral values and not others? Must business serve the social good, for example, or should business people be judged only by their personal virtuousness?

Think of a natural or wild place that you love, like Abbey loves the desert. How would you explain its value to others who had not experienced it? Would a straight-out way be the best? Or would you tell stories, be ironic, what? Try it!

ETHICS IN THE NEWS

Take newspapers—your school paper, say, and the *New York Times*—and pick out articles that involve ethical issues. Then spell out and clarify the moral values involved, as I did in the second section of this chapter.

In doing this over the years with my own classes we have looked at topics ranging from the national and international (surrogate mothering; gay marriage; the Endangered Species Act, the United Nations) to local or college issues (should the food service always have vegetarian options? should the

Greek system be disbanded?). All of these issues reveal unsuspected depths once you begin to seek out the values involved.

Don't expect to "resolve" these issues in this exercise. Very likely you will make the issue more complicated! Just explore the moral values involved. Usually one or at most two will be mentioned in the articles. Clarify them; then ask after others. Don't overlook the values on the side(s) you disagree with—in fact, give them even more attention. You already know what *you* think, but what kinds of values could lead someone to think differently?

READING VALUES STATEMENTS AND STORIES

Look at the mission statements of a variety of organizations: local businesses, national corporations, or nonprofit organizations, like Amnesty International, the Sierra Club, the National Rifle Association (NRA), and the American Civil Liberties Union (ACLU). The latter can be easily found on the Web: e.g., <www.amnesty.org>, <www.nra.org>, <www.aclu.org>.

Once again, spell out the moral values involved. Many of these organizations we know only through a few media stereotypes, or perhaps because they are very visible on one or two controversial issues. Don't assume that you already know who and what they are, and that you don't need to look carefully at what they themselves say they are. Most of them will probably surprise you if you look closely enough.

Look for mission or values statements in your own college or university catalog. The first pages usually offer some larger sense of the institution's mission, often in moral terms. Political speeches and party platforms are a good place to look for values as well. (Full texts can sometimes be found in newspapers like the *New York Times*, or on the Web.) Don't forget the United Nations—look at its founding documents, like the U.N. Declaration of Human Rights. Look at the speeches of ambassadors from places you don't like. For those with a historical bent, look to the great documents and speeches of American history. A useful collection of these is Diane Ravitch, ed., *The American Reader* (HarperCollins, 1990). Look at the encyclicals of the popes (recall the references in Chapter 2).

If your interests run in a more literary direction, look at popular stories in the same way. Children's stories, for example. They often clearly promote moral values, and in fact invite us to spell them out as we interpret the story, as we find the "moral." Useful collections are William Bennett's *The Book of Virtues* (Simon and Schuster, 1993) and his follow-up *The Moral Compass* (Simon and Schuster, 1995).

NOTES AND FURTHER READINGS

Many disciplines study values. The aim may be to classify them, to relate them to each other and to other factors, or sometimes to begin to systematically evaluate them as well. For a useful survey of social-scientific approaches to the question of the nature of values, as well as a survey of typologies and developmental theories of value, see Richard Kilby, *The Study of Human Values* (University Press of America, 1993). Another suggestive survey, more sociological and historical, is Maria Ossowska's *Social Determinants of Moral Ideas* (University of Pennsylvania Press, 1970).

A stimulating and accessible look at values that goes back to the very beginning (how do we know values are even *real?*) is Howard Richards, *Life on a Small Planet: A Philosophy of Value* (Philosophical Library, 1966). For the classic introduction to the philosophical theory of values, see Risieri Frondizi, *What Is Value?* (Open Court Library of Philosophy, 1963). Other classic but more difficult sources are John Dewey, *Theory of Valuation* (University of Chicago Press, 1939) and G. H. von Wright, *The Varieties of Goodness* (Humanities Press, 1963). For more on the definition of the sphere of the moral and its relation to self-interest, an old but incisive piece is W. D. Falk, "Morality, Self, and Others," in Hector-Neri Castaneda and George Nakhnikian, eds., *Morality and the Language of Conduct* (Wayne State University Press, 1963).

◆

CHAPTER 4

Families of Moral Values

As diverse as they are, moral values do not simply form a hodgepodge. Philosophers often distinguish three different *families* of moral values. The families may sometimes overlap, and not all moral values fall neatly into one or another family. Still, categorizing moral values into families, as far as possible, helps us sort them out, and helps us know what to look for when "unpacking" ethical issues. Useful patterns begin to emerge.

THREE FAMILIES OF MORAL VALUES

I will label the three families *Goods*, *Rights*, and *Virtues*—using each term in a fairly careful sense, as we will see. In the most general outline, the families are:

• **Goods.** *Happiness and well-being: satisfaction, pleasure, the relief of pain and suffering; fulfillment. Social benefits (social, political, or economic products, services, or states of affairs that promote happiness and well-being); reduced social costs.*

• **Rights.** *Appropriate respect for the dignity or worth of each person. Fairness; justice; respecting legal, civil, or human rights. Treating others as equals; not acting as though they are somehow less than ourselves.*

• **Virtues.** *Good personal character. Acting as a good person ought to act: responsibly, charitably, honestly, loyally. Living up to the best of what we are.*

Let us look at each family in turn, by themselves first and then in relation to each other.

Goods

Maybe we are wondering how to think, morally, about poverty. What, if anything, should those not in poverty do for those in poverty? What sort of welfare system should there be?

One natural way to think about this issue is to look at *goods*. Poverty can be a grinding, hopeless, self-perpetuating kind of misery, lacking even the basics most people take for granted. Understanding poverty in this way, an argument for a welfare system looks simple: such a system relieves some of this misery, lifts a little of the burden of hunger and homelessness, provides the basics, and therefore can give people a sense of self-worth and a chance to start again. It is *good* for people in the simple and obvious sense that it improves their lives. It relieves suffering and makes them better off.

Of course, many things could be called "goods." In the broadest sense, I suppose, "goods" could include any value at all—anything that is good. In the sense used here, though, *"goods"* are fairly definite, concrete, and visible benefits. Well-being, satisfaction: these things we can verify by experience, at least to some extent. And many of the means to happiness and well-being are "goods" in the economic sense, products or services, say, that are definite and concrete too, often even measurable.

Still in terms of goods, though, there is another side to the argument too. It may be argued that welfare has major social costs. Critics acknowledge the misery and the need, but go on to argue that the welfare system, at least as we know it, actually tends to perpetuate that misery. Some accuse welfare of creating a "culture of dependency" that discourages many people from moving ahead in life. The costs of the welfare program may also dampen the economy—a bad consequence for everyone. So while welfare may genuinely benefit some people, its overall effect, the critics claim, is to make people (many individual recipients, and society as a whole) *worse* off rather than better off.

Suppose we diagram this debate as in Figure 1.

The double arrows in this diagram represent contention. This *is* a debate, after all. People disagree.

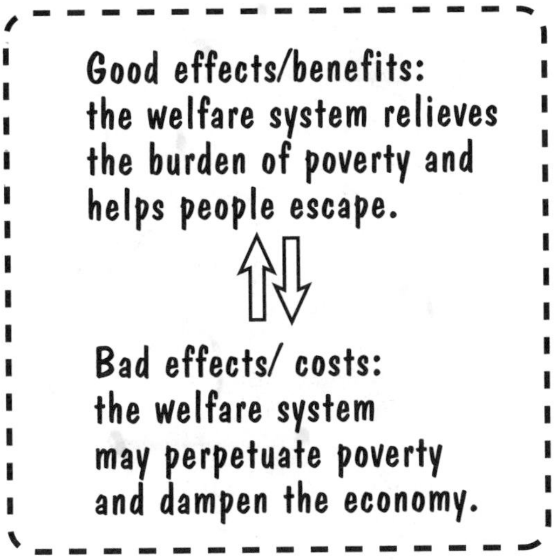

Good effects/benefits:
the welfare system relieves the burden of poverty and helps people escape.

Bad effects/ costs:
the welfare system may perpetuate poverty and dampen the economy.

Figure 1 Ethics and the welfare system: Goods in conflict

Still, this debate takes place in a shared "space," indicated here by the dotted lines around the two poles of the contention. It is framed by certain basic *agreements* about what kinds of moral values count. Again, it's an argument about *goods*: about whether, on balance, the welfare program has social benefits.

Both sides agree that poverty has immense costs. Both sides agree that the costs are morally relevant—indeed, the arguments on both sides appeal directly and solely to the effects of poverty on people. Both want to minimize those costs, to maximize benefits—good effects. They only differ about what the effects of the welfare system actually are, that is, on whether it has the net benefits claimed for it, or perhaps overall does more harm than good.

This way of thinking may seem so very natural that it is not clear that there is any other way to think about such topics. In fact, there is, as we shall see in a moment. The point for now is just that this "natural" way of thinking *is*, in any case, a way of thinking, and a quite specific one at that. "Goods" tell a story—*one* story.

Rights

Consider by contrast another and quite different way of thinking about poverty and welfare.

Is it *fair* for some people to end up living in the streets when others live in mansions? Is it *just* that some people have to work one hundred hours a week merely to keep food on the table while others live in luxury and do not work at all? Many people do not think so. Inequality on such a scale that it threatens people's very lives does not show appropriate respect (or *any* respect, some would argue) for the dignity or worth of each person. No one should have to watch his or her children go hungry or stay with an abusive spouse because there is nowhere else to go. It's just not *right*.

This is a different kind of case for a welfare system: an argument from justice and equality—from what I am calling *rights*. This is not an appeal to goods, at least not in any direct way. We are no longer speaking of lessening the costs of poverty. We are speaking of righting its wrongs.

Note that the word "rights" here is meant in a broader way than we sometimes use it. One way to show "appropriate respect for the dignity or equal worth of each person" is by respecting people's civil or legal or human "rights" in the sense of rights *to* something, as when we speak of the right to life, or the right to some kind of "safety net" when down and out. In the sense used here, though, "rights" include "rights *to*" life, etc., but also go farther. The argument may be that it is the *right thing to do* (it is fair, just, etc.) to help out the poor, to reduce the most radical inequality, and so on, because our fundamental dignity or equality requires it.

Like goods, though, rights in this sense can cut both ways. There is also a case against welfare in the same key.

There are many ways to understand fairness or "doing the right thing." There are many different interpretations of "appropriate respect for the dignity or equal worth of each person." To some it means just that everyone has an equal chance, not that everyone is entitled to succeed. In a ball game, for example, the score may be lopsided, but it doesn't follow that the game was unfair. One team was just a lot better (or luckier) than the other.

So maybe the right or fair thing to do in this case is to be impartial, to avoid acting in a way that is arbitrary or biased. No one should discriminate against poor people, for example—though we're not necessarily obliged to help out. There's a kind of equality here too, but it's not an equality of *result*. What *would* be unjust or unfair in such a case, in fact, would be to take some points from one team and give them to the other even though the second team did not score them. The first team is entitled to all the points they earned, whether the other team scores or not.

Another way to put this is to say that wealthy people have rights to their wealth. People have rights to their property, and therefore to the money that they make. Even if it's a lot more than other people make, it's still theirs. Critics of welfare argue that taxpayers' rights are violated (or: it is not right or fair; they are not being treated with equal respect) if taxpayers are forced to give some of their money to support those who cannot support themselves. Thus we are obliged to respect their rights, even if it means that we cannot do something that would (or might) have social benefits: offer public support to the needy. After all, private (voluntary) support is still possible—and violates no rights.

A diagram of this debate looks rather different. Consider Figure 2. Remember: the double arrows represent contention; the dotted lines mark out

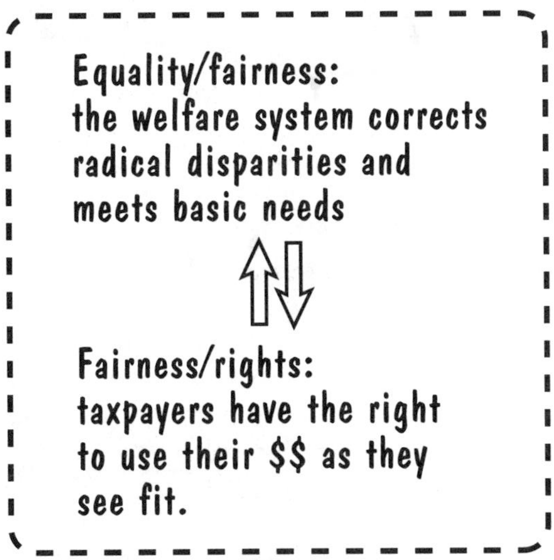

Equality/fairness:
the welfare system corrects
radical disparities and
meets basic needs

⇕

Fairness/rights:
taxpayers have the right
to use their $$ as they
see fit.

Figure 2 Ethics and the welfare system: Rights in conflict

the "space" of this debate—a quite distinct space from the debate about goods outlined above.

Again there is a major disagreement here. What is the right thing to do in the face of poverty? Which takes precedence, the claims of equity or rights to do as you choose with your money? As to values, though, notice once again that both sides agree on fundamentals. This time, both sides agree that the "right thing to do" is the key question—*not* "goods" in the sense of social costs or benefits. What *is* the right thing to do is still a question, but there is no question that what's right is what counts first.

Virtues

There is yet another kind of moral question that we ask—not about goods or rights but about what *sorts of persons we are* or are becoming. And here we come to the third family of moral values: the *virtues*.

Many of us, thinking about poverty, will first think about how we respond to someone in poverty. Do we pull away and deny any connection, or do we respond sensitively, with charity, open-heartedness, benevolence? Think of the stingy, greedy, shrunken-souled Scrooge in Dickens' *A Christmas Carol*—someone we would not like to become.

We may ask the same kinds of questions about our whole society. Are we a society of Scrooges, begrudging the poor every morsel, or can we find in our great wealth the generosity to give freely and without grudge?

That's the pro-welfare side. Thinking about certain other virtues, though, may lead you to oppose welfare. Another virtue we widely recognize and value is self-responsibility: trying to pull your own weight and live within your means. Some needy people refuse to go on welfare, as a point of pride: they believe that the primary virtues are those of self-reliance and hard work, even if poorly rewarded, and that dependence is a kind of vice (the opposite of virtue), to be shunned even if life is very, very tough. Alongside the Scrooge story, there are stories in this other key too. Think of the old stories of families on the frontier, or of the "self-made man."

And so for a third time we can recognize a disagreement within a shared space that defines a family of moral values. Consider Figure 3.

This time the disagreement is about which virtues take precedence and about how to show virtue ourselves (being benevolent) or bring certain virtues forth in others (encouraging self-responsibility). The shared space of the disagreement—the underlying agreements that give it its very terms—is the conviction that the primary moral question is one of *character*—of virtue. Though the term "virtue" sometimes has a quaint ring, it is not at all meant quaintly in our usage here. It points us toward another distinct kind of moral question. In this book, again, the virtues are those moral values concerned with who we *are*, not—right away, anyway—with what we do.

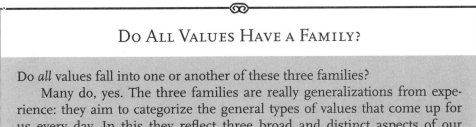

Figure 3 Ethics and the welfare system: Virtues in conflict

There are many (possible) virtues: the ones at stake here are only a few. The Christian Middle Ages had their seven "cardinal virtues": faith, hope, charity, prudence, justice, temperance, fortitude (along with the "deady sins"—vices

Do All Values Have a Family?

Do *all* values fall into one or another of these three families?

Many do, yes. The three families are really generalizations from experience: they aim to categorize the general types of values that come up for us every day. In this they reflect three broad and distinct aspects of our lives. In our lives as embodied, vulnerable beings, the *goods* of well-being and avoiding suffering must be prime concerns. In our lives as socially interdependent beings, *rights*—fairness and justice—are prime concerns. And our special relationships, in families and at work, each carry special demands and expectations, and therefore define *virtues*.

Still, not every value fits neatly into one of these families. Values may arise from other aspects of life. Some writers, for instance, advocate "authenticity," a kind of radical honesty in the face of death and ultimate meaninglessness. Some of these writers formed their views in the midst of World War II, when death was an ever-present reality and it was a real question how to live, knowing that the next day might be your last. They generalized from there. However, it's true for *all* of us all the time, isn't it, that the next day might be our last? Maybe we ought to pay more attention than we do.

In any case, authenticity does not fit any of the three families. It comes closest to virtue, perhaps, but stands apart from the other virtues, embedded as they are in ongoing lives. That is no objection to it, though; instead, it is just a reminder that some values stand outside the three families introduced in this chapter. Sometimes we need a more complicated picture.

Some environmental values also do not fit into any of the three families. Part of the idea seems to be that nature deserves respect, so the rights family might be the best first guess. A well-known historian has even written a history of environmentalism under the title *The Rights of Nature*. Still, the rights family is typically concerned with human social relations, and extending it to nature may be too much of a stretch. Moral values, I have said, connect us to a larger world, but in this case it's a *vastly* larger world, beyond (though including) the human and even animal worlds as a whole. Sometimes the values involved seem to be almost religious in nature: we speak of awe in the face of nature, and the words "sacred" or "holy" sometimes come to mind. It may be that a new family of values is on the horizon—more on this in Chapter 21. (Recall also the reading from Edward Abbey in Chapter 3. Did you find [mainly] goods, rights, or virtues there, or something else?)

By contrast, other "new" values do fit naturally within one of the three families. Philosophers concerned with other animals, for example, divide fairly sharply into those who advocate animal rights—on analogy to human rights—and those who want to relieve animal pain and suffering, whose appeal is chiefly to goods.

The upshot is simply that the three families introduced in this chapter are useful categories most of the time, but we should not try to force every value into them. Some of the most interesting new developments in ethics push beyond these families. Values keep changing!

Another question: does any given value fit only under one category? Could a value belong to several families at once?

It's a matter of interpretation. Some values that appear to be specific may actually be rather vague and varied, and then it becomes a matter of choice whether we should say that the value fits under more than one category, or that the value term really names more than one specific value, each of which may fall into a different family. "Justice," for example, even in the basic lists given in this chapter, shows up twice, in different families: as one of the cardinal virtues and in the category of rights. We might therefore want to distinguish justice as a personal characteristic ("being a just person") from justice as a feature of social institutions ("is the welfare system just?"), and it is somewhat up to us to say whether we have two distinct values here or only one value with several aspects.

Other times it may not be clear how to classify a single value. "Not playing God," for example, may be some sort of obligation, or some sort of virtue (humility?), or maybe both. Or think of "freedom." We speak of freedom (or "liberty," in the Declaration of Independence) as a matter of justice or right, but we also think that freedom is tightly tied up with our well-being and so is a prime candidate for a basic good as well. Perhaps it is a complex single good, a kind of alliance of varied specific values? Or perhaps what we learn from examples like these is that the three families themselves may be deeply interconnected. (Maybe, for example, *all* rights are ultimately justified by their social consequences—a question for Chapter 6.)

In short, there is no need to force every value into one (and only one) family. The reality is probably more complex than that. It is enough that *most* values fit reasonably well into only one. Those that don't, just note separately.

the opposite of virtue: pride, wrath, envy, lust, gluttony, avarice, and sloth). Recent advocates of character education, such as William Bennett, former U.S. Secretary of Education, list ten key virtues: self-discipline, compassion, responsibility, friendship, work, courage, perseverance, honesty, loyalty, and faith. Some feminist thinkers in ethics focus on the virtues of care in relationship. Specific virtues would then include patience, nurturing, trust and trustworthiness, being supportive without being overbearing—essential virtues, in fact, not just for parents and spouses but for teachers, mentors, coaches, health professionals, and many others too.

MAPPING MORAL DEBATES

Values in these three families relate in various ways, from mutual support to open conflict. We can use the kinds of diagrams just introduced to work out rough "maps" of the values involved in different moral debates and how they support or conflict with each other.

Parallel Debates

I introduced each family of values by asking how we might think about the question of poverty and welfare from within each family. Let us stay with the poverty and welfare question, but now picture each of the three welfare debates already sketched—one within each family—side by side.

As before, I use the double arrow to indicate a conflict or tension, and the dotted lines enclose each separate family of values, to mark off its specific space. Figure 4 should make it clear at once that all three families have their own welfare debates, in very different terms. "Pro" goods conflict with "con" goods (or: benefits with costs); "pro" rights conflict with "con" rights; "pro" virtues conflict with "con" virtues.

These are the debates introduced in the first part of this chapter. Here

Figure 4 Ethics and the welfare system: Three parallel debates

each family proceeds separately. These are within-family fights. We have three parallel debates that don't necessarily meet.

Parallel debates like these are common when people mostly speak to other people who share a moral framework—people who mostly draw upon just one family of moral values, either out of temperament or due to the constraints of the discussion. For example, economists and business people are more likely to look at the social benefits and costs of some proposed policy, and often they talk mostly to other economists and business people. The religious community may be more apt to look at virtues or rights, and to talk mostly to others among the religious. In this case, each debate remains a family affair, and there may not be much crossover between the families involved.

Cross-Family Debates

Just as often, values conflict *across* families. We need to draw our arrows in a different direction.

Suppose you argue for welfare on the grounds of its benefits to otherwise destitute people (a "pro" goods argument: an argument about social benefits). Someone responds that the welfare system isn't fair to the people who support it with their tax dollars (a "con" rights argument: an appeal to fairness). The picture then must look like Figure 5.

This time the contention is between values that belong to different families, rather than between two different values within a single family. Here a benefit is opposed not to a cost but to a *right*. Social goods come into conflict with individual entitlements. We have for the first time a conflict that goes beyond the boundaries of one family.

Virtues may get into the fight too. Suppose, for example, that the "con" rights argument against welfare is met in turn with an argument from the virtue of open-heartedness. We might then picture the situation as in Figure 6.

Once again, this is an argument *across* families and not merely *within* one of them. A "con" argument from rights is met with both a "pro" argument from social benefits and a "pro" argument from the virtues of independence and self-reliance.

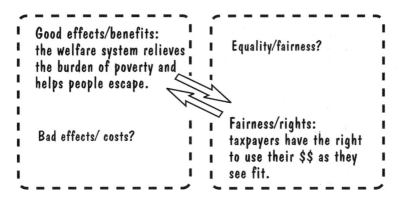

Figure 5 Ethics and the welfare system: A cross-family conflict

Figure 6 Ethics and the welfare system: A conflict across three families

Now the debate is wider. The participants are speaking for fundamentally different types of values, no longer within the same family. For us as individuals, this sort of debate may arise when we speak with people who disagree with some of our basic conclusions, or may agree with (some of) our moral conclusions but not for the same reasons. Likewise, in the larger community, economists and businesspeople sometimes speak (and sometimes *must* speak) with religious leaders and civil rights lawyers, and vice versa. The moral debate widens to include several different communities. Different ways of thinking have to find some way to connect.

Conflicts Between Allied Sets of Values

The overall welfare debate is wider yet. Welfare is debated in society at large; indeed whole political campaigns are waged about it. In this debate, naturally, *all* kinds of reasons come up, from all three families, both pro and con. Proponents of welfare, for example, argue from welfare's benefits *and* its fairness *and* the virtues of charity and benevolence. All of these values are called upon to support a welfare system. Together they make up an allied set of values, even though they come from different families.

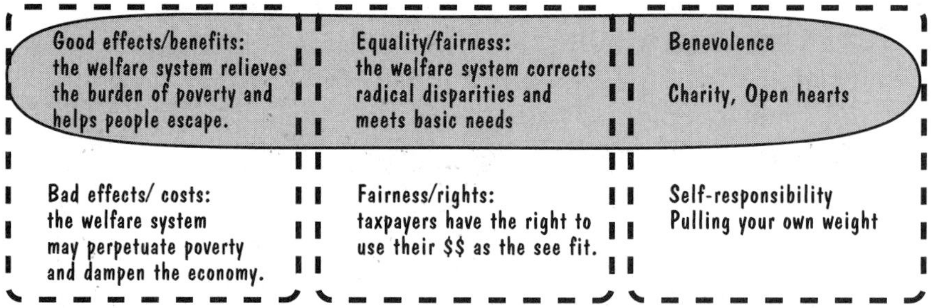

Figure 7 Allied pro-welfare values across families

Picture the situation as in Figure 7.

The solid-line oval now connects pro-welfare values across all the families: it marks out the common pro-welfare *cause*. These values work together; together they confront the other side.

Of course, anti-welfare values also may make common cause. Opponents argue from welfare's social costs *and* the rights of taxpayers *and* the virtues of self-reliance and independence (of avoiding dependence.) Suppose we picture the allied anti-welfare values in the same way, as in Figure 8.

One step now remains. These two allied sets of values, pro- and anti-welfare, of course come into conflict themselves. Rather than conflict between specific values either within or across families, however, conflict here is global in nature. The entire set of pro-welfare values, allied across all three families, conflicts with the entire set of anti-welfare values, again allied across all three families. Picture this as in Figure 9.

Again, the solid-line ovals combined here represent the two allied sets of values across the families. Notice that the arrows of contention run between *them*. All of the other kinds of contention we've looked at—between specific values both within and across families—also remain, of course. But all of that contention can be viewed against the background of the overall debate between the two allied sets of values we have pictured.

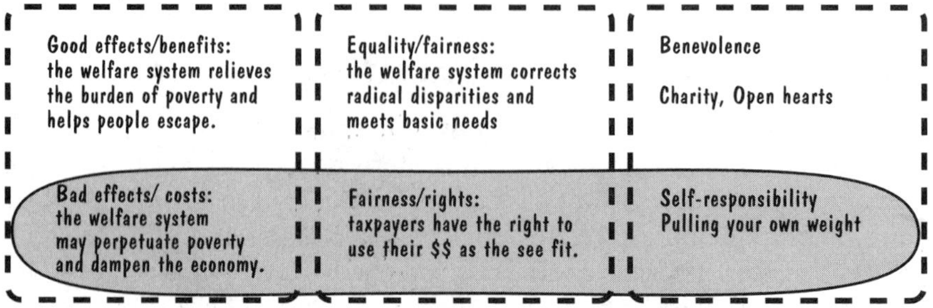

Figure 8 Allied anti-welfare values across families

Figure 9 Allied pro- and anti-welfare values in conflict

Much moral argument is like this. Each side in the debate uses a variety of kinds of reasons, not always clearly distinguished, to argue a case pro or con. Each value invoked thus has affinities both with its other allied values—they all favor or oppose a certain conclusion—and also has affinities with other values in the same family (its "relatives," so to speak) though some of its "relatives" point toward opposite conclusions.

In short, then, both conflict and common cause weave through this (and any) debate. Tension *and* harmony, agreement *and* disagreement, are the natural state of our values. It gets complicated. Remember one more time Chapter 3's guidelines: *expect diversity* and *look in depth!*

Exercises and Notes

Identifying Families and Conflicts

Identify the family or families of moral values involved in each of the following moral debates. Take the conflicts as described (all of them could be interpreted in more complex ways, I'm sure, but here just work from the description offered). Is the conflict within one family, across families, or between allied sets of values across families? Compare your answers.

Here's an example:

> Your freedom to ride your motorcycle without a helmet versus society's wish to require a helmet for your own safety and to keep medical costs down.

Your freedom to ride your motorcycle without a helmet would be a *right*. Regulation for your own good (safety of life and limb) and society's (lowered medical costs) would be a *good*. And this conflict is *across* families: between what's (claimed to be) good and what's (claimed to be) right.

Save your answers to these questions—you'll need them again for the exercises in Chapter 6.

1. Employers' freedom to hire whom they choose, versus fairness to job applicants (non-discriminatory treatment).
2. Rights of accused (and convicted) criminals (to fair trials, against cruel and unusual punishments, etc.), versus the social good (*what* good[s], exactly?) that might be achieved by rapid trials, limited appeals, and cheap jails.
3. Should extra-wide prefabricated homes be allowed on regular highways? Upside: lower costs for manufacturers and purchasers. Downside: more accidents and injuries.
4. Ease of life today versus obligations to the future (e.g., not wasting scarce natural resources, not littering the earth with nonbiodegradable but cheap items).
5. Some of us expect that U.S. presidents will be sterling personal role models. Others ask: isn't it enough if they do what they can to improve the quality of life, the economy, world politics, and so on?
6. Censorship of violence or sex on television. Pro: a safer and more loving society (or is it that people are not portrayed in degrading ways?) Con: censorship limits free expression.
7. Comradeship versus honesty: should academic honor codes require students to turn in fellow students who cheated on an exam?
8. Some colleges are banning fraternities and sororities in order to promote "more respectful relations between the sexes." But don't students have the right of free association too?
9. Sobriety checkpoints on major highways on New Year's Eve, Fourth of July, Labor Day, and other holidays. Pro: safer highways. Con: invasion of privacy?
10. When we buy low-cost imported goods we also end up supporting exploitation overseas and contributing to unemployment here. Is this a moral issue?
11. Zoning laws—property rights versus community goods. If I have the right to own property, does this mean that I can do what I wish with what I own? What if I want to build a store or a duplex or a factory on my lot in a residential district (or tear down a historic building or turn a wild stream into a little lake with pink flamingos)? Suppose I wanted to turn my lot into a nuclear power plant or a rocket launching pad or bomb factory or rock concert stage?
12. How should the government respond to the demands of dispossessed Indian tribes for some kind of compensation or return of ancient ancestral lands?
13. State lotteries do provide some money for good causes (e.g. education) without more taxes. They also send the message that pure chance rules our lives, rather than hard, steady work.

MAPPING MORAL DEBATES

In this chapter I have used one specific moral debate as an example: the debate about poverty and welfare. Now consider some other specific moral questions and "map" the values at stake and their alliances and conflicts in the same way.

Start with a large sheet of scratch paper. Recalling the guidelines in Chapter 3, ask first what values are at stake in the question you are considering. Make a list. Then categorize those values, as far as possible, into the three families we have considered in this chapter. (Remember that some values may not fall into one of these families, and some may fall into more than one.) Diagram them as we did in Figure 4, noting first the ways they conflict *within* their respective families. Then note their typical conflicts *across* families. Finally, ask which values ally with each other across families and to what other cross-family alliances they are opposed.

You should end with a map like one of the figures in the second section of this chapter. For example, consider Figure 10—a map of some of the values involved in the debate over state lotteries (question 13 above, with values from some other families added).

There you have, in quick outline, an introduction to the whole debate. Does this map seem accurate to you? Is it fair to both sides? What would you add or delete? (I couldn't think of any pro-lottery virtues, for example. Can you?)

Note that although there is a lot more on the bottom of this map than on the top, it doesn't necessarily follow that the case for lotteries is weaker than the case against. It might only mean that the case for lotteries is simpler!

You try it now. Here are some issues to consider.

- Should marijuana be legalized?
- Should doctors always tell their patients the truth about their condition, even when in the doctor's opinion the truth may be too depressing for the patient to bear, or may prevent the patient from getting better?

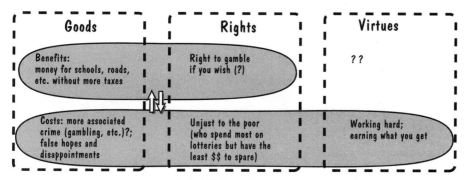

Figure 10 Should there be state lotteries?
Some allied values for (on top) and against (on bottom)

- Should doctors be allowed to help people end their own lives?
- Is the death penalty moral?
- Should the government control the supply and purchase of certain types of guns?
- Should we continue to use animals for food, medical testing, and product-safety research?

A look at any newspaper will suggest many more.

More than the first exercise, this exercise draws on your background knowledge of these moral debates. You may feel that your knowledge of the issue is not up to the task for some questions. Just do the best you can, or move on to the next. But don't give up too soon. Though not every family may offer both pro and con values in every case, at least *ask* about each category in turn.

How do your maps compare with those of your friends and classmates? Can you agree on how to map debates like these even with people who take the opposite view about what should be done?

NOTE

The three-way classification of values introduced here reflects a standard three-way division of ethical theories introduced in the next chapter. I leave all references until then. For more on the moral debate over poverty and welfare, see Chapter 19 of this book.

◯

CHAPTER 5

Some Traditional Ethical Theories

Each family of moral values we've distinguished is a large and loose collection of values. Each family covers a broad range of values and includes all manner of conflicts within itself.

Suppose, though, that underneath all of this diversity and conflict in each family we could come to see a single deep pattern working itself out. Suppose, in other words, that there is a way to systematize, perhaps even unify, all of the values in the family within a single ethical *theory*. What then?

Such theories could give us new and sharper-edged tools. For one thing, understanding each family as a tightly connected and coherent whole would give us ready practical reference points when values come into conflict, at least within each family. In cross-family conflicts, the contending theories in the background could at least help clarify what is actually at stake. Unclear values might be brought into focus and even judged. And as the theories contend with each other we might even begin to glimpse a way to resolve the conflicts between them as well.

Ethical theories in this sense are among the most central interests of moral philosophers. This chapter surveys the three traditional types of theories, corresponding to our three families of values.

UTILITARIANISM

Let us begin with goods—probably the most familiar and seemingly most obvious of the families of values.

Two Claims About Happiness

Most people, on reflection, would say that the ultimate goal of human action is happiness. Though of course we seek many things, day to day, we seek everything in the end for the happiness it promises. What we disvalue, we disvalue in the end because it impedes or counteracts happiness.

If you don't like the word "happiness," use another word. Use "pleasure," "satisfaction," "welfare," or "well-being." Whatever we call it, though, it seems natural to conclude that this state—this positive state of mind—is the single, basic, ultimately good thing. Certainly it seems to encapsulate the sorts of goods we discussed in Chapter 4. When we spoke there of social benefits or reduced social costs we understood that a "benefit" is what serves increased happiness and well-being, and a "cost" is a decrease in happiness and well-being, an increase in pain and suffering or other negative experiences. Economic goods, for example, are products, services, or actions that we seek because they are benefits in this sense.

We can add a second claim. If something is a good thing, more of it is pretty clearly better. If the fundamental good of our lives is happiness, then, best of all must surely be the most happiness. Thus, in general, we should act in such a way as to produce the most happiness. Maximize happiness; minimize pain and suffering.

Many psychologists and (especially) economists believe that this is just what any rational person already does. You may have to do some careful thinking, and even restrain yourself at times—giving up some short-term pleasure, for example, for longer-term gains. Maximizing happiness over a life does not mean that you will be happy every moment of that life.

Suffering, for example, can sometimes actually be a good thing in the long run. Even (some) adversity can sometimes produce more pleasure than pain. You go to the dentist—nobody's idea of a pleasant experience—so you won't suffer more pain later. You sweat in the sauna for the unmatchable rush of pleasure that comes when you leap into the cold water afterward. The trick is to work in just enough adversity to maximize pleasure later. No point in sweating too long or flossing more than you have to. But when a little pain now increases your net happiness in the long run, it's worth it.

The Good of the Whole

So far our unfolding theory may sound like a form of rational selfishness. But there is a crucial third step that turns it into something quite different.

Our concern with happiness seldom stops at the boundaries of our own selves. For one thing, quite simply, it is hard to be happy all alone. Our lives take on their emotional tone from the people around us. Moreover, we naturally seek the well-being of others close to us—spouses, children, parents, friends, lovers, students and teachers, those we work for and those who work for us. Anyone who knows love knows this simple fact. Often we also care for those who are distant, those whose plight or whose successes engage our sympathies or inspire us.

These are psychological, empirical points. Beside them, some philosophers propose a more conceptual argument as well.

When we say that happiness is a morally good thing, remember that we are speaking of the needs—and by extension, goals or ultimate aims—of others as well as of ourselves. Thus, when we recognize happiness as the ultimate good thing, we say nothing about *whose* happiness. I cannot say that others' happiness is of no concern to me simply because I'm me, so to speak, and they're them. Happiness *as such* is a morally good thing, wherever it occurs— and it is good in the same way and to the same extent. We are left, then, with a moral commitment to the happiness of *all*, to the good of the whole, to the "greatest good of the greatest number." This is the moral theory philosophers call *utilitarianism*.

Founders

Two English thinkers advanced utilitarianism as a modern theory of ethics: Jeremy Bentham (1748–1832) and John Stuart Mill (1806–1873.)

Bentham started out as a social critic, concerned for more enlightened legislation, and was a lifelong opponent of the severe British penal codes of his time. It was Bentham who popularized the familiar utilitarian first principle just cited: *Seek the greatest good of the greatest number.* He called it the "Principle of Utility" in ethics—the formula that economists put as "maximize utility," from which the term *utilitarianism* comes.

"Good" for Bentham meant *pleasure*. Moreover, he thought pleasures could be quantified, and he tried to devise criteria for weighing pleasures directly against each other. Bentham actually hoped that we could one day solve moral problems by sitting down with a calculator, figuring up the amounts of pleasure on either side!

Mill inherited the utilitarian project from Bentham and from his own father, James Mill. He gave it his own characteristic twists and developments, but on the key points he is one with them:

> Pleasure, and freedom from pain, are the only things desirable as ends; all desirable things . . . are desirable either for the pleasure inherent in themselves, or as means to the promotion of pleasure and the prevention of pain. . . . Actions are right in proportion as they tend to promote happiness; wrong as they tend to produce the reverse of happiness.

And Mill insists that such an ethic appeals directly to our social nature.

> The deeply rooted conception which every individual even now has of himself as a social being, tends to make him feel it one of his natural wants that there should be harmony between his feelings and those of his fellow creatures. . . . This feeling in most individuals is much inferior in strength to their selfish feelings, and is often wanting altogether. But to those who have it, it possesses all the characters of a natural feeling. It does not present itself to their minds as a superstition of education, or a law despotically imposed by the power of society. . . . This conviction is the ultimate sanction of the greatest happiness morality.

See the box to follow for more from Mill in his own words, including the above citations in context.

EXCERPTS FROM JOHN STUART MILL, UTILITARIANISM

The creed which accepts as the foundation of morals Utility, or the Greatest Happiness Principle, holds that actions are right in proportion as they tend to promote happiness, wrong as they tend to produce the reverse of happiness. By "happiness," is intended pleasure, and the absence of pain; by "unhappiness," pain, and the privation of pleasure. To give a clear view of the moral standard set up by the theory, much requires to be said; in particular, what things it includes in the ideas of pain and pleasure. . . . But these supplementary explanations do not affect the theory of life on which this theory of morality is grounded—namely, that pleasure, and freedom from pain, are the only things desirable as ends; and that all desirable things (which are as numerous in the utilitarian as in any other scheme) are desirable either for the pleasure inherent in themselves, or as means to the promotion of pleasure and the prevention of pain. . . .

The ultimate end, with reference to and for the sake of which all other things are desirable (whether we are considering our own good or that of other people), is an existence exempt as far as possible from pain, and as rich as possible in enjoyments, both in point of quantity and quality; the test of quality, and the rule for measuring it against quantity, being the preference felt by those who, in their opportunities of experience, to which must be added their habits of self-consciousness and self-observation, are best furnished with the means of comparison. This, being, according to the utilitarian opinion, the end of human action is necessarily also the standard of morality; which may accordingly be defined, the rules and precepts for human conduct, by the observance of which an existence such as has been described might be, to the greatest extent possible, secured to all mankind; and not to them only, but, so far as the nature of things admits, to the whole sentient creation.

When it is positively asserted to be impossible that human life should be happy, the assertion, if not something like a verbal quibble, is at least an exaggeration. If by happiness be meant a continuity of highly pleasurable excitement, it is evident enough that this is impossible. A state of exalted pleasure lasts only moments, or in some cases, and with some intermissions, hours or days, and is the occasional brilliant flash of enjoyment, not its permanent and steady flame. Of this the philosophers who have taught that happiness is the end of life were as fully aware as those who taunt them. The happiness which they meant was not a life of rapture; but moments of such, in an existence made up of few and transitory pains, many and various pleasures, with a decided predominance of the active over the passive, and having as the foundation of the whole, not to expect more from life than it is capable of bestowing. A life thus composed, to those who have been fortunate enough to obtain it, has always appeared worthy of the name of happiness. And such an existence is even now the lot of many, during some considerable portion of their lives. The present wretched education, and wretched social arrangements, are the only real hindrance to its being attainable by almost all.

The objectors perhaps may doubt whether human beings, if taught to consider happiness as the end of life, would be satisfied with such a moderate share of it. But great numbers of mankind have been satisfied with much less. The main constituents of a satisfied life appear to be two, either of which by itself is often found sufficient for the purpose: tranquility and excitement. With much tranquility, many find that they can be content with very little pleasure: with much excitement, many can reconcile themselves to a considerable quantity of pain. There is assuredly no inherent impossibility in enabling even the mass of mankind to unite both; since the two are so far from being incompatible that they are in natural alliance, the prolongation of either being a preparation for, and exciting a wish for, the other. . . . When people who are tolerably fortunate in their outward lot do not find in life sufficient enjoyment to make it valuable to them, the cause generally is, caring for nobody but themselves. To those who have neither public nor private affections, the excitements of life are much curtailed, and in any case dwindle in value as the time approaches when all selfish interests must be terminated by death: while those who leave after them objects of personal affection, and especially those who have also cultivated a fellow feeling with the collective interests of mankind, retain as lively an interest in life on the eve of death as in the vigor of youth and health. Next to selfishness, the principal cause which makes life unsatisfactory is want of mental cultivation. A cultivated mind—I do not mean that of a philosopher, but any mind to which the fountains of knowledge have been opened, and which has been taught, in any tolerable degree, to exercise its faculties—finds sources of inexhaustible interest in all that surrounds it; in the objects of nature, the achievements of art, the imagination of poetry, the incidents of history, the ways of mankind past and present, and their prospects in the future. . . .

The deeply rooted conception which every individual even now has of himself as a social being, tends to make him feel it one of his natural wants that there should be harmony between his feeling and aims and those of his fellow creatures. If differences of opinion and of mental culture make it impossible for him to share many of their actual feelings—perhaps make him denounce and defy those feelings—he still needs to be conscious that his real aim and theirs do not conflict; that he is not opposing himself to what they really wish for, namely, their own good, but is, on the contrary, promoting it. This feeling in most individuals is much inferior in strength to their selfish feelings, and is often wanting altogether. But to those who have it, it possesses all the characters of a natural feeling. It does not present itself to their minds as a superstition of education, or a law despotically imposed by the power of society, but as an attribute which it would not be well for them to be without. This conviction is the ultimate sanction of the greatest happiness morality. This it is which makes any mind, of well-developed feelings, work with, and not against, the outward motives to care for others, afforded by what I have called the external sanctions; and when those sanctions are wanting, or act in an opposite direction, constitutes in itself a powerful internal binding force, in proportion to the sensitiveness and thoughtfulness of the character; since few but those whose mind is a moral blank, could bear to lay out their course of life on the plan of paying no regard to others except so far as their own private interest compels.

Utilitarianism in Practice

Utilitarianism's great strength is that it draws attention squarely back to what is actually good or bad for people—to specific consequences for happiness—rather than to the sometimes abstract rules that too often (say utilitarians) are supposed to define what's moral. In this utilitarianism regards itself as no more than systematized common sense. *Do what has the best effects*—surely no one could disagree with so obvious a maxim! All utilitarianism thinks it does is to clarify and systematize it.

We debate about assisted suicide, for example, about whether doctors should be allowed or expected to help people who are aware and rational to die if they so choose. Utilitarians would decide the question by looking at the effects on the happiness of society as a whole. If assisted suicide would promote the social good, all told, then it should be allowed. If it doesn't, it shouldn't. What else (they would ask) could be relevant?

This looks like an empirical question. Maybe we can actually resolve it. The benefits of assisted suicide seem very concrete: relief of suffering—for dying people, who are often in great physical pain and sometimes emotional pain too, unable to secure relief by themselves, and for their families, who also suffer greatly, emotionally and financially, when dying is prolonged and hard. The costs are much more indefinite, by contrast, and do not necessarily have any direct effect on happiness. Some people may feel pressured into choosing assisted suicide, for example, and we might come somehow to "devalue life." Put in the balance with the clear benefits, though, many utilitarians tend to think that these costs, such as they are, will be outweighed.

Likewise, utilitarians who oppose assisted suicide must argue from its likely social costs: that it might snowball into other and less voluntary sorts of "assistance"; that death will come to seem less absolutely bad; and so on. It becomes relevant to look at states and countries where assisted suicide is allowed. Have the feared results materialized? To find out may be hard, but it is not impossible, and it is crucial to a moral decision.

THEORIES OF RIGHT ACTION

Our second family of values is *rights*, remember, meaning not just the sorts of just claims we speak of when we cite the "right to free speech" and the like, but also justice, fairness, and so on—appropriate respect for the dignity and equal worth of each person.

We may agree that certain things are right in practice. But suppose we now probe deeper. What *makes* acts right (or wrong)? Why be fair? Why treat others justly?

It is sometimes hard to find words to answer. After the concrete social benefits just stressed, we sometimes feel tongue-tied when it comes to explaining our sense of what's right. In fact, for that reason we may be tempted to slide back into utilitarianism and just say that an act is right if it maximizes happiness. (Utilitarians themselves would argue for just such a view, as we will see in Chapter 6.) However, traditional (non-utilitarian) theories of right action understand what's right independently of social utility. According to these theories, ethics starts in a very different place.

Ends and Means

When we speak of human dignity, the idea is that there is *something about us* that is supposed to compel respect, and something that we all have equally, so that fair and equal procedures and opportunities are the natural and necessary response. Good so far, but now we have the question: *what* is it about us that compels this kind of respect?

Consider the claim that people are not just "means" but "ends in themselves."

A "means" is a way of getting something. A car is a means of getting around. Money is a means of buying what we want or need to live. The claim, then, is that *people* are not (just) means in this sense.

Of course, to some degree, we inevitably are "means" to each other. A waiter is partly our means of getting food; a parent is partly a means of support. But the claim is that we get the world itself wrong—we mistake reality itself—if we begin to take other people (or ourselves) *just* as means in this sense.

A person is not a thing, and must not be treated as such. The claim sounds (and is) abstract, but it corresponds to real experience too. Cheery salespeople greet you on the phone like your long-lost brother but hang up in mid-sentence when they realize that they are not going to make a sale. How do you feel? "Like a *thing*," we say: a mere means to someone's profit, instantly discarded if we don't buy something. Or again: we get the chills when a certain kind of pornography reduces a woman to her body, or maybe even certain body parts, as if that were all she were. We call this sexual "objectification": literally, once again, making a person into an object, a thing.

There are more extreme cases too. The Nazi concentration camps were designed to turn people into objects, the first step to mass slaughter. Slavery meant the literal treatment of human beings as no more than property, and was partly rationalized by the claim that the slaves did not really feel pain or suffer oppression in the ways the masters would, as if slaves really were more like machinery or animals (who are also often dismissed as mere "things") than like fellow human beings.

Correspondingly, then, what is *right* is to always treat people at least in part as ends in themselves: *not* as mere things, but each as centers of experience and choice as real as we know ourselves to be.

A profound sense of equality follows—and also, in a way, a sense of wonder. The first impulse is one of standing aside, of letting the other person *be*—in the sense of "letting alone," and also, more fundamentally perhaps, in the sense of pure appreciation. Let them *be!* Who and what they are is already complete, worthy, and in at least a metaphorical sense, perfect. The great religious traditions tell us the same thing: they ask us to see each other as "children of God." That is surely to be more than a mere means to some other, or someone else's, ends—even the best ends in the world!

Kant's Theory of Right Action

One philosopher in particular proposed a theory of right action in this sense: the German thinker Immanuel Kant (1724–1804).

Kant was concerned with the basic principle of moral action, which he called the "Categorical Imperative." One form of the Categorical Imperative is:

Always act so as to treat humanity, whether in yourself or in another, as an end and never merely as a means.

Ends in themselves, once again, are distinct from means; and we live in a world full of such ends, a world in which we ourselves, individually—precious as we are—are still but one among equally precious others.

Another form of the Categorical Imperative is:

Act only according to that maxim whereby you can at the same time will that it become a universal law.

This form of the Imperative needs some explaining, but Kant held that it is the most basic of all—the ultimate source, in fact, of human dignity.

Think of the Golden Rule: "Do unto others as you would have them do unto you." Kant's Imperative is not so different. By "maxim" he meant, roughly, the rule you propose to yourself when trying to decide what to do.

The Categorical Imperative is a test to see whether the rule you have in mind can be moral: the test is whether you could consistently will it to be a rule that everyone follows.

Why should we care about *that*? According to Kant, to decide *morally* means to decide as one rational mind among others, as if setting a rule or law for all. Anyone else in the same situation should do the same thing. Only by following a universal rule in this sense (or "law," in Kant's terms) do we express our understanding of and respect for others as "ends in themselves" just as we are. Only in this way do we avoid treating others as mere means to our ends.

Should I lie, for example, to get myself out of an embarrassing or sticky situation? No, said Kant. I cannot will it to be a universal law that *everyone* should lie to get out of a sticky situation, for then no such lie would work. On the contrary: by wanting my lie to work, I am implicitly willing that others *not* lie in the same situation, so that the general expectation of truthfulness will be maintained, that is, so that my lie will succeed. I am only making an exception for myself.

And there's the crucial thing: making an exception for myself. That is the place at which everything goes wrong. For there is no basis for taking myself to be somehow different from or more special than other people in a way that could justify my flaunting a rule that I expect everyone else to follow. Again: others are centers of experience and choice as real as we know ourselves to be. Recognize that, said Kant, and a recognition of equal dignity and equal standing necessarily follows.

See the box to follow for more from Kant in his own words, including the above citations in context.

Theories of Right Action in Practice

Let us take the question of assisted suicide as an example once again. What might a theory of right action say about it?

If we begin with justice or fairness, there may be no strong implications either way, so long as whatever policy we adopt is applied equally to all. The closer we come to *rights* in the sense of "rights to," though, the stronger is the case *for* allowing assisted suicide. One of the most basic of rights in this sense is the right to autonomy—to make the most fundamental decisions of your life for yourself. The "right to choose" pretty clearly implies that assisted suicide should be allowed for those who choose it.

Kant, for his part, would oppose assisted suicide, as he opposed suicide generally. "If [we] kill [ourselves] in order to escape from painful circum-stances," he wrote, "we use a person [ourselves] merely as a means to maintain a tolerable condition to the conclusion of life." Once life offers us no more pleasure, we conclude that our life has no more value. But this move, so very natural for utilitarianism, is for Kant a fundamental mistake. We come back

Excerpts from Immanuel Kant, Grounding for the Metaphysics of Morals

Now I say that man, and in general every rational being, exists as an end in himself and not merely as a means to be arbitrarily used by this or that will. He must in all his actions, whether directed to himself or to other rational beings, always be regarded at the same time as an end.

. . . Beings whose existence depends not on our will but on nature have, nevertheless, if they are not rational beings, only a relative value as means and are therefore called things. On the other hand, rational beings are called persons inasmuch as their nature already marks them out as ends in themselves, i.e., as something which is not to be used merely as means and hence there is imposed thereby a limit on all arbitrary use of such beings, which are thus objects of respect. Persons are, therefore, not merely subjective ends, whose existence as an effect of our actions has a value for us; but such beings are objective ends, i.e., exist as ends in themselves. Such an end is one for which there can be substituted no other end to which such beings should serve merely as means, for otherwise nothing at all of absolute value would be found anywhere. But if all value were conditioned and hence contingent, then no supreme practical principle could be found for reason at all.

If then there is to be a supreme practical principle and, as far as the human will is concerned, a categorical imperative, then it must be such that from the conception of what is necessarily an end for everyone because this end is an end in itself it constitutes an objective principle of the will and can hence serve as a practical law. The ground of such a principle is this: rational nature exists as an end in itself. In this way man necessarily thinks of his own existence; thus far is it a subjective principle of human actions. But in this way also does every other rational being think of his existence on the same rational ground that holds also for me; hence it is at the same time an objective principle, from which, as a supreme practical ground, all laws of the will must be able to be derived. The practical imperative will therefore be the following: Act in such a way that you treat humanity, whether in your own person or in the person of another, always at the same time as an end and never simply as a means.

[*Declaring that we must now see whether such a "practical imperative" can be put into action, Kant considers a range of examples. One of these is the case of the lie in a sticky situation, discussed in the text. Kant considers it in terms of both forms of the Categorical Imperative introduced in the text. Here it is in terms of the "end in itself" form:*]

. . . The man who intends to make a false promise will immediately see that he intends to make use of another man merely as a means to an end which the latter does not likewise hold. For the man whom I want to use for my own purposes by such a promise cannot possibly concur with my way of acting toward him and hence cannot himself hold the end of this action. This conflict with the principle of duty to others becomes even clearer when instances of attacks on the freedom and property of others are considered. For then it becomes clear that a transgressor of the rights of men intends to make use of the persons of others merely as a means, without taking into consideration that, as rational beings, they should always be esteemed at the same time as ends, i.e., be esteemed only as beings who must themselves be able to hold the very same action as an end.

[Here is the same case considered in terms of the "universal law" form of the Categorical Imperative:]

A man in need finds himself forced to borrow money. He knows well that he won't be able to repay it, but he sees also that he will not get any loan unless he firmly promises to repay it within a fixed time. He wants to make such a promise, but he still has conscience enough to ask himself whether it is not permissible and is contrary to duty to get out of difficulty in this way. Suppose, however, that he decides to do so. The maxim of his action would then be expressed as follows: when I believe myself to be in need of money, I will borrow money and promise to pay it back, although I know that I can never do so. Now this principle of self-love or personal advantage may perhaps be quite compatible with one's entire future welfare, but the question is now whether it is right. I then transform the requirement of self-love into a universal law and put the question thus: how would things stand if my maxim were to become a universal law? He then sees at once that such a maxim could never hold as a universal law of nature and be consistent with itself, but must necessarily be self-contradictory. For the universality of a law which says that anyone believing himself to be in difficulty could promise whatever he pleases with the intention of not keeping it would make promising itself and the end to be attained thereby quite impossible, inasmuch as no one would believe what was promised him but would merely laugh at all such utterances as being vain pretenses. . . .

If we now attend to ourselves in any transgressions of a duty, we find that we actually do not will that our maxim should become a universal law— but rather that the opposite of this maxim should remain a law universally. We only take the liberty of making an exception to the law for ourselves (or just for this one time) to the advantage of our inclination. Consequently, if we weighed up everything from one and the same standpoint, namely, that of reason, we would find a contradiction in our own will, viz., that a certain principle be objectively necessary as a universal law and yet subjectively not hold universally but should admit of exceptions. . . . Although this procedure cannot be justified in our own impartial judgement, yet it does show that we actually acknowledge the validity of the categorical imperative. . . .

again to the crucial point: our lives have value *in themselves*, not just as a means to something else, even our own pleasure. We must respect our *own* lives just as we must respect the lives of others around us. This does not mean that we must live passively in the face of suffering, but it does mean that ending our lives to escape the suffering is not one of our moral options.

THEORIES OF VIRTUE

There are many theories of virtue too, though they all have a common logic. Here we briefly consider several.

Aristotle's Virtues

The most influential classical account of the virtues comes from the Greek philosopher Aristotle (384–322 BCE).

Everything in the world, according to Aristotle, has a distinctive and essential function or activity. Trees grow in certain ways depending on their kinds; buildings are made for certain purposes; human artisans have their particular arts.

This function or activity in turn determines admirable or "excellent" characteristics or traits—virtues. "For all things that have a function or activity," Aristotle wrote, "the good and the 'well' [as in: doing a job well] is thought to reside in the function." Good carpenters, for example, are those who build sturdy and beautiful things—and so virtue, in carpenters, is an eye for proportion; skill with saw and plane; a feel for what a piece of wood can and cannot do; and so on.

Similarly, there must be a characteristic or set of characteristics that defines *our* "essence"—the human "function," as Aristotle also put it.

> For just as for a flute player, a sculptor, or any artist, and, in general, for all things that have a function or activity, the good and the "well" is thought to reside in the function, so it would seem to be for man, if he has a function.

According to Aristotle, rational self-regulation is the characteristic activity and therefore "function" of humans. We are, in his famous definition, *rational animals*. What Aristotle meant by "rational," though, is quite different from what Kant meant by the same word. For Aristotle, reason means the ability—the habits and the wisdom and the judgment—that enable us to bring a complex self into order as it unfolds. This vision of balanced self-actualization Aristotle even called "happiness"—a rather different conception from that of the utilitarians!

This essentially human function and activity in turn determines morally admirable or "excellent" characteristics or traits for us—in short, moral virtues. For example, practical reason is in part the capacity to find the "Golden

Mean"—the appropriate middle—between extremes of emotion or action. In responding to danger we may feel either fear or confidence, leading to two opposite failings: either cowardice (too much fear, too little confidence) or foolhardiness (too much confidence, too little fear.) We need to find the appropriate, rational middle—the virtue, said Aristotle, of courage.

Other moral virtues include temperance, justice, and generosity, each of them likewise "means" between extremes. Even a sense of humor is a virtue on this view—the mean between being foolish and being a bore. And moral *vice*, on this view, is *excess*, either way.

See the box to follow for more from Aristotle in his own words, including the above citations in context.

The "Cardinal Virtues"

Aristotle deeply influenced medieval Christian thinkers such as Saint Thomas Aquinas (1224–1274). Aquinas borrowed Aristotle's "logic of virtue," so to speak—deriving virtue from our essential activity or function—but understood our essential activity or function in very different terms.

In particular, for Aquinas, reason is not an end in itself but instead a means to better knowing ourselves and God. Our ultimate purpose is communion with God, which in perfect form is achievable only after death. Aquinas therefore added the "theological" virtues of faith, hope, and charity to the older Greek or "natural" virtues like justice and temperance. Those Greek virtues were also expanded. Temperance, for example, came to include humility, patience, and chastity.

The deady sins, meanwhile—the vices opposite to the cardinal virtues— were those traits considered fatal to spiritual progress. Pride, lust, avarice, and all the rest: to fall into these pits was a sure way of losing salvation.

Virtues and Practices

Aristotle used the example of carpenters or tanners, whose work defines their goals and therefore their virtues (as carpenters or tanners.) Think as well of teachers or doctors or athletes or car mechanics. Each of these professions or activities we entrust with important things; each of them therefore has a moral dimension; and for each of them, that moral dimension is determined by their specific function or goal. Teachers enable and inform; doctors heal; athletes must "play fair"; and so on. Most modern professional organizations have "codes of ethics" that make these goals explicit and work out their implications. (More on this in Chapter 18.)

Here virtue becomes a function of what contemporary philosopher Alasdair MacIntyre calls "practices." Medicine, teaching, and so on are practices, like many other organized, cooperative activities—politics, child-raising, even games. Each of these activities or disciplines has its own "internal goods"—

Aristotle, Excerpts from Nichomachean Ethics

If, then, there is some end of the things we do, which we desire for its own sake (everything else being desired for the sake of this), and if we do not choose everything for the sake of something else (for at that rate the process would go on to infinity, so that our desire would be empty and vain), clearly this must be the good and the chief good. Will not the knowledge of it, then, have a great influence on life? Shall we not, like archers who have a mark to aim at, be more likely to hit upon what is right? If so, we must try, in outline at least to determine what it is, and of which of the sciences or capacities it is the object. . . . Verbally there is very general agreement; for both the general run of men and people of superior refinement say that it is happiness, and identify living well and doing well with being happy; but with regard to what happiness is they differ, and the many do not give the same account as the wise. For the former think it is some plain and obvious thing, like pleasure, wealth, or honor; they differ, however, from one another—and often even the same man identifies it with different things, with health when he is ill, and wealth when he is poor; but, conscious of their ignorance, they admire those who proclaim some great ideal that is above their comprehension. . . .

Presumably, however, to say that happiness is the chief good seems a platitude, and a clearer account of what it is is still desired. This might perhaps be given, if we could first ascertain the function of man. For just as for a flute player, a sculptor, or any artist, and, in general, for all things that have a function or activity, the good and the "well" is thought to reside in the function, so would it seem to be for man, if he has a function. Have the carpenter, then, and the tanner certain functions or activities, and has man none? Is he born without a function? Or as eye, hand, foot, and in general each of the parts evidently has a function, may one lay it down that man similarly has a function apart from all these? What then can this be? Life seems to be common even to plants, but we are seeking what is peculiar to man. Let us exclude, therefore, the life of nutrition and growth. Next there would be a life of perception, but *it* also seems to be common even to the horse, the ox, and every animal. There remains, then, an active life of the element that has a rational principle; of this, one part has such a principle in the sense of being obedient to one, the other in the sense of possessing one and exercising thought. And, as "life of the rational element" also has two meanings, we must state that life in the sense of activity is what we mean; for this seems to be the more proper sense of the term. Now if the function of man is an activity of soul which follows or implies a rational principle, and if we say "a so-and-so" and "a good so-and-so" have a function which is the same in kind, for example, a lyre player and a good lyre player, and so without qualification in all cases, eminence in respect of goodness being added to the name of the function (for the function of a lyre player is to play the lyre, and that of a good lyre player is to do so well): if this is the case, [and we state the function of man to be a certain kind of life, and this to be an activity or actions of the soul implying a rational principle, and the function of a good man to be the good and noble performance of these, and if any action is well performed when it is performed in accordance with the appropriate excellence: if this is the case,] human good turns out to be activity of soul in accordance with virtue, and if there are more than one virtue, in accordance with the best and most complete.

But we must add "in a complete life." For one swallow does not make a summer, nor does one day; and so too one day, or a short time, does not make a man blessed and happy. . . .

We must . . . not only describe [moral] virtue as a state of character, but also say what sort of state it is. We may remark, then, that every virtue or excellence both brings into good condition the thing of which it is the excellence and makes the work of that thing be done well; e.g., the excellence of the eye makes both the eye and its work good; for it is by the excellence of the eye that we see well. Similarly the excellence of the horse makes a horse both good in itself and good at running and at carrying its rider and at awaiting the attack of the enemy. Therefore, if this is true in every case, the virtue of man also will be the state of character which makes a man good and which makes him do his own work well. . . . If reason is divine, then, in comparison with man, the life according to it is divine in comparison with human life. But we must not follow those who advise us, being men, to think of human things, and, being mortal, of mortal things, but must, so far as we can, make ourselves immortal, and strain every nerve to live in accordance with the best thing in us; for even if it be small in bulk, much more does it in power and worth surpass everything. This would seem, too, to be each man himself, since it is the authoritative and better part of him. It would be strange, then, if he were to choose not the life of his self but that of something else. And what we said before will apply now; that which is proper to each thing is by nature best and most pleasant for each thing; for man, therefore, the life according to reason is best and pleasantest, since reason more than anything else *is* man. This life therefore is also the happiest.

goals that define the practice itself, such as health and life for medicine, justice for the law, and so on. Thus, technically, a virtue for MacIntyre is

an acquired human quality the possession and exercise of which tends to enable us to achieve those goods which are internal to practices and the lack of which effectively prevents us from achieving any such goods.

Devotion to the truth, for example, enables lawyers to seek justice. Cool-headedness enables chess masters to concentrate. Liveliness and imagination make a good teacher.

Most virtues, therefore, are relative to practices—some specific, some fairly general. However, according to MacIntyre, there is not necessarily any *single* practice that is common and central to everyone and therefore defines "the" human essence in the way Aristotle or Aquinas proposed. Virtue lives in the details.

The Ethics of Care

Many of the key "practices" of human life arise from our life *together*. We raise families; we support and depend upon our friends and co-workers; we belong to neighborhoods and churches and community groups.

These practices and institutions require working out, and continuing to work *at*, real relationships: face-to-face connections between specific individuals. In families, moreover, the relationships are often between *un*equals (children and parents) rather than legal or political equals. And, perhaps most fundamentally, these relationships run on love, care, and connection, rather than a distant kind of respect or utilitarian calculation. Their internal good, to use MacIntyre's term, is sustaining relationship.

The virtues, on this view, are therefore those traits that sustain and deepen relationship, enable us to raise children well, keep love strong, and build comradeship and solidarity. Thus the psychologist Carol Gilligan describes an "ethics of care," rooted once again in a specific view of the (or *a*) world, this time

> a world of relationships and psychological truths where an awareness of the connection between people gives rise to a recognition of a responsibility for one another, a perception of the need for response. Seen in this light, morality arises from a recognition of relationship. . . .

Believing in "the restorative activity of care," as Gilligan puts it, we come to

> see the actors in [moral] dilemma[s] arrayed not as opponents in a contest of rights but as members of a network of relationships on whose continuation they all depend. Consequently [the] solution to the dilemma[s] lies in activating the network by communication, . . . strengthening rather than severing connections.

Key virtues thus include perceptiveness, imagination, and sensitivity; skill in responding and nurturing; patience and creativity; and acceptance.

Part of Gilligan's claim is that virtues of this sort have too long been overlooked and devalued in philosophical ethics. We do recognize patience, perceptiveness, and so on as virtues, perhaps, but traditionally philosophers have had little to say about them, and they tend to be treated as much less important or interesting than the virtues of the male warrior-citizen that so preoccupied the Greeks. In fact, however, as recent work in feminist ethics has begun to show, the virtues that arise in relationship may be the richest, most vital, and most complex of all.

Virtue Thinking in Practice

By way of illustration let us return for a third and final time to the question of assisted suicide.

Most virtue thinkers oppose assisted suicide. This may be so for several reasons. First of all, facing pain and death calls for certain personal virtues, most notably courage. Pain and death are part of life. Courage gives us a way to take heart in the face of them, rather than trying to deny and suppress them, even to the point of suppressing our own selves in the end.

Humility is important too: that is, not trying to control everything, or thinking we can or should. The inevitability of pain and death also calls for certain virtues in families and communities: caring, responsiveness, hospitality—making suicide less tempting as the only way out. (This is a vital point: the question of moral virtue here isn't exhausted by looking just at the virtues of the sufferer.)

Finally, it's also a serious question whether the healing and life-saving role of doctors should be expanded to include helping people die as well. Doctors' role is to serve life, not death.

As far back as Aristotle, though, virtue thinkers have also insisted that moral choices cannot be made by rule following or calculation. They mistrust single, simple formulas like Bentham's Principle of Utility and Kant's Categorical Imperative, or even the blanket judgment that, say, assisted suicide is always wrong. What we need instead, they say, is good *judgment* in specific situations. Whether to choose to die (and how) or to ask for help (and how) may call for different answers depending on the person and his or her condition. Sometimes quite different virtues—being resolute? knowing when it is time to go?—or different applications of the same virtues, like the courage to choose death or to lovingly accept that choice in others, may carry the day instead. Above all we need the wisdom to know which way to turn when.

Exercises and Notes

APPLYING THE THEORIES

In the last chapter you "mapped" the families of values involved in ethical debates over drug use, medical honesty, eating animals, and others. Now take that work a step farther by asking how you would think about those issues using the theories introduced in this chapter.

The challenge here is to understand the debate in theoretical terms. Put the theories to use. Speak to each issue from "inside" each theory, as I tried to do at the end of each section in this chapter with the issue of assisted suicide. How would utilitarians view the question of medical honesty, for example (and why)? How would Kant view it? What virtues are relevant—and from what larger picture of human nature or specific practices do they spring?

Here's the list again:

- Should marijuana be legalized?
- Should doctors always tell their patients the truth, even when in the doctor's opinion the truth may be too depressing for them to bear, or may prevent them from getting better?
- Should doctors be allowed to help people end their own lives?
- Is the death penalty moral?
- Should the government control the supply and purchase of certain types of guns?
- Should we continue to use animals for food, medical testing, and product-safety research?

Again, a look at any newspaper will suggest many more.

You will get a chance to evaluate, criticize, and defend your favorite theory (if any) below and in Chapter 6. For this exercise, just concentrate on getting the theory right—doing the best by whatever theory you are using at the moment. Understand first, argue later!

WHAT DO YOU THINK?

Now declare yourself. We have considered three types of ethical theories in this chapter. Does one of these types of theories describe how you think (or: how you *mainly* think)? Which one? On any given issue, do you think one kind of theory works better than the others? Which one?

Consider *why* you may have a preference for one kind of theory over the others. Do you think there are good arguments for or against some of these types of theories? (We take up this question further in the next chapter.) Do you think there are features of your upbringing and/or experience that shape your preference? What features? Do you think that people who might prefer one of the other types of theories may have had different kinds of upbringing or experience?

Probably it would be wise to acknowledge that each type of theory has certain special insights. Each theory gets something right. What do *you* think each theory gets right, especially the theories you don't prefer? Do you think there is some way to incorporate the insights of the other theories into the one you prefer?

Some people want to try to combine these three types of theories into a larger overall approach. Are you tempted? If so, how would you combine them? And (don't overlook this question!) how would you prioritize them in cases where they come into conflict? Why would you prioritize them in this way?

NOTES AND FURTHER READINGS

John Stuart Mill is cited from his *Utilitarianism* (available in many editions; I quote from the Hackett Publishing Company edition, 1979), pages 7, 16, and 33. For Kant, see his *Grounding for the Metaphysics of Morals* (James Ellington, trans; Hackett, 1981). Cited here are pages 30, 32–33, 37, and 36 (standard reference numbers 421, 424, 430, and 429, respectively).

Aristotle's key work is the *Nichomachean Ethics* (sometimes just titled *Ethics*). I cite the W. D. Ross translation published by the Clarendon Press. Citations are from Book I, 1097b23–1098a19. Alasdair MacIntyre is quoted from *After Virtue* (University of Notre Dame Press, 1981), page 178. Carol Gilligan is quoted from *In a Different Voice* (Harvard University Press, 1982, 1993), pages 30–31.

Most anthologies in ethics include selections from Mill, Kant, Aristotle, and many others. On-line versions can be accessed through Lawrence Hinman's "Ethics Updates" website at <www.ethics.acusd.edu> or at other philosophical sites linked to it. There are also some accessible short survey books by contemporary teachers, for example Douglas Birsch, *Ethical Insights* (Mayfield Publishing Company, 1999.) More demanding are Richard Norman, *The Moral Philosophers* (Oxford University Press, 1983, 1998) and Alasdair MacIntyre, *A Short History of Ethics* (Macmillan, 1966).

Each theoretical tradition has inspired volumes and volumes of work, far too much to cite here. Just the barest few are the following.

A readable and provocative application of utilitarianism to a range of contemporary issues is Peter Singer, *Practical Ethics* (Cambridge University Press, 1979.) Dan Brock's essay "Utilitarianism" in Tom Regan and Don Vandeveer, eds., *And Justice for All: New Introductory Essays in Philosophy and Public Policy* (Rowman and Allenheld, 1982) is a useful though dense survey of contemporary philosophical utilitarianism. Also see J. J. C. Smart's classic "Outline of a System of Utilitarian Ethics," in J. J. C. Smart and Bernard Williams, *Utilitarianism: For and Against* (Cambridge University Press, 1983.)

On Kantian ethics, start with Onora O'Neill, "A Simplified Account of Kant's Ethics," in Tom Regan, ed., *Matters of Life and Death* (McGraw-Hill, 1986). For a systematic look at respect more or less in its own terms, see R. S. Downie and Elizabeth Telfer, *Respect for Persons* (Schocken, 1970.) A classic theory of the right, much less formal than Kant's, is W. D. Ross's *The Foundations of Ethics* (Oxford University Press, 1939). For a vigorous introduction to contemporary theories about rights, see Lawrence Becker, "Individual Rights" and Hugo Bedeau's essay, "International Human Rights," in the Regan and Vandeveer volume cited above, and Jan Narveson, *The Libertarian Idea* (Temple University Press, 1988).

On the vision of ends and means in theories of the right, a very different approach is Martin Buber's *I and Thou* (various translations: e.g. as translated by Walter Kaufmann and published by Scribner's, 1970). Buber explores how other people (and animals and trees and even God) emerge in our *experience* as ends—those to whom we can and must say "Thou"—rather than mere means—those of whom we offhandedly say "It."

On the virtues, useful introductory collections are Christina Hoff Sommers and Fred Sommers, eds., *Virtue and Vice in Everyday Life* (Harcourt Brace, 1993) and Alexander Hooke, ed., *Virtuous Persons, Vicious Deeds* (Mayfield Publishing Company, 1999). More theoretical is Michael Slote and Roger Crisp, eds., *Virtue Ethics* (Oxford University Press, 1997). On Aristotle's ethics, a classic and accessible treatment is Henry Veatch, *Rational Man* (Indiana University Press, 1966). For Aquinas, see Anton Pegis, ed., *Introduction to St Thomas Aquinas* (Modern Library, 1948). On care ethics, see Nel Noddings, *Caring: A Feminine Approach to Ethics and Moral Education* (University of California Press, 1984) and Sara Ruddick, *Maternal Thinking: Toward a Politics of Peace* (Ballantine, 1989). Two fine collections on Gilligan's work are Eva Feder Kittay and Diana Meyers, eds., *Women and Moral Theory* (Rowman and Littlefield, 1987) and Mary Jeanne Larrabee, ed., *An Ethic of Care: Feminist and Interdisciplinary Perspectives* (Routledge, 1993).

Care ethics is often distinguished from (classical) virtue theory, and it does have certain differences, most notably that care ethics understands the self essentially in *relationship*, rather than in an atomistic and independent way (or in relationship primarily to God). Still, even classical virtue theories give more attention to relationship (e.g. friendship) than the other kinds of theories. Both care ethics and classical virtue theories also appeal to the "internal goods" of practices, and both insist that an ethic of particular and complex judgments is essential, without overarching or formal rules. For a variety of feminist views of ethics (not all of them care ethics, either), see Elizabeth Frazer, Jennifer Hornsby, and Sabina Lovibond, eds., *Ethics: A Feminist Reader* (Blackwell, 1992).

CHAPTER 6

When Values Clash
Theoretical Approaches

Ethical theories have a partly practical aim: to help us deal with conflicts of moral values. Each theory proposes a distinctive approach to such conflicts, though each proposal is different from the others. Here we come to one of the chief areas of attention and controversy in modern philosophical ethics.

UTILITARIAN STRATEGIES: FINDING A SINGLE MEASURE

Utilitarianism's proposal is the most ambitious, and therefore a natural place to start.

Goods Versus Other Goods

When one good conflicts with another good, you know what utilitarianism would say: pick the greater good. Should you finish your degree now, or save the money and time for something else? Each choice has its benefits and its costs. You try to choose in a way that achieves the greatest net benefit (highest total benefit over cost).

It may take some careful figuring. For one thing, you need to take account of the probability of the future benefits and costs (which normally is less than 100%: the future is uncertain!). Perhaps a moderate but improbable gain later is *not* worth the sure bet that you will suffer now. There are elaborate systems for making such trade-offs, but the logic is simple: we still aim to maximize utility.

Suppose that the question is whether to build a dam that will generate electricity and provide irrigation and recreation but will also cost money, displace families or towns, and flood valuable land. How do we decide? Naturally, say utilitarians, we try to quantify the various benefits and costs. How much social good will be gained from the dam? How much will be lost?

Again the figuring can get sophisticated. Usually it is left to the economists, who calculate benefits and costs in dollars. What will the dam cost?

How much money will it take to compensate people who have to move? What is the monetary value of the land that will be lost? All of these costs must be weighed against the monetary value of the electricity produced, the dollar gain in food production due to irrigation, added income from recreation, and so on—as well as the net benefits that could be gained from doing something else with the same resources. More sophisticated calculations factor in the long-run probability of these benefits continuing (maybe high but less than 100%) and consider the costs when the dam's useful life is over (dams eventually silt up and become useless). In the end, though, once again, the aim is still to answer a simple question: which choice has the highest net benefits?

Goods Versus Other Kinds of Values

All of this may seem natural enough. So far, though, we are weighing goods against other goods. The greater challenge comes when we weigh goods against what seem to be other sorts of values: rights or virtues.

But notice I said: seem to be. The usual utilitarian idea is that ultimately *all* values reduce to goods—to benefits and costs. At bottom, utilitarians say, moral values actually don't differ in kind. There really aren't three separate families of moral values, but only one. Underneath, they all belong to the same family. All moral conflict is really about one thing—what will truly achieve the greatest happiness of all, all things considered and in the long run.

Thus, even what seem to be conflicts between goods and other kinds of values are really also just conflicts about utility, utilitarians say, and should be decided exactly as conflicts between goods and other goods should be judged. They really *are* conflicts between goods and other goods, underneath. And so, utilitarians say, we are justified in translating all other values into benefit and cost terms—"cashing them out," so to speak. Happiness becomes utilitarianism's *single measure* for all moral conflicts.

Fairness, for example, looks like quite a different kind of value from maximizing happiness. But couldn't the value of fairness be understood in terms of happiness? Certainly it promotes happiness much of the time. Indirectly, fairness also promotes social stability, which in turn leads to happiness. An unfair social order, unequal and arbitrary, would make a lot of people unhappy much of the time, and it would also be prone to resistance and overthrow, leading to even more uncertainty and unrest: a picture that does not look too satisfying.

John Stuart Mill, for example, explicitly grounded justice on utility:

> Justice is a name for certain classes of moral rules which concern the essentials of human well-being more nearly, and are therefore of more absolute obligation, than any other rules for the guidance of life. . . . [T]hey are the main element in determining the social feelings of mankind. It is their observance which alone preserves peace among human beings. . . .

We should indeed promote fairness, then, but not ultimately for its own sake. We should promote it because it helps maximize utility. It serves the social good.

Utilitarians would say the same of the virtues. No character trait, they argue, is good simply because it conforms to some underlying essence or "function." Rather, good traits are good because they promote utility. Surely we would not really consider care or courage or self-discipline to be virtues if they typically made people *un*happy.

Take honesty, for example. It might seem that dishonesty often has major benefits. Little (or not so little) deceptions can keep you ahead of the crowd and out of trouble. But deception also has costs and dangers. It takes a lot of work. It's emotionally draining to have your guard up all the time. When the deceptions fail, you may lose your friends. Thus, arguably, dishonesty is a bad idea, even on utilitarian grounds. It is not a matter of benefits to you being trumped by some other kind of value, but simply of thinking more carefully about *all* the likely benefits—and costs—in the long run.

Values That Don't "Cash Out"

Some rights or virtues may resist this kind of "translation." For example, some people seem to think that *no* deception can ever be ethical, and propose to tell the truth even to criminals who threaten them and to children too young to understand. But it is not at all clear that this kind of "hypertruthfulness" has positive overall effects.

So what then? Do we give up on truthfulness, or on utilitarian translation? Surely, at least in this case, most of us will answer as the utilitarians do: here is where the value of truthfulness ends. Here, then, the utilitarian "single measure" becomes the *judge* of other values. Those values that don't cash out in terms of utility are not really moral values after all.

Could the same go even for fairness? Utilitarians would say that while fairness is *usually* a good thing, it is not *always* a good thing. It is not a good thing if it irremovably conflicts with social utility. In an emergency, for example, we sometimes cut corners, even violate some people's rights, for the sake of saving greater social goods. Mill again:

> [C]ases may occur in which some other social duty is so important as to overrule . . . the general maxims of justice. Thus, to save a life, it may not only be allowable, but a duty, to steal or take by force the necessary food or medicine, or to kidnap and compel to officiate the only qualified medical practitioner. . . .

So even stealing or kidnapping doctors might be morally acceptable, or even a duty, in a pinch! Strong stuff—but not necessarily implausible, and perfectly natural if you are a utilitarian. In a system where utility rules, no other value can be absolute.

NON-UTILITARIAN STRATEGIES: PRIORITIZING VALUES

In the face of conflict, theories of right action and of virtue take a more modest approach than utilitarianism. They do not deny, for one thing, that there *are* such things as conflicts between genuinely different families of moral values, and they do not dismiss values that resist translation into their favorite terms. They propose a different strategy instead.

Their strategy is to prioritize conflicting moral values. That is, the aim is to try to decide which should take precedence—which need to be honored first—if not all can be honored at once. Utilitarians argue that rational choice requires a single measure for all moral values, but nonutilitarians argue that it is enough if we have an inclusive *ranking* of moral values—it is enough if we know which demands take priority. No single measure is necessary.

Rights Versus Other Rights

When rights conflict, the most basic rights come first. Two children want a toy that belongs to one of them. One says "I want it!" The other says "It's mine!" We don't ask which child would be happier with the toy. We favor the child whose toy it is, while suggesting some other solutions, like trading something else for the toy, voluntarily sharing, and so on. In a pinch, ownership trumps desire.

Likewise, the right to life and to be secure in your own person (free from injury, assault, theft, etc.) take priority over others' rights to freedom. I may not use my gun, say (or car, chainsaw, laser pointer, etc.) in ways that endanger others' lives or bodies, even though I am therefore less free to use my gun (or . . .) as I please. The rights to life and security are more basic. But the right to freedom—say, free speech—in turn takes precedence over the desire to hear only pleasant things said about you. In that case, freedom of speech is more basic.

Two kinds of justice or fairness may also conflict. It's not fair to informed voters, maybe, when people vote who know nothing about the issues or candidates besides what they've heard in a few TV commercials. On the other hand, it would be unfair in a much more basic way to exclude them from voting entirely. Educating poorly informed voters is an option; denying their voting rights is not.

Rights Versus Goods

What about when rights conflict with social utility? How do we establish priority then?

One approach appeals to our "intuitions": to our felt sense of what is and is not right. Specific examples or thought experiments are used to make our intuitions vivid. Here's one:

Imagine that you are a surgeon who comes upon a plane that has just crashed in a remote area. Six people are lying about unconscious. A is fine except for very minor injuries. The other five have potentially fatal injuries, but it just so happens that all five could be saved if each of them had a different organ transplant. B needs a lung; C needs a heart; and so on. And there is A lying there unconscious with all the necessary organs. . . .

Would it be right to cut up A in order to save five other people? At least at first glance, utilitarianism might have to say yes—or so its critics suggest. It's one life versus five. But clearly, in fact, it would be wrong. Among our most basic ethical judgments is that sacrificing one to the many, even if social utility goes up, is not right. Utility matters, of course, but what's right matters first. And how do we know? *We just do.*

Another argument appeals to the concept of morality itself. Kantians claim, remember, that moral thinking must proceed not from one person's particular point of view but from a universal point of view. This already seems to suggest that a moral choice must prioritize equality above social goods.

Imagine people gathered together, says the contemporary Kantian John Rawls, to decide the general ethical and political rules that will govern their interactions. A moral choice must be one in which no one is favored by mere accident of birth or social status, and people must not be able to tailor ethical principles to their advantage (e.g. the rich favoring the rich or the poor the poor). One way to ensure this basic fairness is to make sure that the choosers do not know whether they are rich or poor, white or black, male or female, and so on, until the rules are chosen. So the question is: what rules would people choose under these conditions?

Rawls claims they will *not* choose utilitarian rules. They will not allow the possibility that most will do well if a few are exploited. Since they do not know "who they are," so to speak, it is possible that they themselves will be the ones exploited, an unacceptable risk even if its probability is low.

According to Rawls, people under these conditions will choose rules that establish a basic equality of access to the fundamental goods of society, allowing inequality only when inequalities benefit the least well off segments of society. Thus Rawls concludes that equality has priority, as does an obligation to look to the well-being of the least well off. Only after the requirements of justice are met can we take account of utilitarian benefits and costs.

The Priority of Virtue?

When virtues conflict with other virtues our strategy will be familiar: to try to determine which virtues are more basic. The answer may depend on an underlying theory of human nature or the "function" of human beings.

Aristotle, for example, would consider the rational virtues basic. Aquinas would emphasize faith, communion with God. The answer may also depend on the situation. A mother acting as a mother will set different priorities than a lawyer, even if she herself is also a lawyer.

When virtues conflict with other values, some (but not all) virtue theorists would claim priority for the virtues. Traditionally the arguments were religious. God infused God's own nature into us, it was said, and that nature is ours to try to live up to. This life is only a preparation for the life to come, anyway, and it is our virtues that we will be judged by, not how happy we make ourselves or other people in this life. This is certainly not the only possible religious view (John Stuart Mill speculated that God really is a utilitarian), but it is the view that underlies the priority of virtue as Aquinas saw it.

Modern virtue theories, as we've seen, are more contextual. Virtues may not have priority in general, but specific virtues may have priority over other values in specific situations or for specific people.

A sample argument: Doctors, insofar as they are doctors, serve life and health first, and all other values second. Therefore, doctors should not be expected to help people die (should not take part in or promote assisted suicide), even though it may be a perfectly reasonable thing for a patient to want and request. It may even be perfectly reasonable for a nondoctor to assist other people to end their lives—but not *doctors*, not people for whom life and health are priorities on account of their profession.

Could the virtues have priority in some more general way too, outside of particular or professional contexts? That is harder to say. Most virtue theorists say something more modest: just that virtues also *matter*; that goods or rights should not automatically have priority either. It's a vice (greed?) to try to squeeze every last bit of happiness out of every situation we're in, as utilitarians might. It's also a vice (slavishness?) to follow rules automatically, in the way that Kant is sometimes (perhaps unfairly) supposed to have done. First, or at least in addition, we must be true to ourselves. Virtue, at least, should have more priority than it has lately been given.

WHEN THEORIES STALEMATE

All of this, as you might imagine, is highly controversial.

Can Utilitarian Translation Work?

Non-utilitarians object to the claim that all moral values should be cashed out in utilitarian terms. Is fairness *only* good so far as it serves social utility? Certainly our legal system doesn't think so. Everyone is entitled to a fair trial and to be presumed innocent, for example, even though they may turn out to be guilty. It might be much more satisfying, not to mention cheaper, simply to put away a whole class of criminal suspects without any trial at all. Yet we will not stand for it. It is not *right*—not just, not fair.

Utilitarians do try to defend many important rights. Rights to free speech, liberty, and all the rest serve social utility. They maximize the general happiness—usually. When they don't, though, the utilitarian can only conclude that there simply are no such rights. Mill, remember, even endorsed kidnapping doctors. But what good is a utilitarian kind of right, critics say, if the moment individual rights conflict with social need, utilitarianism no longer stands behind them? The whole point of rights is to stop this kind of thinking—taking a person as a mere means to some social good—dead in its tracks.

Virtue theorists are no happier with utilitarianism's treatment of the virtues. Can pleasure (or "utility" in *any* guise) really be the ethical bottom line? Aren't some pleasures just wrong? And not wrong because they lead to greater displeasure somewhere down the line, but just plain *wrong*—wrong because they are inappropriate for beings of the sort we are?

It's interesting that John Stuart Mill vacillated on this point, speaking at times of "higher" and "lower" pleasures. Higher pleasures are supposed to be better, of course, worthier of human beings. "It is better to be a human being dissatisfied than a pig satisfied; better to be Socrates dissatisfied than a fool satisfied." But it is not at all clear why. If pleasure alone is the good, how can one of two equally pleasurable pleasures still be "better"? It appears that Mill himself wants to introduce some non-utilitarian factors into the mix—a sensible move, for sure, but no credit to utilitarianism!

Problems with Prioritizing

Non-utilitarians do not deny the diversity of values—they do not seek to reduce all values to one type—but only aim to place certain values *first*, before others, when conflicts arise and choices have to be made. This strategy might therefore seem a natural fall-back option if the utilitarian approach fails. But it too has difficulties.

One problem is that most of the arguments for the priority either of rights or virtues work, when they work at all, only in specific situations. Doctors qua doctors (doctors considered purely in their professional capacities) may be bound to give certain values priority, for example, but that does not give much guidance to society as a whole when it tries to set rules for, say, assisted suicide.

Likewise, while it is certainly true that rights and fairness are compelling considerations *some* of the time, they don't offer an effective way to think about *all* moral situations. Often the most pressing moral questions concern our families or friends, for example, where the careful legalism of rights thinking is out of place. We need something richer than that.

The more philosophical arguments sometimes stalemate too. Appeals to intuition, for example, can be met with counterappeals to intuition—and some of our intuitions are utilitarian.

In short, priority is hard to establish. Rights and virtue arguments remind us that certain values—values that are sometimes not so efficient or convenient—are still important, indeed essential. But that does not establish their priority. It may just give us more complexity and conflict. Maybe that's even part of their point!

Conclusions

You can see that these are controversial matters, more controversial than most of the tools in this toolbox. My proposed conclusion (itself controversial, of course!) is that ethical theories are limited tools. Each systematizes *some* of our moral values, and each can help resolve *some* conflicts of moral values, especially conflicts within families. These are genuine and important uses. Subtle and elaborate theorizing continues, as well it should, in each tradition.

When moral values conflict across families, though, theories are much less helpful. They are unlikely to carry us all the way to a resolution. No single theory can prioritize all values or establish a workable single measure. To address some kinds of conflicts we may need other tools, such as those offered in the next chapter.

Of course, many philosophers—maybe you too—will want to (continue to) defend or elaborate one of these ethical theories to meet the objections offered here (and there are others, I'm afraid—see the box to follow). Certainly many thinkers have tried and are still trying.

Still, it seems to other philosophers that the day of ethical theory has passed. At least it no longer seems so likely that one single theory can reach across family lines and plausibly account for all of our values or resolve their conflicts. None has yet succeeded, and given the diversity of sources of our values, it's not too likely that any will. Some philosophers now even claim that theories do a poor job of truly uniting values *within* each family. Here too there is controversy.

Thus, when moral values conflict, especially across families, use your theoretical tools with caution. Try out the theories—see what they can offer—but don't assume that you will or must arrive at a definitive answer. You may learn a great deal about how to think about the problem without necessarily resolving it at all. You may see more deeply without necessarily seeing your way through.

More Arguments Between the Theories

Each theory has its own characteristic way of challenging the others, and, correspondingly, each has its own characteristic difficulties. Here is a brief look at some of these arguments for those interested in going farther.

A

Can utilitarianism take better account of justice and fairness? How? Should it try? What do you think of Mill's endorsement of kidnapping doctors? How about cutting up one unharmed person to save five others in need?

Ought we to be able to criticize some pleasures or happinesses themselves? Some clearly have bad effects: the pleasures of a sadist, for example. But this is a more difficult question than it may look. On the utilitarian view, the pleasures of a sadist are not bad *in themselves*. No pleasure can be bad in itself, since pleasure just *is* the good. Rather, as with everything else on the utilitarian view, the pleasures of the sadist are supposed to be bad because of their effects: more unhappiness for other people than the sadist gains for himself or herself. A better test question would be: would sadistic pleasure be okay (in fact, be good) if no one else were harmed by it (for example, if it were only "virtual," with no likelihood of spilling over into actual harm to others)? Or: what if a sadist had an enormous capacity for pleasure, so that his or her pleasure actually exceeded the suffering of those who were harmed? Would sadism be a good thing *then*? It's hard to see why not on utilitarian grounds. But this certainly seems like the wrong answer.

Some critics of utilitarianism argue that "happiness" and "utility" are such vague terms that it is not clear that we really can measure or even weigh the relative utilities of different courses of action. Seldom am I sure about even what would make *me* happiest, for instance, let alone what makes other people happy—or how to compare my happiness with theirs. Meanwhile, the ripple effects of even the simplest act are almost incalculable, all the more so if the act affects large numbers of people.

Should I spend my vacation at the beach, or helping build houses with Habitat for Humanity? I would probably enjoy the beach more, though I do like to build and to help out too. Building houses would help make the future occupants happier—though the houses will get built anyway, whether I am there or not. Is there any precise way to weigh a sharp and immediate plesure for me—one person—against the smaller and less definite contribution I might make to the quite different and longer-term happiness of others?

And even this is just the beginning. If I go on the Habitat trip, someone else will not go: perhaps the trip would be better for that person than for me? Or maybe that person would up the total happiness more by going to the beach? (Or somewhere else?) Who is this person, anyway? And how do I weigh in the possible benefits to others (my students, say) from my being somewhat better rested after the beach? What about my long-run contribution to beach erosion and the commercial overdevelopment of fragile coast ecologies?

Despite its appearance of hardheaded practicality, then, utilitarianism may actually be useless, or worse, as a practical way to make decisions. What really happens in such cases, critics worry, is that utilitarian language lends itself to offhand self-justification. Whatever I do, I can justify myself by pointing to the happiness I (might) produce or costs I (might) avoid. Just this accusation has been leveled against the monetary calculation of "costs" and "benefits," for example, as in the dam project discussed in the text. It looks very rational and impartial and responsible, but underneath it's all really guesswork, say the critics, dressed up to justify whatever the decision-maker is inclined to do anyway.

If you tend toward utilitarianism, tackle some of these issues. Modern utilitarians have not given up, and they may be onto something. Get a sense of what they are struggling with.

B

Then again, you may agree with the text's criticism of utilitarianism, and (perhaps for that very reason) want to defend a theory of right action instead. Fine—go to it. Here are some questions and challenges for you.

Aren't there *some* limits to rights, *some* circumstances under which we should (or where it is at least not wrong to) treat others as mere means or more or less utilitarian grounds? For example, do you really think it would be wrong, all things considered, to torture a terrorist in order to locate a time-bomb before it goes off and vaporizes a city?

Rights are limited in a variety of ways now. We have the right to hold property, for example, but not to use it for just anything we please. You can't build a gas station or nuclear power plant or even a store on a residential lot, even if you own it free and clear. Why? Not because of others' rights, but because we believe that zoning restrictions serve the public good. Is this a bad thing? Are you prepared to make any rights absolute?

Philosophers often distinguish *negative rights* from *positive rights* (some-times also called "entitlements"). A negative right is a right against something being done to you, say, someone threatening your life. A positive right is a right that requires someone else to do something for you, say, give you food if you are starving.

Often it is argued that negative rights must have priority over positive rights, on the grounds that only a system of negative rights can be consistent. Conservatives argue that the right to life, for example, cannot extend to the requirement that others give up their lives or their freedom (or indeed anything else) to sustain *your* life. The right to life is only a right not to be killed. Others argue in the reverse way—that certain positive rights are necessary if even the basic rights are to make any sense. The right to freedom, for example, makes no sense if you do not have even the bare minimum (education, food) to make use of it.

So what kind of rights do you propose to defend? Are they only "negative," or do they demand more than that? Is there a right to food if you are starving? Medical care if you are sick? If so, why? If not, why not?

Or you may think in terms other than rights: perhaps of justice and equality. These are not exactly the clearest available moral terms either. Are great disparities of wealth morally okay, for example? Some people say: yes, as long as wealth is acquired without lying, cheating, or stealing and the like, but by following the rules of the economic "game": by shrewd marketing, let's say, or by being first to patent an invention, or by good business management. Or by inheritance—someone else's choice to pass on the wealth to you. Economic inequality could therefore be fair under a strict and specific view of fairness or justice.

An alternative view argues that it *cannot* be fair or just, even if all the rules are followed, for some people to end up living in mansions and others to end up living in the streets. Is is fair that athletes make millions of dollars merely for advertising basketball shoes that are assembled by destitute third-world women for pennies a day? (It would take the average worker in Nike's Indonesia plants 45,000 *years* to be paid what Michael Jordan is paid in one year just for advertising Nike's products. Can this be just?)

What do you think? How do you propose to pin down the ideas of justice and equality, in ways that give a plausible answer to questions like these?

C

Virtue theory makes the most modest of the theories' claims to priority, so correspondingly there are fewer objections to it. Still, this does not mean that there is a better case for the overall priority of virtue. Perhaps the opposite: maybe the case is so problematic that it is seldom made in the first place.

Some questions. First, what sort of theory of human nature or roles or relationships would you base virtues on? There are certainly a variety of possible starting points: recall the theories of virtue discussed in Chapter 5.

Once you have settled on a starting point, ask: how far can it go? The text argues that virtue theory is most plausible with regard to specific practices that have clear "internal goods." Assuming this is true, how far do you think virtue theory can be generalized? Does human life as a whole have a clear and specific internal good? What is it? How can you establish this?

Utilitarians sometimes argue that virtue theory is radically incomplete if taken as an overall theory of ethics. We can say, with MacIntyre, that the internal goods of certain practices elevate those character traits that serve those goods. The utilitarians' question, though, would be: what makes those practices themselves good? We would not consider an effective concentration-camp guard to be a virtuous person, even though he or she served ably and well the internal goods of the concentration camp. No—we need some external standard by which to judge social practices as well.

Utilitarians argue that this standard (can only be) social utility. What do you think?

When roles with different internal goods conflict, how do we decide which takes priority? How I respond to a student's needs as a teacher may be very different from how I'd respond as a friend. If I can only respond in one way or the other, which should it be? Often the question of which role takes priority lies at the very core of the ethical issue in the first place. Can you make such a decision without sliding back into utilitarianism? How?

Exercises and Notes

APPROACHING WITHIN-FAMILY CONFLICTS

Look back to your answers to the first exercise in Chapter 4 ("Identifying Families and Conflicts"). Some of the conflicts you identified there were between values in the same family. Now ask how the ethical theory corresponding to that family might help you resolve the conflict. If the conflict is between two goods, can you sort it out using the utilitarians' single measure? If two rights or virtues conflict, how might you prioritize them? Explain your answers in each case.

APPROACHING CROSS-FAMILY CONFLICTS

Some of the conflicts you identified in Chapter 4 were between values in *different* families. Now ask how you might use ethical theories to help you resolve the conflict. If the conflict is between a good and a right, how would you approach it using one or more theories? What would utilitarianism say? Is it plausible? What would a theory of right action say? If a conflict is between a right and a virtue, can you use one or more theories to prioritize them? Which ones, and why? If allied sets of values are coming into conflict, what then? Explain your answers in each case.

WHAT DO YOU THINK?

Between the section "When Theories Stalemate" and the box "More Arguments Between the Theories" you have a lot to chew on in this chapter regardless of which theory you're inclined toward. This is your chance to once again declare yourself in favor of one theory or another, and defend your chosen theory against the various objections and contrasts raised in this chapter. Why is your chosen theory better than the others? Why is it better than working with all three theories together (if you think it is) or better than proceeding without any theory at all (if you think it is)?

Is your theoretical inclination the same as when you answered the parallel exercise in chapter 5? Why or why not?

NOTES AND FURTHER READINGS

On Mill's utilitarian account of justice, see Chapter 5 of his *Utilitarianism* (Hackett Publishing Company, 1979), page 58. On kidnapping doctors, see page 62. On "higher" and "lower" pleasures, see pages 8 to 10. On God as a utilitarian, see page 21. On negative and positive ("welfare") rights, see A. I. Melden, *Rights and Persons* (University of California Press, 1977) and Jan Narveson, *The Libertarian Idea* (Temple University Press, 1988).

John Rawls's views are outlined in his *A Theory of Justice* (Harvard University Press, 1970), Chapter 1. For a vigorous critical discussion of Rawls's project, see Norman Daniels, ed., *Reading Rawls* (Basic Books, 1975). On Rawls's Kantianism, see Kenneth Baynes, *The Normative Grounds of Social Criticism* (SUNY Press, 1992).

For surveys of the recent debate over utilitarianism, two useful professional works are: Amartya Sen and Bernard Williams, eds., *Utilitarianism and Beyond* (Cambridge University Press, 1982); and Samuel Scheffler, *Consequentialism and Its Critics* (Oxford University Press, 1988). For a survey of the debate over applied utilitarianism (cost-benefit analysis), see James Campen, *Benefit, Cost, and Beyond: The Political Economy of Benefit-Cost Analysis* (Ballinger Publishing Company, 1986). For a critical view, with some suggestions about alternative methods, see Herman Daly, *For the Common Good* (Beacon Press, 1994).

Critics of the theoretical turn in ethics are many and varied. On theories' tendency to polarize values in practice, see Richard Zaner, *Ethics and the Clinical Encounter* (Prentice-Hall, 1988), Chapter 1. Albert Jonsen and Stephen Toulmin, in *The Abuse of Casuistry* (University of California Press, 1988), argue that the history of moral philosophy offers a variety of nontheoretical methods for resolving conflicts, though these have been obscured by the twentieth-century's preoccupation with theoretical modes of thinking. For more on this, see the notes to Chapter 10 of this book.

Many contemporary thinkers are working toward a vision of moral judgment rooted in specific situations and life stories. For a feminist version of these arguments, see Margaret Walker, *Moral Understandings* (Routledge, 1998). My own book *Toward Better Problems* (Temple University Press, 1992) warns that the theoretical approach tends to block nontheoretical modes of engagement or problem-solving, such as those offered in the next chapter. Bernard Williams has argued that there is no reason to suppose that the "truth about ethics," if there is such a thing at all, is *simple* in the way that a theory could capture: see his aptly named *Ethics and the Limits of Philosophy* (Harvard University Press, 1985). See also Martin Benjamin's *Splitting the Difference* (University Press of Kansas, 1990), Chapter 4.

◯

CHAPTER 7

When Values Clash
Integrative Approaches

Whatever we conclude about the usefulness of ethical theories, we certainly could use additional tools to help deal with conflicts of moral values. And additional tools are available—tools of quite a different sort.

ANOTHER VIEW OF MORAL CONFLICTS

In nearly every serious moral issue, the truth is that both sides have a point. Or rather, *all* sides have a point, since there are usually more than two. All sides speak for something worth considering. Each side is right about *something*.

This claim may seem totally obvious. Indeed, it *is* totally obvious. In popular moral debate, though, it is rarely recognized. Usually we assume that only one side can be right. On most major moral issues, there are usually supposed to be just two, clearly distinct and opposite positions. "Pro-life" sets itself up against "pro-choice" and vice versa. On gun control, assisted suicide, gay marriage, and a host of other issues, it's always just "yes or no." Almost no other options even get discussed. No ambiguity, no gray areas, no middle ground.

Yet the minute we step back from the heat of debate, we can readily see that both sides could be right in their ways. Most moral conflicts are real, not just mistakes by one side or the other about what really matters. There is genuine good (and/or right and/or virtue) on *both* sides—on *all* sides. Life and choice both matter. Guns have both good points and bad. There are compelling reasons to allow assisted suicide, and other compelling reasons to resist it. That's life. "Only dogmatism," wrote the philosopher John Dewey,

> can suppose that serious moral conflict is between something clearly bad and something known to be good, and that uncertainty lies wholly in the will of the one choosing. Most conflicts of importance are conflicts between things which are or have been satisfying, not between good and evil.

Again, they are choices between one good thing and another. Not "right versus wrong" but "right versus *right.*" We need to start by honoring that fact.

What Is Each Side Right About?

Suppose that we take a new tack in moral controversies. Suppose we begin to ask not which side is right, but what *each* side is right *about.*

Instead of approaching any other view looking for its weak points (according to us), start the other way around. Look for its strong points. Assume that it has some; the challenge is to find them. Even moral arguments that make absolutely no sense to you do make sense to others who are every bit as intelligent and well intentioned as you. There's got to be *something* in them. Figure out what it is.

This takes some practice. We may recognize "right versus right" in principle, but our old habits still say "right versus wrong." And of course the question of "wrong" can also be raised. It's useful to remember that each side, including our own, is likely to be wrong about something. Still, the first and vital step is to seek out the positive on the other side. Indeed, our side and the other side are often two ways of looking at the same thing. What's weak or incomplete (in that sense "wrong") about our own views is often a strong point of (something "right" about) others', and vice versa. We might as well look at it constructively!

Consider, for example, the affirmative action debate, for more than two decades now an intense and polarized debate. The simplest thing to say about it is that both sides are surely onto something important.

On the one hand, we know that racism and sexism are wrong. We know that in many people's minds stereotypes exist that may affect what the people themselves think is unbiased judgment. Certain companies have still never hired a woman or an African American for anything but the lowest-level positions. This isn't fair. It isn't just. And without some outside pressure, it may not change.

The case for affirmative action, then, is not puzzling or unfamiliar. The argument is simply that justice requires some special consideration to "level the playing field" and overcome the legacies of the past. Certain disadvantages are wrong and need to be corrected. We need "affirmative" moves toward equity now.

But of course there's another side too, and it's not puzzling or unfamiliar either. Just as it's not fair to discriminate against a woman or a person of color because of sex or race, so surely it's not fair to discriminate against a man or white person because of sex or race. It's wrong to compensate for one kind of injustice by creating another. No—we need genuine "colorblindness" now—no special preference for any reason.

You've heard these arguments a hundred times, I'm sure. Almost always they are presented as if we must take a side. As if one set of arguments must be rejected and the other defended.

It's better to say: both sides have a point. Both sides are *right*. We have a problem here—it looks like equity and colorblindness collide. Two different forms of justice conflict. But the problem is not really that we disagree about those values. All of us care about justice, and about both equity and colorblindness. Right now it may not be clear how to live up to both at the same time, but as to values we are still basically all on the same page. We're all in this together.

What Is Each Theory Right About?

Generally we assume that we must choose one *theory* over another, too, when theories conflict. But here again, rather than ask which theory is right, we should ask instead what *each* theory is right *about*.

Consider the assisted suicide question. Utilitarians are surely right to stress that one good reason in favor of assisted suicide is the relief of pain. No one is in favor of pointless suffering. Listen to the stories of some of the people who ask for help to die, and your heart goes out to them. They have little to look forward to but unrelenting and debilitating pain.

Theories of right action may go several ways, as we saw in Chapter 5. Shouldn't people have the right to make fundamental life and death choices for themselves? The answer surely is yes—and once again we *all* would agree to that, at least other things being equal. On the other hand, allowing and perhaps encouraging doctors to kill, or even just assist in death, may take a step or two down a path of devaluing life. It makes us uneasy—it makes all of us uneasy—and for good reason. As Kant reminds us, life is a value in itself, even in the face of suffering.

Character matters too in the face of suffering and death. We can respond with courage, humility, resoluteness—virtues. We are called to care and re-sponsiveness in the face of others' suffering as well. When we begin to realize that people sometimes choose suicide out of a pain that is not so much physical as emotional (from bereavement, abandonment, sense of uselessness), we realize that other and more life-affirming responses are also possible.

In short, each theory has a contribution to make. We're not necessarily stalemated if we can't choose among them—we are stalemated only if we assume that we must finally go with just one. But we don't. Each highlights certain values left to the side by the others. They're *all* right in their ways. Each has at least some pieces of of the puzzle.

Naturally, this does not make the problem easier. Still, we end up with a complex situation—many sorts of values that we are trying to live up to together—which is very different from a *fight*. Not a collision between polarized points of view, but instead a shared challenge. And now we can consider how we might try to meet it.

INTEGRATIVE METHODS

The practical question, of course, is what to do after we acknowledge that there is right on both sides. Sometimes we resist acknowledging right on both sides because it may seem that then we'll just be stuck. Are we?

We're not. There are many ways of going on from the acknowledgment that both sides have a point. In fact, people who deal regularly with conflict resolution usually say that only such an acknowledgment makes it *possible* to go on constructively. Moreover, most of the conflict resolvers' methods are familiar. All of them are so eminently sensible that nothing in this chapter will be a surprise, though I hope it may be an inspiration. The task is just to put these methods to use *in ethics*.

Strategies

To integrate values, in general, we need to find a way to acknowledge both (or all) of the contending values. We need to find a way to honor and respond to each of them at least to some extent.

Here we are not trying to rank-order or otherwise prioritize the contending values, as ethical theories might. The aim is *not* for one to "win" and the other or others to "lose." We seek instead "win/win" solutions: *ways in which both sides get something*—perhaps a great deal—of what they most care about.

Here are three "integrative" strategies in this sense.

- When truly opposite values conflict, we can at least split the difference.
- Different values may still be compatible. We can explore them with an eye to finding ways to satisfy both at the same time.
- Most disagreements are framed by deeper shared values. We can work from those shared values toward jointly agreeable resolutions.

Let us start with some simple and everyday examples.

Compromise—"splitting the difference"—is often obvious and easy in everyday conflicts. If tonight we are both at home and you want quiet and I want music, we could have music for a while and then quiet. A little of both. Or we can just work in different rooms.

I could also get a pair of earphones, in which case we could both have exactly what we want. Here we go beyond mere compromise to a truly win/win solution. It may turn out that our competing desires aren't incompatible at all.

Or again: suppose that for vacation my partner wants to go to the mountains and I want to go to the beach. But we live in North Carolina and the mountains are three hours in one direction and the beach is three hours in the other.

This looks like a straight-out conflict of values. Even if it is, though, it is still open to compromise. Maybe this year the beach, next year the mountains. Or maybe we could do a little of each this year, despite the distance. Again, though, we may be able to do better still. Suppose that she and I try to figure out *why* we want to go to the beach or the mountains. Maybe it turns out that she wants to be able to swim and sunbathe, and I want to be able to hike. These goals are not incompatible at all. There are some great lakes in the mountains, and some great hiking trails near the ocean. Both of us can have exactly, or almost exactly, what we want, and at the same time too. Again, win/win.

Notice that these integrative strategies somewhat overlap in practice. We may start out looking for compromises but may end up with something a lot better.

Finally, sometimes when we really look into the values on the other side, it turns out that some of them are not merely compatible but in fact the very same values we hold ourselves. Though we tend to focus on our disagreements, normally there are background agreements that may be far more important. For example, in the vacation question, both of us agree from the start that we want to spend our vacation outside, in nature. It may be that the exact location matters much less than simply being outside, and being physically active. Suppose that we started our negotiation there: on common ground. Basically, once again, we're on the same page. We're in it together. Only the details need to be worked out.

Case in Point: Affirmative Action

All of this may seem hard to apply in ethics. In fact, however, it's easy. All of these strategies are no more than common sense—in ethics too!

Take the affirmative action debate once again. I have argued that both sides speak for important and shared values. Think of it as a shared practical problem, I said, not as a fundamental moral opposition. We care about two different but seemingly incompatible things at once.

Why shouldn't there be practical ways to honor both sides, at least to some extent? At the very least, we could split the difference. For example, suppose we allow *some* preferential treatment at *some* points, possibly earlier points in education or hiring, but not at later points. Give people the chance to show what they can do, offsetting at least in a small way the past disadvantage and/or discrimination that otherwise might deny them even the opportunity. After that, though, fewer and fewer special considerations would apply. You'd get your chance, but then it's up to you.

Yale Law School professor Stephen Carter has proposed this kind of plan. He calls it an "affirmative action pyramid." As in a pyramid narrowing to its top,

> the role of preference narrows as one moves upward. . . . A slight preference is justified in college admissions . . . , as a matter of giving lots of people from different backgrounds the chance—only the chance—to have an education at an elite college or university. But when that opportunity has been exercised, when the student has shown what he or she can do, the rationale for a preference at the next level is slimmer. So [there should be] a slighter affirmative action preference for professional school admission. . . . And when one's training is done, when the time comes for entry in the job market . . . the time for preference is gone.

No doubt the idea still needs work. But it already opens up some new possibilities. At the very least, even on hotly debated and deeply felt issues like this one, we can acknowledge that "both sides are right" in their ways and move on to "walk the talk": to try to reach an agreement that bows in both directions. Each side gets at least something—each side gets, as it were, half of what it wants.

There may also be common ground here, even on this most contentious issue. If we look back at "what each side is right about," one thing we notice right away is that both sides are committed above all to *justice*. They understand the demands of justice differently in the short run, but the ideal of a truly "colorblind" society is shared by both sides—indeed it is the deepest ideal of both sides.

Those who favor affirmative action argue that colorblindness can't be achieved in any reasonable time without at least some preferential measures first. And they may well be right, sometimes. No doubt argument on these points will continue. But aren't there at least some ways in which we can make colorblindness real *right now* — going farther than we go right now, but not so far as (or in a different direction from) setting up preferences? I understand for example that some symphony orchestras audition new players in a truly blind way: the judges cannot see the persons auditioning, and do not hear their voices. They judge the musicians only by their playing.

Granted, this kind of thing can't be done all the time. Usually there is no way to keep a person's race or sex out of the picture if people are inclined to notice them. But where there is a way, why not? There at least we can find common ground. And perhaps we may then find creative ways to go farther.

Other new ideas are emerging too. State universities in Texas and California now guarantee admission to the top 10 percent (or other given percentage) of each high school's graduating class, whether in minority or majority communities. The idea is to reward merit and effort while achieving diversity in state universities in a way much simpler and quite different from the current complex and often resented (also often misunderstood) systems. Everyone seems to win. Again it's an idea that may still need work—objections have certainly been raised, and other states and university systems are looking closely at the results so far—but it's an encouraging sign nonetheless. And what else might we be able to think of if we move beyond the "affirmative action—yes or no?" kinds of arguments we so often hear now?

Case in Point: Gun Control

Sometimes when we take up the question of gun control in my classes we try a surprising exercise. I challenge the class to list all the relevant values that they think are at least partly shared by both sides in the debate. At first no one thinks there are any shared values at all. But then, at first slowly and then with gathering speed, we fill the blackboard with just such values. We get a long list.

There is too much violence around, all sides agree, both involving guns and not involving guns. Too many young children are dying in gun accidents, they say. On the other hand, people need to be able to protect themselves. Freedom is important, but then again, not anyone should be able to own or carry a gun. Not young people, we agree; not people with criminal records; not people untrained in their use. Certain kinds of guns (high-powered, easily concealed, etc.) are much more problematic than other kinds of guns (hunting guns, collectibles, etc.). Crimes that involve guns should be more strictly punished than those that don't.

There is more, but that's a pretty remarkable list already for people who, ten minutes earlier, denied having any common ground with the "other side" at all. And notice how just identifying these agreements—this common ground—immediately opens up certain obvious practical steps as well.

Both sides deplore gun accidents with young children, for example, and for exactly the same reason—young lives are tragically cut short. Both sides can therefore readily agree that more should be done to prevent such accidents. And it is a small step from that recognition to shared initiatives. We should consider gun locks and/or more education and/or legal requirement that guns be stored away from the reach of children, as is the law in some other countries.

Or again: both sides want to reduce the level of violence around us, and again for the very same reason—it threatens all of us. Both sides can therefore readily agree to a wide range of measures aimed at the causes of violence. Reduce unemployment; train kids in conflict resolution early on; create other outlets for competitiveness and thrill seeking. All of these and many more measures might help, and may have other virtues besides.

Of course the causes of violence are in dispute. Opponents of gun control blame human factors (as in the slogan "Guns don't kill people; people kill people"), while the other side blames guns (as in the response: "Guns don't kill people; they just make it real easy").

Both are surely right sometimes. It's not *just* guns—so people on both sides ought to be able to agree on other measures to reduce violence. On the other hand, even the most ardent opponents of gun control have to concede that sometimes the gun makes the difference, and so there is surely a common case for *some* limits: waiting periods, gun locks, and so on.

It's clear from this list, in fact, that we already *have* gun control. Even the National Rifle Association agrees that teenagers or people with criminal records should not be able to buy or carry guns. No one thinks people should be able to own flamethrowers or grenade launchers or the like. In short, we already draw a line, and control many weapons on the far side of it. Despite the popular rhetoric, we seem to agree that such a line is necessary. Of course there are stubborn areas of disagreement too, but still, we are not so impossibly at odds after all. Even on this issue a win/win approach is possible. It may even be *easy*.

WHEN TO HOLD FIRM

Integrative methods do have their limits. Each side is right about something, I have claimed. But there are surely exceptions. Mightn't some issues really come down to right versus wrong? And don't we there want to hold firm? Surely we do not want to split differences or seek common ground with views that truly are *wrong*.

How to Tell?

Sometimes it is easy to tell when a viewpoint can't claim any validity. Seething hatred, needless injury, random violence—these things have no defense.

In real, deep moral disagreements things are not so clear. How can we tell whether we face another view that does speak for something important, even if at the moment we can't see it, or a view that really *is* just plain wrong?

There are some ways. In the first place, keep in mind the basic values we discussed in chapters 4 and 5: happiness, fairness and respect, character and care. If major violations of any of these values are proposed without a reason of equal seriousness proposed as a defense, warning flags should go up. This may not be a situation for compromise or any other kind of accommodation.

Of course, basic values can conflict. That is what creates moral problems in the first place. To serve fairness, the general happiness sometimes may need to be limited, and vice versa. But these are conflicts *between* basic values, not between basic values and something else. To violate rights for the sake of appearances, or to abandon caring obligations because they became a little

Talking the Talk

The methods in this chapter invite us to look at ethical debates in a new way. It takes some getting used to—and some persistence, too, when dealing with people who picture ethical debates only in polarized terms. Consider this dialogue:

> **M:** Are you for or against gun control?
>
> **P:** Yes.
>
> **M:** What do you mean, "yes"? Yes or *no*? Which one? Whose side are you on?
>
> **P:** I think that both sides are onto something. I favor some kinds of gun control, but I also think that gun control by itself partly misses the point.
>
> **M:** In short, you don't really know what you think. Well, let me tell you . . .
>
> **P:** No, I *do* know what I think. What I think is that both sides have some valid points. On the one hand, I think it's pretty clear that cetain kinds of guns do much more harm than good: they make it too easy to kill, or are too prone to accidents. Banning or at least controlling them would be a good start . . .
>
> **M:** So you're for gun control! But if you ban some kinds of weapons then sooner or later we're going to ban all of them! Just let me tell you . . .
>
> **P:** I don't see why we can't stop wherever we choose. The law already says that you can't own an atomic bomb or bazooka or a flamethrower. We already ban some weapons without banning all.
>
> **M:** Well, anyway, guns don't kill people, people kill people.
>
> **P:** That's just a slogan, not very clear either. But I agree that in a deeper way, guns are usually not the real problem. If that's what the slogan really means. Usually the real problem is people's willingness to use such violence against each other in the first place.
>
> **M:** So you're against gun control! Your head's on straight after all.
>
> **P:** I am *for* some effective strategies for reducing violence and accidental shootings. Sometimes that means gun control; but it also means trying to address the underlying causes of killing.
>
> **M:** I'm having a hard time getting a handle on what you think. It seems like you want to satisfy everybody.
>
> **P:** Oh, terrible! Can't both sides be onto something?
>
> **M:** You can't satisfy everybody. Get serious!
>
> **P:** I'll try again. You want the freedom to own hunting rifles and collector's items. I doubt that people are getting murdered by those kinds of guns, so I

don't see why you can't keep them. But the pro-control side wants to ban the handguns that are used in most murders, and lead to the most accidents, and I don't see why we can't do that too. Meanwhile, neither you nor I want to live in such a violent society, and I think if you really mean it about "people killing people," you'd be right there with me supporting the kinds of measures that might actually reduce violence. *You* get serious!

M: It still seems wishy-washy. You need to take a stand.

P: I *am* taking a stand! I just don't think the only way to take a stand is to act like I have the whole truth to myself.

Think about this dialogue. What different assumptions about moral disagreements do M and P bring to it? If the next person to speak were *you*, what would you say?

more expensive than we expected, is not a valid compromise but more like a betrayal.

Also, listen to the people. Normally there are serious people of good will on the other side, people who are reasonable and well intentioned, informed and careful. If you can find such people, you have a good sign that they do indeed speak for something important. If you can't, you have another warning flag.

Of course, to do this you really have to *listen*. Remember that merely disagreeing with your viewpoint does not make another person's viewpoint invalid or the person "uninformed" or "unreasonable." (That would argue in a tight little circle, wouldn't it: I'm right, because anyone who disagrees with me is uninformed and unreasonable, and I know they're uninformed and unreasonable because they disagree with me!) Listening is hard but not impossible; it just takes some honesty and humility on your part. Take your time.

In fact, even when we really are confronted with an evil viewpoint, it is still essential to listen to its advocates. Not because we agree with them, but in order to ask why the evil is so attractive. For example, fanaticism may sometimes arise out of a profound sense of insecurity. Hatred against "outside" groups may arise out of a deep feeling of exclusion and disempowerment. And this feeling too, before it settles on some scapegoat, could be perfectly valid. Just repressing the advocates of such evils leaves the attraction of the evil itself untouched. It may even become more attractive. Even here, then—even when we can genuinely speak of right versus wrong—we need to try to listen, to try to figure out the other side rather than just condemning it outright. We need to try to figure out how the people involved can be reached. That's ethical too!

Drawing the Line in Real Life

Knowing where to draw the line is probably easier in practice than it sounds in theory. Some of the most difficult moral conflicts occur within groups or between people who are in other ways in regular contact and already respectful of each other. Here the other side's intelligence and good intentions are not in question. And, of course, it's easier to listen to them.

For example, many politically liberal secular groups make common cause with Catholics in a wide range of pro-life issues, from welfare and children's rights to environmental causes. The same sides tend to divide sharply over some other issues, especially abortion. Here, though, channels of respect and communication have been easier to keep open. (See Chapter 14 for an example of how.) Neither side can demonize the other—they know each other too well!

Day to day, meanwhile, the people we argue and negotiate with—constantly—are our family and friends and colleagues, whose intelligence and good intentions are not in question either. Here especially the polarized language of "right" and "wrong" is not helpful. Keep a more open mind. There are certainly times to hold firm, but they are the exception and not the rule.

"How to End the Abortion War" (selections)

ROGER ROSENBLATT

When I introduce this chapter in class students always say: well, integrating values might be a fine idea in general, but what about abortion?

What about abortion? The idea is that the abortion issue, at least, is utterly unsolvable. Here, at least, there is no way to say that each side is right about something—no way to split the difference (or no excuse for it: after all, the other side is dead wrong, even evil) or, God forbid, find common ground. We are hesitant to even talk about abortion as a result (and notice that this book has not looked at the abortion issue so far either).

Yet integrative methods *can* be applied to the abortion debate. This short suggestion about "How to End the Abortion War" is a first look at how. Rosenblatt gives the debate some context; cites poll data showing that there is indeed substantial common ground, right now, on abortion; and briefly outlines some practical next steps to dovetail values and build on our shared, though conflicted, feelings about abortion. This is just a start, too; once we have a fuller toolbox, Chapter 17 will look at the abortion debate in more detail.

THE VEINS in his forehead bulged so prominently they might have been blue worms that had worked their way under the surface of his skin. His eyes bulged, too, capillaries zigzagging from the pupils in all directions. His face was pulled tight about the jaw, which thrust forward like a snowplow attachment on the grille of a truck. From the flattened O of his mouth, the word "murderer" erupted in a regular rhythm, the repetition of the r's giving the word the sound of an outboard motor that failed to catch.

She, for her part, paced up and down directly in front of him, saying nothing. Instead, she held high a large cardboard sign on a stick, showing the cartoonish drawing of a bloody coat hanger over the caption, "Never again." Like his, her face was taut with fury, her lips pressed together so tightly they folded under and vanished. Whenever she drew close to him, she would deliberately lower the sign and turn it toward him, so that he would be yelling his "murderer" at the picture of the coat hanger.

For nearly twenty years these two have been at each other with all the hatred they can unearth. Sometimes the man is a woman, sometimes the woman a man. They are black, white, Hispanic, Asian; they make their homes in Missouri or New Jersey; they are teenagers and pharmacists and college professors; Catholic, Baptist, Jew. They have exploded at each other on the steps of the Capitol in Washington, in front of abortion clinics, hospitals, and politicians' homes, on village greens and the avenues of cities. Their rage is tireless; at every decision of the United States Supreme Court or of the President or of the state legislatures, it rises like a missile seeking only the heat of its counterpart.

This is where America is these days on the matter of abortion, or where it seems to be. In fact, it is very hard to tell how the country really feels about abortion, because those feelings are almost always displayed in political arenas. Most ordinary people do not speak of abortion. Friends who gladly debate other volatile issues—political philosophy, war, race—shy away from the subject. It is too private, too personal, too bound up with one's faith or spiritual identity. Given abortion five seconds of thought, and it quickly spirals down in the mind to the most basic questions about human life, to the mysteries of birth and our relationship with our souls. . . .

The oddity in this unnatural silence is that most of us actually know what we feel about abortion. . . .

Seventy-three percent of Ameicans polled in 1990 were in favor of abortion rights. Seventy-seven percent polled also regard abortion as a kind of killing. (Forty-nine percent see abortion as outright murder, 28 percent solely as the taking of human life.) These figures represent the findings of the Harris and Gallup polls, respectively, and contain certain nuances of opinion within both attitudes. But the general conclusions are widely

---

Reprinted by permission of Roger Rosenblatt and the Watkins/Loomis Agency.

considered valid. In other words, most Americans are both for the choice of abortion as a principle and against abortion for themselves. . . .

The fact that abortion entails conflict, however, does not mean that the country is bound to be locked in combat forever. In other contexts, living with conflict is not only normal to America, it is often the only way to function honestly. We are for both Federal assistance and states' autonomy; we are for both the First Amendment and normal standards of propriety; we are for both the rights of privacy and the needs of public health. Our most productive thinking usually contains an inner confession of mixed feelings. . . .

Yet acknowledging and living with ambivalence is, in a way, what America was invented to do. To create a society in which abortion is permitted and its gravity appreciated is to create but another of the many useful frictions of a democratic society. Such a society does not devalue life by allowing abortion; it takes life with utmost seriousness and is, by the depth of its conflicts and by the richness of its difficulties, a reflection of life itself. . . .

. . . Since the end of the Second World War, American society, not unlike modern Western societies in general, has shifted intellectually from a humanistic to a social science culture; that is, from a culture used to dealing with contrarieties to one that demands definite, provable answers. The nature of social science is that it tends not only to identify, but to create issues that must be solved. Often these issues are the most significant to the country's future—civil rights, for example.

What social science thinking does not encourage is human sympathy. By that I do not mean the sentimental feeling that acknowledges another's pain or discomfort; I mean the intellectual sympathy that accepts another's views as both interesting and potentially valid, that deliberately goes to the heart of the thinking of the opposition and spends some time there. That sort of humanistic thinking may or may not be humane, but it does offer the opportunity to arrive at a humane understanding outside the realm and rules of politics. In a way, it is a literary sort of thinking, gone now from a post-literary age, a "reading" of events to determine layers of depth, complication, and confusion and to learn to live with them.

Everything that has happened in the abortion debate has been within the polarities that social science thinking creates. The quest to determine when life begins is a typical exercise of social science—the attempt to impose objective precision on a subjective area of speculation. Arguments over the mother's rights versus the rights of the unborn child are social science arguments, too. The social sciences are far more interested in rights than in how one arrives at what is right—that is both their strength and weakness. Thus the abortion debate has been political from the start.

A good many pro-choice advocates, in fact, came to lament the political character of the abortion debate when it first began in the 60's. At that time, political thinking in America was largely and conventionally liberal. The liberals had the numbers; therefore, they felt that they could set the national agenda without taking into account the valid feelings or objections of the conservative opposition. When, in the Presidential election of 1980, it became glaringly apparent that the feelings of the conservative opposition were not only valid but were politically ascendant, many liberals reconsidered the idea that abortion was purely a rights issue. They expressed appreciation of a more emotionally complicated attitude, one they realized that they shared themselves, however they might vote.

If the abortion debate had risen in a humanistic environment, it might never have achieved the definition and clarity of the *Roe v. Wade* decision, yet it might have moved toward a greater public consensus. One has to guess at such things through hindsight, of course. But in a world in which humanistic thought predominated, abortion might have been taken up more in its human terms and the debate might have focused more on such unscientific and apolitical components as human guilt, human choice and human mystery.

If we could find the way to retrieve this kind of conflicted thinking, and find a way to apply it to the country's needs, we might be on our way toward a common understanding on abortion, and perhaps toward a common good. . . .

. . . For the ordinary private citizen, the elements of a reasonably satisfying resolution are already in place. I return to the fact that the great majority of Americans both favor abortion rights and disapprove of abortion. . . . What most Americans want to do with abortion is to permit but discourage it. Even those with the most pronounced political stands on the subject reveal this duality in the things they say; while making strong defenses of their positions, they nonetheless, if given time to work out their thoughts, allow for opposing views. I discovered this in a great many interviews over the past three years.

Pro-choice advocates are often surprised to hear themselves speak of the immorality of taking a life. Pro-life people are surprised to hear themselves defend individual rights, especially women's rights. And both sides might be surprised to learn how similar are their visions of a society that makes abortion less necessary through sex education, help for unwanted babies, programs to shore up disintegrating families and moral values, and other forms of constructive community action. . . .

Taking a stand against abortion while allowing for its existence can turn out to be a progressive philosophy. It both speaks for moral seriousness and moves in the direction of ameliorating conditions of ignorance, poverty, the social self-destruction of fragmented families, and the loss of spiritual values in general. What started as a debate as to when life begins might lead to making life better. . . . The permit-but-discourage formula on abortion offers the chance to test our national soul by appealing to its basic impulse. Were we once again to work actively toward creating a country where everyone had the same health care, the same sex eduation, the same opportunity for economic survival, the same sense of personal dignity and worth, we would see both fewer abortions and a more respectable America.

Exercises and Notes

"EACH SIDE IS RIGHT ABOUT SOMETHING"

Integrative thinking begins with the acknowledgment that all sides speak for something worth considering. "Each side is right about *something*."

Given our usual habits, it's is a hard message to get. We're too used to debating polarized issues. Just the mere acknowledgment that the other side has some points needs a lot of practice. So that is where we start.

Identify your position on the following issues. (Note that this time we purposely take "hot-button" issues.)

- Capital punishment
- Drug use
- Abortion
- Homosexual marriage

Now here's the challenge: consider the *opposite* position—the *other* side or sides. Ask yourself what the other side(s) is right about—not wrong, but *right*. Where do you actually agree with them? What are their strongest and most important points?

Of course you don't agree with their conclusions—that's a given—but almost certainly you can still find common ground or at least compatible interests. In fact, probably you even share *most* of the other side's values, though you may give them somewhat different weights or rankings. So: what *are* those shared or compatible values? Take your time, be careful, try to put them in a fair way.

Please note: The task here is not just to describe the other side's view. It's tempting to answer by just summarizing what you think they think. This is helpful, but the task here is to go farther. What do they think that *you* think too? What do you actually think they're *right* about? Go beyond "I think . . ." and "They think . . ." to "*We* think. . . ."

In theory this sounds easy, I'm sure, but actually doing it runs right up against all of our habits of argument. We've always been encouraged to stick up for our side and run down all the others. But as you know from the text (and life too, I bet), this is *not* a way to make much progress. Acknowledgment is the necessary beginning instead. Keep practicing.

If you're in a group setting, a variation of this exercise is to make a list together of all of the relevant values that both (all) sides in some debate share, such as the text proposes on the topic of gun control. Usually you can come up with a very long list! That in itself should be surprising—and inspiring.

PRACTICE INTEGRATIVE THINKING

To learn how to actually put the integrative tools into practice—to get a feel for their "logic"—it is useful to start with nonethical issues, or at least issues that are not so hotly debated. Here are some examples:

- Should medical insurance pay for alternative medicine (e.g. holistic medicine, acupuncture, etc.)?
- Should 15-year-olds (or: 85-year-olds) be allowed to drive?
- Should children's TV watching be limited?
- Should elections be held on Saturdays rather than on Tuesdays, so it would be easier for people to vote?
- Should tax money pay for private-school vouchers?
- Should we build more roads to relieve traffic congestion?

In each case, ask first: what are the values that are competing here? What is each side speaking for that is important? Take some time with these questions—don't just name one value on each side. You know from Chapter 3 that the real story is likely to be more complex.

Now bring your integrative methods to bear. Are there ways to split the difference in these debates? What ways? Are "win/win" solutions possible? Is there common ground to be found? What new options then open up?

Now pose the same kinds of questions about moral issues. If you think you're ready, try the issues in the first exercise, or some of these (somewhat) less controversial ones:

- Should political campaigns be publically financed?
- Should there be mandatory drug testing?
- Should employees be encouraged to "blow the whistle" on business or organizational misdeeds or corruption?
- How should gay people be treated in the military?
- Should we allow the testing of new drugs and other products on animals?

Some of the skills introduced in later chapters also help here, especially ways of generating new options and "reframing problems" (chapters 11 and 12) and dialogue skills (Chapter 14). So treat this exercise as a beginning: we will return to questions like it in the chapters to come.

INTEGRATIVE BUMPERSTICKERS

Visit some parking lots and write down the bumperstickers on ethical issues you see. Look for a wide range, including the ones that infuriate you.

Pay attention to the ways in which positions are misrepresented and common ground—shared values—is obscured. Look at the manipulative language, the appeals to authority, the air of finality. Of course, there is a limit to what can be said in a bumpersticker. But how often do we fall into "bumpersticker thinking" even when we could actually say something constructive?

Besides, even bumperstickers may have more possibilities than we think. Take some of the issues you turn up in your survey and try to write integrative alternative bumperstickers. Is there a way to say something pithy that brings us together rather than divides us, that clarifies or connects rather than misrepresents and polarizes?

You will discover a great deal of pro-choice and pro-life sloganizing, for example. GOD HATES ABORTION. ABORTION STOPS A BEATING HEART. IF YOU'RE AGAINST ABORTION, DON'T HAVE ONE. It was an inspiration one day to see EVERY CHILD A WANTED CHILD. Think of that: instead of trashing the other side for the evils of their ways, there is an appeal to the kind of value that unites us. It doesn't insist on one side over the other; it reminds us of what we should *all* aim for in the end. Every child a wanted child—which means: women have both the right and the responsibility to regulate pregnancy. Every child a wanted child—which means: when pregnancy occurs, we need to do everything we can to be sure the potential child *is* "wanted," that is, that the family can sustain the pregnancy and the child. The whole issue appears in a different light. It becomes a collective responsibility, an invitation to try to better the world.

Another one I'd like to see: instead of the current IT'S A CHILD, NOT A CHOICE, how about IT'S A CHILD AND A CHOICE? Here's one I actually saw recently: PRO-CHOICE BEFORE CONCEPTION, PRO-LIFE AFTER. I realize that this is meant to be pro-life the way the debate is now framed, and even a little nasty. But doesn't it have bigger possibilities?

Consider some other issues. Peddle your best ideas to the bumper-sticker makers. Ask your teacher for an A if you sell one.

NOTES AND FURTHER READINGS

The quote from John Dewey in the first section of this chapter is from his essay "The Construction of Good," Chapter 10 of Dewey's book *The Quest for Certainty*, reprinted in James Gouinlock, *The Moral Writings of John Dewey* (Macmillan, 1976), Chapter 5, where the quotation can be found on page 154. The general theme of integrating values is thoroughly Deweyan, as Gouinlock's collection makes clear. See also my book *Toward Better Problems* (Temple University Press, 1992).

Roger Fisher and William Ury's book *Getting to Yes* (Penguin, 1983) is essential practical reading on integrating values. Also useful is Tom Rusk, *The Power of Ethical Persuasion* (Penguin, 1993). On compromise, a careful philosophical treatment is Martin Benjamin's *Splitting the Difference* (University Press of Kansas, 1990). Benjamin systematically contests the various arguments that ethical philosophers have offered (or might offer—the arguments are seldom fully spelled out) against taking compromise seriously as an ethical method. On finding common ground, see the reading in Chapter 14, which is from the aptly named Common Ground Network for Life and Choice, a nationwide organization dedicated to seeking and working from common ground in the abortion debate.

There is an intriguing social-psychological literature on integrative strategies, some of which suggests that competitive, polarized struggles can be defused simply by reconceptualizing the issues at hand as problems that are solvable in a cooperative and mutually acceptable way. The results are demonstrably better for everyone, even by crudely self-interested standards. See Dean Pruitt and Steven Lewis, "The Psychology of Integrative Bargaining," in Daniel Druckman, ed., *Negotiation: A Social-Psychological Perspective* (Sage Publications, 1977). For additional strategies, see J. H. Carens, "Compromise in Politics," in J. R. Penlock and John Chapman, eds., *Compromise in Ethics, Law, and Politics* (New York University Press, 1979).

Stephen Carter is quoted from his book *Reflections of an Affirmative Action Baby* (Basic Books, 1991), page 89. On the values involved with the assisted suicide debate, see Margaret Battin, Rosamond Rhodes, and Anita Silvers, *Physician-Assisted Suicide: Expanding the Debate* (Routledge, 1998).

III

TOOLS FOR
CRITICAL THINKING
IN ETHICS

CHAPTER 8

○

Finding the Facts

WHEN FACTS ARE AT ISSUE

Moral disagreements are much more than differences about values. Many disagreements are about *facts*: about how to produce certain desired effects, for instance; or about what the causes of a current problem really are; or even just about simple and specific information that you could look up in ten minutes in the library. Facts are so crucial in ethics that some philosophers have argued that facts and not values are actually the crux of most moral disagreements. Another set of tools therefore comes into play.

What Facts Are at Issue?

Some people defend the death penalty by arguing that it deters would-be murderers from committing murders. Does it? What does the evidence say?

How would you get evidence for or against the claimed deterrence effect? You could compare murder rates in states with the death penalty to those in states without it, for example. And/or you could compare U.S. murder rates when the death penalty was widely used with murder rates when it was barred. These kinds of studies have been done. What do they say? You need to know before you can decide this question.

Or take the gun control issue. Again: what *facts* are at issue? How many lives, for example, do guns take? You can look this up. Is the toll lower in countries with strict gun control? How much lower? You can look this up too. Is it true, in countries with gun control, that criminals still readily get and use guns? It's not hard to find answers to these questions—and the answers may surprise you.

What will happen if marijuana use were legalized? How can we find out? Are there useful parallels in other countries? Marijuana is legal under controlled conditions in Amsterdam. It's not a disaster. Why not? How is it controlled? Would the results be the same here? And how dangerous is the stuff, anyway?

More questions. What actually have been the results of women in fighting positions in the military, in the Iraq war or in the Israeli Army, for example?

(How many people with strong opinions on the subject actually know?) Do children raised by gay couples grow up sexually confused (any more than the average adolescent)? Do animals suffer pain or terror in laboratories and slaughterhouses? Who actually is on welfare? Do mothers on welfare tend to have more children than the average American family? Do homeless people tend to be drug addicts (or is it that drug addicts tend to be homeless)? Does pornography promote sexual violence?

Again: the answers to all of these questions are primarily factual. That is, actual *evidence* is available, though it can be complex and unclear at times. Many of these questions have been the subjects of thorough study. You can find answers. But it takes looking!

Getting the Facts

A friend and I were arguing about what proportion of the federal budget goes for "welfare." He said 75 percent. I said 5 percent. Big difference.

We met the next day at the library to check it out. In half an hour we had learned some things. If you count strictly "means-tested" entitlements—that is, programs for which eligibility is determined by income—then the answer (for 1996) was 12 percent. This includes food stamps, unemployment compensation, welfare block grants to states, child nutrition programs, and Medicaid (the single largest item).

I believe that this is what conservatives like my friend tend to oppose when they oppose "welfare." On the other hand, my friend sometimes spoke of "entitlement programs" rather than welfare, and "entitlement" is a much broader category. Social Security is included (that's 23% of the budget right there); so are a range of other programs like veterans' benefits, Medicare, earned income tax credits, student loans and grants, refugee assistance, and much more. All of that adds up to about 60 percent of the total federal budget.

So both of us were right, in a sense, though we both exaggerated a bit. We still disagree, but now in a more informed and measured way. We learned a lot about the federal budget too!

Of course, we were lucky in one way. We disagreed about some fairly simple facts. Many factual issues are not so readily dealt with. They may involve more complex studies or interpretations of data. Here too, though, even when the facts are uncertain, looking deeper is necessary.

Take the death penalty issue. One widely publicized study from the 1970s correlated the decline in capital punishment in the United States from 1933 to 1969 with a rise in the number of murders, and therefore concluded that the death penalty does indeed deter murderers. On the other hand, most contemporary studies show the opposite. Many states with the death penalty now have *higher* murder rates than states without it. Others show no difference.

It's hard to know what to make of this. Mightn't other changes (that is, besides the decline in number of executions) from 1933 to 1969 better account for the increase in murder rates in that period? And how do we explain higher murder rates in death-penalty states now? Is it possible that the death penalty actually encourages some would-be murderers? Or is the murder rate now higher in death-penalty states for reasons unrelated to the death penalty? (Could such states have enacted the death penalty *because* the murder rate is felt to be unacceptably high?)

We return to some of these complexities in a few pages. The point for now is more basic. It is useless to go on arguing that "obviously" there is a deterrence effect, or that "obviously" there isn't, without looking at factual data—all of which are widely available and discussed at length in any responsible book or article dealing with the effects of the death penalty. It's just not so "obvious," either way. That's a fact too, and it makes a difference. For example, uncertainties about deterrence have pushed some defenders of the death penalty away from utilitarian arguments and toward arguments about justice. They have also prompted some utilitarians to oppose the death penalty.

It's possible to think intelligently about such issues in the face of complex or surprising evidence. But it's *not* possible to think intelligently about such issues if we don't have any evidence at all. So look for it!

Sources

Go to the source when you can. The federal budget is published every year; my friend and I, debating about the numbers, just looked them up. For other questions, a useful all-around source is the *Statistical Abstract of the United States*. There are similar volumes for other countries. You may need to search for books or articles on the topic that concerns you. Most libraries' catalogues have keyword search systems: using them you can spotlight helpful sources very quickly. Web sites can be useful. Ask for help when you need it.

Look for thorough and careful coverage of the issues in books or journal articles by well-informed people. Check to see who the authors are, and where they get *their* information. What are their qualifications? Are they relatively impartial? On global warming, for example, neither oil-industry publications nor environmental magazines are likely to give you the full story. Neither are popular newsmagazines, which often have their own agendas. The best sources are scientific journals, whose articles are carefully reviewed by other experts and where the norm is supposed to be scrupulous neutrality. Books published by academic presses or large trade presses are more reputable (more carefully and critically reviewed) than books from presses that publish only books promoting a specific point of view.

Cross-check sources, too, to see if other, independent sources agree. Are the experts sharply divided, or pretty much in agreement? If they're pretty much in agreement, theirs is the safe view to take. (At least, if you propose to take a different view, you have some serious explaining to do.) Where even the experts disagree, it is best to reserve judgment yourself too. See if you can argue on some other grounds—or change your conclusion.

Watch the tone of your sources too. Sources that make extreme, simplistic claims, and/or spend most of their time attacking and demeaning the other side, weaken their own claims. On most issues, reasonable disagreement is possible: seek out sources that responsibly and thoroughly engage the arguments and evidence on the other side.

A word about the Internet. Used carefully, it is a great resource—the world at your fingertips. Many websites are very informative. Other sites, however, are pure fabrication. A good academic or even public library has at least some checks on the reliability of the books and other materials they collect, but there are very few (sometimes absolutely no) checks on Internet sites. Don't rely on the Internet alone, then, unless you are dealing with an identifiable and independently reputable source—and don't rely on the Internet *at all* unless you have some idea of what the source is. Ask some questions of any site: who created this site? Why did they create it? What are their qualifications? What does it mean if they don't tell you?

Check out even those claims you think are obvious. Maybe they're not; in any case, you need some evidence. Don't just appeal to what "everybody knows." American fear of crime is at an all-time high, for example, and most people seem to think crime is skyrocketing. In fact, most crime rates are plummeting. Recent TV crime coverage, however, has expanded dramatically. Crime "sells." The specific stories are no doubt true, but overall they create a false impression.

This advice is pretty obvious. But it is surprising how quickly we forget it when it comes to debating ethical issues. It pays to remember.

INFERENCES

We make *inferences* when we move from facts to conclusions. We may generalize from a few cases to many, or use a similar case to draw conclusions about a case that interests us, or notice the correlation of two events and conclude that one causes the other. Each of these kinds of inference can be tricky.

Generalizations

You or I will never know all homeless people, or all women in the army, or all children raised by gay couples, and so on, yet we may need to draw conclusions about populations like these if we are to form an intelligent opinion about certain moral issues. So we have to *generalize*: we take a small sample—limited data, a few examples—to stand for the whole.

But we may generalize well, or poorly. A good generalization

1. cites *specific* and *clear* examples;
2. cites *many* examples; and
3. cites *representative* examples, not all of one type, and gives enough *background information* to allow us to evaluate for ourselves how significant and representative the examples are.

For instance: there are cases in which people on death row, or already executed, have been discovered to be innocent. Suppose someone infers from this that *many* death-row inmates are innocent of the crimes for which they are executed. This is a generalization: the inference moves from a few examples to many, and concludes that execution *often* takes the lives of innocents. But is it a good generalization?

No, or at any rate not yet. Recall requirement 2: many examples are needed. A few examples, even very compelling stories, are not enough. *Some* innocent people executed does not mean that execution often takes the lives of innocents.

As to requirement 3—background information—it's crucial to know what *proportion* of death row inmates turn out to be innocent. If it's one in five, say, capital punishment is a national disgrace. If it's one in five hundred, we may feel unmoved.

As it stands, then, this argument fails. It does not show that innocents are *often* executed. Keep in mind, though, that a failed generalization such as this one does not prove its opposite. This argument, so far, fails to prove that execution often takes the lives of innocents, but its failure does not prove that execution *seldom* takes the lives of innocents. A failed generalization proves nothing at all. Until you can get more information, the question just remains open.

This argument might be improved. You'd have to look at systematic and impartial studies of the problem, especially at the experts' best guesses of what the proportion of innocents executed actually is and what the causes of the mistakes are. Stay open-minded about what you'll actually find out. Some reliable generalizations might be possible, but—once again—finding them takes *work*.

Comparisons

Sometimes we make inferences by comparing one kind of situation with another seemingly similar situation about which more is known. A good comparison

1. cites as a comparison a *clear* case about which *true* claims are made; and
2. cites as a comparison a *relevantly similar* case. That is, the cases compared must be as similar as possible in ways that matter to the conclusion— though they can be very different in other, less relevant ways.

Suppose someone argues that gun control would reduce homicides in the United States because it reduces homicides in Singapore. This is an argument by comparison: gun control in Singapore is proposed as a relevantly similar case to possible gun control in the United States, and the proposed inference is that gun control would be as successful here as it is there. Does the comparison work?

No. Singapore is a highly authoritarian society with no tradition of individualism. Ours, by comparison, is a loosely governed society of nonconformists (or at least we like to think so). Restrictive legislation that would work in Singapore might not work at all here. This is a major relevant difference.

The Singapore case also needs more explaining—part of the point of requirement 1. Exactly what kinds of restrictions are there on gun ownership in Singapore? Must guns be registered, or is gun ownership banned? And what is Singapore's gun-related homicide rate, anyway?

But suppose that the proposed inference is that gun control would work in the United States because it works in Canada. Canada is of course different from the United States too. In relevant ways, though, Canada is fairly similar, much more similar than Singapore. Canada is a fairly open society; we share fairly similar legal and political systems and basic attitudes; Canada too has fairly serious social tensions that may drive some people to violence. But Canada has gun control: mandatory gun registration, screening of all purchasers of guns and a month-long waiting period before guns can be delivered, safe handling and storage requirements, and mandatory minimum sentences for gun-related crimes. And gun-related homicides in Canada are about two hundred per year; in the United States the number is about fifteen thousand.

Questions can still be raised about the proposed inference. Maybe there are subtle but still relevant dissimilarities between Canada and the United States. Maybe Canadians are more tightly repressed than Americans and thus are less likely to turn to violence whether guns are available or not. Maybe so many guns are now in circulation in America that it would take a long time to reach the level of gun circulation in Canada without drastic measures.

These are arguable points. Still, the comparison has some force. A fairly comparable society has achieved a much lower level of gun-related violence. It also doesn't appear that guns are widely used by Canadian criminals, either, as some opponents of gun control worry. Of course there are arguments against gun control too, but this kind of comparison, carefully made, does make a contribution.

Inferring Cause from Correlation

Because two events or changes occur together, we sometimes infer that one causes the other. For example, violence on TV correlates with real-life violence: that is, there seems to be a lot of both. It is often therefore claimed that TV violence *causes* real-life violence. Or again, because a decline in the number of executions from 1933 to 1969 correlates with a rise in the number of murders, it has been argued that the decline in executions caused the rise in murders (and therefore that the death penalty is a deterrent).

A good argument from correlation to cause

1. cites *accurate* correlations;

2. *explains* how the (proposed) cause leads to the (proposed) effect; and

3. argues that the proposed cause-effect relationship is the *best explanation* of the correlation.

The first requirement is obvious but not always easy to meet. For example, it took a great deal of research to establish the correlation cited by the death-penalty argument just outlined. It would also take some work to really show that the level of violence either on TV or in society is unusually high, or higher than it used to be. As usual, just relying on general impressions is not enough.

Proposed cause-effect connections need to be spelled out—that is the point of requirement 2. How the death penalty is supposed to deter, psy-chologically, is pretty clear: it scares people. How burning coal or gasoline is supposed to produce global warming takes more explaining. Filling in such links is crucial: it's what turns a mere co-occurrence into a plausible connection.

Requirement 3 is the hardest to meet. The problem is a general philo-sophical one: *any correlation can be explained in a variety of ways.*

A and B, let's say, are correlated. It could well be that A causes B. It could *also* be that B causes A (instead, or in addition), or that both A and B have a common cause, or that A and B are not causally related at all.

For example, from the fact (let's suppose it's a fact) that high levels of TV violence are correlated with high levels of violence in society, it could well follow that TV violence causes real-life violence. It could *also* be that real-life violence leads to more violence being portrayed on TV. That is, the connection could be the other way around—and the evidence (the correlation) would be exactly the same! Or perhaps certain social changes have led to both more violence on TV and more violence in real life. That is, TV violence and real-life violence may have a common cause. Yet again, it may be that the causes of TV violence (TV's increasing need to sensationalize to keep its audience?) and the causes of real-life violence (a sense of hopelessness, . . . ?) are simply separate: neither really causes the other, even though they both occur together.

It makes a big difference which of these stories is true (or perhaps all of them are partly true?) but it certainly isn't easy to tell which. Therefore, a good argument about causes must both explain how the proposed cause could lead to the proposed effect (requirement 2 again) *and* it must try to show that the proposed explanation is the best or most likely explanation of the observed correlation—requirement 3.

Similar points have already been made about the death-penalty argument. In particular, there have been vast changes in American life from 1933 to 1969. Cities have become crowded, weapons have become readily available, drugs and gangs are widespread. Any of these factors could explain the rise in murders at least as readily as the decline in executions. Inferring from correlation to cause in this case is tricky at best.

Exercises and Notes

IDENTIFYING THE FACTS AT ISSUE

For each of the following issues, pick out two or three factual questions that are central to the debate as you understand it. That is, ask: what sorts of factual claims tend to be made, or presupposed, in this debate? What could we find out, through the appropriate kinds of research, that would make a difference? Be specific!

Remember: the point is not to state your *opinion* on the factual issues, even if you think you know the answers. Ask yourself only what issues central to the debate are chiefly factual questions—specific questions that are resolvable, at least in principle, by impartial research, even if we do not know the answers now. Clarify those questions.

Here are the issues.

- Should states run lotteries to help fund state budgets (e.g. for education or other good causes)?
- Should tax money pay for private-school vouchers?
- Should adoption files be opened so that adopted children and/or parents who gave children up for adoption can find their biological parents/children?
- Should gay people be allowed to marry?
- Should tax money be used for welfare payments to provide food stamps to poor people and aid to poor families with dependent children?
- Should assisted suicide be prohibited?
- Should a parent be encouraged to stay home with preschool children?
- Should throw-away consumer goods be banned in the name of environmental protection and the needs of future generations?
- Should you stop eating meat?

Add your own favorite issues as well!

FINDING THE FACTS

Look back at your list from the preceding exercise. You've identified some factual questions for each of these issues. The next step is to consider how you can begin to resolve these factual questions. What sources can you turn to? What kinds of inferences can you try to make?

Please note again that the challenge is not to construct an argument for your favored conclusion about the whole issue. It is more specific: to consider what kinds of research it would take to resolve the particular factual issue you've identified.

On the vegetarianism issue, for example, you might have said that one central factual issue is how readily people can live without meat. Is a vegetarian diet healthy? If this is your question, a way to find out is to consult nutritionists or nutrition textbooks. (While you're at it, you could also ask: is a *meat* diet healthy? and: what sort of diet is health*iest*?) There may be some disagreement, but with some persistence you should be able to find a reasonably well-informed and neutral answer.

You might find out that a vegetarian diet can be as healthy as or healthier than a meat diet. It would not necessarily follow that you must become a vegetarian. After all, there are other relevant values besides health. The point here, again, is simply to ask how you might resolve the specific factual questions you've identified, not how you might resolve the whole issue. One thing at a time!

Will answering some of these questions require inferences? What sorts of inferences (generalization; comparison; reasoning from correlation to cause; others?) might you have to use? Which is likely to be the most successful?

NOTES AND FURTHER READINGS

Fact finding and inference are enormous topics. There are also other kinds of inference not considered here. Even brief guidebooks to these subjects run to hundreds of pages, and there is a wide range of texts and courses available in "informal logic" and persuasion, rhetoric, argumentative writing, and the like. A very brief introduction is my book *A Rulebook for Arguments* (Hackett Publishing Company, 3rd edition, 2001)—a fine little book indeed, if I may say so myself (note that I am certainly well informed on the subject, but not exactly unbiased!) See also Richard Feldman, *Reason and Argument* (Prentice-Hall, many editions); Wanda Teays, *Second Thoughts: Critical Thinking from a Multicultural Perspective* (Mayfield, 1996); Annette Rottenberg, *Elements of Argument: A Text and Reader* (Bedford Press [St Martin's], 1997); and Timothy Crusins and Carolyn Channell, *The Aims of Argument: A Rhetoric and Reader* (Mayfield, 1998), or any of a great many other textbooks in the same area.

For an introduction to reasoning about causes, see the Feldman book cited above, or Jerry Cederblom and Donald Paulsen, *Critical Reasoning* (Wadsworth Publishing Company, many editions.) More difficult but also richly rewarding and provocative is Richard Nisbet and Lee Ross, *Human Inference: Strategies and Shortcomings of Social Judgment* (Prentice-Hall, 1980).

Does the death penalty deter? For a detailed look at the current evidence, see Ruth Peterson and William Bailey, "Is Capital Punishment an Effective Deterrent to Murder? An Examination of Social Science Research," in J. Acker, R. Bohm, and C. Lanier, eds., *America's Experiment with Capital Punishment* (Carolina Academic Press, 1998). Federal budget data for fiscal 1996 come from Bruce Wetterau, *Desk Reference on the Federal Budget* (Congressional Quarterly, Inc., 1998). Data on gun-related homicides in the United States come from the 1998 *Statistical Abstract of the United States*. Data for Canada come from the 1999 *Canada Yearbook* (Statistics Canada 1999).

CHAPTER 9

◯

Watching Words

Our language can make a difference to how clearly we think and communicate—in general, and in ethics in particular. Here too we may need to pay better attention.

LOADED LANGUAGE

Certain kinds of language can manipulate our feelings, leading us into a prepackaged moral commitment without ever thinking it through. This is called "loaded language."

Drunks who drive are callous and mindless—they are murderers with a dangerous weapon, just as if they'd gone and knifed somebody in cold blood. They should be severely punished.

The language here is exaggerated and depersonalized. People are not even called "people." The terms "drunks" and "murderers" distance us from them, and depersonalize them, so that even the worst punishment becomes imaginable.

Note also that "knifed someone in cold blood" is an inaccurate comparison. Deliberately running someone down with a car would be more analogous—and that would indeed be treated as first-degree murder. Drunk drivers, by contrast, do not intend to kill anybody, though lethal accidents may be a predictable consequence of their behavior. Killing someone while driving drunk is an extremely irresponsible and morally bad act, but still is not the same as killing "in cold blood." Rather than make an accurate comparison, the language of this argument mainly plays on our feelings, and that's the problem with it.

Watch out for terms that are "loaded" in this way. That is, be aware of such terms when others use them, and avoid them yourself. Don't call names; don't describe things with highly charged terms. To put the guideline positively: *use neutral and carefully descriptive language.*

Take the drunk-driving argument again. The actual point is that people do not think enough about the possible consequences of driving while intoxicated. This is what the word "mindless," appropriately neutralized, suggests. The argument can thus be recast, with key points spelled out and inaccurate comparisons dropped:

People who drive under the influence of alcohol may have a poor sense of (or: not care about?) the risk they pose to other people. Strong penalties might remind people of the risks (or: send a message that society takes them seriously?). Thus, we should enact strong penalties for driving under the influence of alcohol.

This is no weaker an argument than the original loaded one. Its virtue is that it makes the underlying idea clear without letting emotion alone make the inference. Strong feeling is fine—the problem comes when we offer nothing else.

WHEN TERMS ARE UNCLEAR

Sometimes the problem is not that terms are loaded but that they are *unclear*. Even some fairly basic categories in ethics are unclear in the popular debate. People who oppose "assisted suicide," for example, often use the term in a very different (and much broader) way than people who favor legalizing it. At times like these, clarifying our terms is crucial.

Often this is easy to do. When a new or specialized term is at issue, misunderstanding can be cleared away just by proposing or agreeing upon a definition. In the case of assisted suicide, for example, the intended definition is: allowing doctors to help aware and rational people to arrange and carry out their own dying. It does *not* include allowing doctors to "unplug" people without their consent (that would be some form of "involuntary euthanasia"— another issue). There may be good reasons to object to assisted suicide so defined, but at least the parties to the argument can ensure that they are talking about the same thing.

Be precise. Don't just replace the problematic word with a synonym—the synonym will be just as confused as the original word. Get technical if you have to.

Keep the dictionary handy. A neighbor of mine in Raleigh was taken to task by the Historic Districts Commission for putting up a 4-foot model lighthouse in her front yard. The symbolism seemed appropriate: she was in the seafood business, and lighthouses are an icon of the state. But city ordinances prohibit any yard fixtures in historic districts. She was hauled before the Commission and asked to remove the lighthouse. A furor erupted and got into the papers. Finally a quick-thinking niece with a dictionary saved the lighthouse. According to *Webster's*, a "fixture" is something that is fixed or attached as to a building, such as a permanent appendage or structural part.

But the lighthouse was moveable, more like a lawn ornament. Hence, not a fixture; hence, not prohibited.

When issues get difficult, dictionaries may be less helpful. Dictionary definitions often just use synonyms, for one thing. Dictionaries also usually give multiple definitions, so that you still have to pick and choose among them. Also, shockingly enough, sometimes the dictionary is wrong. My *Webster's*, for example, defines "headache" as "a pain in the head." This is too broad a definition. A bee sting or cut in the head would be a pain in the head but not a headache.

For some words, then, you may need to make the term more precise yourself. Again: explain *carefully*; use neutral, not loaded terms; and use concrete, definite terms rather than vague ones.

Keep in mind the intended uses of your definition too. Here's an elegant example. Wisconsin law requires that all legislative meetings be open to the public. To exactly what gatherings of legislators are Wisconsin citizens therefore guaranteed access? Here we need a precise formula for deciding, with a minimum of ambiguity or argument, what is a "meeting." The law offers this:

A "meeting" for purposes of this law is any gathering of enough legislators to block action on the legislative measure that is the subject of the gathering.

This definition is far too narrow to define the ordinary word "meeting." But it does accomplish the purpose of this law: to prevent crucial decisions from being made out of the public eye.

WHEN TERMS ARE CONTESTED

Sometimes the term in question is not merely unclear but actually is contested. That is, people are arguing over the term, not just confused about what it means. In this case, you cannot simply stipulate a meaning—for people are disagreeing over what the term *ought* to mean—and the dictionary, wisely staying out of moral issues, seldom does more than suggest synonyms.

Work from the Clear Cases

In this case, you must propose and defend a carefully thought out definition yourself. The rule is: *work from the clear cases.* Here is what I mean.

Whenever a term is contested, you can distinguish three relevant sets of things. One will be those things to which the term clearly applies. Second will be those things to which the term clearly does *not* apply. In the middle will be those things whose status is unclear, probably including the things being argued over. Your job is to formulate a definition that

1. *includes* all the things that the term clearly fits;

2. *excludes* all the things that the term clearly does not fit; and

3. draws the *plainest possible line* somewhere in between, and *explains* why the line belongs there and not somewhere else.

Here is an extended example.

Suppose that in discussing the drug issue we decide that we need a clear definition of the term "drug" itself. What is a drug? Drugs are substances, clearly (as opposed to institutions or actions or animals, and so on), and substances that we ingest (eat, breathe in, snort, or apply to various body parts). But we eat, breathe, and so on many different substances. Which ones are "drugs"?

Clear cases of substances that are drugs in the current moral sense include heroin, cocaine in its various forms, and marijuana.

Clear cases of substances that are *not* drugs include air, water, most foods, sunscreen lotions, and shampoos—though all of these substances are clearly chemicals, in a broad sense of "chemical," and all are ingested or applied to our body parts.

Unclear cases include tobacco and alcohol. It is around some of these that the current debate swirls. Is it fair, for example, to ban marijuana but allow the sale of alcohol, both of which may work on the body in similar ways and which may have at least as bad effects? Should the Food and Drug Administration be able to regulate cigarettes, on the grounds that nicotine is a drug?

Unclear cases in another way are substances such as aspirin, antibiotics, and vitamins, and psychiatric medicines such as antidepressants and stimulants—the kinds of things we may be able to buy in "drug stores" and that we call "drugs" in a pharmaceutical sense. But these are *medicines*, let's say. In moral contexts the word "drug" is used more narrowly.

Is there a definition that meets the three requirements outlined above?

A drug has been defined, by a presidential commission, as a substance that affects mind or body in some way. This definition meets requirement 1: it includes all the clear cases of drugs. But it is far too broad to meet requirement 2. It also includes all the clear cases of substances that are not drugs. (And naturally enough it does not meet the third requirement either, since it effectively draws no line at all.) We need a more limited definition.

We also can't define a drug as an *illegal* substance that affects mind or body in some way. This definition might cover more or less the right set of substances, but it does not meet requirement 3. It does not explain why the line belongs where it is. After all, part of the point of trying to define "drug" in the first place might well be to decide which substances should be legal and which should not! Defining a drug as an illegal substance short-circuits this project. (Besides, if marijuana were legalized tomorrow, would it stop being a drug overnight? Is it not a drug in places, like Amsterdam, where it is legal?)

Try this:

A drug is a substance used primarily to alter the state of the mind in some specific way.

Heroin, cocaine, and marijuana obviously count. Food, air, and water don't, because even though they do have effects on the mind, the effects are not specific, and are not the primary reason we eat, breathe, or drink. Unclear cases we then approach with the question: is the *primary* effect *specific* and on the *mind?* Perception-distorting and mood-altering effects do seem to be what we are concerned about in the current debate about drugs, so arguably this definition captures the kind of distinction that people really want to make.

Should we add that drugs are addictive? Maybe, maybe not. There are some substances that are addictive but are not drugs—certain foods, perhaps. And what if a substance that alters the state of the mind in some specific way turns out to be nonaddictive (as some have claimed about marijuana, for example)? Is it therefore not a drug? It might be better to take addiction to define substance *abuse* rather than "drug" as such.

What Definitions Don't Settle

Definitions help us to organize our thoughts, to group like things with like, to pick out key similarities and differences. By themselves, though, they seldom settle ethical questions.

We may look to a definition of "drug," for example, for guidance about what sorts of substances we should use or avoid and what should be legally allowed or banned. My proposed definition certainly may redraw some lines in ways that surprise or unsettle us. My proposed definition, for instance, includes antidepressants and stimulants as well as alcohol and even coffee. It doesn't follow, however, that all of these are morally problematic or should be banned. We'd need an argument to go that far.

An argument could be made, at least for alcohol. Mike Martin writes:

Alcohol is the most widely used drug; over 100 million Americans drink. Alcohol may cause more harm than all illegal drugs put together. One in ten drinkers—some 10 million Americans—becomes an alcoholic. (By contrast, there are fewer than 500,000 heroin addicts.) In addition, about half of all fatal car collisions, accidental drownings, and violent crimes are alcohol-related. One of the most common severe birth defects, fetal alcohol syndrome, is caused by women who drink while pregnant. And alcohol costs our economy $120 billion yearly in work, property, and medical costs. . . . We would not legalize any currently illegal drug that caused even a fraction of these problems. . . .

This is an argument for restricting alcohol, but notice that it does not depend on alcohol's being a drug. This argument would be damning even if alcohol were not a drug. The definition cannot do that work by itself.

On the other hand, coffee has specific effects on the mind too, may be harmful, and is clearly addictive. Still, it has nothing like the social effects of alcohol, so perhaps we would stop there. And many antidepressants and stimulants, while clearly and appropriately called drugs under the proposed definition, are also legal, under prescription, and have clear benefits to some people.

Again, then: that a substance is a drug is not, by itself, a sufficient reason to object to or ban it, for otherwise we would have to object to and ban coffee and psychiatric medicines as well. The drug in question must also cause a certain degree of personal and social harm, like alcohol, or cocaine. By the same token, just because marijuana, say, is indeed a drug, it doesn't follow automatically that it should be banned. Some people would argue that coffee is a better comparison with marijuana than alcohol—both have relatively mild effects, though both can be misused. And (someone might argue) the best approach might be like Amsterdam's, where marijuana is available but only in coffeehouse-like settings where the amount used can be carefully controlled (perhaps the same restrictions should be extended to coffee?).

Of course, if marijuana is much more addictive than coffee, or if it really is a "gateway" to other and harder drugs, then there may be a good case for its prohibition after all. Or perhaps marijuana is most akin to certain antidepressants and stimulants—the drug-store sorts of "drugs"—medicines that are drugs on the proposed definition too, but call not for bans but for control. The point once again is just that none of these conclusions follows just from the fact that marijuana is a drug.

Nor of course are we entitled to object to or ban *only* substances that are "drugs." Tobacco, for example, may not be a drug according to the proposed definition (it's not clear, at least to me, whether the primary intended effect is on the mind), but it still is addictive and massively destructive (350,000 Americans die every year from its use). Here we come to recognize once again that the question of the morality or legality of substance use is more complex than the question of which substances are drugs. Definitions contribute to clarity, but seldom do they, all by themselves, settle the questions we are asking.

∞

DEFINING A "PERSON"

Defining the most contested terms is a tricky business, but sometimes crucial. A good example is the term "person."

FROM "HUMAN" TO "PERSON"

"Human" seems the natural term to express much that is precious to us. The rhetoric of the abortion debate, for example, often centers around the question whether fetuses are or are not "human." It is assumed that if they are indeed human, they have the same human rights as the rest of us, and that if they aren't, they don't.

This looks like a straightforward question or definition. What is it to be human? Actually, however, "human" is an ambiguous category, which has made for a lot of bad arguments. One common argument goes something like this:

Fetuses are human (i.e. biologically and genetically related to the human species). Therefore, fetuses are human beings (i.e. have the distinctive capacities that give rise to rights).

This argument plays on an ambiguity in the term "human." Human fetuses are obviously *human* fetuses ("what else could they be?," as the popular argument goes) in the genetic and developmental sense. But the same could be said of any part of the human body: human arms, feet, even hair and saliva. The moral conclusion uses the word "human" in a different sense: here it means "human *being*"—a certain sort of whole creature with certain distinctive capacities and therefore rights. But not everything that is genetically human is a human being.

The category "human" is misleading in another way also. Nonhuman creatures might also have the relevant wholeness and the relevant capacities for having rights. Suppose that the whales, or great apes, or some variety of extraterrestrial, turn out to think in the relevant ways very much as we do. This would (might?) imply that they too deserve the kind of moral consideration that rights invoke for us. Note that we cannot confine personhood to humans just by the simple addition of "human" in our definition. That draws an arbitrary line, and thus violates requirement 3 for a good definition.

Philosophers conclude that we need a category other than "human" or "human being" to describe the set of beings who have the special character, and consequently the special ethical weight, that we attribute to ourselves. Currently the term in use is the term "person." Adult, normally conscious humans are taken to be clear cases of persons. Rocks, trees, insects, automobiles, clocks, and so on are taken to be clear cases of nonpersons. Unclear cases will be fetuses and animals, as well as wilder possibilities such as artificial intelligences and extraterrestrials.

DEFINING A "PERSON"

What distinguishes those things that are clearly "persons" from those things that are clearly not? Most proposed definitions center around having a concept of self and the capacity to project a future. The argument is that some degree of self-awareness is what makes a merely reactive being into a "whole being" with serious moral claims: a being aware of suffering (that is, not just a being that suffers); a being with a sense of continuity and a future that can be restricted or denied (by death) altogether; and a being therefore with the capacity to shape its future, its life. Philosopher Tom Regan uses the phrase "subject of a life" for this kind of being, implying both a distinctive kind of self-awareness and the capacities that go with it. A person, in short, is any subject of a life.

From this kind of self-awareness, rights are supposed to follow. According to Kant, a subject of a life must be an end in itself. Beings who can themselves *have* ends (goals deliberately decided upon and pursued) *are* themselves ends, on the Kantian view, for that very reason.

Such a definition fits the clear cases. Normal adult humans are indeed subjects of a life, and for this reason have rights. The definition excludes those things that are clearly not persons, that have no subjectivity at all or at least are not *self*-aware, not subjects of a life. They do not have rights (or at least, if they do have rights, they do not have them on account of being persons in the sense being defined).

As to the unclear cases, some turn out to be persons and some not. Regan argues, in particular, that some adult nonhuman mammals are indeed subjects of a life, and therefore are persons, with rights equal to human rights. Some animals have rights.

Fetuses, howver, are, by this definition, *not* persons. They may have a certain degree of awareness (they move in response to uterine probes, for example), but they do not have *self*-awareness, something that depends not just on further brain development but also, crucially, on a *social* existence: on living among other people who can both bring forth a "self" and stand in contrast to it. This implies in turn—again, on a Regan-like proposed definition—that fetuses do not have rights (or at least, again, if they do have rights, they do not have them on account of being persons in the sense being defined). Therefore, the argument concludes, abortion may be less serious an act than killing an adult human.

THE DEBATE CONTINUES

Many people, naturally, would contest this definition, considering what it seems to imply. But notice that so far, for better or worse, we have at least arrived at a definite result, and with a certain care and clarity and therefore (perhaps, to some) persuasiveness. Those who disagree with this conclusion now need to respond to it: theirs is the burden of proof, as logicians say. The project of defining "person" proves useful at least so far.

As with any complex issue, though, there may be objections, and other possible directions in which the argument can move. Here is a brief survey of a few of these.

The proposed definition may be too restrictive. For example, it makes the status of newborns and infants almost as problematic as that of fetuses. Newborns probably lack self-awareness of the relevant sort too. Therefore a newborn would not be a person either on the proposed definition. Do newborns thus lack human rights? Although some philosophers have said yes, the general view is that newborns are a pretty clear case that any definition of "person" needs to include.

But this may put both (all) sides in somewhat of a bind. Most pro-lifers would like to include fetuses as well as newborns, but they exclude all other animals (except possibly the very most "advanced"). However, it is not easy to define "person" in a more inclusive way—a way that would include fetuses as well as newborns as persons from the start—without including a fair number of other animals. Many animals are far more developed and self-conscious than human newborns, and nearly all animals are more developed and conscious than human fetuses.

Most pro-choicers, on the other hand, want to include newborns but exclude fetuses, and some want to include at least some (maybe many) other animals. *Their* problem is that to include many other animals the standards will have to be low enough that later-term fetuses count too—the same problem as the pro-lifers', actually, except the other way around. People who favor "animal rights," meanwhile, are typically (though not always) pro-choice, so their problem is the same: how to include many or even *all* animals without extending rights to all fetuses as well.

It just may be that *everyone's* views need some rethinking on this question!

AND FINALLY...

This chapter points out that definitions usually don't settle questions all by themselves. This is certainly true of the definition of "person."

Even if the fetus is not a person, for one thing, it may still have strong moral claims—as a *potential* person, for one thing. Maybe potential persons have almost the same rights as actual persons, though this again is a claim that has to be argued (and it is not so clear when "potential" ends: after all, in a sense even an unfertilized egg is a potential person). And suffering too, even without self-awareness, may have a claim on us. People who want to defend animals, for instance, argue that animal suffering is morally bad in itself, whether the animals are self-aware or not.

These last points do not show that fetuses have a right to life, at least as long as rights are tied to (actual) personhood, but it certainly suggests that abortion has moral costs, that it is a serious moral act that needs justification and perhaps might be more tightly restricted as the fetus's potential nears actuality. So there may be a good anti-abortion case even if fetuses are not persons and perhaps don't have rights. Again: definitions don't settle everything!

Exercises and Notes

FINDING A NEUTRAL VOICE

Loaded language comes readily when we're talking with people who share our attitudes. It's also a major barrier when we're talking with people who don't share our attitudes.

To practice avoiding loaded language, pair up with someone who holds the opposite view from you on a particular moral issue (or: pair up with someone and then figure out some question on which you sharply disagree). Now work out *with your partner*

  i. a shareable description of the problem (that is, a detailed answer, agreeable to both of you, to the question: what is this debate about?);
 ii. a shareable description of the strongest argument for your side (that is, an outline of the argument that your partner can acknowledge as a reasonable argument—versus an argument in which emotion does the main work of persuasion—even though he or she will not *agree* with it); and likewise
iii. a shareable description of the strongest argument for your partner's side (same conditions).

Now share your descriptions with others. Do you think you've made progress in understanding the issue and/or in communicating respectfully?

CLARIFYING UNCLEAR TERMS

Not all terms need clarifying, luckily for us. Still, some do. Look around at the ethical debates that currently occupy us. Ask which of them could benefit from careful attention to definition. Where is the meaning of a word or words central to the debate? What word or words are these? How could you begin to define them?

For practice, specify a definition for <u>assisted suicide</u>. What do you think of the definition proposed in the text? Can you do better? You may need to do a little research.

Here's another example: <u>affirmative action</u>. This is a fairly specific term, and it would seem that it could be easily defined. Perhaps it can be. But we seem confused most of the time about what we mean by it. The philosopher Nicholas Capaldi even claims that there are five different definitions of affirmative action current in the discussion. (See his "Affirmative Action: Con," in Albert G. Mosley and Nicholas Capaldi, *Affirmative Action: Social Justice or Unfair Preference?* [Rowman and Littlefield, 1996]). Mosley's companion piece is good as well.) Can you formulate a good definition, or a useful set of distinctions?

Or again, try to define <u>welfare</u> (as in: "welfare programs"). What counts as a welfare program, and what doesn't? Which of our tools do you need to answer this question? (Bear in mind the brief discussion of welfare budgets in chapter 8 as well; you may also want to look ahead to chapter 19.)

A related question is: how would you define <u>poverty</u>? Is your definition suitable for a caseworker to decide whether a given family qualifies for poverty assistance?

Defining Contested Terms

The following terms play major roles in some current moral debates. Try to define each term.

You'll need to work from the clear cases, so start by specifying what they are. Look out for possible ambiguities. Keep open the possibility that for some of these terms there are simply not enough agreed upon clear cases to define the term successfully at all (and if not, are there other useful ways to clarify and focus the debates of which they are a part?). If you think an explicit and clear definition is possible, work it out. Sketch some sort of argument in support, and explore some of its implications in the case(s) in question as well as others.

Here are the terms.

<u>Sex</u>, as in the famous question whether Bill Clinton did or did not lie when he said that he did not have "sex" or a "sexual relationship" with Monica Lewinsky, with whom he later admitted doing various sexual things that did not include penile-vaginal intercourse. Though his accusers claimed that this was an obvious lie, some interesting survey research published at the time suggested that many Americans—interestingly, both older traditional people and college students—would not call Clinton's relationship with Lewinsky a sexual relationship. So what do *you* think? What definition of "sex" or "sexual relationship" would you propose to back up your view? How could you back up your definition?

<u>Selfish</u>, as in the perpetual debate over whether humans are "basically just selfish" or have other motives as well. (Recall also the box in Chapter 3.) Can you define "selfish" in some way that doesn't automatically include all human behavior (for surely we mean *something* when we say of someone that he or she is selfish—it must be possible for someone *not* to be selfish) and on the other hand also does not make selfishness automatically horrible? Once you've defined it in such a way, can you use your definition to actually *investigate* how selfish people really are?

Is affirmative action <u>fair</u>? Well, it depends on what you mean by "affirmative action," first of all, but it also depends on what you mean by "fair." Treating people equally? Maybe, but this is a vague phrase too. To adapt a famous argument of Abraham Lincoln's, it's hardly fair to make a runner run a footrace hobbled by a chain and ball while others run unencumbered. Yet no one blocks the way. The hobbled runner gets a lane in the track just like everyone else. If this strikes you as unfair all the same, how would you specify what fairness is? An equal chance at winning? But that can't be right either, since some people do run faster than others, and that's the whole point of the race!

Natural, in the context of environmental debates. Sometimes people argue that air and water pollution and the pollution of the land with nonbiodegradable wastes (plastics, etc.) is natural in a larger sense because the raw materials after all came from nature ("Where else could they come from?") as did we ourselves. Others argue that this despoilation of the earth is wrong because the materials and maybe the acts themselves are "unnatural." Is there a useful way to define "natural" in this context?

Related is the question of what constitutes "natural" foods. Since all foods come from nature in some ultimate sense, what makes some foods natural and some not natural? The absence or presence of "artificial" ingredients, maybe? Okay, but what makes an ingredient artificial? Isn't that the same question?

The last questions may sound skeptical, but they may well have answers. In any case, don't just dismiss these questions. After all, people are trying to make some sort of distinction with the word "natural." What distinction are they trying to make? If the word "natural" is too ambiguous to carry this kind of weight, what terms would you suggest instead?

Notes and Further Readings

Most "informal logic" texts discuss definition in some detail. Useful treatments can be found in most of the texts cited in Chapter 8, and especially Annette Rottenberg, *Elements of Argument: A Text and Reader* (Bedford Press [St. Martin's], 1997). The "Readings for Analysis" in Rottenberg's Chapter 4 are challenging and useful. For a well-presented classical approach see David Kelley, *The Art of Reasoning* (Norton, 1994), Chapter 3.

Colin McGinn's *Moral Literacy* (Hackett/Duckworth, 1992) offers a vigorous and provocative discussion of drugs, beginning with a proposed definition: see his Chapter 6. The quote from Mike Martin comes from his *Everyday Morality* (Wadsworth Publishing Company, 1995), page 149.

On the logic of "personhood," see Michael Tooley, *Abortion and Infanticide* (Clarendon Press, 1983) and Tom Regan, *The Case for Animal Rights* (University of California Press, 1986). Tooley advances a fairly restrictive definition of personhood; Regan, as the text explains, offers not just an account of animal rights but a person-based theory of the basis of rights in general. On the role of the concept of persons in the abortion debate, see my *Toward Better Problems* (Temple University Press, 1992), Chapter 3.

Some philosophers have argued that it is of the essence of certain very general terms that they not allow any final definition at all. Even the clear cases may be contested, and views may gradually shift. Some such "essentially contested concepts" may even be critical to cultural flexibility. See W. D. Gallie, *Philosophy and the Historical Understanding* (Schocken, 1964); Gallie's examples are terms like "democracy," "justice," "art," and the "good" (and indeed "philosophy"!) itself. For a related line of thought about personhood in the abortion debate, see Jane English, "Abortion and the Concept of a Person," widely reprinted in philosophical anthologies in applied ethics, originally published in *Canadian Journal of Philosophy* 5 (1975): 233–243.

CHAPTER 10

⬡

Judging Like Cases Alike

Kant argued that the essence of a moral judgment is that it must be generalized to other cases. If my act or decision or position is moral, it must be one that I would accept and support anyone else holding in similar cases—and one that I hold myself in similar cases.

In practice, though, we sometimes make judgments about one kind of case without thinking a great deal—or thinking at all—about what our judgments imply for similar kinds of cases not before us right now, or in which we play a different role. If we did think about those other cases, we might end up thinking differently about the one before us. This too, in fact, is our responsibility. Like cases must be judged alike!

CONSISTENCY IS NOT EASY

Applying the Golden Rule

Suppose I am prepared to misrepresent the condition of my car in order to sell it. It's expected, I say. Besides, the buyer can get the car checked herself. The moral question is: would I consider it equally justified for someone else to misrepresent his or her car in the same way and for the same reasons in order to sell it (say, just perchance, to *me*)? If not, then I am not judging like cases alike. I am not doing unto others as I would have them do unto me. As Kant would put it, I really am just "making an exception for myself"—treating others as mere means to my ends.

Would I consider it equally justified if someone else did the same thing to me? The honest answer *could* be "yes." After all, maybe I too would recognize that misrepresentation is expected, and I *could* get the car checked myself. In that I case I do judge like cases alike, and I have done my ethical homework (or some of it, though there may be other moral objections to misrepresenting cars). But this is probably not the norm. Normally we either don't think about it at all, or would judge other people quite differently from how we judge ourselves. Here the Golden Rule has some bite!

"Execution Stops a Beating Heart"

You may have seen a bumpersticker that says EXECUTION STOPS A BEATING HEART. What does this mean?

Literally, it's just a simple true statement. Execution—capital punishment—stops a beating heart. Since stopping a beating heart—that is, killing someone—is usually a bad thing, it's a fair guess that the person who put on this bumpersticker is opposed to the death penalty. But there is more going on than this.

This bumpersticker is an *argument*—in fact a specific challenge. It's an ironic response to the pro-life bumpersticker ABORTION STOPS A BEATING HEART. Essentially it argues: if you are opposed to abortion on the grounds that it's an act of killing, then you also ought to be opposed to the death penalty, since it too is an act of killing. Many people who are pro-life on the abortion issue, however, tend to favor the death penalty. How can this be a consistent position? The implication is: perhaps you ought to reexamine your reasons for opposing abortion or for favoring the death penalty.

This too is a challenge to judge like cases alike. It might be met in various ways, as we will see in a few pages. The first point, however, is that it must be met somehow. You may even have to rethink your views!

Note that the challenge arises the other way around too. Many people who oppose the death penalty tend to be pro-*choice* on the abortion issue. But if "stopping a beating heart" is an objection to execution, why isn't it an objection to abortion?

Respecting Innocent Life

Here is another example, a related bumpersticker:

> WE BRAKE FOR ANIMALS.
> WE SAVE THE WHALES AND THE BABY SEALS.
> WHY DO WE STILL TOLERATE ABORTION?

Good question. To spell it out: one common case for legal abortion rests on the claim that fetal human life is not only less important than nonfetal (born) human life but also less important than many other human needs, for example the need to have a manageable family size or a chance at a career. But people who accept the case for legal abortion also often are committed to saving the whales, protecting animals, and so on. And that commitment seems to come from a very different place—from an unwillingness to subordinate other lives to human needs, at least needs such as fur coats, meat, and new drugs or household chemicals that won't harm us.

In the one case protecting innocent life seems to be a prime value; in the other it does not. The challenge is: how can these two commitments be consistent? Doesn't something have to give somewhere?

∞

Rationalization Alert!

Challenges to judge like cases alike can be irritating. Downright annoying, in fact. It's no fun having our consistency challenged, and it takes work to figure out just what the relevant distinctions are. And of course there's always the danger that we will not be able to find a relevant difference, so that (God forbid) we may even be required to change our minds!

The temptation is to dismiss the challenge—to brush it off as irrelevant, or invent some excuse for treating two apparently like cases in different ways—a form of rationalization, or what Chapter 1 calls offhand self-justification.

Don't do it! An honest and careful attempt to meet the challenge of consistency—acknowledging that it is a real challenge, and that it must be met—is what critical thinking in ethics is all about. Moral principles *are* general in nature. They do apply to other cases besides those that may be in the front of our minds. And if our reasons really are the reasons we are giving, we must be prepared either to draw similar conclusions about those other cases, or change our conclusions in the first case.

You're not obliged to change your mind instantly. It may not even be clear how to answer some of these challenges. The main thing is to keep thinking about the issues. Come back to them when you can. Raise them with others who share (and others who don't share) your judgments of the cases in question. (And don't assume that *they're* so consistent either). Some philosophers say that it's a lifelong task to work out a set of practical reasons that really do consistently apply to all "like cases." Any such reasons are going to be in constant flux as new cases come along and as we grow and learn. And that's probably a good thing, too!

This challenge too works in reverse. People who oppose abortion but tolerate the mistreatment of animals must also consider how their commitments might be consistent. Once again, in the one case protecting innocent life seems to be a prime value; in the other it does not. I once had a neighbor whose car was plastered with pro-life slogans but who was also an avid deer hunter "for fun," as he put it. It didn't sound too pro-life to me. What gives?

HOW TO RESTORE CONSISTENCY

Three Responses

Suppose someone argues that your judgment about one case is not consistent with your judgment about another seemingly like case. There are three possible ways in which you might respond.

- You can argue that the alleged like cases are not really alike. In that case you need to figure out the *morally relevant difference* between the cases and explain what difference that difference makes.
- You can change your judgment about the like case or cases.
- You can change your judgment about the original case or cases.

In short, you can either try to show that your judgments aren't inconsistent, or change one of them.

Take again the question of abortion and capital punishment raised by the EXECUTION STOPS A BEATING HEART bumpersticker. Suppose you oppose abortion but favor capital punishment. Consider your options:

- You could try to establish a difference between the two cases, and explain what difference it makes. For example, a natural response is: fetuses are "innocent" but murderers are not. And innocence makes a difference because the innocent have a right to all the protection we can afford as a society. Those who have killed, however, forfeit the right to that protection (or some of it, anyway: they still have a right to a fair trial and humane treatment in prison). Arguably, those who kill may forfeit their own right to life, a right which all the rest of us, including fetuses on the pro-life view, still have.

Of course, this response might be debated in turn. Many people believe that it may be acceptable to kill innocents in wartime, for example, while others argue that even those who are not innocent still have the right to life. So there are further cases to consider. Still, probably some distinction can be maintained. Maybe the two alleged like cases are fairly far apart in the end.

- You could decide that, all things considered, you should change your mind and oppose capital punishment too. This is an argument made by some modern Catholic moralists who argue for a "consistent ethic of life": that if we are to be pro-life on some issues we need to be pro-life across the board.
- You could decide that, all things considered, you should change your mind and become pro-choice about abortion. The comparison of cases might show you that, in your mind, life is actually not the only or the most important value. You might conclude that your pro-life views about abortion do not reflect your most considered thinking.

There is no automatic way to decide which way to go. Trying to make the most sense of our many moral beliefs and commitments is an ongoing and hard job! You may want to try out all of the possibilities before deciding, and take some time too. Again, though, going in one of these three directions is ultimately necessary. There's nowhere else to go.

Further Examples

We've already noted that the above challenge also holds the other way around. Many people who oppose the death penalty tend to be pro-*choice* on the abortion issue. But again, if "stopping a beating heart" is an objection to execution, why isn't it an objection to abortion?

Can *this* challenge be met? Logically there are the same three options. Perhaps pro-choice people would argue that the cases are not truly like. Many pro-choicers would argue that fetuses are not fully human beings, for example (recall the box in Chapter 9), while murderers *are* fully human beings (though maybe bad ones). Or: some might conclude that capital punishment is morally acceptable too. Or: some might decide that they really ought to become pro-life on the abortion issue.

Again, there is no automatic way to decide, but thinking the question through is necessary.

Another bumpersticker, remember, asks how some people can reconcile great concern for other animals with a seeming lack of concern for human fetuses, which also have a kind of life and awareness but are at risk if abortion is legal. How can there be animal rights, say, and not fetal rights?

Once again, there may be answers. Maybe there is a relevant distinction between the two cases. Maybe it's that other animals are actually born, even adult, and fully conscious of what is happening, unlike a fetus. Or maybe abortion is *not* justified when the reasons are mainly utilitarian (if chiefly for reasons of cost, for example), just as testing drugs on animals is not excusable, according to the animal rights argument, simply because other forms of testing would be more expensive.

This challenge too (like most, you may be noticing) works the other way around too. How can there be fetal rights but not animal rights? If you're pro-life but not a vegetarian, I leave that question for you.

INVENTED CASES

Not all "like cases" need be *real* cases, either. The logic of invented cases is perhaps a little harder to see, but it also opens up intriguing new possibilities.

The Logic of Invented Cases

Consider the Golden Rule case again. The argument, remember, was that I cannot morally misrepresent the condition of my car in order to sell it if I would have objections to someone doing the same to me.

Now notice that it does not matter whether I am actually buying a car or not. It is enough that *if* I were buying a car I would have such objections. Here, then, you have a like case that is not exactly real (suppose I'm not really buying a car right now)—yet it does the work that's needed. A space opens here—indeed the necessity emerges here—for what we could call "moral imagination."

Sometimes we have to go farther.

G: Protests have caused McDonald's restaurants to pull out of many cities in India. I guess the Hindus didn't take too happily to the idea of eating sacred cows. I wonder why McDonald's didn't think of that. . . .

N: I think it's outrageous. McDonald's has the right to offer a legal good for sale. People don't have to buy it if they don't want to.

G: Well, if you were a Hindu you'd probably see it a little differently.

N: I'm not a Hindu!

G: You have certain beliefs that a restaurant could offend, don't you? What if some cannibals started a fast-food chain and opened a take-out place down the street from you. Would you have a problem with that? After all, you don't have to buy it if you don't want to.

N: Outrageous! I'd go down and picket the place myself.

G: I guess that's how the Hindus feel, huh?

It seems to be hard for N to put himself into the Hindus' shoes, at least by imagining himself a Hindu. So G tries something else. G invents a scenario in which someone *else* does to N what McDonald's did to the Hindus, so that N can stay in his own shoes, as it were, and still imagine himself in a situation *like* theirs.

Here the imagination stretches farther, but the logic stays the same. You essentially invent a like case that is relevantly similar (you claim) to the real-life case you are thinking about. Inconsistency can still arise, even if the allegedly like case may be entirely unreal. And the same options arise in response: deny the likeness, or change one of the inconsistent judgments.

The Right to Life and the Unconscious Violinist

Here is a famous example of an argument from an invented case.

On both sides of the abortion debate it is usually assumed that if the fetus has a right to life, then choosing abortion violates that right and is morally wrong. The philosopher Judith Thomson argued in a famous essay that this conclusion doesn't follow. Imagine, she says, that

> You wake up in the morning and find yourself back-to-back in bed with an unconscious violinist. A famous unconscious violinist. He has been found to have a fatal kidney ailment, and the Society of Music Lovers has canvassed all the available medical records and found that you alone have the right blood type to help. They have therefore kidnapped you, and last night the violinist's circulatory system was plugged into yours, so that your kidneys can be used to extract poisons from his blood as well as your own.

If you unplug yourself now, the Music Lovers point out, the violinist will die, and after all the violinist does have a right to life. . . . Yet surely, Thomson argues, you have the *right* to unplug yourself, even so. It might be nice to donate nine months' use of your kidneys to the violinist, but you cannot be compelled to do so.

Suppose you agree; that is, suppose you think that you have the right to unplug yourself in this case. So, even if another being is dependent upon you for life support (and in Thomson's case a being who is clearly a human being—and "innocent," too), and even if that being has a right to life, you believe that you may still, morally, pull the plug. It's still within your rights to refuse to go through with it.

Thomson argues that abortion in some cases, especially if you are pregnant unintentionally or against your will, is exactly parallel to pulling the plug on the violinist. By analogy, then, in the case of abortion, Thomson concludes that the fetus's right to life (if it has such a right) does not necessarily make abortion a violation of that right. You did not ask for this other life to be hooked to yours; you are being asked to make an enormous sacrifice of your time and your body's very energies; you acknowledge that there will be a loss—the dependent being will die—but your right to your own body is the only operative right. You must be allowed the choice.

Comments

This is a pretty wild analogy. It's not something that is actually likely to happen, which is part of Thomson's point. But that it is a completely imaginary case, once again, does not affect the problem of inconsistency. If you would object to being hooked up to the violinist, real or not, then you ought to support abortion rights in at least some cases—so the argument goes.

One nice feature of this analogy is that it puts men into a situation that Thomson thinks is like being unintentionally pregnant. (Notice that only an imaginary case is likely to do this—surely an advantage of the imaginary!) She suspects that most men, even those who are strongly anti-abortion, would insist that they have the right to unplug themselves from the violinist. But then the challenge is acute: can they then consistently be anti-abortion? What's the difference between this case and unintentional pregnancy?

Some deny that being tied to the violinist really is like being unwillingly pregnant. Conservatives argue that a relevant difference between pregnancy and Thomson's case is that pregnancy is a known risk of having sex, even with contraception. In Thomson's case you're simply kidnapped off the street and involuntarily plugged to the violinist, but in the case of having sex, even with contraception, you are quite aware that pregnancy is at least possible. It's not quite so involuntary. You need to take some responsibility.

This is a fair point. Maybe the two cases aren't so like, and we can consistently judge them differently.

On the other hand, this difference does not always hold. In some cases, at least, pregnancy *is* that involuntary. Think of pregnancy caused by rape. Though many pro-life advocates make an exception in this case, not all do. Some still insist that the fetus's right to life has priority. There, at least,

Thomson's analogy has real bite (unless, of course, those pro-life advocates agree that they must stay hooked up to the violinist for nine months too—restoring consistency in another, more extreme and unlikely way).

Thomson or her defenders might also recast the analogy to acknowledge the conservative response. Suppose it was known, for example, that the Society of Music Lovers was looking for someone to hook up to the violinist, and you went out for a nice evening walk even knowing that there was a small probability that you might be kidnapped for this purpose off the street. Maybe you even took an escort. This might be like using contraception—taking reasonable precautions—knowing that there is a small probability that it won't work. Don't you still have a right to unplug?

Thomson would say so. After all, people can't really be obliged to stay inside all the time just because if they go out there is a small chance they might find themselves hooked up to the violinist. You're not responsible, even a little, as long as you take reasonable precautions. It would not be fair to ask more. This might be like saying: women can't be obliged to totally refrain from sex until they are ready to carry through with an unintended pregnancy. Again, you're not responsible, even a little, as long as you take reasonable precautions. It would not be fair to ask more.

Thomson's analogy, and others she proposes like it, have set off a continuing debate among philosophers, much larger than we can review here. You see the point, though: working through like cases, even imaginary ones like hers, is an essential part of moral thinking. It is a complicated business (no surprise), but it can also be intriguing and revealing. Use your imagination!

"Speciesism"

COLIN MCGINN

Philosopher Colin McGinn uses two thought-experiments—extended analogies like Thomson's—to raise questions about the offhand ways we treat other animals.

Often we look at animals as mere objects to be consumed or entertained by or experimented upon, and we justify this practice without considering what our reasons imply about like cases. But suppose we were the *victims* of this kind of treatment rather than its perpetrators? It's not likely that we'd judge it the same way then. Or suppose the victims of it were just a little more like ourselves than other animals are now. What then? At least there would be some uneasiness about it. We'd pay some serious attention, and give the victims' side a little closer look.

McGinn makes these suppositions a bit more vivid: he tells a couple of stories. Of course, these stories are made up, and once again it may be tempting to dismiss them without thinking them through. But take care—there is a serious challenge here. Are we guilty of "speciesism"—a preference for humans over nonhumans merely on the basis of our *being* human, a difference that, according to McGinn, is not a relevant difference when issues of pain and abuse are at stake? If you are passionately convinced (in your guts, let's say) that it would be wrong for McGinn's vampires to suck *you* dry, why are you eating that pork chop without a second thought? Are the cases relevantly different? How?

We have all seen those vampire films, creepy tales of powerful pale predators who live on human blood. Well, let me tell you a story about a particularly successful vampire species. This species is unusual among the run of vampires in that it can live equally well off human blood or orange juice. It is also more in control of its food supply than your average vampire. In addition to producing ample supplies of orange juice, it keeps throngs of humans locked up in huge prisons so that it can get to their necks with minimum effort. The vampires raise human infants in these prisons for the sole purpose of drinking their blood at maturity (and they have been known to do it at tenderer ages too). There is a bit of a snag, though, from the vampires' point of view, namely that you can't drink blood from the same human more than three times without that human's dying, so they are continually needing to replenish their stocks as thrice-bitten humans die off. The humans are powerless to resist because of the superhuman capacities of the vampires. When the vampires aren't dining on human blood (and the occasional glass of orange juice) they do the usual civilised things: go to the movies and the opera, make love, get married, play tennis, whatever.

They also have strict laws governing conduct within their species and are generally law-abiding and polite. They are actually not such a bad lot, generally considered, apart from this human blood business. But they don't see much of a problem about that because, after all, we humans belong to a different species from them and look and act differently; anyway they have been doing it for millennia. They sometimes think it is a pity about the pain and fear the humans feel while their necks are being punctured and drained, not to mention all the death that results, but there is no point in being squeamish and sentimental about your farm animals, is there? And yes, they could live just as well on orange juice—which they actually rather enjoy at breakfast time—but it would be a little monotonous to have only that to drink: they like some variety in their diet. True, also,

Selections from Colin McGinn, *Moral Literacy: or How to Do the Right Thing*, reprinted by permission of Hackett Publishing Company, Inc. and by permission of Gerald Duckworth & Co. Ltd. Copyright © 1992 by Colin McGinn. All rights reserved.

it would be healthier to give up human blood, as some of them are always tediously insisting, but they relish their pint of blood at dinner time and feel that life would be poorer without it. So they don't take much notice of the "juicetarians" among them, a small minority anyhow, who fitfully campaign for humane treatment for humans—and even go so far as to call for complete human liberation! Why, what would become of all the humans if they were set free to roam the land? No, it is inconceivable.

I don't know about you but I find this vampire species a pretty selfish, blinkered and cruel bunch. They have got their values all wrong. If I were a powerful Martian visiting earth and found it dominated by these bloodsuckers, with the human species reduced to the status of mere blood vats, I would insist that they damn well stick to orange juice. Variety, freedom, tradition—don't give me that! Just look what you are doing to these poor humans, the pain and misery and confinement you cause them—and all because you don't fancy orange juice all the time. I mean, honestly, are you really telling me that it is morally acceptable to put that child to a slow and painful death rather than squeeze a couple of oranges? Can the difference of taste be that important to you? Human liberation! That is what I would say; and if I were one of the unlucky human victims I would plead the same case, hoping to appeal to the vampires' moral sense—of which they seem to have plenty when it comes to the welfare of their *own* species.

Here is another example, in which the human role is reversed. Imagine that there are two humanlike species, not one, either naturally evolved or created by God, rather as there are a number of monkey species. We are in the dominant position relative to the other humanlike species—call it the "shuman" species. Shumans, like humans, are intelligent, sensitive, social, civilised—in fact very much on a par with humans in their level of development. However, their warlike prowess is much inferior to ours, and as a result they have been conquered and tyrannised by the "superior" species. Not content merely with enslaving them to do our dirty work, we also use them for food, as subjects of vivisection experiments and in bloodsports. Our exploitation of them gives us a higher standard of living than we would have otherwise. Their flesh is excellent when barbecued; medical science has progressed rapidly by using them instead of lower species which are biologically less like us; and it is jolly amusing to watch them running away from, and being caught by, the starved dogs we let loose on them on Saturday afternoons. Of course, the shumans complain all the time about what we humans do to them, always petitioning the government from their special reservations, trying to work up some emotional sympathy, causing trouble in the streets. We are not impressed, though, because they belong to another species from ours: we can't interbreed with them, they are completely hairless with pointy ears, and the mothers carry the babies for twelve months not nine. Admittedly we don't need to use them in this way—we already have plenty of other species to depend on, as well as the vegetable kingdom—but it can't be denied that we derive pleasure from them that we wouldn't enjoy without exploiting them as we do. So you see it is all right to ignore their interests in order to cater to ours. We don't need to *balance* their interests with ours, treating similar interests equally, since the shumans belong to a different biological group from us. The biological distinction cancels the moral commitments we would have with respect to the interests of members of our own species.

Again, I maintain that this isn't right. We are doing to them what the vampires were doing to us—trampling over the legitimate interests of another group. In essence, we are refusing to take their welfare seriously simply because they belong to a different biological species from us—*and this difference does not warrant that refusal.* There is a word for this attitude, coined about twenty years ago, namely "speciesism." It was coined on analogy with the concept of racism and sexism, and is intended to suggest that what is morally irrelevant or insignificant—species or race or sex—is being treated as if it carried decisive moral weight. The point of my two imaginary examples is to demonstrate that speciesism *as such* is a form of unacceptable discrimination. There is no good moral defence of what the vampires do to us or what we do to the shumans, and to try to base one on a mere difference of species is transparent special pleading. It is simply quite unconvincing as a justification for what looks on the surface like a naked exercise of power designed to benefit one group at the ruthless expense of another. Cruelty is cruelty is cruelty—and a mere difference of species doesn't make it right. Ditto for murder, imprisonment, and so on.

The question we must then ask, returning now to the real world, is whether our actual treatment of animals is founded on a tacit speciesism—that is, whether we would rationally condone it if it weren't for mere species differences. Do we, in other words, accord mere zoological distinctions too much weight in deciding what to do and not do to animals? Is the speciesist attitude the only thing that sustains our exploitative treatment of other species? Could we defend this treatment without reliance upon *naked species bias?*

Once this question is clearly raised, it is very hard to avoid the answer that we do rely, unacceptably, on speciesist assumptions. What tends to obscure this fact is that animals differ from us not *only* in point of what species they belong to; they differ, also, mentally, in terms of their cognitive abilities. They don't have our intellects, our brain power, our moral sense. Their minds are just not as rich and complicated as ours.

But it is easy to see that *this* difference cannot make the moral difference we tend to take for granted—unless, that is, we are prepared to set up a new and pernicious form of social discrimination: intelligenceism. Surely we don't think that mere inferiority of intelligence (by some possibly arbitrary standard) is enough to justify, say, slaughtering the intellectually inferior for food or electrically shocking them for scientific purposes. If we did believe that, we would have the freedom to do these things to human children, mentally backward adults, and senile old people. Indeed, there would be no moral objection to intentionally raising genetically engineered "simple" humans for such purposes. But being intelligent is not what gives you the right not to be abused. The reason it is wrong to cause pain to people is not that they are intelligent or members of the human species. It is that pain hurts, it is bad to suffer it, people don't like to be in pain. If you want to know whether an action is wrong, you have to look at its actual effects and ask if they are bad for the thing being acted on—not ask what *else* happens to be true of the thing. If forced confinement, say, is bad *for* an animal, then it is bad to do this *to* an animal, unless you can think of a reason why this badness is justifiable in the light of a greater good. It isn't a question of the animal's ability to do mathematics or appreciate chamber music—still less of its species per se. It is a matter of sentience, the ability to suffer.

And here we reach the nub of the issue about our moral treatment of animals. *Is* there a greater good that justifies what, considered in itself, appears to be bad? Can we argue that what is bad for the animals is overridden by what is good for us? Is it possible to defend something bad in itself by claiming that the ends justify the means? Note, now, that we are assuming that our treatment of animals would be morally wrong if it were *not* for some supposed greater good.

A clear-eyed look at the facts quickly reveals that there is no such means-end justification, at least in the vast majority of cases. The test to use here is whether you would condone a given form of treatment if it were practised on humans, thus eliminating the speciesist bias from your deliberations. You may also consider "simple" humans in order to eliminate intelligenceist bias. That is, you have to ask whether you would do to intellectually comparable humans what we regularly do to animals. I won't bother to run through the whole gamut of things we do to animals, leaving this as an exercise for the reader; once the principle has been grasped this is fairly mechanical work. But it must be clear enough already that you would not condone killing humans for food in the way we now do animals, or experimenting on humans as we now do on animals, or using them in sports as we do now, or using their skins for clothes as we do now, and so on. You wouldn't even do these things to humans who were mentally *inferior* to the animals in question. The pain, the fear, the frustration, the loss of life—these would be quite enough to deter you. And the reason for these sound moral judgments is simply that the ends do *not* justify the means. A life lost for a pleasant taste gained? Mutilation for some possibly trivial increase in knowledge? Dismemberment in the jaws of dogs for the "thrill of the chase"? Trapped and skinned for an expensive fur coat? We would never accept these calculations if humans constituted the means, so why should we suddenly change our standards when we move outside the human species? Only, it seems, because of the prejudice that declares our species sacred and other species just so much exploitable stuff. Unfair discrimination, in other words.

So what should be done, now that we have seen our treatment of other species for what it is—immorally benefiting ourselves at the expense of other animals? (Actually, it is more that we *think* we are benefiting ourselves, since a lot of what we get from them is bad for us.) We should, at the very least, do everything we can to minimise our dependence on animals, treating their interests as comparable to the interests of fellow humans in the respects relevant to the case at hand. This will mean, just for starters, stopping eating meat if you live in one of the societies in which it is perfectly possible to find other sources of food, i.e. almost everywhere on earth. Don't even think about owning a fur coat. Very few animal experiments, if any. Bloodsports—give me a break. In sum, we have to cease doing to animals what we would not in good conscience do to humans. We must make our morality consistent.

You ask: if it is so wrong, why do people do it? Good question. To answer it, a glance back at history helps. It is a sad fact about human affairs that power tends to rule, and this includes our relation to the animal world. Nor is power always, or indeed often, on the same side as justice. If A is more powerful than B, and A can get something off B which B may not want to give to A, then A is apt to take that something from B by brute force— unless A is a just and moral individual, which he very often isn't. People all too often do what they have the power to do, and to hell with morality. Whenever you have imbalances of power, and a relation of domination that serves one party not the other, then be on the look-out for the kinds of prejudice and ideology that sustain basically immoral arrangements.

Historically, two areas of intense and terrible exploitation stand out, both of which were "justified" by all manner of strange doctrines at the time: slavery and child labour. I need not review these familiar stories of human brutality and moral blindness, since they are now accepted as such, though it is easily forgotten how recently young children were put through unspeakable miseries in supposedly civilised countries like England and slavery was legally permitted in America. My point is that at the time, and for hundreds of years before, these forms of subjugation were widely taken for granted and not regarded as morally dubious. Only now, in enlightened retrospect, do we wag the finger of condemnation at our forebears and marvel at their moral insensitivity. But which of us alive now can be sure that we would have been on the side of the angels had we lived in those benighted days? The pressures of conformity and self-interest and sheer inertia are very strong. May it not now be the case that our treatment of animals, so redolent of the barbarities of slavery and child exploitation, is just one more example of brute power holding sway over natural justice— of self-interest stifling moral decency? But, as with those other cases, it is not always easy to see this when it is all around you. You tend to think it must have *some* justification, even if you can't produce one. But maybe it just doesn't.

Exercises and Notes

PRACTICE

Working through like cases is a way of *thinking*. It is a way of clarifying what's morally at stake in a specific situation, by comparing the situation with other seemingly similar cases to see what the relevant differences are—and aren't. And it is a way of working toward greater consistency and clarity in your moral views generally, by comparing them with each other so as to bring out your general moral commitments.

So consider the following arguments. Begin by spelling out what you think are the key moral values at stake in each one. Be fair, of course (some of the values will need to be carefully phrased). Then ask what some like cases would be. Spell them out: show that they really are "like" the case in question. Make some up too, like McGinn and Thomson. (Have some fun with this.)

And now the question: would you or others judge those like cases in a similar way? Are you or others consistent here? Why or why not? And when inconsistencies show up, how do you think we should respond to them?

Here is an example.

> *If I want to ride my motorcycle without a helmet, I should be able to. After all, if anyone gets creamed, it's just going to be me. It's my right.*

The key idea here is something like: people have the right to do whatever they please as long as no one else is harmed by it. So what would a like case be? How about the so-called victimless crimes: prohibited behaviors that generally occur in private and harm no one, except maybe the person choosing to behave that way. Drug use would be one example; another might be prostitution; wilder examples might include things like dangerous (to yourself) hobbies. Try out some of these analogies. Are they really relevantly "like" cases? Do you judge them the same way? Should you? Would/should others?

These are for you:

- "The Bible condemns homosexuality—it's right there in *Leviticus*. I don't see how you can support anything that God explicitly says is wrong!" [*Hint: recall the discussion in Chapter 2*]
- "The point at which human life begins is not clear. It *may* begin before birth, maybe even at conception. But when something so important is

not clear, the only acceptable approach is to take no chances. Therefore, we should play it safe with respect to fetal life. Abortion should not be allowed." [Hint: how often is "play it safe" an argument in other moral questions?]

- "I have the right to buy whatever kind of car I like. I don't appreciate being guilt-tripped about buying a big, high-gas-consumption car like a sport utility vehicle. If I or my family get in an accident, I want us to walk away alive. If you don't like it, buy a big one yourself!" [Hint: try some science-fiction examples: driving armored vehicles? genetically engineered body armor?]
- "I don't eat anything with a face" (a reason some vegetarians give for not eating cows, pigs, chickens, etc.: the idea is that any creature with a face is an expressive "subject of a life," and thus has moral claims or rights).
- "Affirmative action just gives people a leg up when for so long they've been held down. Isn't it society's responsibility to do something 'affirmative' to counteract the legacies of racism and sexism?"
- "I'm against affirmative action. Everyone should get where they are by sheer hard work. The job just goes to the most qualified person, period."
- "It's a scandal that the law says I can't turn my land into a subdivision. I'm as environmentally concerned as the next guy, but this is my inheritance here. This is America, after all—the right to property is supposed to be sacred!"

THE "CONSISTENT ETHIC OF LIFE"

Modern Catholic moral theologians are not merely pro-life when it comes to fetuses, but argue for what they call a "seamless garment" of respect for life in *all* cases, which to them means being not only anti-abortion but also anti-war, anti-assisted suicide, and anti-capital punishment; and pro-environment, pro-welfare, and pro-animal. In this they differ from many Protestant pro-life activists, who tend to be pro-life on abortion but conservative on most of these other issues.

Consistency drives this argument. If we're going to be pro-life, these moralists argue, we have to be pro-life *across the board*. Thus Catholic moral theology challenges those who wish to be pro-life on some issues but not on others to "judge like cases alike"—to ask if there really is a difference between those issues, and if not to "get consistent."

Of course, there are other possible responses. Perhaps some of those issues *are* relevantly different from abortion, so that defending the fetus's right to life does not necessarily imply defending, for example, a poor person's right to food stamps. It's also possible to get consistent by giving up one's pro-life views on abortion (perhaps one could still be anti-abortion for other reasons), rather than embracing a pro-life view in other similar cases.

Once again, though, meeting the challenge takes some work. What do *you* say to it, at bottom? How many of us really are "pro-life" across the board? Must we be? Should we be? Most of us are probably "pro-life" on *some* issue. But if on some issues, why not *all*?

Notes and Further Readings

Most ethical philosophers agree that we must judge like cases alike, but this requirement may be cashed out in different ways. For many contemporary philosophers, it means arriving at universal principles that can be tested by application and defended against or adapted in the face of possible counterexamples (allegedly like cases where the proposed principle seems to yield the "wrong" result). This approach was first fully laid out by the English philosopher Henry Sidgwick in his *Methods of Ethics* (Macmillan, 7th edition, 1907) and so dominated ethics in England and America that for some time it was simply identified with moral reasoning as such.

Lately there has been criticism, most markedly from philosophers who want to recover a case-based approach that starts with those cases about which there are clear and accepted conclusions, and then explores their analogies—similarities or differences—with confusing or contested cases. On this way of thinking, universal principles seldom come up or get us very far: the aim is to stay more concrete. This is a far older approach, called "casuistry," long a strength of Catholic moral theology, with rabbinical (Jewish) and Islamic parallels too. For a fascinating history and defense of casuistry, see Albert Jonsen and Stephen Toulmin, *The Abuse of Casuistry: A History of Moral Reasoning* (University of California Press, 1988). In this chapter I have tried to present the requirement to judge like cases alike in a way that is compatible with both approaches.

For contemporary Catholic literature on the "seamless garment" or "consistent ethic of life" see Joseph Cardinal Bernadin, *A Moral Vision of America* (Georgetown University Press, 1998). For an evangelical version of a similar argument, see Ronald Sider, *Completely Pro-Life* (InterVarsity Press, 1997). Sider's revealing subtitle is "Building a Consistent Stance." A striking empirical and political work raising similar questions is Jean Reith Schroedel's book *Is the Fetus a Person?* (Cornell University Press, 2000). Schroedel finds that U.S. states and other countries with the most restrictive abortion laws are also the ones *least* likely to protect fetal life or children's lives in any other way—for example by protecting pregnant (and all) women from spouse battering or by providing for poor and needy children's education or even food.

On the trials and travails of consistency, one unusual study is Kimberly Cook, *Divided Passions: Public Opinion on Abortion and the Death Penalty* (Northeastern University Press, 1998). Cook is interested in the relation between people's views on these two hot-button issues. On the face of it, at least, both of the most common pairs of views are inconsistent, as noted in the text. Pro-life people tend to favor the death penalty; pro-choice people tend to be against it. Cook interviews each group and explores the seeming inconsistency and how they deal with it. She identifies two other groups too: people in favor of both the death penalty and legal abortion, and people opposed to both. All groups are interviewed in some depth.

The violinist analogy cited in this chapter comes from Judith Jarvis Thomson, "A Defense of Abortion," apparently one of the most widely reprinted articles in recent philosophical ethics. In Joel Feinberg's collection *The Problem of Abortion* (Wadsworth, 1984), the citation in the text can be found on page 153. Thomson also proposes a number of other striking analogies to other kinds of unintentional and involuntary pregnancy. For commentary, see Rosalind Hursthouse, *Beginning Lives* (Blackwell, 1987), pages 181 to 194.

IV

◆

TOOLS FOR
CREATIVITY IN ETHICS

CHAPTER 11

Multiplying Options

Many times, confronting an ethical problem, we feel stuck. Only a few options come to mind, and none of them are very appealing. Indeed, one of our most immediate associations with the word "moral" seems to be the word "dilemma." Moral *dilemmas*. We are supposed to have two and only two choices, or anyway only a few, and often neither choice is much good. We can only pick the "lesser of two evils." But, hey, that's life. Or so we're told.

Is it? In all seriousness: is it? How many alleged dilemmas are actually only what logicians call "false dilemmas"? How many times, when we seem stuck, do we just need a little more imagination? For one thing, mightn't there be some ready ways of *multiplying options*: of simply thinking up other possibilities, options we might not have considered?

Well, yes. It turns out that there are many good methods to do just that. There are even "creativity experts" who teach such methods, mostly (right now) in industry and managment. Surely they could also make a useful difference in ethics too. Creativity is creativity. It applies everywhere. Ethics is one of the areas of greatest need.

THE NEED FOR INVENTIVENESS IN ETHICS

Consider a famous moral dilemma: the "Heinz dilemma," from the psychologist Lawrence Kohlberg's research on moral development.

> A woman was near death from cancer. One drug might save her, a form of radium that a druggist in the same town had discovered. The druggist was charging $2,000, ten times what the drug cost him to make. The sick woman's husband, Heinz, went to everyone he knew to borrow the money, but he could only get together about half of what it cost. He told the druggist that his wife was dying and asked him to sell it cheaper or let him pay later. But the druggist said "no." The husband got desperate and broke into the man's store to steal the drug for his wife. Should the husband have done that? Why?

Kohlberg used dilemmas like this to probe children's moral reasoning. He claimed that most children go through several different, markedly different stages of moral reasoning—a much-debated theory.

That debate, however, is not our concern here. Our question right now is just: is this a true dilemma or a false one? Does Heinz really have *no* options besides stealing the drug or watching his wife die?

I put this question to my ethics classes after they get a little training in creative problem-solving. Can they think of any other options for Heinz? It turns out that they can, easily. Here are some of their ideas.

For one thing, Heinz might offer the druggist something besides money. He may have some skill that the druggist could use: maybe he's a good house painter or piano tuner or a skilled chemist himself. He could barter, trading the use of his skills for the drug.

For another thing, what about public or charitable assistance? Almost every society in which modern medicine is available has developed some way of offering it to people who cannot afford it themselves. Heinz should at least investigate.

Or suppose Heinz called up a newspaper. Nothing like a little bad publicity to change the druggist's mind. Or to help the sick woman gain a few donations. Think of the appeals you see in hardware stores and community groceries, complete with photos, a town rallying to buy an afflicted child a bone marrow transplant, another chance at life. Once again, a thousand dollars—all that "Ms. Heinz" needs—is not a lot of money in today's world.

And why is the druggist so inflexible, anyway? Possibly he needs the money to promote or keep on developing his drug. But in that case Heinz could argue that a spectacular cure would be the best promotion of all. Maybe his wife should get it free! Or Heinz could buy *half* the drug with the money he can raise, and then, if it works, ask for the rest to complete the demonstration.

Then again: why we should trust the "miracle drug" in the first place is not clear. New life-saving drugs require extensive testing, which evidently has not happened yet in this case. Where's the Food and Drug Administration? Maybe the drug is not worth taking even if the sick woman could get it free. Or maybe she should be paid to participate in a drug test!

In Short . . .

Heinz *does* have alternatives. There are many more possibilities to choose between than stealing the drug or letting his wife die. This is only a partial list, too. I am always delighted by each new group's ability to come up with new options—always there are a few I've not heard before.

I don't mean that there are no moral issues raised by Kohlberg's dilemma. There are. And of course (I add this point for philosophers) *if* one's goal in raising this dilemma is to illustrate the clash of certain ethical theories, or to make certain philosophical points, then it can be altered to foreclose some of the other options. Certainly some situations really *are* dilemmas.

My point, however, is that it is too easy to accept purported moral dilemmas without question, as if somehow dilemmas are the only appropriate or natural form for moral problems. Creative thinking is closed out before we even start. Narrow and limited questions leave us, not surprisingly, with narrow and limited answers.

HOW TO "GET OUT OF THE BOX"

The practical question is *how* to think more creatively. *How* do we multiply options? It turns out that that the creativity experts have a number of very specific suggestions: actual methods for more imaginative thinking, all of them as applicable in ethics as anywhere else. To understand them, we need to begin with a little psychology.

"Set"

Habit is essential to our lives. We can't figure everything out from the beginning every time we need to do something—we'd never do anything. Most of the time we have to rely on our habits to get us through, adding in a little thinking only when necessary. Lucky for us.

But habit also limits us. Sometimes the ruts of habit can be so deep that we can't see over the top of them, so to speak. Then they become *constraints*. Then we *are* "in a rut." Psychologists even have a word to describe these habits and unconscious assumptions: the constraints of the familiar and comfortable— very nice (maybe) and at the same time very limiting. The word is "set."

"Set" can be so powerful that we literally cannot see any other possibilities, even those right before our eyes. For example, for a long time doctors were unwilling to prescribe morphine and other painkillers for people who were dying and in great pain, because morphine and the other painkillers are addictive. Doctors had been so well trained not to use addictive drugs that they simply did not *notice* that it makes no sense to worry about addiction when a patient is about to die anyway. And so people died in pain they didn't have to suffer. Some critics of medicine now wonder if the same thing hasn't happened with regard to assisted suicide: that doctors are so well trained to preserve and save lives that they simply cannot recognize that sometimes the best thing for a suffering person is to die.

In cases like these, of course, "set" has finally been recognized. Now we can see past it. Morphine *is* given to dying patients, and assisted suicide at least arises as a question for doctors (though there may certainly be good reasons to oppose it). The challenge to *us*, however, is how to overcome set in cases where it has not yet been recognized. It's a bit of a paradox: how to overcome a limitation we are not yet aware of.

To break set we need to loosen up, try something new, maybe even something that seems peculiar, embarrassing, or improbable. Doing so may feel forced, but that's just the point: we're trying to force your way beyond your own habits, out of the mental box that confines us, beyond the familiar world that is so comforting but can also be so constraining. We need some ways to shake things up a bit, to see the world in a broader way. So expect some unusual and maybe even awkward methods—that's the way they have to be!

Ask Around

First: *ask around*. Listening to other people is not a bad idea anyway, just to understand them better and broaden your own horizons. Specifically in problem-solving, asking around (asking *anyone* else—friends, children, strangers, oracles, . . .) is an excellent way to get new ideas: to break set. You don't have to follow the advice you get—but others can certainly give you a fresh perspective.

We're often very proud of our own, unaided ability to figure things out. But we get a lot farther with a little help from our friends. Someone else may have had experiences you've not had, or ideas you've not thought of. Even someone's chance half-sentence may give you a perspective you didn't have before—if you ask, and if you listen. Just having to explain the problem to someone else may help you see it in a new light. It's worth a try.

Brainstorm

Brainstorming is another good way to multiply options. Brainstorming is a process in which a group of people try to generate new ideas. (It's like asking around in a more formal and focused way, in a group.) The key rule is: defer criticism.

It is tempting and "safe," of course, to react to any new suggestion with criticism. It won't work, for this or that reason; people won't like it; and so on. Brainstorming asks us to do just the opposite: to consider how some new idea *could* work, not why it probably won't. Even a crude and obviously unrealistic idea, passed around the room, may evolve into something much more realistic, and meanwhile it may spark other new ideas. Ideas hitchhike on each other. But you have to hold back the criticism to let it happen.

Take the problem of littering around fast-food restaurants.

A: Maybe people would recycle if they realized that it takes far more energy to produce those wrappers and cans than you get out of the food or drink!

B: It does? Too bad we can't eat the wrappers and cans!

C: That's silly!

D: No—it's an interesting idea. What if we *could* eat them?

B: Like an ice cream cone—it holds the ice cream while you eat, and then you eat the cone too. No mess.

A: Even if it got dirty, at least the dog might want it . . .

D: Dirt, huh? Maybe wrappers and cans could be made of some material that composts easily—you know, decomposes in a few weeks with water and sun.

B: You can shred up your newspapers and put them right into the garden for mulch. Couldn't we have cans or wrappers like that?

At least two new ideas come out of this little exchange (despite C's offhand dismissal): the idea of edible wrappers and cans, and the idea of wrappers and cans that readily decompose. Each of them could be refined into something "realistic" without a lot of further work.

Random Association

If you're still stumped, problem-solver Edward DeBono has another, truly wild suggestion. Go to the dictionary, or to any book for that matter. Open it to some page and pick out a word at random. Any word will do. Then see what associations that word suggests. The point is: immediately your thinking has a truly new stimulus. You are not just going around in the same old circles. DeBono calls this method "random association."

Once again it may seem silly. Once again, though, some such stimulus is just what we need in order to break set, to get beyond our own habits.

In the face of the Heinz dilemma, for instance, you might turn to the dictionary for random associations. When I did it, the first word I found was "oboe." "Oboe?" I said to myself. "You've got to be kidding!" Then I thought: Well, an oboe is a musical instrument; an oboe-like instrument is used to charm cobras in India; maybe Heinz could somehow charm the druggist? How? Well, I'm not sure, but it seems worthwhile for Heinz at least to talk to the druggist again.

Back to oboes. People play such instruments; people have skills; Heinz has skills: aha! This is how I first reached the idea about bartering skills for the drug. The next word I found was "leaf." Leaf: "Turn over a new leaf"? "Read leaves"? (Hmm—foretelling the future, as people used to do with tea leaves? How do we know that this drug is any good . . . ?) Use leaves instead of drugs? (Are there herbal remedies . . . ?).

DeBono emphasizes that we should not skip around looking for words that give us an immediate idea. This allows set to take over again, to confine our thinking. No: take whatever word comes along and work with it until you find something. "Oboe" seemed pretty unpromising at first, but sticking with it opened up some genuine new possibilities.

The Intermediate Impossible

DeBono proposes another method he calls the "intermediate impossible." Start by imagining what would be the *perfect* solution to your problem. Presumably the absolutely perfect solution will be impossible. Then work backward, toward "intermediate" solutions that *are* possible, until you find a possibility that is realistic. In short, make your very first step a big and wild one—otherwise you may never take a big step at all.

Take the question of assisted suicide. Usually we just ask: should it be legalized or not? Yes or no? But aren't there any other options?

Try the intermediate impossible. One perfect solution (apart from immortality, of course!) would be for people to be able to choose to die in some way that is not so secretive, passive, and (at least in some people's eyes) shameful. Much better is to be able to die in a way that is recognizably good to ourselves and others. So one perfect solution might be a "heroic" death, such as carrying out some sort of "suicide mission"—in space, underseas, in places where those who want to survive can't go—or volunteering to test a new drug or medical procedure. Not that this could be made a requirement; but the idea does, immediately, break set once again. We have something new to work with. Ideas begin to flow.

Once we practice the intermediate impossible we quickly discover that we often do not know what a "perfect" solution to our problem would be. We complain a great deal, we believe things are bad, yet often we have not really begun to imagine, to carefully consider, what we want instead. Maybe when we actually arrive at an idea of what we want, we'll discover that it is not so different from what "the other side" wants. Or not so different from what we have already.

Do we really want to say, for example, that no one should ever want to die, that no one *could* ever want to die so much that he or she should be helped to do so? Is that really the "perfect" answer? Contrariwise, if we agree that some people could justly choose death, then what counts as a "perfect" death? These are not easy questions, and it is natural to wonder whether we are so confused about assisted suicide in general partly because we are so confused about the answers.

Anyway, again, you see how new ideas arise. They are there to be found: the crucial step is to *look*. Confronted with two or three bad choices and the demand to make a decision, start brainstorming. Free-associate. Ask around. Get out your dictionary. Don't let anyone tell you that you have no other options. You won't find any others if you don't look for them.

MORE PROVOCATIONS: "WHAT IF...?" THINKING

Almost any idea or remark can be used to break set. It's up to us. That is, we might choose to treat even obviously "crazy" ideas, or ideas we strongly dislike, not as ideas to be rejected or pushed out of mind, but as potentially useful stimuli, ways to push our thinking in new directions. Sometimes these provocations may be accidents: whatever life happens to offer. Other times we may set them up deliberately. Here are some deliberate methods: ways of asking, "What if . . . ?"

Take a familiar problem like speeding—people driving too fast. This is a practical problem, for sure, and it is a moral problem too, though this is not always obvious. Mishandling a car is one of the prime ways that people put other people's time, bodies, and lives at risk. But how might we reduce speeding, wake up to its implications, or otherwise learn to see the problem in new ways? Can "what if . . . ?" thinking help us here?   7

There is, first of all, what DeBono calls the ESCAPE method. Here we try to identify some "normal," taken-for-granted feature of a situation and then deliberately distort or deny that feature. Roads now are made to smooth cars' way at high speeds. But

What if . . . roads get bumpier at higher speeds?

Crazy, right? But suppose we ask whether any useful new ideas arise from this provocation. For example, maybe little undulations could be built into road surfaces so that unpleasant vibrations are set up in car frames when the speed limit is exceeded. Then roads could enforce their own speed limits!

Try EXAGGERATION. For the sake of provocation, some normal feature of the problem could be pushed to extremes. For example, only some drivers now speed, and only some of the time. But

What if . . . everyone speeds all the time?

Of course, literally, this is just what we don't want. Again, though, in the spirit of exploratory thinking, we ought to ask if there are any useful provocations here. We might be provoked to imagine high-speed freeway lanes in which there is a set high speed (75 mph?) that everyone in that lane is expected to drive. People who want to go fast could do so while other lanes remain at slower speeds, though drivers may enter or exit the high-speed lanes. Passing would not be allowed in the high-speed lanes, since everyone in that lane would drive the same high speed. This should cut down on accidents caused by impatient passing and lane switching. High-speed lanes might be separated by some sort of barrier from the other lanes, with periodic entries and exits.

DeBono also encourages WISHFUL THINKING. "Wouldn't it be nice if . . .", we ask, and make that very fantasy into our provocation:

What if . . . speeding cars announce themselves?

Maybe cars could have a built-in link between speedometer and horn or lights, so that a car exceeding 70 miles per hour, say, would begin honking and flashing its lights, alerting any police car (and all other drivers) in the vicinity, even without radar.

Speaking of radar, here is another EXAGGERATION:

What if . . . everyone has radar?

Not just police, that is. Little radar generators (the read-back part wouldn't be necessary) might be sold to drivers who would rather be surrounded by nice, law-abiding drivers than by speeders, and as more of these came into use, speeders' radar detectors would become useless. (Actually, you can buy such generators now.)

And wouldn't it be nice if cars themselves reminded us of some of the dangers of speed? Perhaps a little ESCAPE would be useful? Rather than cars becoming ever more cushioned, seat-belted, and airbagged,

What if . . . cars are made *less* safe?

That is, the dangers might be made more obvious. Some pretty wild ideas come up here. Suppose that instead of air bags, large spikes are installed in the middle of the steering wheel. *That* would slow people down! Of course, this is not a serious suggestion (after all, even speeders deserve protection, and what of the innocent drivers they hit?). But it may start us thinking about what graphic ways there might be to remind people just how dangerous speed can be. Brainstormers, take it from there. . . .

Exercises and Notes

PROBLEM-SOLVING WARM-UPS

The methods introduced here are useful across the board, not just in ethics. Though the aim is to use them in ethics, you might begin by practicing more broadly.

Try some "novel function practice." Most of us have been asked, in some game or quiz book, how many new and different uses we can think of for some everyday object, like a brick. What can you do with a brick, besides build houses? Obviously, it can be a paperweight or a doorstop. You can make bookcases out of bricks and wood. Are there more creative uses? Suppose you tape on a return-postage-guaranteed junk mail reply form and drop it in a mailbox—a good way to protest junk mail. Suppose you leave it in your yard until you want to go fishing, and then lift it up to collect the worms underneath. (This suggestion is courtesy of one of my students. Brick as "worm generator," he called it.)

So find some other everyday object and practice. What can you do with . . . a cheap ballpoint pen (besides write)? . . . a piece of paper? . . . a rotten apple? . . . a bad joke?

Can you think of ten ways to get water out of a glass without moving the glass or damaging it? (Evaporate it? Soak paper towels or sponges in the water? Suck it out with a straw? And where do you get a straw, right now? How about the casing of of that cheap ball-point pen?) This is fun too, but the crucial thing is to actually use the option-multiplying methods introduced in this chapter, from random word association to the various "what if . . ." methods. Try for ten ways to get water out of a glass; you may be able to think of five or six without being systematic, but after that you have to start using more deliberate methods. If you easily get ten, try for twenty.

To practice random word association, actually generate some words (use this very book if nothing else). Each group can take one as a starting point for brainstorming.

Use "what if . . . ?" methods. Let's see: usually you drink water out of the glass. What DeBono calls a REVERSAL would be:

What if . . . the water drinks *you?*

Does this lead to any ideas? The image is of falling or jumping into a large glass of water. You might notice that some water would be displaced and pushed over the rim of the cup. Could this displacement be mimicked in the small cup? How about adding sand? oil? rocks? another cup? There are four new ideas right there!

Now pick some specific practical problems around your school or area and challenge yourself to add to (let's say, double or triple) the number of solutions usually considered. Here are some sample problems.

- Waste (styrofoam cups, lights left on all the time, newspaper, etc.)
- Alcoholism and other addictions
- Too much television
- Lack of affordable child care for working families with young children
- Lack of inexpensive travel options
- Alternatives to on-the-air fund raising for public radio
- Not enough parking at school or elsewhere
- Difficulties monitoring nuclear test-ban compliance
- Low voter turnout

A look at any newspaper will produce many more.

MULTIPLYING OPTIONS: MORAL ISSUES

Now consider more familiar moral issues, and treat them exactly the same way! Use the option-multiplying methods (random word association, intermediate impossible, "what if . . ." thinking, and all the rest) just as you did with the practical problems above. Once again, challenge yourself to double or triple the number of solutions usually considered.

Pick current issues, or try some of the following:

- Capital punishment
- Gun control
- Assisted suicide
- Drug use
- Blowing the whistle on business or administrative corruption
- The treatment of gay people in the military
- Political campaign finance abuse
- Medical testing on animals
- Rain forest destruction

This will feel awkward at first—it seems not quite serious enough an approach for ethical issues, which we're always taught must be serious indeed. Try it anyway. Give the methods a chance to show what they can do. What alternatives might there be for a convicted murderer besides capital punishment or life in prison? What are the usual processes and assumptions involved with, say, assisted suicide, which you can reverse or distort or exaggerate using the "what if . . . ?" methods? (For instance: how about assisting *non*-suicide: a challenge to doctors or families to do what it takes to make life worthwhile to someone again?)

And don't settle (your teacher shouldn't either) for something that's only a *little bit* different but basically just rings a few changes on a familiar idea. The methods in this chapter can take you farther than that. Get wild!

Go Public

Some brainstorming groups have gone on local radio stations every week or month to offer call-in group problem-solving sessions. One member writes: "Most callers want to solve their problems, and some have ideas for earlier callers, which is what we want from them. But mostly we inspire some people with our attitude about 'considering the possibilities.' "

Now that you have built up some problem-solving expertise, think about going public yourselves. That is, advertise yourselves as a problem-solving or brainstorming group, and invite people to send in problems—especially moral problems. Set up meetings on campus, or elsewhere. Several people in San Francisco have set up a "salon" called the "Brain Exchange" which holds monthly problem-solving sessions, announced in the papers and in mailings to a six-hundred-person mailing list, and charge five dollars at the door to cover costs. Sometimes they throw a potluck at which everyone brings one dish and one problem. Try it yourself!

Notes and Further Readings

"False dilemma" is a classic fallacy in informal logic, and is usefully discussed and illustrated in many informal logic textbooks, such as Howard Kahane's *Logic and Contemporary Rhetoric* (Wadsworth Publishing Company, many editions). The Heinz dilemma is cited from Lawrence Kohlberg, "Stage and Sequence: the Cognitive-Developmental Approach to Socialization," in D. A. Goslin, ed., *Handbook of Socialization Theory and Research* (Rand McNally, 1969), page 379.

Creative methods of generating new options are also discussed very widely, but most of this discussion takes place in literatures unfamiliar to philosophers, such as the problem-solving literature in management and design. For some introduction to problem-solving broadly conceived, see Marvin Levine, *Effective Problem-Solving* (Prentice-Hall, 1988). Edward DeBono has published a wide variety of books on psychology and problem-solving, such as *Lateral Thinking* (Harper and Row, 1970). For an introduction to "what if . . . ?" thinking (he calls it "PO thinking") and the specific methods outlined here, see his *Serious Creativity* (HarperCollins, 1992), especially pages 163 to 176. For more on these methods in practice, see also the exercises for Chapter 20 of this book.

For general information on the Brain Exchange, see *The Book of Visions* (Institute for Social Inventions, 1992), pages 325–326. For a thousand more new ideas to improve our lives—creativity at work!—see the Institute's Web site at <www.globalideasbank.org>.

CHAPTER 12

Problem-Shifting

Our last two tools for creativity are more radical and more powerful, and sometimes it's a little harder to remember to use them. But they also have the potential not just to multiply options but to genuinely transform the whole problem. These are ways of *shifting* problems—which sometimes is far better than *solving* them!

REFRAMING PROBLEMS

Some friends of mine loved to have fires in their fireplace. But they lived in a house so designed that when they wanted to use the fireplace, they had to haul firewood through nearly the whole house to get it. A fire always meant a huge mess, so they didn't have many.

They even multiplied options. They cut firewood into really tiny pieces so it could be carried easily. They thought of buying dirt-free fake logs, or even getting some nice dirt-colored carpet so the mess was less noticeable. But all of these ideas left the problem unchanged. The house itself was awkward. There was no good solution to the problem as it stood.

A precocious cousin visited them one day. Well, she said, why not just knock a hole in the wall right next to the fireplace and put in a little door and a woodbox? My friends were delighted and put in the door that very day. "Why didn't we think of that?" they cried.

My friends were stuck in a specific kind of rut. They missed a simple and "obvious" alternative because they were preoccupied with better ways to haul wood through the house. They had become adept at dealing with a badly designed house. Looking at the problem more broadly, though, *that* was the real problem. The house itself was awkwardly designed. In fact they needed to *change* the house. And notice that once they did so they did not solve the problem of how to haul wood through the house without making a mess. They simply eliminated that problem. Now they don't haul wood through the house at all. There is no problem left to solve!

Opening Up the Problem

This is what I call "reframing problems." You deliberately break out of "the" problem as it may be defined for you by others or by yourself in the past, and ask how "the" problem arises in the first place and what can be done about *that.*

Can't the same thing be done in ethics? That is, rather than multiplying options to solve a problem as it stands, maybe sometimes the best and most creative strategy is to change the problem itself. Maybe we need to look at such problems more broadly.

Take the Heinz problem again for a first example. We worry about whether Heinz should steal a drug that is necessary to save his dying wife. Or maybe Heinz can find some other way to save his wife or get the drug. But there are broader questions—questions about the "design" of the whole health-care payment system—that we should also ask. For example, why does the sick woman have no insurance? Why can't public assistance help her? If either insurance or public assistance were real options, Heinz's dilemma would not come up in the first place.

Indeed this may be the best response of all to the Heinz problem: that there is *no* good solution to the problem as it stands, and therefore the best thing we can do is to try to prevent such dilemmas from coming up at all. The best strategy is to head it off next time, or try to transform it into something more easily manageable. An ounce of prevention is worth a pound of cure.

Of course, the old questions can still be asked too. There is poor Heinz, after all, who must do something right now. Maybe ethics can help him. Or maybe not. Anyway, even though Heinz could use some advice, figuring out an answer to a "given" situation like his is not the only thing ethics can be doing, and is certainly not the most creative response to Kohlberg's dilemma. Sometimes we need to change focus.

Reframing the Drug Problem

Consider "the drug problem." It's a large and puzzling issue. By way of response, though, we are usually invited to consider only enforcement or resistance (how kids can resist pressure to take drugs). Sometimes "the" drug problem is even reduced to the question of how to get dealers off the streets. Longer jail terms, mandatory sentencing, more police.

We need to ask: what is the bigger challenge? Are there ways to rethink and shift the problem itself? Suppose we ask this: why is it that so many people are tempted by drugs in the first place? What combination of social pressures, hopelessness, the wish to experiment, and so on, are at play, perhaps on the part of different people and with respect to different drugs?

Surely part of the allure of drugs is that they offer some excitement in the midst of an otherwise uninteresting life. Then one bottom-line question is: are there less lethal ways to make life interesting? Yes, obviously. Well, *what* ways? What can we do to make life so interesting that people are no longer tempted to escape through drugs?

Now *there's* a fine question—no longer punitive; widely engaging; more promising for all of us. Here too, of course, the old questions remain, but they are no longer the *only* questions. A new sense of freedom opens up, and maybe of hope as well.

Thinking Preventively

Consider capital punishment. Society is consumed by the question of whether killing murderers is right or wrong. But perhaps the best answer comes from a different direction entirely. Why not refocus our energies toward reducing the number of murders in the first place?

We do understand something about what drives people to kill other people. Everything from emotional and social stresses (unemployment for example) to the easy availability of weapons makes a difference. But too often we seem preoccupied with results and not causes. Here, though, as in a great many other cases, we know that prevention in advance is far better than punishment afterward. Besides, a great many *other* goods would also be served if weapons were less readily available, if unemployment were lower, and if people were enabled to deal with conflicts and anger in more constructive ways.

Of course, once again, reframing the problem in this way doesn't answer the moral question of capital punishment itself—any more than cutting a hole in the wall solved the problem of how to haul wood cleanly through the house. The point is that problems like this may not *have* "solutions," at any rate, no solutions a tenth as good as trying to head the problem off in the first place. Even so, we will not eliminate all murders, and therefore we will still have a moral question about capital punishment. But why are we spending so much energy on that question and so very little energy where it could do much more good?

MAKING THE PROBLEM AN OPPORTUNITY

Here is yet another tool for problem-shifting—perhaps the wildest but also, sometimes, the most creative of all.

The method is this: to take the seeming problem as an *opportunity* rather than a problem in the first place. Perhaps rather than eliminating or reducing it (whatever it is), we can make use of it in some new and unexpected way.

No Way—How Can Problems Be Opportunities?

Here is a practical example. Suppose you're out digging one fine hot day, excavating for a house that is partly to be built underground. You hit an

Think of How the problem Started and how to change or avoid it.

enormous rock, so big that your backhoe can't even budge it. Immoveable; like a wall. What do you do?

Maybe you call for dynamite and bulldozer. So a week or two later, after a huge investment of time and energy and explosives, you are ready to dig again. Or maybe now you have a hole that is too big, and you have to spend more time filling it partly back in, maybe with fragments of the rock you've just laboriously blown to bits.

Well, that's life, right?

You already know from the last chapter that there are probably other options. Ask around, brainstorm, random associate, and so on, to find better ways to get rid of the rock. You could attach chains and pull it out. You could grind it up, just taking out what you need to remove. You could. . . .

Notice, though, these answers are only concerned with moving the rock. That's how "the" problem is framed: the rock, or some of it, needs to go. But maybe, just maybe, it's the real essence of creativity to challenge and rethink the alleged problem itself. For there's at least one other way to frame this problem. Instead of asking, how do we move the rock? suppose we ask, what if we do *not* move the rock?

New possibilities emerge the minute we ask this new question. Most obviously, we should ask whether it is possible to move the *house*—to build it away from the rock. Must the house be right there? Six feet to the right or the left, maybe, and there would be no problem.

But it is also possible to shift this problem still farther, to the point that it is no longer even a problem. Ask instead: is there some way to use this unexpected obstacle to *advantage*? Maybe the new situation has possibilities— positive possibilities, that is.

An immoveable rock, like a wall, eh? Let's see. . . . Suppose it *were* a wall? How about building the house around the rock? Redesign the house, make a fireplace in the "natural" rock wall. . . . Now the house might be far more dramatic and intriguing, not to mention less expensive, than it would have been otherwise. *Why not?*

And in Ethics . . . ?

Could some moral problems also be opportunities, just like the (seeming) problem of the immoveable rock, if we think about them creatively enough?

Try this one: go to any nursing home and you will find people longing for something constructive to do. There are some organized games and other activities, but the overall feeling is simply that time is being filled. Trained professionals are even hired to find ways to keep old people busy—disguising what we normally assume to be the simple fact that really there *is* "nothing for them to do." There is no one even to hear their stories.

In the meantime, many young parents are desperate for good-quality child care—for a setting in which children can be cared for and can learn and grow into the larger community in richer ways than they might at home. And therefore, in another building possibly quite near the nursing home, trained professionals are again hired, this time to find ways to keep children busy and maybe even teach them something. Once again the normal assumption is that there is nothing especially constructive for children to do either. Just play or, in the cheaper day care centers, watch TV.

Do you see any connection? Here are two serious social problems, both enormously costly and controversial, both major burdens on many families, sometimes at the same time. Yet we have not begun to ask if each might not be the answer to the other. Each has its hidden opportunities.

Why not bring the very young and the very old *together* in a setting in which they can help each other? The old can tell their stories to the very people who above all love stories. And the young can help tend to the needs of the old, learning something of life cycles and of service in the process. In every traditional society in the world the elders are the ones who initiate the young into the life and history and stories of the culture—and the young are not shielded from the fears and losses that the end of life brings. They help the old. What these two age groups could offer each other!

No doubt this idea, like all brainstorms or "what if's," needs work. We'd have to rethink some things. Probably we should. In any case, examples like these give you at least a glimpse of what might be possible. Even our *problems* have creative possibilities!

Don't Settle for Too Little

I have been teaching problem-shifting strategies for years, both in my ethics classes and in public talks. My experience has been that people almost immediately see the point, and even consider it a little obvious.

But what happens next is quite remarkable. I find that people consistently *settle for far too little* when given the opportunity to reframe real problems. Somehow these strategies are obvious only in theory. The minute an actual, practical problem shows up, habit kicks in and it's the same old thing: maybe we come up with a few new options, but basically we resign ourselves to "the" problem as defined for us in advance.

It's worth working through a detailed problem and some sample responses to recognize how little we usually settle for and how much more we might ask.

WASTE WATERS

Stand where Big Alamance Creek meets the Haw River, near the city of Burlington in North Carolina's central Piedmont, and you can watch the sooty waters of the creek swirl into the much cleaner waters of the Haw. The Haw is quickly overloaded with pollutants and nutrients as it flows into the middle of the state, into the drinking-water reservoirs for downstream cities, and then on to the sea and the saltwater marshes where shellfish once bred but now barely hang on.

All across America, the volume of wastewater is vast already and is increasing steadily. Municipal treatment plants are overwhelmed. Here, just upstream on the creek, is the last of Burlington's series of outdated sewage-treatment plants that work poorly even in the best of times and regularly spill raw sewage into the river when there is a hard rain or when the power goes out (the pumps fail).

Burlington is about to build a new sewage drain system. It will replace the old, leaky pipes and unreliable pump stations with a much bigger and gravity-operated system that does not rely on pumps. The pipes will be placed along the lowest points in the land so they can drain without the help of pumps.

Sounds good so far. But there is a rub. The lowest points in the land, naturally, are already occupied. To put sewage there means digging down the middle of about 20 miles of relatively pristine streams. At some points the pipe can be located stream-side, though even then usually within the 50-foot buffer zone that ecologists consider the minimum necessary to keep the stream banks from eroding. Mostly, though, it will have to be buried in the creek bed itself, since everywhere else is too rocky or otherwise unsuitable.

The effect will be to destroy the creek, and to create massive downstream pollution once again, this time soil and particulate matter from the construction. The economic costs will be enormous, and the designs aren't guaranteed to last very long (subjecting a pipe to stream flow, for one thing, dramatically reduces its life expectancy). State water-quality regulators are not wild about the stream damage but are inclined to approve the plan anyway, because Burlington's sewage system is a shambles and the area is growing rapidly. What else can they do?

SOME SAMPLE RESPONSES

Sometimes I describe this problem to my classes and assign it as a short overnight exercise for practicing problem-shifting skills. Some students take it and run. But a more common kind of response is an essay like the following (excerpts).

> For one thing, I think it is highly important that the public know what the new sewer will mean for the creeks. After hearing all the effects that the gravity system will have on the environment they may not want to continue the system.

There are also many alternatives to the gravity system. The city could just purchase a new pump altogether or use a more recent system that is a little more advanced. Research would have to be done on these types of systems, but it could turn out to be more profitable.

I don't think there are other ways to reframe the situation since so many limitations and restrictions have already been put upon it. Such as that the ground around the streams is unsuitable and the previous pumps have failed a good number of times. . . . I'm sure there is a good solution somewhere, but it will take a good deal of research to figure one out.

This is a nice response in many ways. It is clear, to the point, sensible, and well meant. Some ideas do come up, and a few directions for research are suggested. These are natural, commonsensical things to say.

But they also barely begin to reframe the problem. No "preventive" questions are raised, for example. I guess the problem would be prevented in some sense if the city bought new pumps (though the pipes would still be too small and leaky), but that is only to say that buying new pumps is one response to (part of) the problem as it stands. Genuinely preventive thinking would try to *change* the "problem as it stands."

The author proposes more public awareness. "After hearing all the effects that the gravity system will have on the environment, they may not want to continue the system." Maybe not. But what could they (we) do instead? They (we) may feel just as trapped as the state water-quality people, after all, who already know what the effects will be. The idea in reframing a problem is to offer a real alternative.

In fact, this writer even claims that there is no real alternative. "The" problem is already too limited and restricted, she says. Well, maybe. But we are trying to learn to take limited and restricted problems as invitations to creative thinking. Are there no other possibilities here?

Here is another sample response.

When studying a case like this you are going to hear only why each side of the argument is right, but the key to trying to resolve this problem is to find a way that both sides can compromise on. The issue should be brought back to a public forum to see if there is any other way to build a sewage system without so much damage to the land. I would bring in somebody who was not attached to the design of the original sewage system and see if they can find a way to build an effective system that would not damage the land. . . .

Again this response has something to recommend it. Once again, however, it also makes only the barest first step at reframing the problem. It too takes "the" problem to be just the problem given: how to build a system that doesn't damage the creek. Its very sensible suggestions about compromise and calling in experts still offer no specific ideas about what other kinds of solutions there might be. "See if there is any other way . . ."—well sure, but the assignment was to actually think of some other way!

EXPECT MORE

I think part of what's happening in such cases is that we don't trust ourselves to think of something new. Instead my students do what we are often encouraged to do in this age of authorities and mass politics: fall back on "the experts" or on the local equivalent of "60 Minutes." "If people only knew!" "Maybe the experts will think of something." We do not believe that we *ourselves* can "think of something."

But we can. The problem we're offered is two bad choices to get rid of Burlington's growing volume of sewage. To reframe the problem your very first move should be to ask a preventive or "big picture" question. *Why is there so much sewage in the first place?* Is sewage a "given," or could that itself be changed?

Of course there's something a little distasteful about sewage, so maybe we're not inclined to think much about it. But that's exactly the problem. The minute the question is raised, new possibilities come to mind.

Waste flows can be greatly reduced. For example, until recently most toilets used up to 7 or 8 gallons of fresh water per flush. New toilets use only about a gallon and a half, reducing water usage and sewage volume by more than 80 percent. Federal law now requires these toilets for all new or replacement installations. Maybe Burlington's money would be better spent subsidizing the replacement of its toilets, rather than building a massive new sewer system to accommodate the old ones?

A lot of wastewater can also be reused. So-called "grey water"—water used in showers, washing dishes and laundry—can be minimally filtered and then used to water gardens or the lawn, wash cars, or flush toilets. Right now grey water is the second biggest category of residential wastewater flow after toilet flushing. Reusing it might eliminate the waste almost completely, not to mention that using it to replace fresh water drawn for all these purposes would greatly reduce water demand as well.

There are still other options: neighborhood-scale treatment facilities, for example, that could produce water clean enough to release right into the creeks. No need for piping wastes long distances in special pipes to enormous treatment plants. Maybe our problem is that we think too *big*. . . .

Is the volume of sewage also in some way an opportunity? Sounds unlikely, doesn't it? Well, does sewage have any uses? Sure it does: fertilizer. Farmers in ancient China set up competing outhouses along the major public roads, each trying to tempt travelers into depositing their wastes. The farmers needed the fertilizer. The modern analogy is the "composting toilet": a toilet that uses no water at all and sends *no* wastes into the sewage systems, but turns it into compost that you can periodically shovel out and put on your garden. All perfectly sanitary and legal. Couldn't the city of Burlington do the same thing—even financing the system, maybe, by selling fertilizer? Imagine the advertising campaign!

So there are useful ways to reframe this problem. They are not even that hard to think of, especially if you do a little research. You just have to ask the right questions, and not settle for the habitual, small-change sorts of answers. Don't assume that "someone [else] will think of something." *You* do it!

Exercises and Notes

PRACTICE REFRAMING PROBLEMS

Consider again a list of practical problems around your school and area— you'll remember this list from the exercises in Chapter 11. There you practiced multiplying options. Now try to *reframe* these problems. What things need to be changed so that the present problem does not come up, or comes up in a more manageable way than it does now? Would changing the problem in some of these ways be preferable to leaving the problem as it stands and trying to solve it as such?

- Waste (styrofoam cups, lights left on all the time, newspaper, etc.)
- Alcoholism and other addictions
- Too much television
- Lack of affordable child care for working families with young children
- Lack of inexpensive travel options
- Alternatives to on-the-air fund raising for public radio
- Not enough parking at school or elsewhere
- Difficulties monitoring nuclear test-ban compliance
- Low voter turnout, especially for primaries

Preventive options in some of these cases might seem easy. We might try to prevent alcoholism, for example, by banning alcohol. But simple bans, in this and other cases, are unlikely to work, and they leave unaddressed the deeper drives that create the problems in the first place—as I tried to say in the text about drugs. Try to address those drives themselves.

We could prevent crowded roads by building more roads. But again, try to think more creatively. Look deeper. We can't keep building roads forever: they have massive social and economic costs, and they tend to create even more demand. Are there ways to reframe the whole problem? Maybe this: is there a way we could reduce the amount of required travel itself? For example, could we begin to locate work and shopping closer to home, so people need to drive less in the first place? *There's* a preventive strategy that is also creative, and offers a vision of a better life for all of us.

The need for reframing may seem obvious in theory, but it is not so easy to overcome our old "straight-ahead" habits in practice. If you are writing a response to one of the problems listed above, look it over when you're done, after reviewing the sample responses in this chapter's box, and be sure that you really have used your reframing tools. No vague language ("see if we can find a better way"), no appeals to experts ("they'll figure out something")—just specific, concrete, practical new ideas.

PRACTICE REFRAMING PROBLEMS IN ETHICS

Now pose the same kinds of questions about moral issues. Again the list from Chapter 11 might be useful:

- Capital punishment
- Gun control
- Assisted suicide
- Drug use
- Blowing the whistle on business or administrative corruption
- The treatment of gay people in the military
- Political campaign finance abuse
- Medical testing on animals
- Rain forest destruction.

Or again, pick your own. The key question remains: How can these problems be prevented from even arising? Can they be "solved" by being *changed*—or perhaps eliminated entirely? What would we have to do to achieve this?

Be sure that you really do use your reframing tools. Don't just talk about how you might use them—use them!

PRACTICE OPPORTUNISM

Now take the same issues once again—first the practical ones and then the moral ones—and try to shift them in another way: by asking in what ways each problem may be an opportunity. Opportunity *for what*? How can we see it in a more positive and constructive light? What would we have to do differently?

Again, don't settle for easy answers. Amost any problem is an opportunity to learn something ("don't get in this mess again!"), for example, but there may well be much richer possibilities too, as I have tried to show. Take some time to look for them. Brainstorm, random associate, and so on if you get stuck. See what happens. The results may surprise you!

NOTES AND FURTHER READINGS

For general background on reframing problems, see the works of Edward DeBono cited in Chapter 11. The idea of "problems as opportunities" is now widespread in a number of practical fields: for one example (to which I owe the example of the recalcitrant rock, and which also is a fine resource for reframing the problem outlined in this chapter's box), see Bill Mollison, *Permaculture* (Island Press, 1990). Also widely discussed is the idea of "proactive thinking": looking ahead to potential problems and working now to head them off—as opposed to "*reactive* thinking," which waits until they arrive as full-blown problems and then struggles to find some response. On proactive thinking, see Stephen Covey, *The Seven Habits of Highly Effective People* (Simon and Schuster, 1990), Habit 1. Notice that Covey subtitles his book *Restoring the Character Ethic*. Proactive thinking for him is a moral virtue!

Philosophers who want more argument for the importance of reframing problems might consult my book *Toward Better Problems* (Temple University Press, 1992), where it is mostly called "reconstructive thinking," using John Dewey's term. The classical source is Dewey's *Reconstruction in Philosophy* (Beacon Press, 1948). See also Caroline Whitbeck's article "Ethics as Design: Doing Justice to Moral Problems," *Hastings Center Report* 26 (1996): 9–16.

V

PUTTING ETHICS
INTO ACTION

CHAPTER 13

○

Picking the Right Tools

Congratulate yourself—you now have a pretty reasonable ethical toolbox. From an open mind through your ethical theories, from integrating values to shifting problems, from evaluating inferences to judging like cases alike, you're nearly ready to jump into the pressing moral questions of the day.

What you need now is some strategy. After all, having great tools by itself doesn't make a person a great surgeon or a great car mechanic or a great contributor to moral understanding either. You also need to know *which* tools to use *when*. At different times and for different purposes, you will need to use your ethical toolbox in different ways.

This chapter suggests some strategies. The aim is to help you plan your approach to whatever moral issues you take up. Don't jump in half ready. This last step isn't hard, but it certainly is essential.

KNOW WHAT YOUR GOALS ARE

If you don't know where you're going,
you're not likely to get there.

——Old saying

To decide which tools to use when, you need a clear sense of your *goals* in coming to the problem with the toolbox in the first place. Take the time to consider "where you are going." As you approach any moral issue, clarify your goals—your aims, your hopes—in coming to this issue at this time. *What are you trying to accomplish?*

Here are four possible goals, all quite different. There are others too, of course; these will at least help lay out some of the possibilities.

Goal 1: To Explore the Issue

One goal is: to explore the issue. And *just* to explore it.

Maybe some moral issue intrigues you, and you want to know more about it. Or you are taking a class in ethics, exploring along with others who share your curiosity and a commitment to learning together. Your goal, either way, is to satisfy your curiosity, learn more, broaden your sense of the world. You want to understand better; you want to learn. That's a worthy goal all by itself, and oftentimes hard enough.

Notice in this case that you are not looking for some kind of knock-down argument or final conclusion. You are not looking for a "position" on the question that you can take into debates with others. Indeed you are not really looking for debates with others at all. True, having debates is one way to explore some parts of an issue with others, but it is certainly not the only way. Better, usually, is a more open-ended kind of exploration in which you and your classmates look into all of the relevant values, factual arguments, and options without feeling that you have to be personally committed to one view or the other. Explore first, commit later—if you have to commit at all.

Goal 2: To Get Unstuck

Another possible goal is: getting yourself or helping to get a group or a community past some of the sticking points in the debate as it stands.

In particular, we are often "stuck" over options. We don't think we have many. As Chapter 11 points out, we tend to speak of moral "dilemmas," as if we expect moral problems always to take the shape of two opposed and fairly unsatisfactory options. Legal abortion or illegal abortion; gun control or no gun control—on issues such as these two polarized options dominate our thinking. Other issues are often similar.

You have the tools to make a real contribution to stuck debates such as these. Help get them *unstuck*. You can multiply options and reframe problems. You can also look to the contending values with an eye toward finding common ground or compatible values or at least acceptable compromises. You can pay careful attention to *all* the values at stake and help both sides acknowledge values that, in the midst of their polarized debate, they may have trouble even hearing.

Notice that in this case you are not arguing for or against a position either. You elect to serve instead as a kind of creative facilitator, trying to take account of all of the contending arguments and positions. This is a worthy role too. It is so rarely done well, or done at all, that it can be a first-rate contribution—sometimes the most vital contribution of all.

Goal 3: To Make a Case

Then again, you may want (or be required) to take one side in a moral debate and defend it. Sometimes making an argument will really be your goal. Maybe you will be taking part in a public debate on some moral topic and will be assigned or will choose one "side" to defend. Or perhaps you will be assigned an ethics paper to write in an argumentative style. You are asked to *make a case*.

Here you want to advance the kinds of values and factual arguments that will persuade others to join your cause. You want to give those values an eloquent voice; to trace a compelling and natural path from those values to the course of action you are defending; and to show that the concerns others have raised about it (that is, objections to your case) are not the serious drawbacks the objectors claim they are. Even so, of course, you don't want to overlook good points on the other side(s) or "win" by playing on others' emotions or misrepresenting the known facts. Public argument—making a case—is not a game for its own sake. It's in service of finding the best way, together. Tracing a path from compelling values to practical action can do just that.

Goal 4: To Decide for Yourself

Some moral problems confront us with a personal urgency. We have to do something: we must decide what we ourselves, at least, should do. Do you work honestly when others around you are getting ahead by cutting corners? Should you blow the whistle on those who are cutting corners? Use drugs? Have an abortion? Support a friend who has chosen abortion? Eat meat? Support the latest war?

Here your goal is not just to explore the issue, and it is not to make a constructive contribution to a larger debate (though that may also happen). It is to *decide a question:* to take a stand, to settle the question, for now at least, for yourself. And to do it right—carefully and with due consideration of all the relevant values and inferences and options.

For some people it seems that moral discussions are always about taking a stand. But I think it may be fairly rare that we actually *have* to take a stand. Often we may not know enough to take a meaningful stand; more exploration may be called for first (back to goal 1). Or the situation may call for some other response, some creative thinking for example (goal 2). So take a little care here: be sure that when you insist on taking a stand that you really have to do so, and are in a position to do so intelligently. It's hard enough to do it well when you have to!

MATCHING TOOLS TO GOALS

The following chart (p. 206) gives you a quick overview of how to match your ethical tools to the four goals just laid out. The numbers in parentheses refer to chapter numbers in this book. Study the chart before you read on.

Exploring an Issue

If your goal is to explore an issue, begin by being as clear as you can about what exactly the issue is about. Get specific. Maybe you want to think about poverty generally, in its many dimensions. On the other hand, maybe what you really want to consider is whether there should be governmental welfare programs. That is quite different! Likewise, don't just say "abortion" if what

GOALS	TOOLS		PITFALLS
	Main move	**Follow-up**	
TO EXPLORE AN ISSUE	Pay attention to values (3,4)	Pay attention to factual issues and terms (8,9)	*Don't stop too soon - i.e. expect diversity, look in depth (3)*
TO GET UNSTUCK	Multiply options, shift problems (11,12)	Pay attention to values (3) to open up new possibilities for integrating values (7)	*Don't slight the other sides - i.e. don't just be creative with **your** values*
TO MAKE A CASE	Make the key values explicit (3-5)	Defend/define key factual claims and terms (8,9) Consider key objections: -fr. other theories (6) -re. key inferences (8)	*Don't overlook better options (11,12)* *Be sure to judge like cases alike (10)*
TO DECIDE FOR YOURSELF	Prioritize or integrate the key values (6,7)	Seek new and creative options (11,12) Check facts and inferences (8)	*Don't close your mind (1) - maybe the question isn't settled for good*

you want to consider is only whether the government has the right to regulate abortion. A little precision at this point makes life a lot simpler later on.

Main Move

Your key move is to pay attention to the central moral values at play in your issue—and on all sides, not just those you happen to agree with (Chapter 3). Ask after each of our three families of values: goods, rights, and virtues (Chapter 4). Does (and where does) the social good come in, for instance—the greater good of the greater number? Consider what *are* the relevant "goods." Ask how wide a net is cast—ask for example whether the goods of all the affected people (perhaps even other creatures) are considered.

Likewise, are rights in conflict here? What (whose) rights? Is it a question of treating people as ends and not means? In what sense? What people? Ask too about character. Is "who we are" at issue in any way? How? Ask what virtues are called upon, or vices condemned. You may want to make a "map," as in Chapter 4, identifying values by family and sorting out their conflicts and the larger allied sets of values across families. Remember that the families are not necessarily equally represented (or sometimes represented at all) in every conflict.

You may move into later chapters in the values section (chapters 5–7) by asking how the conflicts between these values are currently addressed. Is there an effort at finding a "common measure" or at prioritizing values? Is there an effort at integrating the contending values?

Follow-up

Follow up by exploring what sorts of facts are crucial to this debate (Chapter 8). What factual issues are real points of contention? Are there areas where more research would be a good idea? Are there key but problematic inferences? Why do you think the debate is hung up over such points (if it is)?

Watch the language—the concepts—as well (Chapter 9). Does the debate turn on the appropriate use (or the unwitting use, perhaps) of certain concepts and terms: "human," for example, or "natural," or "person," or something else? Try to identify the different uses of the problematic concepts or terms.

Pitfalls

Finally, a word of warning. Don't just pick out the obvious contending values or key facts and then stop. As you know from Chapter 3, there is almost always a lot more going on than that! Sometimes what *isn't* discussed may be as crucial as what is. As Chapter 3 reminds you, expect diversity, and look in depth.

You may be asked to write up your results as a kind of "survey" of the issue, a sort of report of what the debate is really about. If so, remember again that you are not taking a position here. You're just trying to understand the issue and the debate over it. You are not required also to "solve" it—not required to weigh up the values or declare yourself or come up with new options or anything else. It may be enough for your purposes to simply have mapped and outlined and noted the main points of contention.

Again, this is the stage of *learning*. Don't go farther unless you need to— and until you have another, further goal clearly in mind.

Getting Unstuck

Your goal might be to help get a debate "unstuck." Here too there is a useful step before you take out your main tools. To get past a sticking point, you must first identify it. So don't slight your exploration of the issue in a rush to get your creative thinking tools into action. A good exploration can be the basis of everything else: it's what keeps you from focusing on some aspect of the problem that really isn't that important and overlooking some aspect that is. So: begin by carefully identifying some of the sticking points in the issue or debate as it stands. Be prepared to explain your choices.

Main Move

To help get the debate unstuck, your main move is to pull out your tools for creativity: for multiplying options and shifting problems (chapters 11, 12). Use all of them: "what if . . . ?" thinking, taking the problem as an opportunity, and all the rest. Don't rush! Remember that some of the set-breaking and free-association methods take some time. You may need to provoke your imagination from a few different directions.

Also: have fun. Even though this is ethics, after all, and ethics is supposed to be "serious." It is. But here you have a good excuse: breaking set *requires* playfulness. And the sense of freedom that comes with multiplying options can sometimes be exhilarating. Eventually it can be a powerful contribution in the most serious of ways. First, though, you have to open things up. Let down your guard a little.

Follow-up

Your chief follow-up is to look to the contending values with an eye toward *integrating* them (Chapter 7)— which again is a way of multiplying options and opening up the problem. Look for common ground or win/win solutions or at least acceptable compromises.

This too asks you to do something usually not expected in ethics. You are asked not to determine which side is right or wrong, but instead what each side is right about—and to look from there for compatible values and common ground. You may need to be explicit about this. All too often people expect that the only way to enter a public debate is to take a side and defend it. Even if you do have a side, though, your aim here is not to defend it so much as to offer all of us a more creative or clear-headed way through the problem as a whole. You may need to remind yourself and others that that is what you aim to do.

Anyway, even if your aims may be hard for some people to credit, your results should be appealing to everyone. Good new creative and integrative solutions are generally well appreciated all around. Sometimes it may be best to focus on results.

Pitfalls

Don't use your creativity in only one direction. I have seen students use the problem-solving tools very creatively to come up with original and imaginative ways of putting *their* values into action, but with nary a look toward anyone else's. To get a debate unstuck you need to take account of the other side(s) too. Again, using your integrative tools will help: from the start you want to look for ways to connect across viewpoints and contending values. Creative facilitation is your role here—and that means not just speaking from a single point of view.

Don't give up too soon, or settle for too little. As you begin, the problem may seem insoluble. You think: how could I possibly think of something new? But take heart, try. Remember that before we think of a new option, a problem will always seem unsolvable. No surprise if yours does. After you find one, the typical reaction is: why didn't anyone think of that before?

Don't be too cowed by the "experts," either, especially those who say that there is nothing to be done. For one thing, they probably got to be (recognized as) experts by being conventional—to the point that now they are very "set" indeed. Usually it's the outsider and the newcomer who can think more creatively. Besides, if you really begin to explore options you will quite likely discover that there are alternative "experts" too—people who are well versed in alternative ways of doing things. They aren't often featured as experts because the media are often rather on the conventional side too!

Small steps are fine. Don't expect to resolve the entire problem or try to unstick every sticking point. Just one constructive contribution would be quite something. Take one aspect of the problem and see if you can make some progress. That's enough—that's a *lot*—all by itself.

Making a Case

If your goal is to make a case, to argue a position, a preliminary step once again is clarity. Carefully lay out what your position actually is. Be specific and don't overstate. It's probably not enough to say "abortion" or "sexual freedom." If you wish to defend abortion, what you probably wish to defend in fact is keeping abortion legal under certain circumstances. Specify the circumstances. Will there still be limits, for example? What limits? Why? If you are opposed to abortion, also say what you're *for*.

Main Move

Now make your key values explicit (chapters 3–5). What are the most fundamental reasons supporting your position? If a specific proposal is involved, what is the basic need it meets or value it promotes? Be explicit about the underlying moral values, and back them up with explanations using the ethical theories we've examined when you can.

Don't underestimate the power of just *naming* the moral values you are calling upon. Too often we feel embarrassed publicly declaring ourselves for certain values, and so we leave them unspoken and "stick to the facts." This may be reasonable enough when the implicit values favor your side, though even then it is clearer to be more explicit. Often, though, the implicit values in public debates are more or less utilitarian, and the values that need to be spoken for belong to one of the other families. In this case you have to be explicit. Other things matter too: it's up to you to point them out.

Follow-up

Now lay out and defend the key factual claims your case needs to succeed. Cite the strongest sources you can; spell out your key inferences and your basis for them clearly; clarify and define any problematic terms (chapters 8, 9).

You also need to acknowledge and respond to the most important *objections* to your position or proposal. Any case worth making has a downside too.

After all, in making a case you join an ongoing debate, and there are other sides too: other moral values of concern, other beliefs about the facts, and so on. No complete case can be made that ignores such difficulties or dismisses the sorts of reasons people have for objecting to your proposal or favoring some other position.

So: where do the problems lie? What will the chief objections be? Outline them and respond. Check out and back up your most important factual claims if necessary. Again, analyze sources and inferences (chapters 8, 9). Acknowledge any conflicts of values the proposal may create. Can you draw on theoretical strategies—prioritizing values, or an appeal to a common measure—to resolve them (Chapter 6)? Can you use integrative strategies like seeking win/win solutions or finding common ground (Chapter 7)?

Pitfalls

Take care not to overlook better options. A good case must show that its position or proposal is the *best response* to the problem or need.

For example, suppose you want to defend the death penalty. Maybe you claim that it does indeed deter some murders. This is an arguable point, as we've seen, but even granting it, you have more to show. It's surely true that the death penalty is a better deterrent than doing nothing at all. But the question is whether it deters murders *better than alternative punishments*— for example, an automatic life sentence without parole. An alternative case could even go farther and propose required community service as a form of restitution, which might be just as effective a deterrent while also drawing better on some additional values, like respect for life (the state wouldn't be in the business of killing people; and restitution would allow even murderers a chance to redeem themselves). Is the death penalty better than *that*? Maybe, but it takes some showing.

Also, be sure you are judging like cases alike (Chapter 10). The stronger and clearer your position, the more directly it will invite comparison with other situations where your arguments might also apply. If you're pro-life on abortion, are you also pro-life on issues of militarism, welfare, environment? If not, why not? If you favor gay marriages, what other out-of-the-mainstream lifestyle choices would you also want the law to allow or affirm? There are no automatic and simple answers to these challenges—remember there are three quite different ways to respond to alleged inconsistencies—but the point once again is that they need to be considered.

Deciding for Yourself

If your goal is to decide for yourself, your preliminary step once again is to explore the issue, already discussed above. Don't prejudge the issue, though. The point of the exploration is to help you begin to decide, not to rationalize a decision you've already made. Don't concentrate on the values for just one side. Be clear and honest about *all* the values involved.

Main Move

You'll end your exploration with a good sense of the key values whose tensions make the question difficult. Your main move now is to ask whether you can find a way to prioritize or integrate these values in a way that points in a clear practical direction.

You have some theoretical tools for dealing with conflicts of values (Chapter 6). Maybe the values at stake are all of one type, so that a "single measure" can be used to weigh them against each other. Ask yourself then whether a utilitarian single measure will work. Or will you pick some other? Maybe the values at stake can be prioritized. Ask yourself which values take precedence. Which rights are the most basic, the strongest, the most relevant in this case? Which virtues matter most—are most essential to who you are and want to be? If values from several different families are involved, ask, can they be prioritized? Is one clearly more important than the others?

Or perhaps neither a common measure nor a complete prioritizing of values is possible in this case. Turn then to integrative strategies (Chapter 7). Is there a middle ground between the contending values? Look for ways in which they might be compatible. Can you find a balance between them, or some "center of gravity" for yourself?

A nurse, for example, may believe that she owes all of her patients the same high level of care. On the other hand, she may also fear for herself when regularly in contact with patients who have very dangerous diseases. So sometimes she is tempted to withhold the touch, to keep her distance. Yet that may feel as wrong as rushing headlong into the risk. How should she decide?

The tools she needs are the integrative ones. Maybe she can straight-forwardly split the difference, offering "dangerous" patients somewhat more contact than prudence alone would suggest, but less than she offers others less threatening to herself. Or maybe she can integrate her values more fully. Suppose that she comes to see herself as a caring person trying to respond to different needs, her own needs included, with appropriately different kinds of care. Thus some coherence within her values emerges, in this particular case and also more broadly. She has found a liveable way of going on.

Follow-up

Now look back to your creativity skills again, your "what if . . . ?" thinking and other ways of multiplying options and shifting problems (chapters 11, 12). See if you can find unexpected or imaginative ways around or through the problem. Ask around: get other people's advice. You can always ignore their advice if you wish, but you may also learn something, or get a new perspective on the whole question. People you know have probably been in similar circumstances: what did they choose? how did it work out? Are there other people whose advice has always been helpful, minister or rabbi, parent, friend? Just explaining the problem to someone else—actually doing it, working it all out as you go, not just imagining what you'd say—can often clarify it far more than many hours thinking alone. (In other words, it's not just what *they* say that may help you, it's also what *you* say!)

Don't forget your critical thinking skills either: you may need to check key facts and inferences (Chapter 8). Make sure that your information is the best it can be!

Pitfalls

Finally, look out for closing your mind (Chapter 1). Even if you must decide a question right away, remember to leave some space for more learning later, maybe even for a different choice next time.

Our nurse, for example, might assign herself the special task of finding out more about just how dangerous her allegedly dangerous patients really are. Fear of catching AIDS, for example, panicked some health-care workers for a time in the 1980s, but it soon became clear that the actual risks of transmission to doctors and nurses are very low. Part of a good decision in a hard case like hers is precisely to keep on thinking about this very sort of case. Her decision, and yours, may still change down the line.

And, of course, good luck!

❧

WRITING AN ETHICS PAPER

College courses in ethics often require writing a term paper as part of the work of the course. If your course requires such a paper, then you come to the toolbox with an additional goal in mind: to write a good one!

GETTING STARTED

The first rule in writing any academic paper is: *understand the assignment*. You need to consider what kind of audience you should address and what topic or range of topics should be covered.

You will almost always write more clearly and consistently if you keep in mind a vivid picture of a person or kind of person for whom you are writing. Besides it's much easier to imagine yourself talking to your roommate or maybe even your senator than addressing an abstract void. So pick someone to write *to*. It may even be an actual person who will in fact read your paper.

In one sense, obviously, you are writing for your teacher or professor. That is the bottom line. But your instructor is usually not the best audience to keep in mind as you write. What you need to say in your paper is not necessarily what you would say to your teacher person to person. For example, teachers generally expect that student papers will competently review the subject matter, but the subject is seldom news to the professor. Imagine writing to someone who could really use the explanation. I tell my students to imagine writing for a friend or roommate who is not in the class but who is, like them, intelligent and interested. In fact, when you have a presentable paper, show it to that friend or roommate—see how well you're doing.

If the appropriate audience is not clear, ask!

SETTING YOUR GOALS

Just as in any other use of your toolbox, setting specific goals for your paper is essential.

Sometimes your goals will be assigned. Many philosophy professors expect their students to *make a case* for some moral conclusion, or at least to analyze some aspect of an applied moral argument or a debate between two theories. Here your critical thinking or theoretical skills come to the fore. Other professors may ask you to *explore a problem* without necessarily taking a position or analyzing arguments. If your paper's goals are assigned, be sure you know exactly what they are. If they're not clear, ask!

Or maybe you get to choose your own goals. Remember then that this chapter offers you four ways of organizing your paper, corresponding to four different goals you may bring to it. You may explore the problem, or try to make a practical suggestion to help get the debate unstuck, or argue a case, or decide for yourself. There may be others besides. Each goal has its attractions.

Here, in short, the clarity about goals must come from *you*. Don't get going until you know, at least roughly, where you want to go. Then look back to this chapter, and through it to the toolbox as a whole, or organize your paper and begin to gather your ideas. You may also need to be very clear about your goals in the paper itself.

QUESTIONS OF STYLE

Style may vary too. Many college professors, especially philosophers, expect a kind of argumentative impersonal writing as a matter of course—but many others don't. Don't assume that an argumentative style is your only option. Look at some of the readings in this book for other kinds of examples: at Edward Abbey's ironic and irascible approach to wilderness in Chapter 3, for one; Roger Rosenblatt's attempt to mediate the abortion debate in Chapter 7; Colin McGinn's wild analogies in Chapter 10; and—to come—

the essays by Jason Schultz (Chapter 16) and Rayna Rapp (Chapter 17), which are personal narratives with general ethical reflections; and the interview with Violet Woodsorrel Oxalis in Chapter 21.

There are many other styles of writing in ethics too: sermons, parables, letters to the editor, even plays and short stories. Try a new one occasionally! Once again, if you are unsure about what would be appropriate, check in advance with your instructor.

SET A CONSTRUCTIVE TONE

Whatever kind of paper you write, be sure that your writing sets a constructive tone. Avoid polarizing values and dismissing other positions or values other than those you most wish to promote. Convey an open mind through your writing, and a willingness to reframe problems and find common ground. In short, make your paper itself *ethical*—not just a paper *about* ethics.

Consider this (very short) sample paper on the subject of ethics and the elderly.

> I have heard that half of all the Medicare money spent in America goes to provide medical care for people in the very last stages of life, in the last two months of life.
>
> This is a crying shame when so many other people have medical needs that are not being met: people who could get a heart transplant or bypass surgery, let's say, and live long and productive lives. The tough fact is that we do die eventually, and trying to fight it off for the last few months just isn't worth it to society.
>
> I don't really see any options. Maybe there could be a cap or ceiling put on how much surgery and other medical care is done for the really old, per year or per hospital or something. But then they would have to recognize that there are other people with needs too, and we have to make the hard choice to put our money where it will do the most good—like the unitarians say.
>
> Imagine a three year old child who needs a kidney transplant to live. But there is no kidney available because the last one just went to a 90-year-old patient who is barely able to get around on her own and is already a little senile. The 90-year-old may have Medicare to pay for the surgery, or may have good medical insurance. The 3-year-old's family may not have the money to pay for medical care, and the organ may not be available anyway. I don't think this is right. We have to recognize that some lives are more valuable than others. When you've lived a long and full life, then it's just time to go.
>
> People do die eventually. We need to get used to that fact and stop acting like we can put it off forever. My uncle died on a respirator after his cancers made him unable to talk or do anything, even stay awake. But he wanted everything possible to be done. Meanwhile, who knows what

other person could have benefitted from all that medical attention? I don't see much else that can be done, besides just saying that we can't all live forever!

This essay has some strengths. It's direct, no beating around the bush. It's clear on the one basic value or ethical theory it appeals to (utilitarianism, though it gets the spelling wrong: "Unitarians" are a religious denomination). It's concrete: it gives examples, and the examples are on the point.

But—a very big "but"–this is a poor use of the toolbox.

Only one kind of value is considered. Surely there are other sides too. We know from the presence of a moral controversy in the first place that there are a number of values in tension. Where are the rest of them?

The tone is dismissive. "It's just time to go" isn't exactly a considerate piece of advice. And the essay overstates. Do we really act as though "we can put [death] off forever"? How many 90-year-olds get major transplants? This essay is also careless at unfortunate points: misspelling "utilitarianism," for example, and using data without support, for example in the opening sentence (because the writer has *heard* this claim, is it true?). You can do better!

Consider a second sample answer.

It's hard writing about old people. Everyone in this class is young—it is hard to imagine how life will feel at the other end. We see old people as rigid, stuffy, stuck at home, and a little bit funny—not anything like ourselves, of course! They also remind us of death, which we'd rather not think about. . . .

Different and even conflicting values are involved. The whole society sees the old as a little bit funny (the doddery old "gramps" character), also as pretty stuck in their ways. We want to be free of them. On the other hand, the old are our parents and grandparents, our teachers and their teachers, etc. We respect them because they are the ones who gave us life and everything else that we have.

No one should end their life abandoned and alone, left to the care of strangers and professionals and possibly abuse too. These are real people, just like us—and we will *be* them, someday—and they have done their part. Yes, the younger generations need their chance and their freedom too, but we ought to ask how we can meet our needs without short-changing the needs of others!

Are there creative options? I think so. For example, part of the problem of abandonment, the loneliness of the old, is that old people's homes are cut off from the rest of their communities. There is no need for this! Old people's homes could be at the center of community life: they are the ones who have time to spend with the young ones, like you said. They can start the seedlings for gardens, they can teach what they know. Rather than pushing them aside, society needs to brainstorm how the old can remain a vital part of life.

Really old people can still be creative and active. One of my best dance teachers is in her 80s and more limber than most of the class. The architect Frank Lloyd Wright designed some of his best buildings in his 90s. It's only when people lose their community, their friends, contact, and stimulation that they grow stale and stuffy. Sure, brains age too, but I think a lot of senility is a *social* problem. If they can stay more active, they will also stay more alert and involved.

This is a fine essay for its length. It clearly surveys the whole problem: from why we are often inattentive or closed-minded on this subject, through the variety of values involved, to some creative options. About each aspect it carries us a few steps beyond where the debate is stuck at present. The only improvement I would suggest is more development of these main points— something that would come in a longer version.

You get the idea. The tools in your toolbox can transform your paper—but, of course, you have to *use* them!

Exercises and Notes

PRACTICE, PRACTICE, PRACTICE

Each of the four ways into the toolbox outlined in this chapter can and should be practiced.

Practice taking real issues and helping the contending sides get unstuck, for example. Go to a City Council or Planning Commission or school board meeting. Pay attention to the moral concerns that come up, and how they are handled. What kinds of contributions could help? What can *you* do? Or watch for public comment meetings on local, state, or national policy matters. Usually there will be notices in the papers. Some of these will be local meetings; some will have Web sites; some will involve national "Town Meetings." Go to the meetings or visit the Web sites. Ask the same questions. What kinds of contributions actually help? Which do not? Why? What can *you* do?

In the newspaper, compare a variety of editorials and Letters to the Editor. What are their apparent goals? What are some ways that they succeed—and fail? Do they make effective cases? What kind of letter or editorial might you choose to write on similar topics? Why don't you write it?

Look around for people who have made constructive contributions. How did they do this? My college has a program each year in which students nominate people they know as "Hometown Heroes," people who have made real contributions to their communities. Winners are invited to campus to speak to classes. Whom would you nominate for such an honor? What kind of contribution did they make? What can you learn from them? What kind of hero do you think you could be?

Exploring Moral Decisions

Interview your parents, friends, and elders about specific moral decisions they've made. How did they arrive at their decision? How did it work out? Would they do it again differently? Why or why not?

Some of my classes have made a class project out of such interviews. Each student interviewed someone, wrote up the results (leaving the interviewee anonymous whenever requested), and reported back to the class. We heard some fascinating stories!

Consult biographies and autobiographies with the same questions in mind. Pick people you admire (and some you don't) or find intriguing: find some good books by them or about their lives. Consider the decisions they made, how they made those decisions, their reasons, and the results. Find some people whose moral choices puzzle you and do the same thing—try to figure them out.

Think about your *own* past decisions too. Ask the same questions.

Notes and Further Readings

For several related ways of organizing a moral toolbox, see Ronald McLaren, *Solving Moral Problems: A Strategy for Practical Inquiry* (Mayfield Publishing Company, 1989) and Marvin Brown, *The Ethical Process: An Approach to Controversial Issues* (Prentice-Hall, 1999).

A useful and inspiring book on our potential contributions as citizens is Frances Moore Lappé and Paul Martin Dubois, *The Quickening of America: Rebuilding Our Nation, Remaking Our Lives* (Jossey-Bass, 1994). On persuasively entering the realm of public argument, see Annette Rottenberg, *Elements of Argument: A Text and Reader* (Bedford Press [St. Martin's], 1997) and Timothy Crusins and Carolyn Channell, *The Aims of Argument: A Rhetoric and Reader* (Mayfield, 1998)—two textbooks and anthologies cited also in Chapter 8— and Chaim Perelman's study *The Realm of Rhetoric* (University of Notre Dame Press, 1982).

○

CHAPTER 14

Dialogue: Learning by Talking

One chief way that we put the ethical toolbox into action is by *talking*—in dialogue with others: to persuade, to negotiate, to learn. But we can talk more or less effectively. Usually we can do a lot better. As we turn toward contemporary moral issues in the chapters that follow, we need to pay some careful attention to dialogue itself.

Dialogue is also an occasion, remember, to put ethics itself into action. Effective dialogue reflects an ethical relationship: it reflects ethical attitudes toward others and a commitment to shared solutions. In the view of this book, at least, ethics is not only or even mainly about holding the "right" opinions about controversial issues. Much more important is how we *engage* such issues. Ethics lives just as much in the ongoing process.

HOW TO HAVE A FRUITLESS DEBATE

A meets B in the cafeteria line, one thing leads to another, and a familiar kind of verbal fistfight begins . . .

A: Eating meat is natural! Humans have always done it. I wish all you vegetarians would get off my back. You want to go against nature.

B: Oh right, I suppose people have always lined up at McDonald's for their quarter-pounder with shake and fries.

A: Well, what do you want, to line up at some juice bar for your little organic carrot with spring water? Give me a break! Besides, you animal rights fanatics want to stop all medical research. What about the cures for so many diseases, found through experiments on animals? If it weren't for those experiments, you wouldn't even be here to bad-mouth them.

B: Why do we need all those new cosmetics and toilet bowl cleaners? That's what 99 percent of animal testing is about! You're just rationalizing torture.

A: I bet you don't even like pets. You're telling me I don't love my dog?

B: You think that your dog wants to live stuck in some tiny little apartment all day? You call it "love" when you pen up a dog? Talk about unnatural!!

And so it goes—a fruitless debate. This one is only slightly exaggerated from the kinds of real-life debates we have all the time. Each side aims primarily to shut the other side up, or to put the other side down. Potentially helpful points come up, but they are immediately dropped like hot potatoes. The actual arguments don't connect.

If put-downs and "winning" are your goals, you may deliberately try to create such debates. We could even spell out some of the "rules" both sides seem to be following. One is:

- **Take All the Room You Can.** Talk *loud* and talk a lot. Fill all the space you can with *your* thoughts and opinions. Worry about your *comeback*. Restate your opinion; Use a lot of "I think that . . ." statements. After the other person is done, come right back with "Yeah, but. . . ."

Neither person really listens or tries to understand what the other person is saying. Both are angry; they have a lot to say on the subject; they cannot wait to jump back in with some new peeve or assertion. If one side raises a good point, the other one would not think of acknowledging it or trying to respond. Neither is willing to give an inch. Apparently the best defense instead is just to change the subject. Having a comeback is everything.

Second:

- **Separate and Polarize.** *Polarize:* that is, exaggerate differences. Emphasize what you and the other side disagree about. Define the other person's view as simply the opposite of yours. Always *assume the worst. Stereotype* the other side ("You're just a . . ."). Use *black/white labels* ("pro-life," "pro-death"). Try to define your opponents before they can define themselves. Make your stereotyped labels stick.

Either all medical research or none; either a quarter-pounder or carrot sticks for lunch. No space for possible agreement is explored, no shared values are acknowledged or sought. Polarizing in this way reinforces the put-downs generally: the other side is made to look silly and stupid by constant exaggeration, as if they could not be in favor of anything sensible or balanced. Again there is no attempt to understand what the other person might actually mean. Instead the worst is assumed, and then attacked and mocked.

Finally, two related further "rules":

- **Exploit all Weaknesses or Openings.** Take *potshots.* Follow "red herrings." Pounce on any small discrepancies or other difficulties; don't engage the main point. *Run down partial solutions.* If an idea is not a perfect solution, attack it as no solution at all. Protect yourself by avoiding constructive thinking or making suggestions. Always be *against* something than *for* something.

- **Go for the Quick Kill.** Talk in *slogans and sound bites.* You'll infuriate the other side and everyone will remember your brilliant pithiness. Use facts only as *weapons.* Only seek out the ones that support your side; deny and suppress any others. *Disengage quickly* once you have secured an advantage. Demand closure; expect "final" answers; pull out as soon as you can claim you're "right."

Slogans and labels abound (like "you animal rights fanatics") and all sorts of assumptions are made with no thought of checking them out to see whether they're true or not. Does B really know that A's dog is penned up all day? Does A really know what B thinks about medical research? No—each just makes an assumption and blasts away.

The whole debate is a series of potshots and changes of subject. Often the comeback is on a subject different from the one just being discussed. They start out talking about meat eating; then about medical research; then about pets. A's opening claim is mostly about whether eating meat is natural. B responds in a sarcastic way, though B does have an argument of sorts. Not surprisingly, A in turn responds chiefly to the sarcasm, derides what A *assumes* to be B's alternative, and then changes the subject to medical research.

What's Wrong with That?

Debators know these rules and use them often. For some purposes they may even be useful. For other purposes it is at least useful to know about them: they may help you fight back, or avoid getting caught in such a debate in the first place.

But these rules do *not* work well when we are trying to think constructively about a problem. For one thing, they are ineffective, at least at persuasion. They don't really persuade, they only dominate and silence. The "loser" in such debates goes away angry, frustrated, maybe self-blaming; certainly not feeling understood.

Second, they don't expand or develop ideas. They give us no way of cooperatively improving an idea. Quite the contrary: since the whole aim is to gain some personal advantage from criticizing any weakness in the other side's ideas, putting forward any kind of proposal is the last thing these rules encourage. Tentativeness, hope, enough trust to take up a rough idea and brainstorm together: this is just what these rules *prevent.*

In short, debate in this key drives people apart; it does not promote understanding; and at bottom *it is not ethical itself!* It is not committed to listening, open-mindedness, cooperation, careful and responsible attention to values or arguments or concepts. It does not show respect, honor fairness, seek the common good, or bring people together in constructive ways. Yet this is what ethics asks of us. How can we debate about ethical issues in a way that itself is so flagrantly unethical? We need to find another way.

HOW TO HAVE A USEFUL DISCUSSION

Toward a Different Kind of Dialogue

Now imagine a dialogue on the same subject in exactly the opposite key: careful listening, respect for the other side, the desire to learn something and perhaps even to change one's opinion as a result. Not mere acceptance ("Well, whatever . . ."), which leads to no dialogue and no learning at all. No: a real discussion, even disagreement, but in a constructive key. What would the discussion look like then?

A meets B in the cafeteria line, and the debate begins again.

A: Eating meat is natural! Humans have always done it. I wish all you vegetarians would get off my back. You want to go against nature.

In the very first place, a good listener would notice the defensiveness in this statement. "I wish all you vegetarians would get off my back." This is a clue that more is at stake for A than just a disagreement about the facts. You might guess that A has felt put on the spot, or put down, for eating meat. You could easily predict, too, that A will therefore find it hard to hear and acknowledge even the best arguments against meat eating. So although B's first impulse might be to mock A's argument and put A down even more cleverly, this is exactly the wrong strategy. Better to deal with the anger before taking up any arguments at all.

B: So someone's been on your case, eh? Sorry about that. For my part, I'm really not interested in playing guilt games, though I know it happens with subjects like this . . .

B's response in the original dialogue did raise an important point. But B should raise this point in a way that is clearer and (obviously) not sarcastic. In the original, remember, A said that eating meat is natural, that humans have always done it. B responded

B: Oh right, I suppose people have always lined up at McDonald's for their quarter-pounder with shake and fries.

B may have been thinking that humans may *not* always have eaten meat, at least in the way we do now. Generalizations about what has "always happened" are often made in a pretty offhand way, more as a rationalization than anything else. Is this what B suspects? If so, B could make the point a lot more effectively: by asking a question, for example. Suppose B said instead:

   B: I'm not so sure that people have always eaten meat. We're not built for it, biologically: our teeth are the munching sort, not the tearing teeth of real carnivores. At least, I doubt that humans ate so *much* meat as we do now. What kind of diet do you think humans evolved with?

Now consider the next exchange. In the original, A mocked B's point in turn, and then went on to something else. Remember:

   A: Well, what do you want, to line up at some juice bar for your little organic carrot with spring water? Give me a break! Besides, you animal rights fanatics want to stop all medical research. What about the cures for so many diseases, found through experiments on animals? If it weren't for those experiments, you wouldn't even be here to bad-mouth them.

My students, analyzing this exchange, point out: (1) it would be more useful for A to ask B what kind of diet B actually proposes, rather than respond to the sarcasm with more of the same; (2) A should stay on the subject (the naturalness of meat eating) rather than shift to something else; and (3) A should *ask* B what B thinks about medical research rather than assuming B's against all of it. Suppose A said:

   A: I'm pretty sure our ancestors ate meat when they could get it, though you might be right that it wasn't very often. But I'm interested in what you propose instead. Eating no meat at all, ever? What about people who need to eat meat to survive in their environments, like the Eskimo? This also makes me think of the debate about using animals in medical research. Are you also opposed to that? Always?

These are good questions, and once again have the effect of opening up a thoughtful discussion rather than closing the talk down into "comebacks." Notice also that A no longer assumes that B must hold the most extreme possible position. Instead, A *asks* B what B thinks—and raises the question of just how far B will go.

   B in turn can respond in a more constructive way.

   B: Probably many people did eat meat when they could get it. And yes, maybe some people have to. But *we* don't have to. My real point is that it's not exactly natural to eat meat like we eat meat, anyway. Not meat at every meal, and the fattiest meat at that!

A has helped B to get to the *real* point—now we are getting somewhere!

Notice that in B's original response, B never answered the question about medical research: B talked only about product testing.

B: Why do we need all those new cosmetics and toilet bowl cleaners? That's what 99 percent of animal testing is about! You're just rationalizing torture.

B might now be able to answer that part of A's question more thoughtfully too:

B: I'm troubled by how much pain animals are put through for even the most minimal human gain. What right do we have to do that to animals even if there *is* a gain for us? This relates to the question of product testing too. If some new kind of shampoo or cosmetic or cleaner can only be brought out if it is tested on animals, then maybe it just shouldn't be brought out. We shouldn't be causing so much suffering when we don't have to.

This last discussion is in place of B's passing remark in the original debate about "torture." No longer is it merely a passing remark. Now it opens up new aspects of the issue to explore.

Notice how shared values begin to come into view. For example, A is unlikely to think that unnecessary suffering is morally acceptable. A does not want to be responsible for imposing needless suffering on animals. This is why many people have stopped eating veal, even though they may eat other animals and use animal products. A would probably argue that in other cases the suffering isn't needless—that in some way it is necessary—or that the animals don't really suffer so much. In any case, this is now a constructive discussion, and it is beginning to sound like "ethics" in a more familiar sense: trying to spell out and apply shared values. It's a mutual exploration, no longer a fight.

Rules for Constructive Talking

Ethics *could* be like this. No part of the discussion in the last few pages, I trust, has been a new revelation. All of the skills, and the possibilities they open up, are familiar. We just need to learn how to put them into practice at the right times.

The beginning of this chapter spelled out "rules" for fruitless debates. We can now spell out four corresponding rules for constructive talking.

- **Slow Down and Listen.** Speak *calmly* and listen a lot. *Avoid the automatic comeback.* If you find yourself too ready with the "Yeah, but . . . ," stop and take a deep breath. Then say, "Let me see if I understand you. . . ." Watch the surprise (and appreciation). And work for better *understanding*. Ask questions, and mean them. Restate others' views to make sure you "get it"—later you can ask for the same consideration back. Expect that you have as much to learn as the other side does.

In the revised dialogue, instead of taking all the room they can, A and B show some interest in each other's views, and take the time to understand each other. They put their points carefully, admit uncertainty, and identify conflict without escalating it.

- **Connect.** Seek *common ground*. Approach differences against a background of probable agreement. (Differences may emerge as interesting against this background. They certainly emerge as *solvable*.) Recognize *complexity* on the other side (and yours). Don't polarize. There are no simple "yes" and "no" positions. Keep the focus on the *main points*. You might even help other people clarify and develop their thoughts and avoid distraction.

In the revised version, A and B are not preoccupied with their differences, but explore them carefully while also identifying key points of agreement. They try to "integrate values," recognizing that each side speaks for something important. It's up to us to figure out what it is.

Finally, two more related rules:

- **Welcome Openings and Opportunities.** Look for *first steps* and *partial measures*. No problem is going to be easily resolved all at once. Think constructively; make suggestions. Always be *for* something and not just *against* something.

- **Stay Engaged.** Think of discussion as a collaboration in search of better understanding and creative ideas. Try to speak in a careful, open-ended, and helpful way. Avoid slogans or soundbites. Treat facts as *tools*. They're probably also more ambiguous than either side makes it seem. Keep exploring. Expect the key questions to remain *open*. There is always more learning to do; the discussion will continue.

Instead of taking potshots and seeking to disengage the moment they have an advantage, A and B now take a much more exploratory approach, and don't imagine that they are going to settle things once and for all. And thus, oddly enough, they actually get much farther than the debaters for whom finding a final and "right" position, right now, is everything. Debaters lock themselves into their positions and then cannot budge. Collaborators, interested in a constructive discussion and making at least *some* difference, can *move*.

And notice finally, as I have been insisting throughout, that these are *moral* rules too. Unlike the first set of rules, these rules reflect a commitment to listening, open-mindedness, cooperation, careful and responsible attention to values or arguments or concepts. They show respect, honor fairness, seek the common good, and bring people together in constructive ways. They offer a way to talk about moral issues that is itself moral.

∞

WHEN DIALOGUE FAILS

Dialogue sounds wonderful in theory. But what if you are talking with some-one who is not interested in dialogue? Or someone who does not know how to have one, or does not trust you or the situation enough to listen or believe he or she will be listened to?

DON'T GIVE UP TOO SOON

Sometimess ethical discussions reduce to fruitless debates because some of the participants have no idea that there is any other way to talk, or, even if they do, don't trust anyone else to try it.

In that case, clearly, the thing to do is to try it. Create an alternative. Set alternative ground rules for discussion (such as the "Common Ground Rules" in the reading in this chapter). Anyone who thinks that debate is the only way to have an ethical discussion will be pleasantly surprised—and so will you, when people who appeared to be interested only in debate turn out to prefer something else, once given a choice. The point is that *you* may have to be the one who creates that choice—*you* may have to set the alternative ground rules, formally or explicitly or gently by example. You do not simply have to accept whatever kind of discussion you find yourself stuck in.

Even habitual complainers can be lured onto more constructive ground. To the people whose main mode of discussion seems to be criticism and complaining, ask: "So, what's *your* idea?" Show some interest. Make positive suggestions safer. Create a setting in which creativity and openness are rewarded and carping is not.

RESISTERS

Some people just *love* to argue, so much so that they do not even notice, and certainly do not respond to, invitations to dialogue. They automatically turn any discussion into a debate.

You can leave this kind of discussion. You are not obliged to keep trying dialogue forever. Usually you can pull out in a way that isn't "losing," but just refusing to play the game.

You might also challenge the debate rules. Point out what is happening, and ask your partner or the group if this is really how they want to proceed. This is uncomfortable, of course, and not subtle at all. But it may sometimes work. At least it keeps people from falling into debate as if it were the only possible way to discuss things.

Some people enter dialogue in bad faith. People may use dialogue as a means of stalling. The idea might be to talk an issue to death so that nothing really changes—an appealing option for those who like things the way they are. So you need to be sure that all parties to the dialogue enter it with some good faith. If they don't, you are again entitled to pull out.

Or stay but refuse to play along. You might still make some progress. Stallers may find it hard to keep polarizing values and grandstanding when you are speaking carefully and in general refusing to play "debate." Try it once or twice: it can be rather fun. If you have low expectations at least you won't be disappointed.

Some people may join a dialogue (or may have to, for example in a classroom) but be unwilling to speak honestly and openly in it. I have seen students in discussions of homophobia or racism or other kinds of prejudice unwilling to express views they actually hold, especially if they are afraid of seeming even the least bit prejudiced. But then many useful questions never get asked, stereotypes never get addressed, and some people leave feeling oppressed by a general atmosphere of "correctness."

This is a way of resisting dialogue too, though often well intentioned. Some indirection might help. *You* name the stereotypes, so at least they're out on the table. Find a story or movie whose characters bring them up, so the class or group can discuss them in the third person. Encourage others to bring up views in the third person too, as in: "Someone might say that . . . ." or "It's not my view, but. . . ."

SILENCING

Some people go into dialogue easily and feel welcomed and rewarded. Others go into the same space disadvantaged and with well-established habits of deference and silence. The results are very uneven patterns of participation and influence.

Usually the advantaged ones are blissfully unaware of this imbalance—it's just "the way things are," to them—and if it is brought up by the disadvantaged (who are generally well aware of it) the reaction typically is denial and anger. So, naturally, it is seldom brought up. Things just go on as before.

Still, dialogue fails when only some members of a group do all the talking: only men in gender-mixed groups; only whites in racially mixed groups; only teachers when teachers and students are together. Phyllis Beck Kritek, a nurse-administrator experienced at "negotiating at an uneven table," gives another example.

> I once served on a statewide committee looking at maldistribution of health care services. . . . There were several Native American reservations in this state. Health care needs on these reservations were profound. Historically, these needs had been easily rendered invisible. . . . An honest effort was made to change this pattern, to invite representatives from the tribal councils to the table. They attended the first organizational meeting.

The tribal councils, of course, had a well-developed model for deliberating on conflicts: requesting all parties to speak their minds on the issue one by one and uninterrupted, in a deliberative fashion; consulting the elders; seeking guidance from spirits . . . ; reflection. The approach to conflict offered by the statewide committee was open discussion and political posturing, a tug of war between competing agendas. The tribal representatives sat silently watching, saying nothing. Later one participant commented to me privately that the American Indians were sure not going to get their fair share if they didn't participate better. No one asked them to speak their mind during this time. They would only have had the opportunity to speak if they had chosen to participate in the competition for airtime. At the second meeting, they were absent. . . .

IF YOU FEEL SILENCED

When you find yourself silenced or disadvantaged, here are some suggestions.

For one thing, again, don't assume that you must play the game by the prevailing rules. Maybe the prevailing rules are the *problem*. You might try to bring up this problem directly, or you might try to subvert the rules in a less direct way. For example, if the advantage of others is sustained partly by a distinctive language or jargon, request translations. Use your own language sometimes and translate for others. As Kritek says, this at least " highlights the inequity structured into the negotiation that requires you to sit at an uneven table speaking someone else's language." Things get more complicated—as they should.

Democratic talk needn't be the kind of "free-for-all" that Kritek describes. There are many other traditions and styles of dialogue. Native Americans often used a "talking stick," giving the holder an uninterrupted "floor," passed around to everyone in turn so that each voice could be heard and each voice had its "space." Try it. At least, if debate is not a style that you can even enter, ask for a different kind of hearing from your group. If they care to hear you out, they will agree (or at least discuss it). If they don't, then at least you know where you stand—and they will have to admit where *they* stand.

Classrooom settings can be changed too. Talk to your instructor; find a way to raise the issue for the class. In a class that uses this book, refer to this chapter.

WHEN YOU ARE ADVANTAGED

Suppose you are one of the advantaged. Your job first of all is simply to recognize the problem. Advantage is usually invisible to the advantaged because the space of dialogue does not seem constrained to *them*. It is easy to enter when you know you will be listened to and taken seriously. It is hard to imagine that others could feel any differently. "Well, why don't they just *talk?*"

But of course it is not so simple from the other side. It may help to remember those times when *you* felt intimidated from saying anything, or when you felt that no one would really listen or care anyway. Recognize now that others may be feeling the same way in a discussion that feels entirely open and natural to you.

Second, raise the problem with your group as a whole. Point out the unequal pattern of participation. State as directly and honestly as you can *your* interest in hearing from those who have been silent. Ask on behalf of the group (step up to leadership here) in what ways the group can change so as to lessen the barriers to participation that others may be feeling. Maybe you need a talking stick? Maybe . . . ?

Once again, the challenge may be to *you* to move yourself—and to move *first*. You may have to disrupt and challenge familiar and comfortable ways (to you, anyway) and make things more difficult. There may even be dialogues that you conclude aren't possible right now. Trust must first be built in other ways, maybe; of perhaps some other kind of institutional or personal change is necessary. Things don't get easier! But they might, slowly, get better.

The Common Ground Network for Life and Choice, "Common Ground Rules"

Here is a seemingly impossible example of dialogue in practice. The Common Ground Network for Life and Choice was formed in 1994 to bring together activists from the opposing sides in the abortion conflict in the hopes of creating real dialogue, understanding each other better, and finding common ground that the two sides could build upon together rather than frustrating each other's every move.

The reading that follows comes from the group's manual, *Finding Common Ground in the Abortion Conflict,* by Mary Jacksteit and Adrienne Kaufmann, published by the Common Ground Network (1601 Connecticut Avenue NW, Washington, DC 20009) in January 1995. The "spirit of common ground," they say, is dialogue—a good in its own right as well as a precondition for actually working together to promote shared goals. For more information, check out the Network's web site at <www.searchforcommonground.org>.

WHAT IS THE COMMON GROUND APPROACH?

FOR MANY PEOPLE the idea of searching for common ground in the abortion conflict is strange and unbelievable—even unthinkable. Some people can only imagine that you are inviting them to engage in an activity in which they will have to "compromise" their values and beliefs. Viewing the conflict as a black or white contest to see which "side" will "win," the only alternative they can envision is the creation of some shade of gray in which their values and concerns are diluted and diminished. For some, the idea of any conversation with "Them" is dismissed as an act of betrayal.

Because the very idea of "common ground" in the abortion conflict is foreign and radical to many people in this society, we are offering a variety of approaches to answering the frequently asked questions "what do you mean by common ground?" and "what is the common ground approach?"

The Spirit of Common Ground Is the Spirit of Dialogue

The practice of dialogue lies at the heart of the common ground approach. Dialogue is different from debate. Debate is about persuading others that your views are "right" and that the views of others are "wrong." Debate tends to create winners and losers and often leads to pain and divisiveness when the subject is sensitive and people's views are as heart-felt as they tend to be on the issue of abortion.

Dialogue is a gentler, more respectful process than debate. The spirit of dialogue is to acknowledge and honor the humanity of *all* persons present regardless of their points of view. The goals of dialogue center around increasing understanding and being understood rather than persuading others and being "right."

When dialogue is attempted in a sustained and polarized conflict, a primary goal is to change the relationship between those who see each other as demonized adversaries. When an issue is explosive and relationships are already highly strained, dialogue is more likely than debate to lead to understanding and trust. A carefully constructed dialogue process can enable hard issues to be addressed without leading to bad feelings.

The Common Ground Approach Is a Search for What Is Genuinely Shared

The idea of common ground can be illustrated by two interlocking circles. Each circle represents a point of view about abortion (one circle, pro-life: the other, pro-choice). A common ground process recognizes the integrity

From Mary Jackstelt and Adrienne Kaufmannn, *Finding Common Ground in the Abortion Conflict* (Washington, DC: Common Ground Network, 1995).

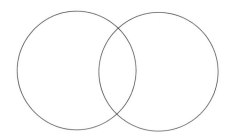

of each circle as a complete set of concerns, beliefs, and values around this issue. A common ground process primarily focuses attention on and explore the *area of intersection*. Through the search for concerns, beliefs, and values that are *shared*, a platform of understanding is built.

When participants stand together in the area of genuine intersection, they can also look at their *differences* with fresh eyes. The differences remain the same as before, but the perspective on these differences has changed. The angle of vision is from the common space looking out, instead of from the areas of difference where adversaries glare at one another across the submerged and unseen area of what is shared.

Common Ground Is not Compromise

Searching for common ground is not about compromising to reach a middle position but about focusing on areas of *genuinely* shared values and concerns. People are not asked to change their views on abortion or sacrifice their integrity. Participants in a common ground process seek to understand one another, not to force or pretend agreement where it does not exist.

A Common Ground Approach Encourages Looking Beyond the Labels and the Stereotypes

A common ground approach assumes that even in a polarized conflict, people's views fall on a continuum.

Pro-life _____ Pro-choice

When people identify themselves as "pro-choice" or "pro-life," they are only placing themselves *somewhere* on the continuum other than the exact center.

The idea of a continuum encourages awareness of how little we can assume about another person's set of beliefs if all we know about them is that they choose one label over the other. It opens us to look for diversity on both sides, and to imagine that two given people with different labels may be as similar as two other people with the same label. It fosters curiosity about the views of the particular individuals on the "other side" encountered within a common ground approach.

A Common Ground Approach Encourages Connective Thinking

Debates tend to focus attention on the weaknesses of a speaker and to encourage a search for the flaws in what is said. Dialogue encourages *connective thinking* that focuses attention on the *strengths* of the speaker and encourages a search for the gems of wisdom, or pieces of truth, in what is said. Over time, the practice of connective thinking in a group can lead to the creation of a web of shared knowledge woven from the threads of truth contributed by its members. Connective thinking fosters the building of constructive relationships and the development of community because it ties together the best wisdom of each member of the group. It is an important practice in the search for common ground.

A Common Ground Dialogue Encourages the Sharing of Personal Experience

A common ground dialogue usually begins with the sharing of personal experiences. Life has been experienced by each person in a unique way. Personal experiences cannot be argued about nor agreed or disagreed with. They *are*. Sharing life stories invites understanding responses from those who hear them. They are a constructive place to begin.

A Common Ground Dialogue Encourages Genuine Questions

Genuine questions are questions asked in a spirit of real curiosity and a sincere interest in hearing the answers. Rhetorical or leading questions are **not** genuine questions. They are questions for which we already know the answers. We usually ask them not to learn but to test or trap someone whom we view as an opponent. The posing of genuine questions and the omission of all other kinds is a trademark of common ground dialogue.

The Search for Common Ground Acknowledges Our Shared Membership in This Society

Common ground involves acknowledging the connections that exist between people related to one another by shared community, faith, and/or citizenship. This approach can allow us to see how we are all affected by stressful and troubling circumstances in the larger social environment. It can enable participants to relate to one another as "all of us against the problems we face" rather than "part of us against the rest of us."

ANSWERS TO FREQUENTLY ASKED QUESTIONS

In this section we offer ingredients for answers to questions that are frequently asked of us or members of the Network.

Why Do People Get Involved in Common Ground?

People have become involved in common ground activities for a variety of reasons. Prominent among those reasons are desires to promote a civil democratic society, effective problem-solving on important social issues, and peace. More specific motives frequently offered include:

- A belief that the level of confrontation over abortion is "out of hand" and destructive.
- A perception that the conflict is getting in the way of needed social change and is not helping the powerless and disadvantaged.
- The sense that the tone of the conflict is uncomfortably "out of sync" with a personal systems of beliefs.
- A painful experience of division—division between people of faith, between women, between family members, between community members—and a belief in reconciliation, reconnection, and the need for people to learn to live in community despite serious differences.

What Frame of Mind Does It Take to "Search for Common Ground?"

Not everyone is willing or able to join in the search for common ground at the moment they are invited to do so. Ideally, a person participating in common ground brings:

- A willingness to respect a human being who disagrees with you on the abortion issue and pledges to respect you in turn.
- An ability to listen to statements and views with which you strongly disagree without trying to convert those on the "other side" to your way of thinking and without feeling compromised by the act of listening.
- A belief in the importance of finding out what each person knows and understands about an issue.
- A desire to meet the human beings behind the stereotypes and media images.
- An openness to the unexpected, to the potential of "connecting" with an "adversary."
- A belief that conflict can be a positive opportunity for growth and understanding.

- An ability to handle skepticism and criticism from people on one's "own side" who view common ground as compromise and a dangerous way of conferring legitimacy on the "enemy."

Few people have all these qualities fully or equally developed when they enter into a common ground process. What is essential is that participants be committed to respecting the ground rules that govern the dialogue process.

What Sort of People Are Interested in Common Ground?

- Women and men, of different ages and different backgrounds, in widely separate parts of the country.
- Catholic and Protestant Christians, Jews, people of all faiths and those who have no religious orientation.
- Committed and active advocates on the abortion issue.
- People who have a position on abortion but are not activists, and people who feel "in the middle" on this issue.

What Are People Actually Doing?

Around the country, pro-life and pro-choice people in local communities are coming together in a number of different ways—in small informal groups, in workshops, in structured dialogues with facilitators, in retreats, in joint endeavors to solve real problems. To date, efforts to find common ground on abortion have been happening primarily at the grassroots level where people are trying to create community at a face-to-face level. This is a "bottom-up" change in the dynamics of the conflict.

How Do People Search for Common Ground on Abortion?

- They set aside generalities and rhetoric.
- They meet and talk within a framework of ground rules based on a willingness to listen, to speak with respect, and to keep what is said confidential.
- They speak as individuals, not as repesentatives of advocacy organizations.
- They share personal experiences and beliefs about abortion.
- They explore areas of common concern as well as difference.
- They confront the stereotypes, perceptions, and misperceptions that people on each side hold about those on the other.
- They may organize to work on a specific project or issue of mutual concern.

Exercises and Notes

REWORKING DYSFUNCTIONAL DIALOGUES

A good way to practice dialogue skills is to rework dialogues that have gone bad. Below are a number of "dysfunctional dialogues"—short exchanges that never rise above the level of fruitless debates. Each of them, however, also presents some opportunities for new directions, for more constructive conversations. In fact each could be taken in many different constructive directions.

In class, read each dialogue aloud. Then identify the places where the dialogue goes bad. What are its failures? Why does it so quickly turn fruitless? Next identify its missed opportunities. Where are some of the places it could have gone better? Are there interesting ideas the opposed sides could explore together? Do points of possible agreement come into view? Are questions asked that could be understood as genuine questions, and answered without more rhetoric?

Finally, rewrite the dialogue in a more constructive key, and read the new dialogue aloud for the whole group. Comment on the methods of dialogue you are trying to use.

Business Ethics

R: "Business ethics" is a contradiction in terms. The business of business is to make money, not to be nice to people.

P: Besides, business *is* pretty ethical. I know a lot of business people, they're not out there breaking laws and screwing people just to make an extra buck.

Q: Oh yeah? Think of all the scandals. The military contractors that overcharge a thousand percent for screwdrivers and deliver faulty equipment that endangers service people's lives. Oil companies that ravage the rain forests. Companies like WalMart that deliberately destroy whole downtowns while pretending to be such patriotic American citizens. It makes me sick.

P: Well, like I always say, the exceptions prove the rule.

Q: Then there are all the scandals that we don't even know about. I bet we've only scratched the surface.

R: The real problem is all the self-proclaimed whistleblowers who keep accusing businesses of scandals just so they can get some attention. I think they're damn troublemakers. Should keep their heads down and their mouths shut.

Q: You're swearing. Upset?

P: You started it!

Homelessness

M: I just saw a homeless guy holding his sign out at the intersection.

N: It's disgusting how people like that come and put themselves on display and play on your sympathies and tie up traffic too.

M: So what should he do, just go off into the woods and die quietly?

N: He should get a job! I'm tired of these welfare bums eating up my tax dollars.

M: If he's homeless I doubt he's on welfare. He's probably one of the ones that you and your Bible-thumping right-wing friends threw off welfare to fend for themselves. Now look what you've done. Now he has absolutely nothing. You call that Christian?!

N: There's plenty of work in this country if people just got out and did it.

M: Oh right, the way corporations are downsizing jobs around here, you should be glad *you've* got a job. Maybe that will be you out there in the intersection in a couple of years. You think I'll stop for you?

Wasteful Ways

A: The amount of waste around us is just incredible. Every time the college has a party, look at all the plastic forks and spoons and styrofoam cups— thousands and thousands of the things, and they last forever. We just throw them out. Then people go back to their muscle cars and drive two blocks that it would be healthier to walk, wasting gas too. Not to mention that the stupid cars themselves are deliberately designed to go out of style and even stop working after a few years. Then we have to buy a new one. And already there are more cars than people in America.

B: Oh, lighten up. People choose to buy these things. It's their right— that's what America is all about. They *know* it will be out of style in four years. They choose to change it.

A: Do you know that advertising is the biggest industry in this whole country? They're spending millions of dollars to make you want this stuff. You don't object to that, you think that's just fine. . . . But if *I* have an opinion, but not a million dollars to spend promoting it, you get mad!

B: Well, people choose to watch the ads, don't they? Besides, what do you want? Ban them all? OK, let's make a law: no ads, no new models, everyone has to buy the same boring old car, keep it ten years at least. . . . Give me a break!

A: Give *me* a break! I bet you're going into advertising yourself. Good luck with your life after you find yourself stuck in your oh-so-well-advertised junkheap!

Rich and Poor

T: I can't believe the insensitivity of some people. Everywhere there is hunger and need. Twenty thousand children in this world die every day of starvation or diseases that are easy to prevent. Yet we waste and waste and waste.

M: Yeah, but the poor will always be with us. You're ranting and raving about how terrible we are, but if you think about it, the poor in America are rich compared with even the rich in other countries. Whole families in Africa may get less money in a year than one welfare mother in Chicago gets in a month.

T: Oh, right, I'd like to see *you* try to live on it, even for a *week*.

M: I certainly wouldn't sit around all day feeling sorry for myself. I believe in *work*—that's how to get ahead in America. As my grandfather used to say, if you need a hand, look at the end of your arm. God helps those who help themselves.

T: What a crazy idea of God! It seems to me that a really sensible God would help those who *need help*.

M: That just shows what a Communist you are. Go back to Russia!

T: Russia?! Are you kidding? These days Russia is more capitalistic than we are. They also have an incredibly large poor population—much larger than ever before. *You* go back to Russia—that seems to be what you want!

A CLASSROOM DEBATE

Here is a more complex dialogue that occurred in a recent ethics class. More people are involved than in the above dialogues, and more possibilities also open up. Comment and revise as above.

A: Food stamps will pay for basic necessities, generic goods, things like that. They're not meant for name-brand items or things people don't really need.

B: That's not true! I've seen people buy just about anything with food stamps.

A: That's not how it's *supposed* to work. Probably it isn't policed very well. Besides, how many cashiers are going to tell people to their faces that they can't buy certain things with their food stamps?

C: How common is this? Does anyone know? Or are we just working from stereotype here?

D: It would be pretty hard to know. What could you do—stop people and search through their groceries?

E: That is what really bugs me. Here are the rest of us paying taxes, money we earned, so that some people who did not earn that money can buy whatever they want, when I might have to cut back because my taxes are so high.

F: Me too!

G: Wait a minute! Who says "buy whatever they want"? Food stamps aren't a blank check. You only get so much—not very much, either—and then that's it.

H: Besides, most people who get food stamps also have jobs. They earn their own money too. Are you going to tell people that because they accept some public aid that the rest of us have the right to tell them what they can and can't buy? Just buy generics or bulk diapers or whatever?

G: Oh right, how many of *us* buy generics?

E: Well, shouldn't there be *some* limits? I resent paying for other people's bad spending habits! They should live within their means.

G: Live within their means? You or I live don't within *our* means—but we think we have the right to go and tell poor people what they do and don't need?

F: That isn't unfair—after all, it's *our* money!

I: Maybe if you're a single adult and you are just buying for yourself, it's OK for you to buy whatever you want, even if it's unhealthy or whatever. But I don't think it's right to shortchange your kids.

C: It can't be that common. We're back to stereotypes here. I suppose it happens sometimes, but who's going to shortchange their kids?

A: I don't understand why you are all attacking me. All I said was that it probably isn't policed very well. . . .

NOTES AND FURTHER READINGS

One helpful practical book on ethics and dialogue is Tom Rusk, *The Power of Ethical Persuasion* (Penguin, 1993). Rusk "applies the ethical principles of respect, understanding, caring, and fairness . . . to high-stakes conversations often threatened by strong emotions and defensive reactions." Many of Rusk's themes parallel this chapter's, though his focus is chiefly on one-on-one conversations about professional or personal matters, rather than, as here, larger conversations about moral issues.

This chapter's box draws upon an intriguing book by Phyllis Beck Kritek, *Negotiating at an Uneven Table: Developing Moral Courage in Resolving Our Conflicts* (Jossey-Bass, 1994). The story about Native Americans comes from her page 36; about "using your own language" from page 279. There is much other useful advice. A detailed treatment of goals and styles of ethical action in organizations is Richard Nielsen, *The Politics of Ethics: Methods for Acting, Learning, and Sometimes Fighting with Others in Addressing Ethics Problems in Organizational Life* (Oxford University Press, 1996).

Many groups are working on the problem of communicating across the barriers of advantage, stereotype, and silence that limit so much of our public discourse. One fine example is the National Coalition Building Institute (1835 K Street NW, Suite 715, Washington, DC 20006; <www.ncbi.org>).

CHAPTER 15

⬡

Service
Learning by Helping

CALLS TO SERVICE

Making a Difference

When it's a real puzzle what we should do, ethics is primarily about figuring it out. That's why this toolbox tells you how to find the facts and integrate values and reframe problems and all the rest.

But ethics is also about helping out. Moral values, remember, are those values that give voice to the needs and legitimate expectations of others. The bottom line is to listen and respond to those needs and expectations. Ethical theories may debate with each other about the hard cases, for example, but all agree that the point of ethics finally is to *act*.

A lost child at the store or the airport needs reassurance and aid. A struggling child at school needs tutoring. There is an accident on the highway. In situations like these there is no puzzle at all what to do—the point is just to do it. Your grandmother has stories to tell but no one to listen to them. After a storm trees are down on people's houses all over the neighborhood, and you have a chain saw. There is famine in Africa, and the Amazonian rain forests are still burning—don't you have a little money to spare? No puzzle here.

Even about controversial and unclear matters, there is usually a lot to do that isn't controversial or unclear at all. Don't use the debate as an excuse for staying away. Welfare programs may be controversial, for example, but it's clear that there are many poor people who need help. No one disagrees about that. And many are not getting that help now. Your church may run a soup kitchen or provide meals to a homeless shelter; you can join in. Maybe you are hiring people—why not someone in special need?

"Service-Learning"

Service can also be a kind of *learning*—so much so that many high schools and colleges are now beginning to speak of "service-learning" not just as a combination of two different things but as *one* kind of thing, where the learning is integral to the helping and the helping is integral to the learning. In fact, many schools are beginning to require it.

You learn about life from very different perspectives. You get to know people quite different from yourself. Work in a soup kitchen, tutor under-privileged children, answer a suicide prevention hotline, and you begin to understand what life is like for some other people. Situations and needs that might have been easy to dismiss, that may never have been more real than a quick glimpse in a TV news report or a politician's speech, now are right before you. Real people. You learn what their struggles involve. The world begins to look a little different.

You learn what is possible for people past the usual labels and assumptions. Only by meeting different people and working with them can you crack those stereotypes, can you begin to see them as actual *people*: individuals just like yourself, with their own distinctive struggles and needs, humor and depth.

The Special Olympics World Games came to town last summer. Mentally handicapped people from all around the world came to compete and be honored—so many that it took three hours just for all the teams to march into the stadium. Thirty years ago the mentally handicapped were kept out of sight, not believed capable of physical skill or speed or grace. Now there are Special Olympics marathoners and swimming teams and horseback riders and soccer and volleyball teams, many of whom also compete with nonhandicapped athletes in open competitions. Last summer it seemed like every store in the state was sponsoring a team or highlighting its own mentally handicapped employee-participants. They were visible, and proud. Thousands of volunteers did the behind-the-scenes work, met the athletes, and found themselves looking at the mentally handicapped in a new way.

You learn to remember what really matters. Volunteer in a hospital or deliver meals to the sick or old, and you realize how precious is the ability to just walk down the street. Work at a homeless shelter and every time you get into your car or open your front door you will remember what an amazing freedom you have. Make a child laugh, and life's little frustrations go back to the corners where they belong.

Personal Challenges

Helping is not necessarily easy. Especially when it is face to face, service can be upsetting and unsettling, an uneasy experience. Collecting money for charity feels pretty safe; but serving meals to the homeless or showing a mentally retarded South African the town may feel like a real stretch.

Yet it is precisely when we "stretch" the most that we learn the most, especially about ourselves. Ram Dass and Paul Gorman:

Often we reach out to help one another and succeed. Natural compassion comes easily and we're equal to the challenge. But . . . deep questions of identity and relationship are going to arise much of the time we are caring for one another. The more wrenching the situation, the more likely such issues will be central. Who *are* we to ourselves and each other?—it will all come down to that.

Will we look within? Can we see that to be of most service to others we must face our own doubts, needs, and resistances? We've never grown without having done so. This wouldn't be the first time we've fought the inertia of conditioning. . . .

"Doubts, needs, and resistances"—yes. First there are the little nagging things. Maybe we think that it's not our job to help. Don't we pay taxes to hire other people to do this? Or: how will we know what to do? Or maybe we're too used to holding aloof even from family and friends. Sharing life stories with a stranger is asking a lot! Or maybe we're afraid of being rejected. What do we really have to offer?

Worries like these don't last long once you begin helping. There's certainly enough to do, taxes or no, and often it's the simplest things—sometimes just being with someone, or pulling fallen branches off a lawn, or serving up supper. And rejection is very rare if you respond to a clear call for help and remember your basic courtesies. Anyway, asking ourselves what we really have to offer is probably a useful thing from time to time: it is a way of taking stock of our own lives.

The deeper worries are the harder ones. Maybe we fear our *own* weakness and suffering, seeing in others' suffering what may await us in turn. In that case helping is a hard thing indeed, but can also be a path back to a kind of moral recognition: acknowledging and accepting suffering, our own included, as part of life. There is no way around the pain; the only way is through.

> I have a friend, a chemotherapy nurse in a children's cancer ward, whose job it is to pry for any available vein in an often emaciated arm to give infusions of chemicals that sometimes last as long as twelve hours and which are often quite discomforting to the child. He is probably the greatest pain-giver the children meet in their stay in the hospital. Because he has worked so much with his own pain, his heart is very open. He works with his responsibilities in the hospital as a "laying on of hands with love and acceptance." There is little in him that causes him to withdraw, that reinforces the painfulness of the experience for the children. He is a warm, open space which encourages them to trust whatever they feel. And it is he whom the children most ask for at the time they are dying. Although he is the main pain-giver, he is also the main love-giver.

Maybe the deepest worry is that once we open to suffering and needs like these, they may eat us alive. We can come face to face with suffering on a scale so unexpected and enormous that we do not know what to do. It may even be

How Much Is Enough?

There are people who give their lives, in one way or another, to service. Mother Theresa, who dedicated her whole life to helping the outcast of India. "St. John of the Trees," a man who devoted decades to reforesting parts of the Alps, each day and every day, one seedling at a time. The ordinary and unnamed heroes of some catastrophe, like the unidentified passenger in a Washington, DC plane crash a few years back who, as his plane was sinking into the ice-filled Potomac, pulled passenger after passenger out of the cracked fuselage and into a helicopter lift until the plane went down for good and took him with it. Countless parents and teachers and many, many others in all walks of life who keep life going by daily small acts of self-sacrifice and spunk.

Examples like these may inspire us—and they may also make us feel guilty. Is such selflessness really morally required of us all? Once we acknowledge the need for service, doesn't it sometimes seem that we are being asked to hand over our lives as a kind of moral blank check? Is there any legitimate and honest way to draw a line?

Yes there is. Christian moral tradition, for one, draws such a line. We are obliged, naturally, to do our duty by others—to respect others, keep our promises, follow the law, and so on. We are *not* obliged, however—or rather, not *obliged*—to go farther than that. Great acts of generosity or sacrifice are certainly good things to do, but they are not *required*. You do not have to make such sacrifices to be a moral person. These are the acts of "saints": what moral traditions calls "supererogatory" acts—above and beyond the call of duty.

In short, it's not required that we take the whole burden of the world on our shoulders. It's not required that we do absolutely everything we can, whatever the cost to ourselves, to help others. Ordinary morality calls for something more like a balancing act.

Notice that each of our ethical theories both urges us toward service and also suggests certain limits. Utilitarianism, for example, asks us to serve the greatest good of the greatest number, but we must include ourselves and those close to us—families, friends, co-workers, communities—among that number. And often we ourselves and those close to us are the people whose happiness we can most directly affect. At moments of great need or emergency, real sacrifice may be called for, but normally our own needs and the needs of those close to us are a pretty major part of the picture.

What's *right*, likewise, requires justice and fairness to others but also gives some voice to the self. We have our own rights just as do others. And virtues too point in both directions: independence and self-sufficiency are virtues as important as attentiveness, generosity, and open-heartedness. Even for the sake of better serving others, some kind of space for the self is also necessary, some kind of breathing room, some sense of a center.

Morality, then, is not infinitely demanding. The real story is more complicated, and more humanly realistic. We need at least to pay attention to the needs and legitimate expectations of others as well as ourselves—remember, that is our very definition of morality—and we need to respond to those needs and expectations at least to some extent. But the best way to respond, and how far we should respond, may vary with each of us and with each of our situations.

As a broad and rough general guide. Christian moral tradition challenges us to consider "tithing": that is, to give about 10 percent of our income—and by extension, perhaps, 10 percent of our time and energy—to others beyond self, family, and friends. It's interesting to note that American volunteerism runs at just about this level. About half of all Americans over age 13 volunteer an average of three and a half hours a week—which is about 10 percent of the average work week.

The most important point, though, is that "helping" and "self" are not necessarily at odds. So it's not quite as though the tradition tells us that we can morally have 90 percent of our time and energy to ourselves as long as we give 10 percent "away" to others. No: the tithing idea is instead a kind of reminder that among the many forms of giving and receiving in our lives there needs to be a level of conscious giving beyond one's immediate self, family, and friends. And we also "receive" in the same way. Making the extra phone call, coaching a kids' soccer team, welcoming the new neighbors with a surprise dinner—these can sometimes open up whole new possibilities, new dimensions of life for us. They serve the self as well—as long as the "self" is not narrowly defined in opposition to "others."

More than a few of my students have spoken of Habitat for Humanity house-building trips, or working at the homeless shelters, as among the richest experiences of their college years. Think of it: all of that struggling through classes, and all of that work to pay for it, and yet the best parts are free. . . .

that there *is* nothing that anyone can do. We want to run away, to retreat into a safe world where there is hope and laughter and love.

But even here we can help. There may be nothing else to do, but we can almost always just *listen*. Often that is what people really want above all—just a chance to tell their story, to be heard. And as a listener you can accept the story as a kind of gift, not as an added burden. It is not as though the weight somehow shifts to you. No, but it does lighten for the other person. Funny thing about us: sharing actually helps.

VISITS TO A HOMELESS SHELTER

Ten minutes from my semirural oasis of a college campus is a small city's shelter for the homeless. Half an hour on the freeway takes us to a large urban shelter. My students and I go to both places to help—and to learn.

Today we are standing in the lobby of Weaver House, a shelter run by Greensboro Urban Ministries in Greensboro, North Carolina. We have already run a kind of gauntlet to get in here, a gauntlet, at least, of our stereotypes: inner city, people hanging around the door, "The Homeless." We're uneasy, glad we are here in numbers. Yet there is something else here too: a sense of reality, and of need, need so palpable as to hang in the air. After all, this place is the only thing standing between most of these people and sleeping on the streets, hungry. We begin to see the world a bit through their eyes. Are *we* the gauntlet that the homeless all too often have to run?

"The primary objective of Weaver House," says the shelter's mission statement,

> is to provide Greensboro's homeless with the necessities for basic human survival on a temporary basis, including: food, refuge, clothing, medical and spiritual counseling. In addition to the above, Weaver House seeks to empower those homeless persons who wish to be empowered by providing them with the programs, the linkage to service agencies, and the advocacy that is needed to generate a new start.

This statement is part of a Volunteer Information Sheet written by Paul Davis, the shelter's director and our guide today. In it Davis spells out certain values in an extraordinarily precise way—and not in the way we probably expected.

You might expect an appeal to pity. Certainly that is how the homeless are often presented—as pitiable—and how charity often goes. But Davis is talking about *respect*—respect and fairness, equality and rights. To speak of "basic human survival" is a plea for the most fundamental equality, and the words themselves have weight and an echo: Basic. Human. Survival. These are the most minimal but essential things, he says. How could they be too expensive for the richest society on earth? How could they even be grudging?

Guests

"All people who come are guests," the statement goes on, "sojourners for whom God demands hospitality." The overriding message of this way of putting things is not the religion. (This place calls itself a *ministry*, after all, where religious language comes naturally, but it is not the only language one could use.) No: the point is that at bottom we are not so different. We are *all* "sojourners" along the way. To say that "God demands hospitality" might for some invoke the image of a stern, commanding figure. It might also simply remind us that just as each of us is sometimes vulnerable and in need, so too each of us has a certain right to be here, to walk the earth and know something of the joys this life can bring—sojourners all.

> We seldom ask why a person has come. All people who come are guests. . . . Most of our guests are wonderful. Some cannot follow our rules and must leave. Some cannot follow our rules and we will bend them to be hospitable. Our guests, in short, are just like us, only they are more poor, under stress, and are forced to make more difficult choices than most of us face.

For this reason, people who stay in the shelter are never labeled as homeless (or even "clients"—that's social-service agency talk), just, always, "guests." They are not made into objects of pity by our very language.

Seventy-five to eighty percent of Weaver House's guests have jobs, Paul tells us. More have two jobs than have none. Some are highly trained. An aerospace worker, displaced when his company abruptly left town. One of the masons who built the latest classroom building on our own campus. Most have a college education: sometimes we meet guests who were graduates of our own college (one night, hearing where my students are from, one guest pulls out his old college ID card for them). Some will only stay until they get enough money together to move into a place of their own.

People are shocked. This is not what the stereotypes tell us. We wonder how a person working two jobs still can't manage to make it. Paul's answer is that the pay is low and the conditions are bad, and even people who move into their own apartments are one disaster away from the shelter again. Kid gets sick, car breaks down, and they're destitute again.

Others can never seem to do it, he says. They can't handle money, never learned how to keep a checking account, can't seem to understand that it might be better to take a job that pays more money less often rather than daily work that pays little but right now. A whole range of people.

And, yes, some are no longer interested. Think of it as another culture, Paul says. Many of the homeless want just what these students want: a good job, money, a house, a nice comfortable middle-class life. But not all do. In much of the rest of the world there are cultures in which these things might be nice but are not worth working for and worrying about all the time. Homeless culture, or part of it, Paul says, can be like that too. Besides, if you have worked hard for twenty years and still have nothing, why would you still want to work? Why indeed.

Listening

"Talking with the guests," says the Volunteer Information Sheet,

> is probably the most important thing you can do at Weaver House. Just listen and be polite. You may feel the need to "fix" some problem, and indeed fixing is very important. But, listening is even more important. Our guests are rarely

listened to, and it is our privilege (and sometimes our burden) to listen to another person's story.

It is hard to welcome or deal with those who remind us of vulnerability, those whose needs are too great or too unfamiliar. My students sometimes wonder how they can help out here, what difference they can really make in these people's lives, not realizing yet that simply being here, willing to help and to listen, is already the biggest step they can take. And that they too will learn in the process.

"My experience at Weaver House," wrote one student,

> was not what I expected. . . . I went in with a narrow mind. I thought I was going to see a bunch of drugs and drunken men in horrible dirty and ripped clothes. Now I cannot believe I went in with an attitude like that. . . .
>
> I was afraid to go up to someone to start a conversation, but I did anyway. I ate dinner with a woman while we talked. She was an interesting lady. You could tell she was very lonely and had no friends or family. She talked about when she was younger. She seemed to be very happy then. . . . I do not know what happened to her. It is probably better that I don't know, but I am broken up to hear how someone who seemed to have such a "normal" life could end up like her. Maybe she got into drugs or whatever, but she appeared to have a very good heart. . . .

"I did not know what to think," she concluded, "because if my grandmother was in a situation like that I would cry my heart out." She went home and cried her heart out anyway. Then she went back.

"Our guests," says Paul, "are just like us. . . ." We know that too, but usually only in the abstract. Here in the shelter it gets more real.

> All of my insecurities were running through my head as I approached the door and had to be let in by one of the guests. Some people were gathered by the TV and it's funny to me now, but the first thing I thought was, "Hey, I watch that show too!" It's embarrassing to look back now at how nervous I was because then it hit me that homeless people are just the same as me. . . . Right away I was so glad I had come.

Again and again the students encounter people their own age—and see themselves.

> Just before the doors closed at eight o'clock a young girl walked in. She handed me her card and walked into the dining hall. I could not help noticing how young she looked—like me. I looked her up in the book. She and I are only two months apart by birth. I could not imagine being in her situation.
>
> When dinner was over and it was time for a smoke break, she walked out the door with the others for a cigarette. I don't smoke but I really wanted to

talk to her so I got a cigarette and followed them out the door. I sat down next to her and asked her if she had a light. Then we started talking. She told me that she was born in Texas, then her family moved to Greensboro. She attended NC State for the first month of school but had to drop out for medical reasons. She and her mother did not get along and that was why she had come to the shelter. I asked her if the people at the shelter ever intimidated her. She answered without hesitation "yes." I then questioned why she didn't go home . . . if the shelter scared her and her mother wanted her to go home. She responded that she wanted time on her own. Later she got up and called her mom.

I'm not sure what she will end up doing—whether or not she will go home or return to school. What I do know is that I saw myself in her. . . .

Learning

Other things happen—puzzling, provocative, scary, painful. In one shelter there are small children. Thinking of their lives is very hard for some students. "Why do we allow children to live on the streets?"

Sometimes the reality is more complicated. One pair of kids is in day care while their mother works, and day care costs enough that she can't afford an apartment. So, in effect, homelessness is the price of working. In the evenings one of my students finds herself rocking the little ones to sleep while their mother studies for her GED. It is certainly not an easy life, but it is not a dead end, and they are not "living on the streets" either. They live at the shelter. One child has so many friends at her shelter that it is really, for her, an extended family. Let in early, on a cold night, she cries until all her friends get in too. ("Home is where the heart is," one student wrote after a night like this.)

People at Weaver House often have only one bag of things to their name. Volunteers have to check their bags when they come in. They discover to their amazement that many bags are filled with *books*. "The very things students like us take for granted," writes one, "are the prize possessions of people who have nothing." Another writes:

> Up in the laundry room they have a shelf of books. . . . B. [a guest] came in and began looking through them and asked if I had ever read any of them . . . not these in particular but just any at all. It felt awkward to answer "no," but that was my answer. He then replied, "These are good, you should read them sometime. Right now these are pretty much all I got and when I read them, in my mind I do have opportunity, and that is what keeps me going."

This student concludes: "It took me a few seconds to realize that a 22-year-old, just like me, who has fallen upon hard times had basically made me feel like I have pretty much cheated myself out of a semester of top-quality education. . . ."

Some students are brought up short when they assume that a well-dressed person in the shelter must be another volunteer, only to find that he or she is a guest. "At that moment," says one, "I realized that *I too* could be here. . . ." It also happens in reverse: "A young black man came in and stood at the counter talking with some of the guests. I felt completely embarrassed after I had asked him his name to check him in and he told me he was not a guest. . . ." He was, in fact, the *manager*.

Sports-minded students go for the ballgames. They could stay at home and watch by themselves in their dorm rooms or a bar, but they go to the shelter, help out, and then sit and watch the game with the guests.

> All of the guests' eyes were glued to the TV. One man was even decked out in Duke accessories. . . . He and K. [another student volunteer] had a bet for the evening that the person whose team lost would have to fall to their knees after the game and admit that the other was the best. I sat in the room the entire game, talking to the guests sitting in chairs next to me. The scene was one I will never forget: a group of about 15 homeless men and K. and I sitting around and watching basketball. We would get excited and disappointed together. . . .

"When I signed up for this course," writes another,

> I didn't really think that the highlight of the term would be spending Monday night watching football with a bunch of homeless people in a shelter in Greensboro. I mean, what would my parents think? "Bunch of lazy bums," my dad always says. I don't know, though—I actually think he'd have a good time here. He sits around just like this too. Maybe his mind wouldn't snap shut so fast. The world looks so different from here. . . .

Of course there are hard times too. Some guests are rude or angry; people are turned away if drunk or stoned; there are fights and hard words. Most of my students do not think they themselves would survive the guests' situation, emotionally or even physically. They are amazed at the guests' relative good humor, all things considered. Some remark that the guests are better mannered than, for example, people at the country club where some students also work.

We may or may not conclude from our experiences at the shelters that governmental welfare programs as we know them are necessarily a good idea. For one thing, these are private shelters, supported by local churches and synagogues, and sometimes pretty tough on the guests too. Students are often motivated to come back on their own time, or bring their friends, or talk their parents into sending boxes of food or clothes to help out. Those opposed to governmental welfare programs often favor just such actions. Yet one is left wondering if private and local initiatives can be enough. The realities can be overwhelming, and what shelters can offer is very partial. We carry away questions and uncertainty too.

"Compassion: The Witness Within"

RAM DASS AND PAUL GORMAN

Dass and Gorman's *How Can I Help?* is an eloquent study of service, mainly in helpers' own words. It is also a practical how-to manual. Dass and Gorman point out, as I also have briefly suggested in this chapter, that the biggest challenges to those who would help are often the emotional challenges, and most of these we put up ourselves. Denial, evasion, and pity all can become obstacles to true compassion. So can even "professional warmth"—cool efficiency, impersonal friendliness—or its opposite, a kind of hyperactivity that never stops to listen.

These, Dass and Gorman say, are "a few of the ways in which the mind reacts to suffering and attempts to restrict or redirect the natural compassion of the heart." As we reach out, then pull back, "love and fear are pitted against one another." And, as Dass and Gorman also say, "As hard as this is for *us*, what must it be like for those who need our help?"

How can we respond with true openness and compassion, keeping the interference from ourselves in the background? In this brief excerpt Dass and Gorman give their answer, bracketed by two helpers' stories. Can you see what they mean by "cultivating a dispassionate Witness within"?

AS I WALK INTO THE SANATORIUM, *I have a little exercise. I know that I'm to be presented with evidence of terrible pain. It's all right there, right in front of me. And I know that it's probably going to blow me away the minute I go in, no matter that I've worked there six years. So I'll take note of all that, as if it were a sign on the front door. It gives me a certain amount of sobriety—preparation for entering.*

In doing that, I find I get a feeling of deep respect for those inside who are suffering from the kinds of pains they're dealing with. Basic respect for their dignity and their worth. They're here, they're equally as human as I am, and their suffering calls my attention to that fact.

Sometimes I also find myself honoring them. Not just respect, but honoring them for what they are and what they're enduring. I'll try to bring that feeling in the door with me. This gives me strength. And it just starts simply from taking account of what's going on in me, in the sanatorium, in those inside it.

From *How Can I Help?* by Ram Dass and Paul Gorman. Copyright © 1985 by Ram Dass and Paul Gorman. Reprinted by permission of Alfred A. Knopf, a division of Random House, Inc.

Our tendency when we acknowledge qualities in ourselves like fear of suffering or loss of control may be to judge ourselves. Found selfish, uncaring, impatient, unworthy . . . we're embarrassed and uncomfortable at the recognition of our "weakness." We have not taken to heart the example of the biblical Paul, who said, "My strength is made perfect through weakness." Yet this often turns out to be the case in our efforts to care for others. Acknowledging our weakness can soften our defensiveness. We're not so busy protecting ourselves all the time. We're much more likely to be there for anyone who is wrestling with his or her own sense of weakness, unworthiness, or fear. We'll hear each other. To acknowledge our humanness, with its mixture of empathy and fear, strengthens our helping hand.

But we must do so with compassion for ourselves and a supportive appreciation of our own predicament. Such compassion can come forth more easily when we appreciate that *it is the openness of our heart, after all, with which this all began.* Our fear is awakened not just by the suffering but by the intensity of our heart's reaction to it. The ego may have been frightened into all kinds of defense mechanisms to control our innate generosity. But mercy and kindness were our first impulses. Natural compassion was our starting point.

This compassionate self-acknowledgment may start out with a simple reflection. "I'm really uncomfortable when I visit Uncle Harry because he's suffering so much. I want so much to help him, but there doesn't seem to be anything I can do. I see how phony I get when I'm around him. And that's okay." But it's more than okay. This act of acknowledgment begins to go to work for us. The phoniness usually starts to fall away the minute it's owned up to. Discomfort in the presence of suffering is usually less toxic and infectious when it's no longer denied. This quality of unjudging awareness not only frees us and others from the consequences of our reactivity; it allows us to enter more consciously into the experience of suffering itself. We're no longer running away, glancing over our shoulder. We can stop and face what's right before us. We can look at *what is.*

But we must be quiet to do so, quiet to hear. Yet the first thing we notice when we try is that we're not quiet at all. We're a torrent of reactions, and reactions to reactions, one piling in upon the other. Such agitation is hardly the best ground from which to observe the subtleties of any situation. It would be so much easier if we weren't in the presence of all this suffering. But then again, wasn't it the suffering and our reactions to it that we set out to observe in the first place?

So we have to find tranquility even in the midst of trauma. What's required is to cultivate a dispassionate Witness within. This Witness, as it grows stronger, can see precisely how we jump the gun in the presence of pain. It notices how our reactions might be perpetuating denial or fear or tension in the situation, the very qualities we'd like to help alleviate.

The Witness catches us in the act, but gently, without reproach, so we can simply acknowledge our reactivity and begin to let it fall away, allowing our natural compassion to come more into play. The Witness gives us a little room.

Not only does it notice our own reactivity, but it also brings into the light of awareness the actions and reactions of other parties in the situation. Now we can begin, perhaps for the first time, to hear *them*. Less busy pushing away suffering, less frenzied having to do something about it, we're able to get a sense of what *they're* feeling, of what *they* feel they need. We may be startled to discover that what they've been asking for all along is entirely different from what we've been so busy offering: "All I want is for you to sit down here next to me. I don't care about the nurse; the IV is working fine; the bed is comfortable. Just sit with me." Quieter now, we can recognize such a need—often without it having to be expressed, perhaps even before it's consciously felt. We'll just come into the room and sit down and say "Hello."

This process of witnessing is dispassionate. It's not committed to one result or another; it's open to everyting. Because it has, so to speak, no ax to grind, it is more able to see truth. As the Tao Te Ching says, "The truth waits for eyes unclouded by longing."

The Witness, however, is not passive, complacent, or indifferent. Indeed, while it's not attached to a particular outcome, its presence turns out to bring about change. As we bring *what is* into the light of clear awareness, we begin to see that the universe is providing us with abundant clues as to the nature of the suffering before us, what is being asked, what fears have been inhibiting us, and finally, *what might really help*. All we have to do is listen—really listen.

Such investigation and inquiry into *what is* infuses a situation with a quality of freshness and possibility. As we see how reactive we have been, we find ourselves opening to new responses. It was our own reactivity unacknowledged that cut off the spontaneity of our helping heart. Once it is acknowledged, however—and once we begin to work with it—a whole new level of creativity becomes possible.

I used to have to walk through it automatically. You don't bother to look. You certainly don't let much of it in. But it was the children themselves who began to open me up. Once it started, it began to pull me in gradually but steadily. It was very powerful, but you have to take it at your own pace. Because here, in a neonatal intensive care unit, you see incredible beauty and unbearable pain. And you have to figure you how to be with both.

The children are beautiful because you just get to know them. You can't nurse them, really nurse them, without knowing them. And you can't know them, really know them, without seeing their beauty. What can be more beautiful than innocence? And that affects all their features: their tininess, the eyes, the fingers, the sound of their heart—just their breath can move you with its beauty. Part of it seems to come from how fragile they are, how uncertain it is how long they'll be here—the cliché metaphor of the flower that blooms for a day. It's like a garden of that in here.

The picture on the surface, though, is also terribly grim. A room full of these little ones, many of whom are right on the edge of life and death, and some of whose faces and movements are pretty distressing. And then their parents: there on the other side of the window, with the most desperate and stricken faces looking in, so helplessly, such pain. It's something to be inside a picture that's being looked at with such expressions. But you look back, just to let them know someone's in here.

It was the use of machines and extraordinary medical measures that moved several of us to see how much distance we were putting between ourselves and the infants. Even if the machines weren't there, though, there was that tendency to keep it impersonal, to keep your distance, and you knew that wasn't any good for the children—for the children least of all.

So a group of us began to talk about it, to open up to our feelings, to decide to be with the children more, and when it got too hard and we'd break down, we'd support each other and talk it over. The more we opened up, it just became natural that we began this new practice of holding infants when the time would come for them to die. It wasn't a decision as much as something we'd become ready to do. So at the end we'd take them off the monitors and into our arms in a rocker. And we'd sit with them in their final moments.

It tears you apart, because holding them, sometimes you can feel them go. And the death itself is different. On the machines, it's monitored as brain death. In your arms, it's the heart and the breath.

It's so—what's that word—poignant. You feel ten dozen things at once. Terrible sadness, because you'd become attached to the child. But glad too, because their suffering is about to end. Maybe anger, at the world, at God, at whatever, for allowing this to happen. And such empathy for the parents. And somehow like awe and wonder; like there must be some kind of explanation for all this which you don't yet understand. But patience too, that things become more clear in time. And peace of mind, because you're doing the best you can. And humble, to be present at such a moment. All of the above, often at once.

*You're sitting with these feelings, as well as sitting there with the child. In fact, you come to see that you're sitting with all of it **on behalf of the child.** You're doing it for yourself, simply to stay cool. But it's a final act for them as well. You're offering whatever peace you've come to. And it creates such intimacy, impossible to describe, you're so right with them.*

It's unbearable and beautiful at the same time. How do you explain that? It's just the part of you that's with them is getting ripped up. But the part of you that's, like, trying to understand it all . . . well, that's beautiful because you see that you can be, we all can be, in the presence of great pain, but still appreciate life, even in its last moments. Especially then.

Exercises and Notes

GET OUT AND DO SOMETHING

There is no substitute for actually going out and helping. Pick some way to help that is genuinely face to face. Tutor a struggling child. Volunteer at a local homeless shelter or soup kitchen. Work with retarded citizens. Read to children at an inner-city child care center. Teach a class at a community center or a nursing home. Help build a house with Habitat for Humanity.

The mechanics are usually easy. Making the arrangements only takes a phone call. Most homeless shelters are desperate for volunteer help, and have staff coordinators to arrange volunteers' dates and times. Many consider public education part of their mission: they regularly run orientation and training sessions. When floods or storms strike, many cities or counties set up volunteer hotlines to match willing volunteers with people in need of help. Community newspapers often run appeals for help. School offices schedule community volunteers and tutors.

Most colleges and universities have offices that match community organizations' needs and student volunteers. Find yours and use it. My school even has a volunteer fair at which community organizations in need set up information tables and sign up people.

For better or worse, it's not hard to find the opportunities. Start with the readily-available ones: be on the lookout for the less visible opportunities that may arise only after you are actively involved.

NOTES AND FURTHER READINGS

The quotations in the first part of this chapter come, like the chapter's reading, from Ram Dass and Paul Gorman's book *How Can I Help?*, pages 14 to 15 and 86 to 87. Greensboro Urban Ministry's Weaver House, whose Volunteer Information Statement is cited here, can be reached at 305 W. Lee Street, Greensboro, NC 27406. My students also work at the Alamance County Allied Churches Emergency Night Shelter, PO Box 2581, Burlington, NC 27216. Students quoted in this chapter include Tracy Cournoyer, Lee Hawley, Andrew Hendryx, Becky Rosso, Christine Sanlorenzo, Jennette Schorsch, and Emily Tucker.

On service as a form of learning, a useful place to start for both students and teachers is David Lempert's *Escape From the Ivory Tower* (Jossey-Bass, 1995). "In eight years of higher education at Yale and Stanford," Lempert complains,

> I had read about poor people but had never spoken with them. I read about crime and prison life, but I had never visited a prison or talked with an inmate. I had studied law for three years but had hardly ever seen the inside of a courtroom. Though I was completing a business degree, I had rarely been

on a factory floor, and I had never had a chance to speak to workers, union leaders, or consumer advocates. I had studied economics before that, but I had never spoken with a farmer or spent any time on a production line. I had taken humanities classes in which I had almost no contact with humans . . .

So Lempert set about to do things differently: his book is largely an account of how. See also Jane Vella, *Learning to Listen, Learning to Teach: The Power of Dialogue in Educating Adults* (Jossey-Bass, 1994). Both books offer useful teaching suggestions too. On service in general, see Robert Coles, *The Call of Service* (Houghton-Mifflin, 1993) and John McKnight, *The Careless Society: Community and Its Counterfeits* (Basic Books, 1995). Coles' book is highly personal and narrative; McKnight's has a provocative political dimension.

VI

CONTEMPORARY ISSUES

CHAPTER 16

○

Sexuality

Sex! Even the word creates a tingle. Probably there is no topic of more interest to young people. Probably there is also no topic on which the culture gives more mixed messages. Can our toolbox help?

WHO CARES ABOUT SEX?

We could start with this question: why does sex matter, anyway, at least in ethics? After all, there are many things, even quite wonderful things, that ethics is not much concerned about. There are also many things that ethics has been concerned about but probably shouldn't be. Sometimes we get moralistic when we shouldn't. Is sex really any of ethics' business?

Why Sex Matters (in Ethics)

Sex *is* ethics' business, and here's why. In the first place, it has genuine positive moral values.

Sex can be intensely pleasurable, of course. It must be high on any utilitarian's list of *goods* for this simple reason. And it is worth being very clear that sex therefore has *moral* value. Utilitarians fear that the moral tradition has been too quick to turn negative or prudish about sex, that moralists have too often become sexual killjoys. And there may be good reasons for caution. Still, surely, the first thing to say is that sex is a good thing, indeed a wonderful thing, at its best an almost unmatched source of pleasure and celebration.

It is not crude to celebrate sex in this way. We get crude, maybe, when we reduce sex to nothing but the immediate pleasure or release of tension. But there is more to it than this even in terms of its pleasures. Sex involves the many pleasures of companionship and mutual appreciation; of touching and simple physical togetherness; of gracefulness and humor too. The needs it can fulfill are not just passing and physical but go to the very core of our beings. Nothing crude about that.

Considered in "ultimate" terms, moreover, sex is the desire to unite with another person, to go beyond the limits of our own being and solitude. In this way we can understand sex as a fitting completion of our natures, both as animals and as social and spiritual beings. In the most everyday terms too, sex is part of what brings us into connection, and transmutes physical desire into loyalty, sharing, family, love.

Looked at this way, sex lives among the *rights* and *virtues* as well. Rights, because by its unparalleled ability to call forth love it can put us and keep us deeply in touch with the reality of another person as end and not mere means. Virtues, because almost any voluntary sexual union calls forth certain legitimate expectations (remember our definition of moral values). It offers a kind of trust, for example, which calls for trustworthiness in return.

In this sense it may really be true that sex is a kind of rite of passage into adulthood. Actually making a sexual relationship work takes time and effort, but it is also a genuine moral achievement. Yes, it takes a lot of adjustment and practical skill, but more than that too. It is coming into part of the richness and fullness of human life—a richness and fullness we cannot find alone.

Cautions and Limits

But sex *also* matters in ethics because, frankly, it has immense destructive power too. Moralists have good reason to be concerned with the need for sexual limits and caution. Things get complicated. Here are some of the reasons.

Utilitarian Cautions

Utilitarians may celebrate pure physical pleasure. But few things in life are "pure" in the sense that they have no implications for anything else. Sex certainly does. Part of the very reason that sex is so pleasurable is that sex is a social thing: something that we do *with* others (usually). As we've just been saying, sexual pleasures are tied up with the pleasures of companionship and communion. But then what's good for others becomes part of what's good for us, and vice versa. There's more to think about.

Certain limits and cautions thus emerge even for the most "sex-positive" utilitarians. Sexual communication, for one thing, becomes critical to sustaining and deepening a relationship or a marriage. Hedonistic self-seeking, oblivious to the needs of others, becomes self-defeating even on its own terms.

Sex also creates feelings that did not exist before. It is no accident that we call sexual intercourse "making love." Questions of attachment and love are unavoidable. Besides, since sex is how we reproduce, other people (at least other possible people) beyond you and your sexual partner(s) are involved too. Again there's more to think about: your readiness or willingness for parenthood, forthrightness about contraception, and so on. Utilitarianism celebrates pleasure, yes, but it is not a hedonistic or "go with the flow" philosophy. Have fun, it says, but don't turn off your brain.

Responsibility

Sexual intercourse is an act of profound vulnerability and trust. We give of our bodies, which can be treasured and honored or hurt or infected or impregnated; and of our feelings, which can be shared and deepened or betrayed or manipulated. From the point of view of the virtues, therefore, *responsibility* is a prime concern. We are called to take care with the gift of another's trust; to offer back the same; to honestly live up to our partner's (and others') legitimate expectations. Irresponsibility—carelessness, deception, coercion— is the complementary vice.

Sexual communication is vital here too, though in a somewhat different way than for utilitarians. Disregard for your partner, disinterest or inattention or deliberate misunderstanding, not only typically have bad consequences but violate the "internal goods" (as a virtue-oriented moralist would put it) of sex itself. They violate the trust and mutuality that sexual expression requires.

Some virtue thinkers argue that sexual relationships must be understood in the context of family and child-raising. The prime implied virtues are fidelity, commitment to the family, and monogamy. From this point of view, sex sometimes seems to be a kind of loose cannon in the human make-up, something that must be kept tightly under control in the name of larger human goods. Some versions of this view also imply that homosexuality is immoral, an issue we take up in later in this chapter.

Respect

"You're just treating me like an object," we may complain. Sexually, this means: you are just treating me as a means to your pleasure. Or: you are making me feel like I am just a body to you. Or: you are so fixated on certain of my body parts that you are missing me as a whole person (you don't even see me as a whole *body*).

This is sexual *objectification* — treating another person, sexually, as if they were just an object, just a thing.

Sex may be especially prone to objectification. The French existential philosopher Jean-Paul Sartre believed that objectification is unavoidable, since, as he put it, in sexual expression and lovemaking we literally turn ourselves into bodies (put all of our subjectivity into our *skin*, as it were) so as to be fully present to the other person. Maybe it's no surprise that we slide so readily into treating a person as only a body.

Language reflects and promotes this objectification too. Think of how many of the most common terms for women are derogatory and reductive. "Chick," for example—a helpless and mindless animal; or "doll," a plaything. Think of how slang words for genitals of either sex are used to talk about the whole person ("He's such a dick"). They're degrading *because* a person is being reduced to one body part, to be taken and used. Likewise, most of the popular terms for sexual intercourse not only put women into passive roles ("John screwed Jane," we say, but seldom vice versa) but conceive that role to be the object of *hurt* or exploitation ("screwed," "nailed," . . .).

Meanwhile, pornographic magazines outsell all others on the newsstands, pornographic videos and posters are everywhere, and pornographic imagery has steadily entered mainline advertising too. "Using sex to sell" is now almost trite, so universal and obvious is it—and it gets more and more explicit.

Many people, from feminists to conservatives, argue that all of this teaches a profoundly immoral lesson: that sex is a relation between a person (usually, male) and something that is less than a person (body part, plaything, . . .). At the very least, they say, it makes it extremely hard to create and live out a sexuality based on mutual respect. We come to believe not only that objectification is *sexy* (normal, natural, "hot"), but also that it is just *sex* itself— the only kind of sex there is.

For theories of right action, remember, the key ethical idea is that a person is *not* a thing, and must not be treated as such. We are not mere "objects"; we each demand respect as genuine centers of experience in our own rights. We need to imagine and create a sexuality that responds to that, to each other as whole persons. How shall we do that?

CAN WE BUILD ON SEXUAL COMMON GROUND?

Disagreements emerge here, for sure. By and large, though, what's more remarkable is how much we *agree* about sexual values. (At least, I think we do: this is a hypothesis you should check out.)

We agree that the pleasures of sex have a lot to do with its value. Most of us would also agree that sex is a deeply compelling expression of our natures both physical and spiritual (broadly speaking). We agree that sex also requires personal responsibility. We agree that people ought not to treat each other as objects. Even the pornographers' official line is that pornography is just a way for loving couples to heat up their sex lives.

Certainly few of these values are incompatible. Quite the contrary: most people's sexual ideals include them all. They even draw on each other. The utilitarian argument begins with pleasure, for example, but ends with something very like the virtues. Responsibility in turn arguably expresses respect. Each family of values has something to contribute.

Couldn't we build on this compatibility and common ground? Are there ways to help get the sex-and-ethics debate, such as it is, usefully unstuck? Here are a few possibilities to think about.

Reimagining Sex?

Surely we need to become more aware of the power of objectifying sexual language and of pornography. This may or may not translate into outright bans, say, on certain kinds of pornography (for one thing, difficult civil liberties issues come up). But awareness has power all by itself. We can't resist pornography—we can't even think it through—if we pay no attention to it at all.

We need to begin to reimagine sex itself. One of the worst effects of treating sex as "dirty" is that mainstream culture has virtually abandoned the imagination of sex to the movie industry, advertisers, and pornographers. And so we learn early on, and often below the level of consciousness, that "sex" must be hot, quick, purely genital, precautionless, and, usually, objectified. Even mainstream culture, as prudish and repressed as some people think it is, could do better than that.

Meanwhile, the same traditional views of sex as dirty have made it hard for many people to talk about sex even with the people with whom they themselves are *having* sex, which leads to another large set of problems, such as "date rape." Men and women seem to have radically different understandings of what even the simplest words (such as "no") actually mean, and what the other person actually wants. Again, surely we can do better than this.

The challenge, then, is to create and promote alternative and more moral visions of sexuality: sex based upon mutual understanding and respect, sex not cut off from larger kinds of sensitivities and communication, sex that allows us to respond to each other as whole persons, sex that takes our responsibilities to others seriously—*and sex that is also sexy.*

I almost wrote "*nonetheless* also sexy." But why should we suppose that it wouldn't or couldn't be sexy—even more sexy, maybe, than sex as it is so often pictured now? We speak of "good sex" in a physical sense—sex that is most physically fulfilling and satisfying—but we also can speak of it in a moral sense: and we might just venture as a guess that the two are not so distinct. Imagine sex that is truly a union with another person fully present to you and you to them; fully conscious; fully mutual. Isn't that the ideal—far better than a sexual encounter with the same person as mere body? When objectified sex seems to be the only "sexy" sex (or the only way to have sex at all), isn't that part of the *problem?*

Retooling Marriage?

Another example: maybe we could re-approach the vexed question of marriage in a more integrative spirit.

With the divorce rate over 50 percent and rampant spousal abuse, it can hardly be said that marriage as it now exists is an unqualified success. On the other hand, we do seem to have a need for institutionalized companionship. Half of all marriages end in divorce, yes, but 90 percent of all eligible Americans marry despite the odds, and even 80 percent of those who divorce remarry within five years. Some energy would be well spent trying to improve marriage.

For one concrete proposal: it's time to acknowledge that people often need help living together, at least living together in a productive and fulfilling way. Marriage counseling could become the norm—something expected, something we sometimes even do for each other rather than go to a therapist— rather than the embarrassed last resort we consider it now. As part of the marriage ceremony, friends and family could pledge to "be there" for the new couple when they need help.

Some people have proposed "trial marriages," in which partners commit themselves to each other for a specific period of time (say, five or ten years), to see if it will really work with that person (no children). If not, at the end of the trial period the marriage dissolves, on prearranged terms (no lawyers). At a time when the vast majority of couples live together before marriage anyway, and divorce is so very common, it is arguable that we live in a "trial marriage" society anyway—only unrecognized, unsupported, and made unnecessarily difficult and unhappy. There is no good reason for all the hindrance.

Besides, if it does work out, you get to marry the same person twice, in effect! Sweet. If you don't like that idea (or even if you do), how (or how else) would *you* propose to improve marriage?

"PERVERSION"

One of the most contested contemporary questions about sexuality has to do with the idea of sexual "perversion" and its application to the question of homosexuality. Here we need our critical-thinking tools in particular. Can we make some progress?

Definitions

Can you pervert sex? Philosopher Colin McGinn points out that to "pervert" something, according to *Webster's*, is to "turn it aside from its proper use or nature." We can pervert justice; we can pervert sport; what about sex? "Can you deflect sexual desire," McGinn asks, "from its true or proper course?" His answer is *yes*.

"To make sense of this," he begins, "we obviously need some concept of what the 'proper use or nature' of human sexual desire is." Here is his proposal.

> From a purely biological perspective, the human sex drive has as its primary object sexual activity of a kind that would lead to conception if it occurred in the right circumstances. . . . But of course there is more to sexual desire than this purely biological function; it also has an emotional or personal side. Sex makes us relate in certain ways to other persons *as persons*; it is connected in all sorts of respects to our nature as social beings. I would like to suggest

that the proper nature of sex, from a psychological point of view, involves a desire for another person as a sentient and physical entity: it is a complex passion aimed at another person conceived as possessing a sensual nature.

If we conceive the object of sex in this way, it turns out that we can fairly readily define what "perversion" could mean.

That sensual nature is the proper object of sexual attraction—a living body capable of sexual feelings and desires. If sexual desire becomes detached from such an object, it can be said to have been perverted from its proper course.

Certain examples are obvious. McGinn mentions sex with things, which are not living and have no "sensual nature" of their own at all. Sex with animals is another example, where responding to and being responded to as a "whole sensual nature" is not possible.

Sex with other humans can be perverted too, by this definition. Here too, sexual desires can be "detached from the whole sensual nature" of the other person.

I think we generally appreciate that certain elements in [the structure of our sexual desires] shouldn't be allowed to take on a life of their own, squeezing out the rest. The focus must remain on the other person as a complete sensual being, and not shift to something that lies to the side of the person, or is a mere part of him, or is quite impersonal. . . .

"Sexual tunnel vision," then, is the essence of sexual perversion according to McGinn. Perversion is a failure (or inability?) to respond to another person as a *person*—thus a failure of respect as well.

McGinn argues that this definition has plausible parallels in related areas of life. Eating, like sex, also has both biological and social functions, and a wide range of foods and eating styles are possible and natural enough. But eating can also be perverted "if, say, you eat only to cure depression, thus overeating; or if certain foods are consumed solely in order to irritate your mother. . . ." Or again: curiosity, a natural enough drive, can be perverted into an interest "merely in gossip about soap-opera celebrities." That too is a form of tunnel vision. Here too perversion means that there is "something funny somewhere," as McGinn puts it. Desire has wandered off target, has become fixated on some small part of the larger whole that matters.

The Question of Homosexuality

Call someone a "pervert" in the culture at large, of course, and what you will be understood to mean is "homosexual." Even as studies suggest that up to 10 percent or more of the population may be primarily homosexual (and more may be bisexual), there is a vast well of uneasiness, condemnation, and hostility toward anyone perceived to be a "pervert" in this way. What can ethics say to this?

One starting point is this. Even if homosexuality *is* clearly and deeply "perverse," there is no justification for the hatred and violence that are sometimes acted out against gay men and lesbians. It's pretty hard to justify hatred and violence in any case, and surely impossible when they are directed against people whose only offense is to show love (of all things!) in ways that certain others are uneasy with.

Moreover, even if homosexuality is "perverse," it is arguably a person's legal right to engage in it—just like most other "perversions," sexual or otherwise. To use McGinn's example, it may be perverse to watch soap operas too, but it's not the law's business. We hold dear the right to do what we want with consenting others within pretty broad limits. To recognize the right, of course, does not mean that you have to approve of everything people do with it. But the right still exists. We understand this well enough when it comes to free speech or choice of private activities. Should sexual orientation be any different?

But the question remains whether homosexuality actually *is* perverse in the first place. Is it truly a case of desire wandering "off course"?

On McGinn's analysis, clearly it is *not*. Homosexual desire can respond to the "whole sensual nature" of a person just as can heterosexual desire. Likewise, both homosexual *and* heterosexual desire may *fail* to respond in this way—may become "tunnel visioned," fixated, or objectified. But there is nothing in homosexual love as such that makes it necessarily objectified, any more than heterosexual love. Neither orientation has a monopoly on objectification.

Sexual tunnel vision, in short, is perverse wherever it occurs. The pornography addict and the person who hits on someone only to "score" are perverse whether gay or straight. On McGinn's account, sexual perversion simply *has nothing to do with sexual orientation*. It has everything to do with sexual *ethics*.

Can the Sexual-Orientation Debate Make Progress?

Again disagreement must be acknowledged. Some people believe that the familiar heterosexual roles are "given" in some fundamental way, ordained by God or nature, and may even feel that their own sexual identity is tied up with them. Or maybe it could be argued that homosexuality is perverse for some other reason. Maybe McGinn's analysis has missed something (what do *you* think?).

Yet possibly a somewhat settled "center" is beginning to emerge on this issue. Many Americans in the polls say that they are unattracted to, perhaps faintly uncomfortable with, a homosexual life for themselves, but also say that they believe others have the right to choose homosexual relationships without prejudice if they so wish. When push comes to shove, we put rights first.

"Natural" Sex

We all seem to want to believe that what we do is "natural"—and of course we believe that what's "natural" is also *right*. But "natural" is a notoriously hard word to define, and it is never so hard as when it comes to sex.

Is there a way to find out what's "natural." One way might be to try to find common sexual practices across all human cultures. If we could find them, we'd have a strong argument that those practices are natural in the sense that they have some deep basis in our shared nature.

But universal sexual practices are hard to find. Even the physical act of sex itself varies among cultures. The so-called "missionary position"—still the only legal position for sexual intercourse in many American states, by the way—got its name because it was so unheard of (and so amusing) among the Africans to whom European and American missionaries were sent. They named it after the only people they knew who did it that way.

Sex and gender roles that seem second nature to us vary too. In some cultures women are much more sexually forward than men. In others, men spend hours on makeup and clothes in order to win the favor of women. Psychological research suggest that all of us have traits that are both male *and* female. It's even possible that we're all naturally *bi*sexual!

One argument for the "unnaturalness" of homosexuality appeals to biology. Some argue that the natural purpose of sex is reproduction; so homosexual sex can't be natural because it can't lead to reproduction.

This is one of those arguments that doesn't apply to "like cases" quite as its proponents might expect. For one thing, it seems to imply that the use of effective contraception is unnatural too. Catholic moralists usually accept that implication, though most non-Catholics do not. It also seems to imply that any heterosexual sex that takes place when the woman is not fertile is not natural either. A few (very few) people take this view, but it is far too restrictive for the usual understanding of sexual appropriateness.

Notice that the same goes for marriage. If you oppose gay marriage on the grounds that gay or lesbian couples cannot "naturally" bear children, then logically (it seems) you must also object to heterosexual marriage between partners one of whom is infertile or sterilized, or who choose to remain childless or who adopt children not "naturally" their own. Once again, this seems far too restrictive.

Maybe "natural" means "normal." Well, normal in what sense? That which is most common statistically? This seems like a nonstarter too. A very long list of other things would become "unnatural" too. Homosexuality, yes; but it's also not statistically normal to be a left-hander or a college student or a Christian or for that matter even a male (52% of the U.S. population is female).

Besides, it seems quite clear that if "normal" means just the statistically most common, this meaning of "natural" also cannot carry much moral weight. All kinds of horrible things are statistically common.

At bottom I think it would be more honest to admit that most of our talk of "naturalness" or "normality" really reflects an unfamiliarity and uneasiness with homosexuality on the part of some (but by no means all) "straight" people. Chapters 1 and 3 of this book have argued that feelings such as these should not be discounted simply because they are feelings—but Chapter 1 also insists that they be *thought through*, not treated as though they are justifications all by themselves, or furiously rationalized when challenged. You have the tools to think them through more carefully!

Stereotypes are changing. Gay men and lesbians have been stereotyped in certain all-too-familiar ways, a product of many factors: media attention on the most florid behaviors, for instance, and the suppression of any traces of the homosexuality of many people in the past. Now more gay people are openly affirming their homosexuality, and turn out to be the people down the street, your lawyer or nurse, your favorite artist or aunt. My students write again and again of overcoming the stereotypes when their boss or close friend or teammate turns out to be gay. Even when many of the stereotypes are true (of the boss, friend, etc.), something changes for these students. They can see a homosexual as a whole *person* and not merely as a being defined by sexual orientation.

Recent research on the biological roots of sexuality seems to make a difference to many people. Though we have thought of of sexual orientation as a choice, some studies now suggest that it has a strong neurological basis. So perhaps it's not something we can "help." Each of us is just born with certain sexual inclinations and not others. This new understanding is reflected in the recent change in language from "sexual preference" to "sexual orientation."

Yet it is also a matter of debate in the gay community. Gay people don't want to be *forgiven* for their sexual orientation, as if it were some sort of genetic burden or liability. The very thing that might make it more acceptable to (some) straight people, then, is a sticking point for (some) gay people.

There is also a persistent unwillingness in "straight" media to recognize the implications of the very same research for *hetero*sexuality. If the research is right, it's not just homosexuality that is biologically determined, but sexuality as such. If there are "gay genes" then there are also "straight genes." This seems to be a sticking point for (some) straight people.

People, in any case, are more than their sexual orientation. To respond to each other as "whole persons," we *all* need to avoid defining each other by sexual orientation alone. Maybe we're beginning to find our way to at least that much common ground. Even Catholic doctrine, for example, though strongly opposed to homosexuality, makes a clear distinction between the behavior and the *person*, who is someone larger than his or her sexuality and deserving of love and respect as such. And that is not so different from a gay friend of mine, asked whether he prefers to be called "gay" or "homosexual," who always answers: "Just 'human being' would be fine."

"Bachelor Party"

JASON SCHULTZ

Suppose you take seriously some of the themes of this chapter and aim to live a life in accord with them. If you are, say, a heterosexual man, you'll try for a life of equality and respect for your partner(s) and for women generally. Simple, right?

Maybe not. In this essay Jason Schultz struggles just to create a bachelor party that does not play into what he calls the "typical anti-women, homophobic male-bonding thing." To plan such a party that is also fun, even "sexy," turns out to be a real challenge. Getting free of the usual stereotypes proves to be hard indeed. What's sexy and what's oppressive still seem to be uncomfortably close together, even in our day-to-day habits and old traditions.

Would it, maybe, be easier for you? Think about how you would plan such a party. If you're a straight woman, or gay, how would *you* plan such an event? Do you think you are any more free of the usual stereotypes? Why or why not?

MINUTES AFTER MY BEST FRIEND TOLD ME HE WAS GETTING married, I casually offered to throw a bachelor party in his honor. Even though such parties are notorious for their degradation of women, I didn't think this party would be much of a problem. Both the bride and groom considered themselves feminists, and I figured that most of the men attending would agree that sexism had no place in the celebration of this union.

I wanted to include at least some of the usual elements, such as good food and drink, great music, and cool things to do. At the same time, I was determined not to fall prey to traditional sexist party gimmicks such as prostitutes, strippers jumping out of cakes, or straight porn. But after nixing all the traditional lore, even *I* thought it sounded boring. What were we going to do except sit around and think about women?

Copyright © by Jason Schultz.

"What about a belly dancer?" one of the ushers suggested when I confided my concerns to him. "That's not as bad as stripper." I sighed. This was supposed to be an occasion for the groom and his male friends to get together, celebrate the upcoming marriage, and affirm their friendship and connection with each other as men. "What does hiring a female sex worker have to do with any of that?" I shouted into the phone. I quickly regained my calm, but his suggestion still stung. We had to find some other way.

. . . I thought about renting some gay porn, or making it a cross-dressing party, but many of the guests were conservative, and I didn't want to scare anyone off. Besides, what would it say about a bunch of straight men if all we could do to be sexy was act queer for a night?

Over coffee on a Sunday morning, I asked some of the other guys what they thought was so "sexy" about having a stripper at a bachelor party.

"Well," David said, "it's just a gag. It's something kinda funny and sexy at the same time."

"Yeah," A.J. agreed. "It's not all that serious, but it's something special to do that makes the party cool."

"But *why* is it sexy and funny?" I asked. "Why can't we, as a bunch of guys, be sexy and funny ourselves?"

" 'Cause it's easier to be a guy with other guys when there's a chick around. It gives you all something in common to relate to."

"Hmm. I think I know what you mean," I said. "When I see a stripper, I get turned on, but not in the same way I would if I was with a lover. It's more like going to a show or watching a flick together. It's enjoyable, stimulating, but it's not overwhelming or intimate in the same way that sex is. Having the stripper provides a common emotional context for us to feel turned on. But we don't have to do anything about it like we would if we were with a girlfriend, right?"

"Well, my girlfriend would kill me if she saw me checking out this stripper," Greg replied. "But because it's kind of a male-bonding thing, it's not as threatening to our relationship. It's not because it's the stripper over her, it's because it's just us guys hanging out. It doesn't go past that."

Others agreed. "Yeah. You get turned on, but not in a serious way. It makes you feel sexy and sexual, and you can enjoy feeling that way with your friends. Otherwise, a lot of times, just hanging out with the guys is pretty boring. Especially at a bachelor party. I mean, that's the whole point, isn't it—to celebrate the fact that we're bachelors, and he"—referring to Robert, the groom—"isn't!"

[I was beginning to] realize that having a female sex worker at the party would give the men permission to connect with one another without becoming vulnerable. When men discuss sex in terms of actions—who they "did," and how and where they did it—they can gain recognition and validation of their sexuality from other men without having to expose their *feelings* about sex.

"What other kinds of things make you feel sexy like the stripper does?" I asked several of the guys.

"Watching porn sometimes, or a sexy movie."

A.J. said, "Just getting a look from a girl at a club. I mean, she doesn't even have to talk to you, but you still feel sexy and you can still hang out with your friends."

Greg added, "Sometimes just knowing that my girlfriend thinks I'm sexy, and then talking about her with friends, makes me feel like I'm the man. Or I'll hear some other guy talk about his girlfriend in a way that reminds me of mine, and I'll still get that same feeling. But that doesn't happen very often, and usually only when talking with one other guy.

This gave me an idea. "I've noticed that same thing, both here and at school with my other close guy friends. Why doesn't it happen with a bunch of guys, say at a party?"

"I don't know. It's hard to share a lot of personal stuff with guys," said Adam, "especially about someone you're seeing, if you don't feel comfortable. Well, not comfortable, because I know most of the guys who'll be at the party, but it's more like I don't want them to hassle me, or I might say something that freaks them out."

"Or you're just used to guys talking shit about girls," someone else added. "Like a party or hanging out together. They rag on them, or pick out who's the cutest or who wants to do who. That's not the same thing as really talking about what makes you feel sexy."

I said: "So it's kind of like if I were to say that I liked to be tied down to the bed, no one would take me seriously. You guys would probably crack up laughing, make a joke or two, but I'd never expect you to actually join in and talk about being tied up in a serious way. It certainly wouldn't feel 'sexy,' would it? At least not as much as the stripper."

"Exactly. You talking about being tied down here is fine, 'cause we're into the subject of sex on a serious kick and all. But at a party, people are bullshitting each other and gabbing, and horsing around. The last thing most of us want is to trip over someone's personal taste or start thinking someone's a little queer."

"You mean queer as in homosexual?" I asked.

"Well, not really, 'cause I think everyone here is straight. But more of queer in the sense of perverted or different. I mean, you grow up in high school thinking that all guys are basically the same. You all want the same thing from girls in the same way. And when someone like you says you like to be tied down, it's kinda weird—almost like a challenge. It makes me have to respond in a way that either shows me agreeing that I also like to be tied down or not. And if someone's a typical guy and he says that, it makes you think he's different—not the same guy you knew in high school. And if he's not the same guy, then it challenges you to relate to him on a different level." . . .

According to the prevailing cultural view, "desirable" hetero men are inherently dominant, aggressive, and, in many subtle and overt ways, abusive to women. To be sexy and powerful, straight men are expected to control and contrive a sexuality that reinforces their authority. Opposing these notions of power subjects a straight guy to being branded "sensitive," submissive, or passive—banished to the nether regions of excitement and pleasure, the unmasculine, asexual, "vanilla" purgatory of antieroticism. Just as hetero women are often forced to choose between the images of the virgin and the whore, modern straight men are caught in a cultural tug-of-war between the Marlboro Man and the Wimp.

So where does that leave straight men who want to reexamine what a man is and change it? Can a good man be sexy? Can a sexy man be good? What is good sex, egalitarian sex?

. . . What about the sensitive guy? Wasn't that the male cry (whimper) of the nineties? Sorry, but all the media hype about sensitivity never added up to significant changes in behavior. Straight male sexuality still remains one of the most underchallenged areas of masculinity in America. Some men *did* propose a different kind of sexuality for straight men in the 1970s, one that emphasizes feelings and sensitivity and emotional connection. But these efforts failed to affect our ideas in any kind of revolutionary way. Now, instead of a "sexy" sensitive guy, men's magazines are calling for the emergence of the "Post-Sensitive Man."

Why did sensitivity fail? Were straight women, even feminists, lying to men about what they wanted? The answer is "yes" and "no." I don't think sensitivity was the culprit. I think the problem was men's passivity, or more specifically, men's lack of assertiveness and power.

In much of our understanding, power is equated with oppression: images of white supremacists dominating people of color, men dominating women, and the rich dominating the poor. But power need not always oppress others. One can, I believe, be powerful in a nonoppressive way.

In order to find this sort of alternative, we need to examine men's experience with power and sexuality further. Fortunately, queer men and women have given us a leg up on the process by reenergizing the debate about what is good sex and what is fair sex. Gay male culture has a long history of exploring nontraditional aspects of male sexuality, such as crossdressing, bondage and dominance, and role playing. These dynamics force gay men to break out of a singular experience of male sexual desire and to examine the diversity within male sexuality. . . . Gay culture has broader and more inclusive attitudes about what is sexy and a conception of desire that accommodates many types of sex for many types of gay men. For straight men in our culture, there is such a rigid definition of "sexy" that it leaves us few options besides being oppressive, overbearing, or violent.

. . . Many straight women (both feminist and not) still find an aggressive, dominant man sexy. Many straight women still desire a man to take charge when it comes to romance or intimacy, especially when initiating intercourse. Yet many of the same straight feminist women constantly highlight the abuse and discrimination that many of these men inflict. They often complain about a man who is misogynist while affirming his desirability. This is confusing and frustrating.

Admittedly, much of my frustration relates to my own experience. I've always found fierce, independent women attractive—women who say they want a man to support them emotionally, listen to them, and not fight them every step of the way. Yet in reality, these women often lost respect for me and for other men who tried to change our sexuality to meet these needs.

I'd try to play the game, moving in as the aggressive man and then showing a more sensitive side after I'd caught the person's attention. But more often than not, the result was frustrating. I didn't catch a clue until one night when I had an enlightening conversation with one of these women who called herself a feminist. I asked her why guys who tried to accommodate the political desires of straight feminists always seemed to lose out in the end. She said she thought it was because a lot of young straight women who confront gender issues through feminism are constantly trying to redefine themselves in relation to culture and other people in their lives. Therefore, if they pursue relationships with men, many consciously seek out a *traditional* man—not only because it is the kind of man they have been taught to desire, but because he is familiar to them. He is strong, stable, predictable, and powerful. As the woman's identity shifts and changes, she can use the man she is dating as a reference point and source of strength and stability.

If she chooses to become involved with a feminist man who feels the same need to examine assumptions about gender (including his own masculinity) on a political and personal level, both partners are in a state of flux and instability. . . .

. . . We need to find new, strong values and ideas of male heterosexuality instead of passive identities that try to distance us from sexist men. We need to stop trying to avoid powerful straight sexuality and work to redefine what our power means and does. We need to find strength and desire outside of macho, antiwomen ways of being masculine.

. . . Our cultures tell us that being a "real" man means not being feminine, not being gay, and not being weak. They warn us that anyone who dares to stand up to these ideas becomes a sitting target to have his manhood shot down in flames. . . .

Not becoming a sitting target to have *my* manhood shot down was high on my mind when the evening of my best friend's bachelor party finally arrived. But I was determined not to be silent about how I felt about the party and about new visions for straight men within our society.

We decided to throw the party two nights before the wedding. We all gathered at my house, each of us bringing a present to add to the night's activities. After all the men had arrived, we began cooking dinner, breaking open beer and champagne, and catching up on where we had left off since we last saw each other.

During the evening, we continued to talk off and on about why we didn't have a stripper or prostitute for the party. After several rounds of margaritas and a few hands of poker, tension started to build around the direction I was pushing the conversation.

"So what don't you like about strippers?" David asked me.

This was an interesting question. I was surprised not only by the guts of David to ask it, but also by my own mixed feelings in coming up with an answer. "It's not that I don't like being excited, or turned on, per se," I responded. "In fact, to be honest, watching a female stripper is an exciting and erotic experience for me. But at the same time, it's a very uncomfortable one. I get a sense when I watch her that I'm participating in a misuse of pleasure, if that makes sense."

I looked around at my friends. I couldn't tell whether the confused looks on their faces were due to the alcohol, the poker game, or my answer. "Ideally, I would love to sit back and enjoy watching someone express herself sexually through dance, seduction, flirtation—all the positive elements I associate with stripping," I said. "But at the same time, because so many strippers are poor and forced to perform in order to survive economically, I feel like the turn-on I get is false. I feel like I get off easy, sitting back as the man, paying for the show.

"And in that way, it's selling myself short sexually. It's not only saying very little about the sexual worth of the woman on stage, but the sexual worth of me as the viewer as well. By *only* being a viewer—just getting off as a member of the audience—the striptease becomes a very limiting thing. If the purpose is for me to feel sexy and excited, but not to act on those feelings, I'd rather find a more honest and direct way to do it. So personally, while I would enjoy watching a stripper on one level, the real issues of economics, the treatment of women, and the limitation of my own sexual personae push me to reject the whole stripper thing in favor of something else."

"But what else do you do to feel sexy?" A.J. asked.

"That's a tough question," I said. "Feeling sexy often depends on the way other people act toward you. For me, right now, you guys are a huge way for me to feel sexy. [Some of the men cringe.] I'm not saying that we have to challenge our sexual identities, although that's one way. But we can cut through a lot of this locker-room macho crap and start talking with each other about how we feel sexually, what we think, what we like, etc.

. . . All right, I thought. Here we go. "What makes me feel sexy? I'll tell you. I feel sexy when I say how much I like licking chocolate off a partner's back. Not just that I like to do it, or talking about how often I do it, but that it feels amazing to taste her sweat and her skin mixed in with the sweetness of the chocolate. I feel sexy when I think about running my fingers through her hair in the shower, or watching her put a condom on me with her tongue. I feel sexy remembering how my muscles stretch and strain after being tied down to the bed, or the difference between leather, lace, and silk rubbing up and down my body. That's some of what makes me feel sexy."

The guys were silent for a few seconds, but soon afterwards, the ice seemed to break. We agreed that, as heterosexual men, we should be able to share with each other what we find exciting and shouldn't *need* a female stripper to feel sexy. In some ways it may have been the desire to define their own sexuality that changed their minds; in others it may have been a traditionally masculine desire to reject any dependency on women. In any case, other men began to speak of their own experiences with pleasure and desire, and we continued to talk throughout the night, exploring the joys of hot sex, one-night stands, and even our preferences for certain brands of condoms. We discussed the ups and downs of monogamy versus "open" dating and the pains of long-distance relationships.

Some men continued to talk openly about their desire for straight pornography or women who fit the traditional stereotype of feminity. But others contradicted this, expressing their wish to move beyond that image of women in their lives. The wedding, which started out as the circumstance for our gathering, soon fell into the background of our thoughts as we began to find common ground through our real-life experiences and feelings as straight men. In the end, we all toasted the groom, sharing stories, jokes, and parts of our lives that many of us had never told. Most importantly, we were able to express ourselves sexually without hiding who we were from each other.

. . . Some of the most amazing conversations I have had have been with other straight and bisexual men about the *pleasure* of sex with women. These conversations have been far from passive, boring, or placid. They have ranged from the many uses of cock rings to issues of consent with S/M and B&D acts to methods of achieving multiple male orgasms. The differences between these conversations and typical sexist male dialogue is that our discourse strives to bypass the mythological nature of straight male bravado and pornographic fantasy and to emphasize straight men asserting themselves as strong voices for equality *and* pleasure in cultural discourses on sexuality.

These public dialogues have been immensely helpful in dispelling overemphasized issues like impotence and premature ejaculation; such conversations have also allowed us to move past the degrading and pornographic lingo used in high school locker rooms to describe sex with women and have pushed us to focus our energy on honest questions, feelings, and *desires*. These are the kinds of voices straight men must claim publicly.

When it comes to sex, feminist straight men must become participants in the discourse about our own sexuality. We have to fight the oppressive images of men as biological breeders and leering animals. We must find ways in which to understand our diverse backgrounds, articulate desires that are not oppressive, and acknowledge the power we hold. We must take center stage when it comes to articulating our views in a powerful voice. I'm not trying to prescribe any particular form of sexuality or specify what straight men should want. But until we begin to generate our own demands and desires in an honest and equitable way for feminist straight women to hear. I don't think we can expect to be both good *and* sexy any time soon.

Exercises and Notes

Sex at Antioch College

Sexual pressure and coercion, up to and including "date rape," seem to be widespread on college campuses. Most colleges now offer some warnings about sexual miscommunication and coercion at least as part of standard orientation presentations. Some administrations have formalized policies for dealing with allegations of sexual coercion.

A few have gone farther. At Antioch College, in Yellow Springs, Ohio, the entire community—students, faculty, administration, and staff—has formulated and tested a policy meant to deal with, and prevent, "sexual offenses" such as this.

The statement begins with values:

> Antioch College has made a strong commitment to the issue of respect, including respect for each individual's personal and sexual boundaries. Sexual offenses are dehumanizing. They are not just a violation of the individual, but of the Antioch community.

Sex must be *consensual*, the policy insists. That is, participants must "willingly and verbally agree to engage in specific sexual behavior." Participants need to share enough common understanding to be able to request consent and to clearly consent or not, and also must not be so intoxicated or threatened that consent or the request for it is meaningless. Moreover, and crucially, "silence and/or non-communication *must never be interpreted as consent.*"

Consent is understood to be an *ongoing process* in any sexual interaction. The most controversial part of the policy is this:

> Verbal consent should be obtained with each new level of physical and/or sexual behavior in any given interaction, regardless of who initiates it. Asking "Do you want to have sex with me?" is not enough. The request for consent must be specific to each act.

The policy continues (it's a longish document) with definitions of key terms ("sexual conduct," for example) and enforcement procedures.

What do you think about this policy? Does sex at Antioch sound exciting? If fully mutual sex with explicit consent at each stage does *not* sound sexy, why not? What does it say about *us* (about what we assume sex *must* be like) if we can't imagine sex like that?

Is there even a way to make the requirement of consent at each stage into a kind of *opportunity* (remembering Chapter 12)? One of my students recently wrote, in response to the above questions: "Actually, I think whispering to someone, communicating, and asking permission to do fun things is pretty cool."

Consider the pros and cons of such a policy for your own school. How would it change or not change sexual interactions for you and your fellow students? How would you write such a policy for your own school? Should your class try it? Can men and women in your very own class actually communicate about these things? Why or why not? If communication breaks down, where do you think it breaks down, and why?

From Pornography to "Erotica"

Pornography is a hotly debated topic among feminists because it is hard to see how to limit it without raising grave civil liberties concerns. Restrictions on sexually explicit materials also put at risk any descriptions or pictures of sex from nonstandard points of view, and have in fact been used disproportionately against lesbian and gay materials. Many antipornography activists are not in favor of censorship in most cases.

One such critic, David Steinberg, writes:

> What is needed, in my opinion, is not an attempt to drive pornography underground, socially or psychically. If pornography becomes outlawed (again), it, like prostitution, will only come to represent the notion that sex is dirty, even more than it does today. What is needed instead is the development of sexual materials that take the best of the pornographic tradition—sexual openness, exploration, and celebration—and add to these egalitarian values, imagination, artfulness, respect for ourselves, and respect for the power and beauty of sex itself. . . .

Some people have proposed a different name for this sexually explicit but different-from-pornography kind of material: "erotica." There might be many different types of erotica, depending on your tastes, sexual orientation, interest in fantasy, and so on—but erotica, whatever else it is or isn't, is *never* degrading or abusive.

What do *you* think? What would erotica or "feminist pornography" (Steinberg's term) look like? Is it possible to distinguish morally acceptable erotic materials from morally unacceptable ones? If you think so, how would you propose to draw the line? Why?

KEEP ON THINKING

Is there (more) overlooked common ground in the sexual ethics debate?

Take the "gay marriage" issue, for example. This entire debate comes up in the first place because many gay men and lesbians *want* to be married. We're not disagreeing about the value of marriage itself. Mightn't it then be possible to affirm the value of heterosexual marriage and child-rearing families (the central concern of many conservatives) without excluding the possibility of affirming *other* kinds of institutionalized relationships too (as we already do in allowing people to marry who cannot or choose not to bear children)?

France has recently offered a new kind of legal status to unmarried couples, both gay and straight, that extends to them the same rights as married couples in such areas as housing, income tax, inheritance, and social welfare—but differs from marriage in other ways, such as the ease with which it can be dissolved and nonprovision for parental rights. These are called "civil solidarity pacts," which the French government describes as "not marriages but a new form of legal coupling that recognizes the needs of people today." Why couldn't we do something along the same lines? Marriage as we know it is surely not the only way two people could choose to be together, and recognizing an alternative form of "coupling" might calm down people who want to keep traditional, heterosexual, family-oriented marriages distinct from gay or other kinds of long-term, commited sexual relationships. A little compromise might be in order.

I have tried to point out some fundamental areas of agreement throughout this chapter, and suggested some possible steps forward based on those agreements. Go back and look at those suggestions. Do you agree? Why or why not? Do you think trial marriages are a good idea? How about investing some energy in helping people communicate better in relationships, deal with day-to-day frustration constructively, and so on?

Religion, especially religious conservatism, often comes up as a sticking point when my students survey ethical issues about sexuality. But is the Bible really "antisex"? It's not so clear. Saint Paul did think it only barely better to be married than to burn in hell. Jesus, though, did not express such views (nor did he condemn or even mention homosexuality). The Torah/Old

Testament's stated penalties for sexual transgressions tend to be severe, but when Tamar seduces her own father-in-law she is not condemned but honored. The adulterers David and Bathsheba beget the wise king Solomon. Solomon himself authored *Song of Solomon*—a rather steamy bit of Scripture, by the way!

I don't mean that the Bible is necessarily "pro-sex" either; just that, as usual, it's arguably more richly ambiguous than some people say.

Another point: regardless of what we think about homosexuality, we need to pay more attention to the question of homo*phobia* (fear and hatred of homosexuals) too. After all, despite all of the drum beating about the dangers of homosexuals, it's the homo*phobes* who are out there threatening, beating up, and sometimes even murdering gay people. Nothing justifies hatefulness so drastically off the scale.

Once again, I think this is a recognition the larger society shares, even as we struggle over sexual orientation itself. But the questions it raises go deep. What accounts for such intense fear and hatred? And why is it a response to a kind of *love*? "I cannot tell you how astonished I am," writes one lesbian, "when heterosexuals see our love as unnatural. In a world that glamorizes war and graphic violence, I would think that any expression of love would be welcome." Why isn't it? This is a real and difficult question. Give it some thought.

NOTES AND FURTHER READINGS

Useful philosophical anthologies on sex and ethics include Alan Soble, ed., *The Philosophy of Sex* (Rowman and Littlefield, 3rd edition, 1997); Robert Baker, Kathleen Winninger, and Frederick Elliston, eds., *Philosophy and Sex* (Prometheus, 3rd edition, 1998); and Robert Stewart, ed., *Philosophical Perspectives on Sex and Love* (Oxford, 1995). This chapter draws upon several selections from *Philosophy and Sex*, especially Robert Baker, " 'Pricks' and 'Chicks' ": A Plea for 'Persons.' " Also included in *Philosophy and Sex* is the full text of Antioch's "Sexual Offense Prevention Policy" and a discussion of the debate over Antioch's policy by Matthew Silliman. A detailed and provocative treatment of objectification, challenging and deepening what is said here on that theme, is Martha Nussbaum's essay "Objectification," in Soble's *The Philosophy of Sex*. For texts of some other philosophical treatments, an extensive bibliography, and a wide variety of useful links, go to Lawrence Hinman's "Ethics Updates" website at <ethics.acusd.edu> and select "Sexual Orientation."

Colin McGinn is cited from his essay "Sex," in *Moral Literacy* (Duckworth/Hackett, 1992), pages 60 to 64. Bertrand Russell was first to propose trial marriages. For a contemporary version, see E. M. Adams, *A Society Fit for Human Beings* (SUNY Press, 1997), page 82. On "civil solidarity pacts" in France, see Suzanne Daley, "France Gives Legal Status to Unmarried Couples," *New York Times*, 14 October 1999, page A3; and Peter Ford, "French Stretch Law to Fit Post-Modern Mores," *Christian Science Monitor*, 23 November 1999, page 1. The quote at the end of exercise #3 ("I cannot tell you how astonished . . .")

is from Sonia-Ivette Roman, "What Will We Teach the Children?," in Robert Goss and Amy Adams Squire Strongheart, *Our Families, Our Values: Snapshots of Queer Kinship* (Haworth Press, 1997).

A provocative book on all of these topics is John Stoltenberg, *Refusing to Be a Man* (Penguin, 1989). A useful video on the objectification of women in advertisements is Jean Kilbourne's "Still Killing Us Softly," available from Cambridge Documentary Films, P.O. Box 385, Cambridge, MA 02139. On pornography, see the first two philosophical anthologies cited above; and Michael Kimmel, ed., *Men Confront Pornography* (Meridian, 1990). David Weinberg is quoted from his essay "The Roots of Pornography," on page 58 of Kimmel's collection. On the censorship debate, see Susan Dwyer, ed., *The Problem of Pornography* (Wadsworth, 1995).

On sex and religion, an excellent starting point is Adrian Thatcher and Elizabeth Stuart, eds., *Christian Perspectives on Sexuality and Gender* (Wm. B. Eerdmans Publishing Company, 1996).

CHAPTER 17

⬡

Abortion

BACKGROUND

A Very Brief History of the Abortion Debate

Folk medicine long offered certain ways of trying to terminate a pregnancy. These were far less effective than modern medical methods, though, and were often lethal for the pregnant woman. Trying to terminate a pregnancy was a risky and uncertain business.

Moralists disapproved, but not mainly because of the abortion. They disapproved because the cause of any pregnancy that would drive a woman to such extreme measures was probably illicit sex, which was harshly regarded indeed. Legally, abortion itself was not taken so seriously. English common law allowed abortion at any stage of pregnancy. Early American law followed suit.

The Catholic Church originally did not condemn all abortions either. Before the seventeenth century, terminating a pregnancy was not prohibited in the earliest stages—not until quickening, about eight or nine weeks into pregnancy, when Saint Thomas, following Aristotle, believed that we acquire human souls. Even abortion after quickening, though disapproved, was not condemned wholesale. It was not considered comparable to killing a full-fledged human being.

The Church's view changed when early biologists came to believe that conception immediately produced a tiny but perfectly formed new person (a "homunculus"), which just got bigger through the course of pregnancy. Only then did abortion start to look like killing a human being from the very beginning. The Church changed its view, and has held to a blanket prohibition ever since. The homunculus theory, though, is long gone, a product, it seems, of primitive microscopes.

No laws prohibited abortion in the United States until the mid-nineteenth century, when a coalition of doctors and early feminists lobbied successfully to bring it under medical control. Their motive was to take it out of the hands of midwives, who were pictured as unskilled and unclean (and who, of course, competed with doctors). Still, even when it was legal, medical abortion was probably not common. It wasn't exactly a choice in the modern sense that you could be assured of a relatively safe and quick outcome. (Of course, neither was childbirth—or sex.)

Abortion then continued fairly uncontroversially under medical control until 1962, when a pregnant woman was denied abortion by a U.S. Air Force hospital after discovering that her baby was deformed by thalidomide poisoning. She went public to warn other exposed military wives of the dangers. Some people were outraged to discover that she could not get an abortion even under such conditions (she eventually did get an abortion abroad). Others were outraged to discover that abortion was available at all. At the same time the sexual revolution brought many sexual issues into public attention—and created more demand for abortion too. There were between 200,000 and 1.2 million illegal abortions by year in the late sixties (more exact figures, not surprisingly, are hard to come by).

By the late sixties and early seventies momentum was building for liberalizing abortion laws. Conservatives tended to favor legalizing it as a means of population control. Many churches were moving toward acknowledging that abortion could be a moral choice under some circumstances. In the end, though, change came abruptly and not through legislation. In 1973, the Supreme Court's decision in *Roe* v. *Wade* declared abortion a constitutionally protected privacy right in the first trimester of pregnancy (the first thirteen weeks); states could regulate it for the sake of maternal health in the second trimester (the second thirteen weeks) and prohibit it in the third (the final thirteen weeks).

Roe has been controversial ever since, both as an exercise of state power and as an assertion of the priority of privacy rights over other rights and/or other relevant values. The Supreme Court spent much of the eighties and nineties hedging a bit, but it is fairly clear now that barring any major changes in the makeup of the Court, the basic framework of *Roe* v. *Wade* will stand. A variety of restrictions, such as waiting periods, parental notification, and so on, have been allowed by the Court; some have been rejected.

Current Statistics

There were 1.3 million abortions in the United States in 1995, down from 1.5 million per year in the early nineties; the numbers continue to fall. This represented an abortion rate of 350 per 1000 live births. Counting fetal losses from other causes as well, the percentage of all pregnancies ending in abortion was about 23 percent in 1995.

About 50 percent of the pregnancies among American women are unintended (82% among teenagers). Both American abortion rates and unintended pregnancy rates are much higher than those of most comparable countries: five times the rates in the Netherlands, for example.

TERMS OF THE DEBATE

Even basic terms in the abortion debate have become oversimplified and loaded. We need to take care with them.

It's not even agreed what to call the postconception, prebirth subject of abortion itself. On the pro-life side, it is almost always called a "baby," invoking all the protectiveness usually associated with babies, appropriate enough at late stages but misleading early on. A bean-sized metamorphosing embryo is not analogous to a baby, whatever claims it might nonetheless have on us.

Pregnant women, meanwhile, are called "mothers" by the pro-life side, as if their choice is essentially made already—which is just what's at issue. Abortion itself is called "murder," which automatically makes anyone who chooses abortion or performs one, no matter how thoughtful or agonized or desperate, a "murderer." And the other side is usually labeled "pro-abortion," as if they really thought abortion were a good thing.

The pro-choice side is no more fair. Rather than being called a baby, the subject of abortion is sometimes called just the "products of conception"—a clinical term that tries to deny that there is any moral question at all—or an "embryo," appropriate enough at early stages but misleading later. By the end of pregnancy we are no longer just embryonic. The term "fetus" is better, though it is most appropriate in the middle of pregnancy.

The pregnant woman may be called just a "woman," as if her choices about pregnancy are no more momentous than her choices about anything else. Abortion itself is called a "procedure"—again too purely medical and sterile a term for what's really at stake. And the other side is usually called "anti-abortion," as if the whole position were exhausted by what it opposes.

We need terms that are not so loaded and do not presume one view or the other before we can even start to think. In this chapter I will use "fetus" to name the subject of abortion—what it is that a pregnant woman is pregnant with. It's not perfect, but at least it's reasonably neutral. I will use "pregnant woman" for those who bear fetuses, again a reasonably descriptive term, not presuming to do our thinking for us. For abortion itself I will just use the term "abortion." And for the contending positions I will stick with "pro-life" and "pro-choice," which at least have the advantage of identifying what each side is *for* rather than what each side is against.

Note that no one is really "pro-abortion." Pro-choice people believe that abortion should be a legal option, that at least sometimes it is the best option available. No one believes that abortion is a good thing all by itself. This is a fairly powerful recognition, I think, because the familiar loaded terms obscure just this major point of agreement. More on this in the next section.

The majority of women seeking abortions are young (26% teenagers), unmarried, poor, and white. Seventy percent intend to have children in the future. One in six is a born-again or evangelical Christian. Catholic women have abortions at about the national average. Ninety percent of abortions take place in the first thirteen weeks of pregnancy; 50 percent within the first eight weeks. Medical risks of abortion are minimal—less than 1 percent produce major complications—and have declined dramatically since abortion was legalized in 1973. Childbirth is more than ten times as risky.

In some places, (e.g. the District of Columbia) the abortion rate is higher than the birthrate; in other places (states such as West Virginia, Mississippi, and South Dakota) it is only a tiny fraction of the birthrate. Both figures are probably distorted by decreasing availability in many places. More than 83 percent of the counties in the United States—home to a third of the child-bearing population—have no abortion provider at all, and many women seeking abortions have to travel to other cities or even states.

And, of course, intense controversy continues.

KEY VALUES

Many of the arguments, pro and con, are familiar, maybe all too familiar. Still, we need to revisit them here. What is crucial, though, is that we revisit them in a different spirit. Even in the abortion debate—*yes, even in the abortion debate*—we can ask what the other side (whichever it is) is *right* about. We can look for the common ground rather than the gulf between. Both sides have something to tell us. Can we finally hear it?

Core Arguments

Life

Life has value, says one side: life is a precious thing.

Surely it is. They're right. We are *all* pro-life in some basic sense. Life is the condition of all other goods. It is what makes love and community and beauty and everything else possible. Those acts associated with creating and preserving and honoring life—sex, childbirth, nurturing a baby, caring for the sick, mourning the dead—are among the deepest and most profound of life's experiences.

So why shouldn't the preciousness of life extend to the very beginnings? Prenatal human life is precious too. Maybe that preciousness is not the whole story, but certainly it is *part* of it.

Outside of the context of the abortion debate, at least, we recognize this preciousness already. When a couple loses a child to miscarriage, we recognize a loss, even if it is not the same as the death of a full-term baby. It's not just a disappointment, it's a *loss*.

Life is a shared value even *in* the abortion debate. One sign: pro-choicers are almost as uneasy as pro-lifers with repeat abortions—with people who use abortion as a form of birth control. Kristin Luker reports in her landmark study of pro-choice activists that some activists, particularly those helping women have abortions, reported feeling like failures when a woman comes back to them for a second or third abortion. The first time perhaps the pregnant woman lacked the information or the resources to avoid unwanted pregnancy. After the first abortion, though, having been given contraceptive services and counseling, the woman who gets pregnant again and seeks abortion is seen as irresponsible. Irresponsible to herself, for sure—but also irresponsible to *life*.

Choice

And just as we all, really, value life, so too do we, *all* of us, value choice. Freedom, self-determination, the right to control what happens in and to our own bodies—these are basic values too.

This is no surprise either. Outside of the abortion debate the value of choice is almost axiomatic. In the economic sphere it is our reigning ideal. Politically, our democracy is defined as a system in which the people as a whole choose representatives and therefore, at least indirectly, the laws. Morally, we insist on the *right* to choose what we want even if our own or other's lives are at stake: to eat badly; to read or watch whatever trash or hatefulness we choose (pretty much); to commit suicide; to ride motorcycles without helmets or drive without seat belts (and not buckle up the kids either) or to install radar detectors and speed with impunity.

Yet seat belts and speed limits are trivial restrictions compared with pregnancy. Pregnancy induces nine months of profound physical changes, and in many ways the mother's body will never be the same. How could she *not* have the right to choose there, when her very body is at stake? Even most of the pro-life movement acknowledges this, which is why pregnancies caused by rape are usually allowed as exceptions in otherwise strict anti-abortion laws. Fetuses are no different whether conceived by rape or not, yet here we almost all acknowledge that something else also matters, and matters more, actually, than the fetus's right to life.

Forms and Limits of the Core Arguments

Both sides also raise good critical points about the other. Having acknowleged that each side is right in certain fundamental ways, might we now also be able to look at each side's limits in a little more open-minded way than usual? Could we not acknowledge some limits too?

Limits of Pro-Life Arguments

Fetal life is precious, yes, but is its preciousness really the same as that of a full-fledged human being's? The point is at least arguable. That a human fetus is *human*, for instance, as opposed to belonging to some other species, is of course true. But it doesn't follow from this that it is a human *being* or has human rights, especially not in the early, embryonic stages.

That fetal development is gradual is sometimes supposed to imply that the fetus must be a human being from the start. Where but conception could we draw the line? But you could turn the argument on its head with equal justice and ask: where but *birth* could we draw the line? A more sensible view would be that the fetus begins with fairly minimal claims that gradually increase to nearly the significance of a baby's at the end—and then we'd have to look more closely at the research on fetal development to map its growing claims more exactly.

After all, there's not much in life that happens in one single stroke. Maybe we need to make some conceptual room for *partial* human beings, and *developing* ones, whose moral claims, like their humanness, develop over time.

As Chapter 10 notes, there is also the question of "life" in the case of other animals. Can "innocent life" be the overriding value in one case and not even show up on the moral radar in the other? Even if we see animal issues as trade-offs between competing values (human needs versus animal suffering, for example), why are parallel trade-offs not allowable with respect to abortion? Here too, maybe, "life" does not always have the last word.

It may be that insisting so single-mindedly on the full humanhood of fetuses was an unwise line for the pro-life movement. I think the underlying concern is really the issue of violence. All of us are concerned about the growing harshness and lack of care in our lives, often expressed in casual violence all around: in the schools, at home, between men and women, toward nature. Pro-lifers see this casual violence reflected and intensified in our attitude toward prenatal life: it's another innocent and helpless form of life now treated as disposable, readily devalued and cast aside.

And surely about this they are right. Violence, on all fronts, is a real concern. But it is a concern *whether or not* the fetus is a full-fledged human being. Wouldn't the point be clearer without raising the issue of just what makes us human?

Limits of Pro-Choice Arguments

Choice also clearly has limits. Despite the rhetoric of choice above all, we can't choose just anything, especially not when other people's lives are involved. Even people who are pro-choice on abortion are not necessarily pro-choice about, say, gun ownership or speed limits or even fairly humdrum things like zoning laws or food-safety inspections.

Even where choice really is a right (a "right-to," in the language of Chapter 4), it is not necessarily the right thing to do. Modern critics argue that a morality of "rights-to" alone creates a world in which we are too isolated from each other, and misses entirely the values of care, community, family, shared traditions, and civility. Even if it is true that we have a right to do something that involves certain kinds of violence, in other words, it doesn't follow that the violence is somehow morally neutralized. It's still violence, and still should be avoided whenever possible.

I think that the pro-choice movement's underlying concern is with power issues, especially the disempowerment of women in a male-dominated society and the double disadvantage of women with children. After all, we live in a society in which children are still assumed to be women's responsibilities while women are also expected to perfom as well or better than men at work. Women still get paid on the average only 75 percent of what men in comparable jobs get paid (which is not just unfair but also affects women's abilities to have a child and remain afloat economically). High-quality child care is hard to find and expensive, and is routinely attacked by the same people who attack abortion. Rape and sexual coercion are widespread, and in countless more subtle ways too women are not in full control of their own fertility. Against this kind of background, abortion begins to look like a last chance for *some* sort of control. Maybe it is a violent, desperate, and last-ditch form of control, but some women may understandably feel that it is all they've got.

Are the Core Arguments Compatible?

If I am right that the core concerns of the two movements are overgeneralized and misrepresented by the rhetoric of "life" versus "choice," then we already have values that are somewhat compatible. Reducing violence is certainly not at odds with empowering women. In fact the two require each other.

Moreover, even if we stick with the usual rhetoric, "life" and "choice" are not incompatible. They both just limit each other—they require some balancing. I think that the intensity of the usual disagreement obscures the fact that most of us already balance them in practice.

Sometimes I divide my students into pro-life and pro-choice groups. Case studies of unintended pregnancy are suggested and each group is asked to work out their reaction, and also to guess how the other group will react to the same cases. The results surprise everyone. Pro-life groups assume that the pro-choice side will more or less automatically opt for abortion when the going gets tough. In fact, the pro-choice groups consider abortion only as a last resort. Similarly, pro-choice groups assume that the pro-life group will be against abortion no matter what. But they're not: they make exceptions too.

The most common view I find among my students is that "I probably wouldn't choose abortion myself, but I think the choice should be there for others." This would probably be classified as a pro-choice view, as the usual categories go—but those categories may hide more than they reveal. There's middle ground here, *between* the usual views. *Both* sides acknowledge that abortion can be a painful and tragic but also (sometimes) necessary choice.

What's more, national poll figures show the same thing. For the last twenty years, while the abortion debate raged all around us, the U. S. population consistently has divided into about one-quarter strongly anti-abortion, one quarter strongly in favor of abortion rights, and the remaining half probably against abortion for themselves most of the time but also in favor of allowing abortion as a limited legal right. About 60 percent continue to support the *Roe* v. *Wade* framework.

In fact, then, despite the painful and persistent debate between two single-minded sides, most people recognize that abortion choices pit two genuine values against each other in a case where *both of them count*. Both of them are right in their way. How to put them together is still a (hard) question, but at least we can find here a kind of shared starting point.

CAN WE GET THE ABORTION DEBATE UNSTUCK?

If we leave the question at "Should abortion be legal, or not?," we may be condemned to yes-or-no kinds of answers and therefore to more rounds of the familiar painful debate. But if we begin to multiply options and reframe the problem, we may be able to get unstuck in a hurry.

Reducing Unwanted Pregnancies

In the reading in Chapter 7, Roger Rosenblatt suggests that a widely acceptable approach is to "permit but discourage" abortion. Recent Democratic party platforms hold that abortion should be "safe, legal, and *rare*." Many others, looking for common ground, end up in the same place. As Julie Polter writes in *Sojourners*, a liberal Catholic journal, "If pro-life people know that one abortion is too many and many pro-choice people can at least agree that there surely shouldn't be as many abortions as there are, shouldn't we do what we can in the scope of that common territory?"

Already, then, we could ask a different question from the usual ones. *How can we prevent or reduce the demand for abortions themselves?* Is there any realistic way to prevent the number of unwanted pregnancies, and/or to keep those unintended pregnancies that do occur from being unwanted?

More than half of all women seeking abortions used no contraception. Why? We need to find out. Lack of access? Lack of education? These things can be changed. Changing them might not even be controversial. Not even the Catholic Church opposes all ways of regulating pregnancy.

And what about the other half, women who used contraception and still got pregnant? Again we need to find out why. Poor or difficult-to-use methods? Resistance from spouses and lovers? But these things can be changed too, with a fraction of the energy and intensity put into the present abortion debate.

Schools, clinics, and even the media can teach people about contraceptives and promote their use. Of course, there are formidable barriers. Many people who oppose abortion also oppose sex education and public discussion of contraception. But if sex education and expanded access to contraception could be seen as directly reducing the abortion problem, would the opposition be so intense? It's hard to imagine that more sex (if that really would be a result) could really be as bad as more murder.

We might even imagine a grand compromise along these lines. Suppose abortion itself—the medical procedure—were tightly controlled and limited, but that birth control were widely promoted and available? Each side would have to give up something. The pro-life side would have to embrace birth control; the pro-choice side would have to allow abortion to become much less available. But both sides would gain their most important and shared goal: greatly reducing the actual number of abortions by reducing the number of unintended and unwanted pregnancies.

I know, I know—a half-dozen objections come immediately to mind. Fine: it's meant to be a rough idea, a starting-point, a "what if . . . ?" provocation, opening up the issue in an unexpected way. Maybe *you* can take it somewhere now, or think of something else.

Making Unplanned Child-bearing Possible

Still there will be unexpected, unintended pregnancies. What can be done about the demand for abortion then?

Reframers should ask: why does abortion sometimes become so desperate a need? Why would a child, or another child, or a child at the "wrong" time, sometimes be a disaster for a mother or family? And what can be done about *that*?

Some on the pro-life side answer: the real problem is that we think we can have everything. We want to control every aspect of our lives. Maybe we ought to be more humble in the face of life's mysteries. When we speak of "unintended" pregnancy, for example, we set it up from the start as a failure of control and therefore a problem, a potential disaster. Some people propose to speak of "surprise" pregnancy instead. A surprise is not necessarily a disaster—it can also be a kind of gift, an opportunity.

But *still*: surprises can be unpleasant. More must be said. Why is the surprise sometimes unwelcome?

One answer is: because women confront fairly inflexible expectations about career tracks, work schedules, and schooling. Though some in the pro-life movement believe that women should not aspire to careers, most would surely agree that careers ought at least to be one option for women. Women have a right to seek that kind of life—and to have a sex life too. But then the trap seems to close. How to have a baby when it would mean two or three years out of school or part-time at work, long-term financial costs, and permanent, deep emotional commitments elsewhere?

This is a fixable problem. We need more flexible expectations and alternative work and schooling patterns that do not punish or impede women (and men) who also choose major family responsibilities. Most European countries are far ahead of the United States in this area. It's not so hard to work out the details.

The same goes for schools. One of my ethics classes was discussing the abortion issue with our college chaplain. He remarked that in his decade or so at the college he had seen only three or four students carry pregnancies to term and stay in school too. A (male) student then said:

> I'm pro-life, but I can't blame a fellow student for getting an abortion when the choice is between the abortion and finishing college. Your whole future is at stake. I think the real question is: why should she be put in that position?

Why indeed. So the question to us is: what can *we* change—teachers, students, chaplains—so that fewer women are put in this position in the future? Class schedules, assignments, how financial aid is calculated? How hard would that be?

Economic Factors

Over 80 percent of American women seeking abortions are unmarried, and most are either working or attending school or both. Their desperation is partly economic: they can't afford a child, or another child.

This is a fixable problem too. Equal pay for women is, or ought to be, our goal. Shared child-raising has everything to recommend it. At the very least, fathers should be expected (required) to support their children financially (at present, even with greatly expanded enforcement, only 37 percent of unmarried fathers contribute anything at all). Paid parental leaves are the norm in Europe. Community support for affordable child care could be mobilized precisely as a way of helping to break the deadlock over abortion.

When the welfare laws were up for revision in 1996, conservatives proposed to deny assistance to children born of mothers under age 18 or currently on welfare, or whose paternity hadn't been established. Many of these limits are now law. But a remarkable thing happened along the way. Nearly all major organizations on *both sides* of the abortion issue campaigned against the bill, including the National Right to Life Committee, Planned Parenthood, the U.S. Catholic Conference, and the National Organization of Women (NOW). Both sides feared that the results would be to coerce abortions among poor women. Both sides made the connections back to economic conditions. Pro-choice and pro-life organizations even jointly designed a comprehensive child-support reform plan. Common ground emerged—even a detailed common agenda—in the face of a common threat. Maybe next time we shouldn't wait.

"XYLO"

RAYNA RAPP

I first encountered this story in a collection of stories intended to illustrate "how varied, complex, and personal are the factors surrounding reproductive choice, and . . . the suffering that results when choice is denied." (The book is Angela Bonavoglia, ed., *The Choices We Made* [Random House, 1991].) If you are single-mindedly looking to classify this story as pro-life or pro-choice, you'd probably conclude from the part about choice that this story has a pro-choice "moral." But it would be wiser to suspend judgment on that question and pay more attention to the first phrase: *how varied, complex, and personal are the factors surrounding reproductive choice.* Could we read the story just for that? Could we note both the overwhelming importance of *life* to Rayna Rapp and her partner and her parents too, and their conviction, nonetheless, that choice—choosing abortion in this case—is necessary too? Could we note all the ways in which social factors beyond their control, especially the lack of "decent humane attention and services for other-than-fully-abled children and adults," also seem to compel that choice? Is it just possible, then, that this story, tragic as it is, helps to show us a way *out*—beyond the current opposition of "life" versus "choice"?

MIKE CALLED THE FETUS XYLO, XY for its unknown sex, LO for the love we were pouring into it. Day by day we fantasized about who this growing cluster of cells might become. Day by day, we followed the growth process in the myriad books that surround modern pregnancy for the over-thirty-five baby boomlet. Both busy with engrossing work and political commitments, we welcomed this potential child with excitement, fantasy, and the rationality of scientific knowledge. As a Women's Movement activist, I had decided opinions about treating pregnancy as a normal, not a diseased condition, and we were fortunate to find a health-care team—obstetrician, midwives, genetic counseling—who shared that view.

The early months of the pregnancy passed in a blur of exhaustion and nausea. Preoccupied with my own feelings, I lived in a perpetual underwater, slow-motion version of my prior life. As one friend put it, I was already operating on fetal time, tied to an unfamiliar regimen of enforced naps, loss of energy, and rigid eating. Knowing the research on nutrition, on hormones, and on miscarriage rates among older pregnant women, I did whatever I could to stay comfortable.

Rayna Rapp, "XYLO." Reproduced from *Test Tube Women*, edited by Rita Arditti, Renate Duelli Klein, and Shelly Minden (London: Pandora Press, 1984).

I was thirty-six when XYLO was conceived, and like many of my peers, I chose to have amniocentesis, a prenatal test for birth defects such as Down syndrome, Tay-Sachs disease, and sickle-cell anemia. Both Mike and I knew about prenatal diagnosis from our friends' experiences, and from reading about it. Each year, many thousands of American women choose amniocentesis to detect birth defects. The procedure is performed between the sixteenth and twentieth weeks of pregnancy. Most obstetricians, mine included, send their pregnant patients directly to the genetic division of a hospital where counseling is provided, and the laboratory technicians are specially trained. Analysis of amniotic fluid requires complex laboratory work, and can cost between five hundred dollars and two thousand dollars.

It was fear of Down syndrome that sent us to seek prenatal diagnosis of XYLO. Down syndrome produces a characteristic physical appearance— short, stocky size, large tongue, puffy upward-slanting eyes with skin folds in the inner corners—and is a major cause of mental retardation, worldwide. People with Down syndrome are quite likely to have weak cardiovascular systems, respiratory problems, and run a greater risk of developing childhood leukemia. While the majority of Down syndrome infants used to die very young, a combination of antibiotics and infant surgery enables modern medicine to keep them alive. And programs of childhood physical-mental stimulation may facilitate their assimilation. Some parents also opt for cosmetic surgery—an expensive and potentially risky procedure. Down syndrome is caused by an extra chromosome, at the twenty-first pair of chromosomes, as geneticists label them. And while the diagnosis of Down spells mental retardation and physical vulnerability, no geneticist can tell you how seriously affected your particular fetus will be. There is no cure for Down syndrome. A pregnant woman whose fetus is diagnosed as having the extra chromosome can either prepare to raise a mentally retarded and physically vulnerable child, or decide to abort it.

On the February morning Mike and I arrived at a local medical center for genetic counseling, in my nineteenth week of pregnancy, Nancy Z., our counselor, took a detailed pedigree (or family tree) from each of us, to discover any rare diseases or birth defects for which we could be tested. She then gave us an excellent genetics lesson, explained the amniocentesis procedure and the risks, both of the test and of discovering a serious genetic defect. One third of one percent of pregnancies miscarry due to amniocentesis. Most women feel fine after the test, but some (perhaps 10 percent) experience uterine cramping or contractions. Overall, about 98 percent of the women who go for amniocentesis will be told that no fetal defects or anomalies have been found.

After counseling, we descended to the testing area, where an all-female team of radiologist, obstetrician, nurses, and staff assistants performed the tap. In skilled hands, and with the use of sonogram equipment, the tap is a rapid procedure. I spent perhaps five minutes on the table, belly attached to sonar electrodes. Mike holding my feet for encouragement. The radiologist snapped Polaroid pictures of XYLO, and we had our first "baby album"— gray blotches of a head and spine of our baby-in-waiting. She located the placenta, which enabled the obstetrician to successfully draw a small, clear sample of amniotic fluid (less than one eighth of a cup). The tap felt like a crampier version of drawing blood—not particularly painful or traumatic. We marched the fluid back to the genetic lab where it would be cultured, and went home.

The waiting period for amniocentesis results is a long one, and I was very anxious. Cells must be cultured, then analyzed, a process that takes two to four weeks. We wait, caught between the late date at which amniocentesis can be performed (usually sixteen to twenty weeks); the moment of quickening, when the woman feels the fetus move (roughly eighteen to twenty weeks); and the legal limits of abortion (very few of which are performed after twenty-four weeks in the United States). Those of my friends who have had amniocentesis report terrible fantasies, dreams, and crying fits, and I was no exception: I dreamed in lurid detail of my return to the lab, of awful damage. I woke up frantic, sobbing, to face the nagging fear that is focused in the waiting period after amniocentesis.

For the 98 percent of women whose amniotic fluid reveals no anomaly, reassurance arrives by phone, or more likely, by mail, confirming a negative test. When Nancy called me twelve days after the tap, I began to scream as soon as I recognized her voice; in her office, I knew only positive results (very negative results, from a potential parent's point of view) are reported by phone. The image of myself, alone, screaming into a white plastic telephone is indelible. Although it only took twenty minutes to locate Mike and bring him and a close friend to my side, time is suspended in my memory. I replay the call, and my screams echo for indefinite periods. We learned, after contacting our midwives and obstetrician, that a diagnosis of a male fetus with Down syndrome had been made. Our fantasies for XYLO, our five months' fetus, were completely shattered.

Mike and I had discussed what we would do if amniocentesis revealed a serious genetic condition long before the test. For us, the diagnosis of Down syndrome was reason to choose abortion. Our thinking was clear, if abstract, long before the question became reality. We were eager to have a child, and prepared to change our lives to make emotional, social, and economic resources available. But the realities of raising a child who could never grow to independence would call forth more than we could muster, unless one or both of us gave up our work, our political commitments, our social existence beyond the household. And despite a shared commitment to coparenting, we both understood that in this society, that one was likely to be the mother. When I thought about myself, I knew that in such a situation, I would transform myself to become the kind of twenty-four-hour-a-day advocate such a child would require. I'd do the best and most loving job I could, and I'd undoubtedly become an activist in support of the needs of disabled children.

But other stark realities confronted us: to keep a Down syndrome child alive through potentially lethal health problems is an act of love with weighty consequences. As we ourselves age, to whom would we leave the person XYLO would become? Neither Mike nor I have any living kin who are likely to be young enough, or close enough, to take on this burden after our deaths. In a society where the state provides virtually no decent, humane services for the mentally retarded, how could we take responsibility for the future of our dependent Down syndrome child? In good conscience, we couldn't choose to raise a child who would become a ward of the state. The health care, schools, various therapies that Down syndrome children require are inadequately available, and horrendously expensive in America; no single family should have to shoulder all the burdens that a decent health and so-cial policy may someday extend to physically and mentally disabled people. In the meantime, while struggling for such a society, we did not choose to bring a child into this world who could never grow up to care for himself.

Most women who've opted for amniocentesis are prepared to face the question of abortion, and many of us *do* choose it, after a diagnosis of serious disability is made. Perhaps 95 percent of Down syndrome pregnancies are terminated after test results are known. Reports on other diseases and conditions are harder to find, but in one study, the diagnosis of spina bifida led to abortion about 90 percent of the time.

In shock and grief, I learned from my obstetrician that two kinds of late second-trimester abortions were available. Most common are the "installation procedures"—saline solution or urea is injected into the uterus to kill the fetus, and drugs are sometimes used to bring on labor. The woman then goes through labor to deliver the fetus. The second kind of mid-trimester abortion, and the one I choose, is a D&E—dilation and evacuation. This procedure demands more active intervention from a doctor, who vacuums out the amniotic fluid, and then removes the fetus. The D&E requires some intense, upsetting work for the medical team, but it's over in about twenty minutes, without putting the woman through labor. Both forms of late abortion entail some physical risk, and the psychological pain is enormous. Deciding to end the life of a fetus you've wanted and carried for most of five months is no easy matter. The number of relatively late second-trimester abortions performed for genetic reasons is very small. It seems an almost inconsequential number, unless you happen to be one of them.

Making the medical arrangements, going back for counseling, the pretests, and finally, the abortion, was the most difficult period of my adult life. I was then twenty-one weeks pregnant, and had been proudly carrying my expanding belly. Telling everyone—friends, family, students, colleagues, neighbors—seemed an endless nightmare. But it also allowed us to rely on their love and support during this terrible time. Friends streamed in from all over to teach my classes; I have scores of letters expressing concern; the phone never stopped ringing for weeks. Our community was invaluable, reminding us that our lives were rich and filled with love despite this loss. A few weeks afterward, I spoke with another woman who'd gone through selective abortion (as this experience is antiseptically called in medical jargon). She'd returned to work immediately, her terrible abortion experience unspoken. Colleagues assumed she'd had a late miscarriage, and didn't speak about it. Her isolation only underlined my appreciation of the support I'd received.

My parents flew a thousand miles to sit guard over my hospital bed, answer telephones, shop, and cook. Filled with sorrow for the loss of their first grandchild, my mother told me of a conversation she'd had with my father. Despite their grief, they were deeply grateful for the test. After all, she reasoned, we were too young and active to be devastated like this; if the child had been born, she and my dad would have taken him to raise in their older years, so we could get on with raising other children. I can only respond with deep love and gratitude for the wellspring of compassion behind that conversation. But surely, no single woman, mother or grandmother, no single family, nuclear or extended, should have to bear all the burdens that raising a seriously disabled child entails. It points out, once again, the importance of providing decent, humane attention and services for other-than-fully-abled children and adults.

And, of course, parents of disabled children are quick to point out that the lives they've nurtured have been worth living. I honor their hard work and commitments, as well as their love, and I think that part of "informed consent" to amniocentesis and selective abortion should include information about parents' groups of Down syndrome children, and social services available to them, not just the individual, medical diagnosis of the problem. And even people who feel they could never choose a late abortion may nonetheless want amniocentesis so they'll have a few extra months to prepare themselves, other family members, friends, and special resources for the birth of a child with special, complex needs.

Recovering from the abortion took a long time. Friends, family, coworkers, students did everything they could to ease me through the experience. Even so, I yearned to talk with someone who'd "been there." Over the next few months, I used my personal and medical networks to locate and talk with a handful of other women who'd opted for selective abortions. In each case, I was the first person they'd ever met with a similar experience. The isolation of this decision and its consequences is intense. Only when women (and concerned men) speak of the experience of selective abortion as a tragic but chosen fetal death can we as a community offer the support, sort out the ethics, and give the compassionate attention that such a loss entails.

For two weeks, Mike and I breathed as one person. His distress, loss, and concern were never one whit less than my own. But we were sometimes upset and angered by the unconscious attitudes toward his loss. He was expected to "cope," while I was nurtured through my "need." We've struggled for male responsibility in birth control, sexual mutuality, childbirth, and child-rearing, and I think we need to acknowledge that those men who do engage in such transformed practices have mourning rights during a pregnancy loss, as well.

Nonetheless, our experiences *were* different, and I'm compelled to recognize the material reality of my experience. Because it happened in my body, a woman's body, I recovered much more slowly than Mike did. By whatever mysterious process, he was able to damp back the pain, and throw himself back into work after several weeks. For me, it took months. As long as I had the fourteen pounds of pregnancy weight to lose, as long as my aching breasts, filled with milk, couldn't squeeze into bras, as long as my tummy muscles protruded, I was confronted with the physical reality of being post-pregnant, without a child. Mike's support seemed inadequate; I was still in deep mourning while he seemed distant and cured. Only much later, when I began doing research on amniocentesis, did I find one study of the stresses and strains of selective abortion. In a small sample of couples, a high percentage separated or divorced following this experience. Of course, the same holds true after couples face a child's disablement, or child death. Still, I had no idea that deep mourning for a fetus could be so disorienting. Abortion after prenatal diagnosis has been kept a medical and private experience, so there is no common fund of knowledge or support to alert us as individuals, as couples, as families, as friends, to the aftermath our "freedom of choice" entails.

Which is why I've pierced my private pain to raise this issue. As feminists, we need to speak from our seemingly private experience toward a social and political agenda. I'm suggesting we lift the veil of privacy and professionalism to explore issues of health care, abortion, and the right to choose death, as well as life, for our genetically disabled fetuses. If XYLO's story, a true story, has helped to make this a compelling issue for more than one couple, then this five short months of fetal life will have been a great gift.

Exercises and Notes

CRITICAL REACTIONS

Below are some critical student reactions to this chapter. Consider them, and consider your own reactions too. Take this as an occasion to step back a bit and evaluate your ethical toolbox in action. How far can we really transform a debate like the abortion debate? How well have I used the toolbox in this chapter? Am I showing a pro-choice or pro-life bias? If so, how might the results differ if the same tools were used by someone from the other starting point?

> You probably think that the Civil War could have been avoided too if people had just used your Toolbox. It's way too rosy a picture for me. These disagreements about abortion are *really deep*. People feel very strongly. And the differences extend to radically opposed views of the family, the meaning of sex, and on and on. Abortion is just the tip of the iceberg. Abortion is part of America's culture wars. It's the real "Civil War" of our time. It's not going to go away just because we can do some nice things to cut down on unwanted pregnancies and things like that.

> Isn't there a point sometimes to standing firm, to making it a struggle, making it a fight? What if the Civil Rights Movement, which you seem to admire, had tried compromise instead of (peaceful) confrontation? I don't think you'd approve of that, and I don't think they would have succeeded half as well as they did. Well, for pro-life people (and I'm one of them) the civil rights of the fetus are precisely the issue. No one has the right to assure their quality of life by owning or suppressing someone else, and no one has the right to assure their quality of life by aborting another.

> My friends and I tried to guess before class whether you were really pro-choice or pro-life. They all said you were pro-choice. But I think you just don't get it about pro-choice people. We want abortion to be a matter of right— not something so hedged, "discouraged," some kind of disgrace that needs excuse. Choice is a right. You're not a woman, maybe that's why you can't see it. . . .

TALKING THE TALK, CONTINUED

Integrating values, remember, requires us to look at ethical debates in a new way. As Chapter 7 said, it takes some getting used to, and some persistence too, when dealing with people who picture ethical debates only in polarized terms. And of course the abortion debate is even more polarized than most.

The box in Chapter 7 offered a sample dialogue for illustration. Here is the beginning of another, specifically on abortion. This one is for practice. How would you carry it on?

L: So what are you, pro-life or pro-choice?

A: Both.

L: Oh give me a break!

C: You can't be both. What are you, joking?

A: Yes I *can* be both. I am in favor of life and I am in favor of choice. Aren't you? I mean, who *isn't* both?

C: I've never heard of this before.

L: I'll tell you why you can't be both. It's totally obvious. They conflict. You have to go one way or the other. Are you going to let women kill their unborn babies just for convenience, or not?

C: Whoa—hold on. Don't you mean: are you going to allow Bible-thumpers like L here tell women what they can do with their own bodies?

What would *you* say next if you were A? Why?

KEEP ON THINKING

Chapters 11 and 12 claim that we can think more creatively about *all* of our ethical problems—that we feel stuck far more often than we really are. Abortion, of course, is the very model of a stuck ethical issue. Therefore I have dedicated a whole section of this chapter just to options: to give an immediate and clear sense that this issue too is far more open than we often think.

And even this is only a beginning. We haven't begun to use some of the more radical methods of reframing and "provocation" offered in chapters 11 and 12. I hereby challenge you to go farther still.

For example: no doubt it seems that abortion is the least likely of any moral controversy to yield to "opportunistic" thinking. Is there any sense in which the demand for abortion is actually an opportunity?

An opportunity *for what?* One group of student brainstormers came up with this idea: it is an opportunity to find a source for embryos for infertile couples. Suppose that women who did not want to continue their pregnancies gave the fertilized embryos to infertile women who did want to get pregnant. Suppose that instead of "abortion" we had "embryo donation." Could we not thereby take two problems—abortion on the one hand and infertility on the other—and find in them one solution?

Of course, this is still a raw idea: it would need a lot of refinement, as well as more medical research, and is not a total solution. But it certainly opens up a sense of possibility that is not there now!

Here is another example. Reflecting that only women have abortions, we might try as a provocation:

What if . . . men have abortions too?

This might set you thinking of Judith Thomson's violinist analogy in Chapter 10. Or you might try to construct a better analogy yourself. Or you might go in some other direction.

Me, it reminds of a famous remark of Gloria Steinem's: "If men could get pregnant, abortion would be a sacrament." Her claim, somewhat like Thomson's, was: men wouldn't think of imposing similar requirements on themselves. Quite the contrary: getting free of impediments and not being tied down are sometimes treated almost as imperatives or duties for males, thus, in a sense, "sacraments."

You may or may not find Steinem's point persuasive. Take it as a provocation, though, and you might generate some useful new ideas from it whether you agree with it or not. For example: what if we took it quite literally and considered the possibility that abortion could be accompanied by a kind of sacrament—a ritual of loss? Acknowledging that the choice is tragic but that sometimes abortion may be the least bad choice: a ritual, then, of acknowledging and letting go. How would things be then? Might we think about it differently, perhaps better?

In fact, the Japanese have such a ritual. For more information, go to the "Ethics Updates" website at <ethics.acusd.edu>, select "Abortion," and look for the subsection on "Mizuko Kuyo."

Now it's your turn. What might other "what if . . . ?" provocations yield? Where else in this debate might some creativity make a difference?

NOTES AND FURTHER READINGS

The first section of this chapter draws upon the 1999 *Statistical Abstract of the United States* and various "Facts in Brief" reports from the Alan Guttmacher Institute (2010 Massachusetts Avenue, Washington, DC 20036). See also Kristin Luker's *Abortion and the Politics of Motherhood* (University of California Press, 1984), an excellent survey of the history of the abortion debate as well as an exploration of the minds of the activists.

For general background, trying to give a fair voice to each side, see Robert Baird and Stuart Rosenbaum, eds., *The Ethics of Abortion* (Prometheus Books, 1989) and Sidney and Daniel Callahan, eds., *Abortion: Understanding Differences* (Plenum, 1984)—especially interesting because the editors, a married couple, are on opposite sides of the debate. Two earlier readings in this book also bear on the abortion debate: Roger Rosenblatt's essay "How to End the Abortion War" in Chapter 7, and the Common Ground Network for Life and Choice's "Common Ground Rules" in Chapter 14. In addition to further information on "Mizuko Kuyo," as cited above, Lawrence Hinman's "Ethics Updates" website at <ethics.acusd.edu> offers an especially extensive set of links and other resources on the abortion issue, including texts of major articles and a number of helpful links. Go to the main site and select "Abortion."

For some unfamiliar but intriguing ways of thinking of the debate, see Jane English, "Abortion and the Concept of a Person," widely reprinted in philosophical anthologies in applied ethics and originally published in *Canadian Journal of Philosophy* 5 (1975): 233–243; Peter Wenz, *Abortion Rights as Religious Freedom* (Temple University Press, 1992); and Sally Markowitz, "A Feminist Defense of Abortion," in James Sterba, ed., *Morality in Practice* (Wadsworth Publishing Company, 5th edition, 1997). Though the Catholic Church is in the forefront of the fight against abortion, there are some pro-choice (again, remember: not pro-*abortion*) Catholics too. See for example Daniel Maguire, *Abortion: A Guide to Making Ethical Choices* (Catholics for Free Choice, 1983, 1998). Correspondingly, though all feminists are assumed to be pro-choice, there are pro-life feminists too, who argue among other things that the availability of abortion has contributed to the sexual objectification of women. See Karen Gustafson, "The New Politics of Abortion," *Utne Reader* (March/April 1989).

There is a large but not yet so visible literature on the possibilities for compromise and constructive resolution of the abortion issue. See, for example, Elizabeth Mensch and Alan Freeman, *The Politics of Virtue: Is Abortion Debatable?* (Duke University Press, 1993) and Celeste Michelle Condit, *Decoding Abortion Rhetoric: Communicating Social Change* (University of Illinois Press, 1989). Both books are careful to avoid the usual polemics, and both dig deeply into recent historical developments (and twentieth-century theology, in Mensch and Freeman) to deepen their cases.

◯

CHAPTER 18

Business and Professional Ethics

ETHICS AND PROFESSIONS

You're a doctor whose patient has just been diagnosed with cancer. You believe that radical surgery is her best option. You also know that she does not make decisions quickly and will be tempted to delay and grasp at straws, so that by the time she accepts the need for surgery it may well be too late. Should you tell her about other options anyway, or insist that surgery is the only possibility?

It isn't right to lie to her. The truth, however, may, indirectly, kill her. What do you do?

You're a psychotherapist whose patient confides to you that he plans to murder his ex-girlfriend. Should you alert law enforcement? his intended victim? Should you commit him against his will? What about your obligation to confidentiality in the therapeutic encounter? Without it, he might not have confided in you in the first place. How can you violate his trust?

You're a newspaper reporter investigating a new make of car. You discover that the car has some very dangerous features. The car's manufacturer advertises lavishly in your paper. If you report your discovery, your article will be spiked by your editors, who are unwilling to lose the advertising revenue and the company's good will. You may even lose your job. Should you water down your article to ensure that it gets published and the public is at least minimally informed? How far are you required to stick out your own neck?

How about stretching the truth to make a vital point? For a report on badly placed gas tanks in 1992 GM trucks, NBC's *Dateline* staged collisions to try to get footage of gas tanks blowing up. When the collisions didn't blow up the tanks, they used a few explosives to help out. Nothing was said about the explosives on the air. Was this unethical? NBC thought so: the people involved were fired. But the trucks *were* dangerous. . . .

Professional Codes of Ethics

The Hippocratic Oath

Many professions have developed code of ethics to address questions like these. Doctors' famous Oath traces back to Hippocrates, a Greek physician of the fifth century BCE. The core of the Hippocratic Oath reads:

> I will apply dietetic measures for the benefit of the sick according to my ability and judgement; I will keep them from harm and injustice.
>
> I will neither give a deadly drug to anybody if asked for it, nor will I make a suggestion to this effect. Similarly, I will not give a woman an abortive remedy. In purity and holiness I will guard my life and my art.
>
> I will not use the knife . . . but will withdraw in favor of such men as are engaged in this work.
>
> Whatever houses I may visit, I will come for the benefit of the sick, remaining free of all intentional injustice, of all mischief, and in particular of sexual relations with both female and male persons, be they free or slaves.
>
> What I may see or hear in the course of the treatment . . . which on no account one must spread abroad, I will keep to myself. . . .

There are more modern medical codes of ethics too. The Hippocratic Oath does not deal with questions of truthfulness, for example, but the American Medical Association Principles of Medical Ethics (last revised 1992) requires that "a physician . . . deal honestly with patients and colleagues." The International Council of Nurses Ethical Code as well as the Constitution of the World Health Organization require "respect for life . . . unrestricted by considerations of nationality, race, creed, age, sex, politics, or social status." Many codes also oblige the medical professional to try to improve the profession, including "establish[ing] and maintain[ing] equitable social and economic working conditions" (International Council of Nurses), as well as contributing to the community at large.

Journalists' Code

The Society of Professional Journalists, in like spirit, has something to say to the reporter discussed above.

> Members of the Society of Professional Journalists believe that public enlightment is the forerunner of justice and the foundation of democracy. The duty of the journalist is to further those ends by seeking truth and providing a fair and comprehensive account of events and issues. . . .

> 1. Journalists should be honest, fair, and courageous in gathering, reporting, and interpreting information.
>
> 2. Ethical journalists treat sources, subjects, and colleagues as human beings deserving of respect.
>
> 3. Journalists should be free of obligation to any interest other than the public's right to know.

4. Journalists are accountable to their readers, listeners, viewers, and each other.

Each of the numbered points is spelled out in detail. Under (3) we find, among other points, that

> Journalists should deny favored treatments to advertisers and special interests and resist their pressure to influence news coverage.

Likewise (1) is spelled out with a variety of specifics, such as "Never plagiarize," "Identify sources," "Give voice to the voiceless," and "Distinguish between advocacy and news reporting." Bearing in mind cases like NBC's, the code also specifies that a journalist must

> avoid misleading re-enactments or staged news events. If re-enactment is necessary to tell a story, label it.

The Logic of Professional Codes

These codes make explicit the *virtues* of a good doctor or nurse or journalist, and they begin to show us how these virtues flow from what virtue theorists like Alasdair MacIntyre would call the "internal goods" of the practice of medicine or journalism.

Take medicine. Medicine serves health—it is practiced "for the benefit of the sick"—therefore, medical professionals must put their patients' health above all other goals, including the professional's own enjoyments or income and even, sometimes, personal safety. The doctor must above all "do no harm." A doctor also enters a person's life at moments of great vulnerability—sickness and death—and is therefore bound to utmost respect for the patient and all of his family and household, including confidentiality. "What I may see or hear in the course of the treatment . . . I will keep to myself. . . ."

Take journalism. Again the proposed list of virtues flows directly from the "internal goods" of the profession. The aim of journalism is to inform people and by so doing to help promote democratic decision-making. Therefore, telling the truth is crucial. Some attempt to present both (all) sides of a dispute is crucial too, especially when most of the established powers stand on one side. Careful distinction between news and "advocacy" allows people to make up their own minds.

Once you understand professional codes of ethics in this way, you can begin to outline ethical standards for almost any profession. Teachers nurture the young, open minds, inform and enable: hence teachers must be supportive, must not indoctrinate, should be accurate and clear, and so on. Airline pilots must remain alert at all times and keep themselves well trained and ready. Same for truck drivers. Accountants must be objective, avoid conflicts of interest, and report clearly and accurately.

Beyond Professional Codes

For better or worse, codes of ethics do not resolve all ethical questions in the professions. You always need to think for yourself too (surprise!). Other tools also come into play.

Why Professional Codes Are not Enough

In the first place, most codes tend to be *general*. They lay out basic values and large ideals. Applying them to specific cases is still tricky. The Hippocratic Oath, for example, require doctors to work only "for the benefit of the sick." But often what *is* the benefit or best interest of the sick person (lying to her family? keeping him alive but immobilized on life support?) is the very question we need to answer.

Codes can also come into *conflict* with each other, or even themselves, as when the Journalists' Code requires both telling the full story and protecting the confidentiality of sources. Sometimes you can't do both.

Third, codes *evolve*. The Hippocratic Oath, for example, is dated in some obvious ways. Modern doctors do surgery, for example, and sex with household slaves is not exactly an issue. Older codes of the American Nurses Association required nurses to always follow doctors' orders, whereas more recent versions stress responsibility to patients and sometimes may even require nurses to become "patient advocates" *against* doctors. Now on the way out may be the assumption that patients do not want to be fully informed about their options or conditions, even when that information may be frightening or painful. Surveys show that doctors still overwhelmingly think so—but patients overwhelmingly want to know.

Finally, there is debate about certain aspects of some professions' codes of ethics, especially requirements that seem to set lower or different ethical standards for professionals than for ordinary people.

Are lawyers, for example, obliged to defend clients whom they know or discover to be guilty? The Code of Professional Responsibility of the American Bar Association says yes: lawyers are to defend their clients' interests "as vigorously as possible within the limits of the law." The adversarial procedure, they say, is the best way to find out the truth. Moreover, even guilty parties deserve the protection of the law. A system that would allow lawyers to judge clients themselves puts the lawyer's private judgment in place of judges and juries, where judgment really belongs. It also raises thorny questions about confidentiality (suppose a client tells his or her lawyer the truth in confidence . . .).

Still, many moralists have been critical of these arguments. Purely adversarial procedures are not the only or even the best way to arrive at truth (compare scientific method, for example). Certainly justice is not served when lawyers seeking the best settlement for guilty clients stall or complicate lawsuits or raise prohibitive barriers for poor plaintiffs. Even confidentiality is not absolute. In cases of imminent threat to others, courts have ruled that professionals have a duty to protect those threatened, even if they must violate confidentiality to do so.

Obviously this is a complicated issue. My point here is only that it (and others like it) *are* issues. Even a well-established professional code of ethics can still be challenged on ethical grounds. Reconsidering and debating about such codes from a larger ethical point of view may be one of the obligations of a professional too.

Reframing the Problems

By nature these codes are virtue centered. They address individual behavior in more or less "given" contexts. They tell doctors to serve the best interests of those patients they find themselves with; journalists to report their stories as accurately as they can.

As you know from Chapter 12, however, part of our ethical task is to examine and perhaps change those seemingly given contexts themselves. For example: journalists must indeed report their stories accurately. But it may also be part of a journalist's responsibility to examine and question the way stories are assigned in the first place. In the case of the dangerous new car, for instance, suppose that the newspaper just pulled all reporters off any stories about auto safety, or never assigned such stories in the first place. Is our hypothetical reporter then off the hook? Can she go on with a clear conscience to reporting about garden club meetings?

Likewise, if major changes in the organization of American medicine are undercutting adequate medical care for many people, as many doctors believe, shouldn't they step forward *as doctors* to sound the warning?

Traditionally such "social" questions have been ignored in professional codes, but things may be changing. The AMA's Principles of Medical Ethics now conclude with the statement "A physician shall recognize a responsibility to participate in activities contributing to an improved community." Nurses' codes do the same. The Code of Ethics for Legal Professionals also says that lawyers "should assist in improving the legal system." Given the wide range of views on these questions within the professions, perhaps this is all these codes *can* say. Yet for that very reason they don't give us the guidance we may need on the bigger questions.

Finally: no professional code can succeed without supporting practices and institutions. A journalist who has to worry about the influence of advertisers on editorial policy will hardly be reassured by a code that tells her that she should not bow to such influence. No code by itself will get her article published or save her job. To do that requires that newspapers commit themselves to the journalist's code too—that they commit themselves publicly, for one thing, and that they establish some hearing board or other forum at which alleged violations of the code can be considered. Her professional association should also establish such a forum, so that there is a professional check on the individual employers of journalists as well as a real check on individual journalists. Teaching ethics in journalism school would also help. Only when the industry as a whole *shows*—and not just declares—that it takes such codes seriously will they really carry the necessary weight. And the same, of course, goes for medicine, truck driving, teaching, and all the rest.

ETHICS AND BUSINESS

Suppose you design ads for a cigarette company. Would you make an ad encouraging smoking? How about an ad specifically targeting young people or certain especially vulnerable minority groups? Why or why not?

Would you make an ad for a war toy using hyperviolent imagery that you know will create an attractive "aura" for the toy and increase sales? Is it your responsibility to ask what happens when the young users of such toys graduate to real guns? Should ever-more-violent war toys be manufactured at all? How about new gun toys based on the latest school massacre? Where would you draw the line? Why?

There are few areas where unethical behavior can have such widespread consequences as in business. The A.H. Robins Corporation, maker of Chapstick, Robitussin, and other household drugs, also produced the Dalkon Shield, an intrauterine device that caused infection, sterility, and death in many of the 10 million women worldwide who used it in the 1970s. The Ford Pinto had an easily corrected fire hazard that the company declined to fix at the cost of five to ten dollars per car, knowing that hundreds of people would burn to death as a result. General Electric, with $60 billion in revenues America's fifth largest corporation, paid fines or settlements in sixteen cases of fraud in government contracting since 1990, is responsible or potentially responsible for pollution in seventy-two Superfund sites, and is on trial for trading scandals, diamond price fixing, and concealing defects in its jet engines. Corporate price fixing, by some estimates, costs Americans more each year than all robberies, larcenies, and burglaries combined.

What should be done about such behavior? Was it right that lawsuits eventually drove Robins into bankruptcy? (Should there be, as it were, capital punishment for corporations?) Wouldn't preventive strategies (but what strategies?) work better? And suppose that *you* worked for one of these corporations and had some hint, or more, of what was happening. What could you do to stop it? Are you obliged to step forward or go public with ethical concerns, even at personal risk? And what should companies do to protect such "whistleblowers" and create channels for internal and *preventive* whistleblowing?

Corporate Credos

No single code of ethics has been developed for business as a whole (though developing such a code was proposed by some CEOs in the 1970s). Instead most businesses have developed their own code of ethics or values statement. One sterling example is the "credo" of the pharmaceutical maker Johnson and Johnson:

> We believe our first responsibility is to the doctors, nurses, and patients, to mothers and fathers and all others who use our products and services. In meeting their needs everything we do must be of high quality. . . .
>
> We are responsible to our employees, the men and women who work with us throughout the world. We must respect their dignity and recognize their merit. They must have a sense of security in their jobs. Compensation must be fair and adequate. . . . Employees must feel free to make suggestions and complaints. There must be equal opportunity for employment, development, and advancement for those qualified. . . .
>
> We are responsible to the communities in which we live and work and to the world community as well. We must be good citizens—support good works and charities and bear our share of taxes. We must encourage civic improvements and better health and education . . . protecting the environment and natural resources.
>
> Our final responsibility is to our stockholders. Business must make a sound profit. We must experiment with new ideas. Research must be carried on, innovative programs developed, and mistakes paid for. . . . When we operate according to these principles, the stockholders should realize a fair return.

Notice that of the four responsibilities listed, J&J lists its responsibility to its stockholders last. This may not be what we expect. Some people argue that a business's only responsibility is to its stockholders. But from J&J's point of view, that appears to be a settled debate. As a provider of vital goods to "doctors, nurses, patients, mothers, fathers . . ." and a part of local and world communities, J&J believes that only if its responsibilities to these "*stake*holders" (those who have a *stake* in what J&J does) are fulfilled will stockholders earn a fair return.

They mean it, too. After seven people were poisoned by cynaide-laced Tylenol capsules in Chicago in 1982, J&J pulled twenty-two million bottles of Tylenol off shelves across the country, offered to exchanged any old capsules for tablets, made executives available to the media to forthrightly spell out the company's response, and reintroduced Tylenol only slowly and in tamper-resistant packaging that has since become an industry norm. Despite $100 million in losses, they also saved the brand, which quickly reclaimed more than 80 percent of its previous market share—proving that doing the right thing by *stake*holders also benefits *stock*holders too.

Other Corporate Codes

Ninety-one percent of large U.S.-based firms developed a code of ethics by 1994; 53 percent had values statements. So many now exist that you can even find collections of them, such as Patrick Murphy's aptly titled *Eighty Exemplary Ethical Codes for Business*.

Levi-Strauss & Co., the apparel maker, commits itself to trust, diversity, honesty, fairness, and even compassion ("an awareness of the needs of others"; acting to "meet those needs whenever possible"; minimizing harm . . .), and in this spirit became, in 1991, the first multinational company to establish "Global Sourcing and Operating Guidelines" for its trading partners overseas, banning the use of child labor, forced labor, exceptionally long work weeks, and unsafe working conditions.

Many statements, like J&J's, acknowledge "stakeholders" beyond (and *before*) stockholders: customers, employees, and the larger community. The Caterpillar Corporation, a heavy-equipment maker, identifies three different kinds of "possible social impact by business":

> First is the straightforward pursuit of daily business affairs. . . .
>
> The second category has to do with conducting business in a *way* that is socially responsible. It isn't enough to successfully offer useful products and services. A business should, for example, employ and promote people fairly, see to their job safety and the safety of its products, conserve energy. . . .
>
> The third category relates to initiatives beyond our operations, such as helping to solve community problems. . . . Each corporate facility is an integral part of the community in which it operates. Like an individual, it benefits from character building, health, welfare, educational, and other activities. And like an individual, it also has a citizen's responsibility to support such activities.

In this spirit Caterpillar and other corporations have created company foundations for charitable gift giving, often contributing at levels far beyond the tax advantageous and minimal (Borg-Warner Corporation even speaks explicitly of "reaching beyond the minimal" and of "responsibility to the common good"). The Dayton-Hudson Corporation has given 5 percent of its pretax income to charity every year since 1946. Others take seriously their environmental responsibilities, again far beyond what the law requires. As far back as 1975, when concern over ozone depletion was just beginning to arise, Johnson Wax Company withdrew all of its fluorocarbon-based products from the market, nearly a decade before a ban was even considered by the FDA.

Even the sacredness of profits comes in for reconsideration. J. C. Penney (whose original choice for the name of his stores, by the way, was the Golden Rule Stores) wrote an ethical code (the "Penney Idea") in 1913 that includes the explicit commitment "to expect for the service we render a fair remuneration and *not* all the profit the traffic will bear." Levi-Strauss explicitly declares its commitment to "commercial success in terms broader than merely financial measures" and in 1993, on the basis of its "Global Sourcing and Operating Guidelines," decided not to begin what would have been a very profitable partnership with some Chinese enterprises.

Not all businesses, of course, live up to their official sentiments. GE, for example, has an inspiring ethics code but a miserable record. Yet actions like J&J's show that living up to ethical standards is not only possible but profitable. Indeed, a famous 1983 study by J&J concluded that over a thirty-year period companies with a strong public service policy have profits more than double the profits of the average Fortune 500 company.

Employees Within the Company

Like professional codes of ethics, these corporate ethical statements certainly don't resolve all of the specific questions that arise in day-to-day practice. They are often too general to help, and/or come into conflict with themselves or other values.

Once again, though, they at least point out a useful direction. They establish certain virtues for corporate employees generally and sometimes for employees of a specific company in particular. Integrity, fairness, creativity, cooperation, trust, and respect are very widely cited. Like other virtues, they make sense given the nature and goals of the enterprise. Businesses recognize that ethical statements make for effective teamwork and therefore corporate success.

These statements also raise new issues and difficulties. For one, how are employees to deal with conflicts between a company's ethical commitments and its actions in practice? How far, in the name of a company's own ethical commitments, are employees obliged to stick their own necks out to resist the "corporate culture"? Or suppose an engineer's or doctor's or journalist's professional organizations' codes say one thing but their employers—businesses—expect another. What then?

One widely agreed on point is that companies should set up internal mechanisms for addressing employee's ethical and other concerns, before the person feels obliged either to "shut up and put up" or go public ("blow the whistle"). Many companies have set up help lines, anonymous telephone numbers, ombudspersons, and so on, and encouraged employees to share their concerns. Cummins Engine Company's "Statement of Principles" is typical:

> If . . . you are uncomfortable with a particular action; if you would be unwilling to tell persons you love and respect; if you would not want to see it reported on the front page of your major newspaper; then DON'T DO IT!

The statement follows up with names and phone numbers of people to contact for guidance.

Protecting the whistleblower against reprisals (harassment, job loss) is crucial too, of course. Some laws are beginning to address this issue, and some fired whistleblowers have regained jobs or compensation in the courts.

Potential whistleblowers themselves are often (justly) conflicted. Loyalties to the company—to one's friends and colleagues, especially, who usually are one's co-workers—conflict with other loyalties. One may worry about personal resentments, vendettas, knowing only part of the story, and other ways in which individual judgment may be clouded. Professional loyalties (say, as a nurse) may conflict with organizational loyalties (say, as an employee of a drug company). Borg-Warner's ethics statement eloquently acknowledges this: loyalty, it says, "can flow in many different directions." There is no easy way to sort this out, but it would at least be useful for all parties to realize that no *dis*loyalty is necessarily implied by raising questions. The challenge is to make it instead a source of organizational strength through self-correction.

Building More Ethical Business

How can corporations become *more* ethical (and *more* corporations become ethical)? And how (remembering our problem-shifting tools) can we prevent the sorts of abuses that create the need for whistleblowing in the first place?

Just the formulation of corporate ethics statements is a major first step. Employees and customers then have an ethical reference point: expectations are created and commitments made. The company declares, at least officially, that it is willing to be held to certain standards.

Training programs, executive progress reports, and other practical applications are the next step. These too are becoming widespread. Companies need to signal in day-to-day ways that their ethical commitments are taken seriously and make a difference.

But corporate *structure* may have to change too. For example, better "feedback mechanisms" may be crucial. Some of the worst problems come about because no one in a company is made responsible for quality checks: for listening to reports back from the field. The Dalkon shield, for example, was the A.H. Robins Company's first venture into medical devices, and partly for this reason the company had no mechanism in place to collect and evaluate the reports of difficulties that began to pour back from doctors. Years passed before it became clear that a disaster was unfolding.

This is an ethical failure too. People sometimes have trouble blaming a whole company for product failures like the Dalkon shield, because in a badly organized company there may be no single identifiable individuals who failed to do their jobs. But then, surely, the company is at least to blame *for its bad organization.*

Also outrageous in Robins's case was that higher-ups in the company who *did* begin to suspect that the shield was dangerous did nothing to stop its promotion but did quietly tell their families and friends not to use it, and did not use it themselves. This is a pretty clear violation of the Golden Rule—of the Kantian idea that you cannot ethically make an exception for yourself to rules or practices that you expect (in this case even encourage) others to follow.

This may lead to another suggestion. What if we began to expect that all the higher-ups in a company would use the company's products? Not a specially checked and top-of-the-line model, either, but a random model right off the assembly line, just like all the rest of us get. If the Ford executives who approved the Pinto knew that they or their children would be driving one themselves, would they have declined to add a cheap part that would have eliminated the fire hazard? Would Robins' executives have allowed ten million *other* people to use the Dalkon shield if they'd had to use it themselves? Here a little applied ethics might go a long way.

" 'Obviously a Major Malfunction' "

LISA NEWTON AND DAVID SCHMIDT

Morton Thiokol Industries (MTI) was the lead contractor for the solid-fuel boosters that powered the American space shuttle launches in the 1980s, and the builder of the booster that exploded seventy-three seconds into flight on January 28, 1986, destroying the *Challenger* space shuttle, killing its crew of seven and shocking the world.

At first the disaster seemed simply a cruel act of fate. As investigation began, however, a more complicated story began to emerge. Some of MTI's engineers strenuously opposed the launch, fearing just such a explosion, but were overruled by NASA officials and their own higher-ups at MTI in a crucial teleconference just hours before the launch. Thus the "major malfunction" of the spacecraft (as NASA's public affairs officer put it right after the explosion) may have been a sign of a major malfunction in corporate and professional decision-making as well. What emerged in the investigation that followed was a long story of missed opportunities and ignored warnings.

How did it happen? Could it happen again? Notice that the answers are not at all simple. There are no obvious villains here, as there sometimes are in clearer cases of corporate or professional misdemeanor. The "malfunction" lies in the underlying structures of decision-making themselves. What do you think can be done (what should have been done? what should be done next time?) to correct them?

THE TRAGIC EXPLOSION OF THE
SPACE SHUTTLE CHALLENGER

The following was taken from a *New York Times* transcript of the last moments of the Space Shuttle *Challenger*, before and after liftoff:

PUBLIC AFFAIRS OFFICER: Coming up on the 90-second point in our countdown. Ninety seconds and counting. The 51-L Mission is ready to go. . . . T minus 10, 9, 8 7, 6, we have main engine start, 4, 3, 2, 1. And liftoff. Liftoff of the 25th space shuttle mission and it has cleared the tower. . . .

MISSION CONTROL CENTER: Watch your roll, *Challenger*.

PUBLIC AFFAIRS OFFICER: Roll program confirmed. *Challenger* now heading down range. [Pause.] Engines beginning throttling down now at 94 percent. Normal throttle for most of flight 104 percent. Will throttle down to 65 percent. Three engines running normally. Three good cells, three good ABU's. [Pause.] Velocity 2,257 feet per second, altitude 4.3 nautical miles, down range distance 3 nautical miles. [Pause.] Engines throttling up, three engines now at 104 percent.

MISSION CONTROL: *Challenger*, go with throttle up.

FRANCIS R. SCOBEE, *CHALLENGER* COMMANDER: Roger, go with throttle up.

PUBLIC AFFAIRS OFFICER: One minute fifteen seconds, velocity 2,900 feet per second, altitude 9 nautical miles, down range distance 7 nautical miles. [Long pause.] Flight controllers here looking very carefully at the situation. [Pause.] Obviously a major malfunction. We have no downlink [communications from *Challenger*]. [Long pause.] We have a report from the flight dynamics officer that the vehicle has exploded.[1]

January 29, 1986, marks the day the Space Shuttle *Challenger* exploded. Only seventy-three seconds into its flight the *Challenger* disintegrated in a catastrophic explosion. All seven astronauts aboard died, including Christa McAuliffe, a teacher from Concord, New Hampshire, who was to have been the first ordinary citizen to travel in space. At the launch site and at home before their television sets, Americans watched in disbelief, scarcely able to comprehend what had just happened before their eyes. . . .

Something Was Not Right

The following is an account of the final shuttle flight procedures from that morning[2]:

From *Wake-Up Calls*: Classic Cases in Business Ethics, by L. H. Newton and D. A. Schmidt. © 1996. Reprinted with permission of Wadsworth, a division of Thompson Learning.

January 28, 1986, 1:30 A.M. to 3:00 A.M. at Kennedy.   The ice crew reports large quantities of ice on pad B. The spacecraft can be damaged by chunks of ice that can be hurled about during the turbulent rocket ignition.

5:00 A.M. at Kennedy.   Mulloy [Chief of Solid Rockets at NASA's Marshall Center] tells Lucas [Director of NASA's Marshall Center] of MTI [Morton Thiokol] concerns over temperature and resolution and shows the recommendation writen by MTI.

7:00 A.M. to 9:00 A.M. at Kennedy.   The clear morning sky formed what glider pilots call a "blue bowl." Winds dwindled to 9 mph. During the night temperatures fell to 27 degrees Fahrenheit. The ice crew measures temperatures at 25 degrees Fahrenheit on the right-hand solid rocket booster, 8 degrees Fahrenheit on the left. They are not concerned as there are no Launch Commit Criteria relating to temperatures on rocket surfaces.

8:00 A.M. at Kennedy.   Lovingwood [NASA] tells Deputy Director of Marshall (Lee) about previous discussions with MTI.

9:00 A.M. at Kennedy.   Mission Management Team meets with Level 1 and 2 managers, project managers, and others. The ice conditions on launch pad are discussed, but not the O-ring issue.

10:30 A.M. at Kennedy.   The ice crew reports to the Mission Management Team that ice is still left on booster.

11:18 A.M.   A Rockwell engineer in California watching the ice team over closed-circuit television telephones the Cape to advise a delay because of the ice. Kennedy Center Director Smith, advised by the ice team that there is little risk, permits the countdown to continue.

11:28 A.M.   Inside *Challenger's* flight deck (about the size of a 747), Commander Scobee and pilot Smith run through their elaborate checklists. The orbiter's main computer, supported by four backup computers, scans data from 2,000 sensors. If it detects a problem, it will shut down the entire system. In June 1984, the computer aborted four seconds before the rocket ignition. This time, it doesn't.

11:30 A.M.   Thousands of motorists pull off highways to face toward the ocean.

11:37 A.M.   The launch platform is flooded by powerful streams of water from 7-foot pipes to dampen the lift-off sound levels, which could damage the craft's underside.

11:38 A.M.   Flight 51-L is launched. Two rust-colored external fuel tanks, each 154 feet high, carrying 143,351 gallons of liquid oxygen and 385,265 gallons of liquid hydrogen power the rocket. They will burn until the fuel runs out.

11:39 A.M.   Everything looked like it was supposed to look. As one MTI engineer watched the rocket lift off the pad into a bright Florida sky he thought, "Gee, it's gonna be all right. It's a piece of cake . . . we made it."

Among those watching the launch were engineers responsible for the rocket boosters who opposed the launch, and their reactions to the initial moments of liftoff reflected their anxiety. According to another account of the *Challenger's* liftoff:

> On January 28, 1986, a reluctant Roger Boisjoly watched the launch of the *Challenger*. As the vehicle cleared the tower, Bob Ebeling whispered, "we've just dodged a bullet." (The engineers who opposed the launch assumed that O-ring failure would result in an explosion almost immediately after engine ignition.) To continue in Boisjoly's words, "At approximately T+60 seconds Bob told me had just completed a prayer of thanks to the Lord for a successful launch. Just thirteen seconds later we both saw the horror of the destruction as the vehicle exploded.[3]

As these accounts reveal, there had been a debate over the potential risks posed by the unseasonably cold weather that morning. In particular, there was concern about the effects of the cold on something called an "O-ring." These accounts also indicate that there were several parties to the debate within NASA and between NASA and Morton Thiokol, the manufacturer of the solid fuel rocket boosters for the space shuttle program. The debate about the safety of the O-rings under cold conditions had been brewing for some time. However, this debate failed to postpone the *Challenger's* January 28 launch date, for a variety of complex reasons. The Presidential Commission on the Space Shuttle *Challenger* Accident later described the cause of the explosion as follows:

> The consensus of the Commission and participating investigative agencies is that the loss of the Space Shuttle *Challenger* was caused by a failure in the joint between the two lower segments of the right Solid Rocket Motor. The specific failure was the destruction of the seals that are intended to prevent hot gases from leaking through the joint during the propellant burn of the rocket motor. The evidence assembled by the Commission indicates that no other element of the Space Shuttle system contributed to this failure.[4]

Growing Concern About O-Rings

It was fully one year before the *Challenger* explosion when Roger Boisjoly began to have serious questions about the safety of the solid rocket boosters that Morton Thiokol manufactured for NASA's space shuttles.[5] Boisjoly was senior scientist at Morton Thiokol with twenty-five years of experience as an aerospace industry engineer. On January 24, 1985, he observed the launch of Space Shuttle Flight 51-C as part of his responsibility for the safety of the solid rocket booster joints. The air temperature that day was unseasonably cool. The launch appeared to go off without a hitch. The solid rocket boosters separated from the *Challenger* after they had burned their fuel and fell to the ocean. They were later recovered and inspected by Boisjoly. He detected something in the solid rocket boosters that worried him.

The boosters are so large that they are made up of separate segments. The connecting joints between the segments are sealed by a rubberlike material called the O-rings. These seals must not leak during launch or an explosion is very likely to occur. Boisjoly discovered while inspecting the primary O-ring seals on two field joints that the joints had been damaged by hot combustion gases. Part of the primary O-ring had eroded. As far as Boisjoly knew, this was the first time a primary seal on a booster field joint had been penetrated by hot gases. He found a large quantity of blackened grease between the primary and secondary seals, which alarmed him even more. Boisjoly learned from a postflight analysis that the ambient temperature of the field joints (the temperature in the area surrounding the joints) at the time of launch was fifty-three degrees. He remembered how cold it was the day of the launch. For the first time, Boisjoly suspected that there might be a connection between the damage to the O-rings and the low air temperature. He reported his suspicions to engineers and managers at NASA's Marshall Space Flight Center. However, the association of low temperature with evidence of hot gas leakage through a field joint was termed as "acceptable risk" by key NASA officials.

In March Boisjoly conducted laboratory tests on the O-ring seals, working with Arnie Thompson, Supervisor of Rocket Motor Cases. The tests supported his theory that low temperatures prevented O-ring seals from forming an adequate seal on solid rocket booster joints. Boisjoly and Thompson did not know with certainty the temperatures below which it would be too dangerous for a safe flight. They only knew that at very cold temperatures neither the primary nor the secondary O-rings would seal. The consequences of this double failure would be a catastrophic explosion. Boisjoly's concerns were reported to key engineers and managers at NASA and Morton Thiokol.

Even though a Seal Erosion Task Force was informally created in July, Boisjoly was increasingly frustrated by what he perceived to be a lack of progress in fixing the problem. At that point, Boisjoly wrote a memo labeled "Company Private," which he sent to Robert (Bob) Lund, vice president of engineering at Morton Thiokol. The memo, which Boisjoly intended to express the extreme urgency of his views, contained the following passages:

> This letter is written to insure that management is fully aware of the seriousness of the current O-ring erosion problem. . . . The mistakenly accepted position on the joint problem was to fly without fear of failure . . . is now drastically changed as a result of the SRM 16A nozzle joint erosion[,] which eroded a secondary O-ring with the primary O-ring never sealing. If the same scenario should occur in a field joint (and it could), then it is a jump ball as to the success or failure of the joint. . . . The result would be a catastrophe of the highest order—loss of human life. . . .

> It is my honest and real fear that if we do not take immediate action
> to dedicate a team to solve the problem, with the field joint having the
> number one priority, then we stand in jeopardy of losing a flight[,] along
> with all the launch pad facilities.[6]

Following the memo, in August Lund formally established the Seal
Erosion Task Team. However, the Team consisted of a mere five full-
time engineers (there were 2,500 Morton Thiokol employees working
on the space shuttle program). To some engineers at Morton Thiokol, it
appeared that the Seal Erosion Task Team was never adequately supported
in its implementation. Moreover, there were indications that senior Morton
Thiokol managers did not take seriously the Team's concerns. For example,
the members of the Seal Erosion Task Team met with Joe Kilminster
(vice president for boosters) on October 3, 1985, to raise their concerns
about the lack of corporate support. "Boisjoly later stated that Kilminster
summarized the meeting as a 'good bullshit session.' "[7] During the next two
months leading up to the launch of the Space Shuttle *Challenger*, Boisjoly
and the Seal Erosion Task Team apparently made little headway against
the indifference and even opposition that they perceived among certain
Morton Thiokol executives.

The Teleconference Between Morton Thiokol and NASA

The debate over the safety of the O-ring seals came to a head during a key
telephone conference call between Morton Thiokol and NASA just before
the launch of the Space Shuttle *Challenger* on January 28. The day before
the launch, the weather forecast for conditions at the launch site predicted
temperatures as low as eighteen degrees. The situation was monitored
closely by Morton Thiokol personnel at the Marshall Space Flight Center, as
well as by their counterparts at the Kennedy Space Center. The debate over
what to do culminated in a three-way telephone conference call beween
three teams of engineers and managers. The call took place at 8:15 P.M.
eastern standard time the evening before the scheduled lanuch.

In this teleconference, Boisjoly and Thompson presented their scientific evidence about the effects of cold temperatures on the O-ring's ability to
maintain a reliable seal. Based on their findings, they recommended against
the launch of the *Challenger*. The key facts supporting their position follow:

> Although there was some leaking around the seal even at relatively high
> temperatures, the worst leakage was at 53 degrees. With a predicted
> ambient temperature of 26 degrees at launch, the O-rings were estimated
> to be at 29 degrees. This was much lower than the launch temperatures
> of any previous flight.[8]

It is important to note that the engineers could not state with precision the
exact temperature at which the O-rings would be too cold for a safe launch.

It is also pertinent that engineers are trained to err on the side of caution when assessing risk.

Bob Lund summarized Boisjoly's and Thompson's report, saying that it was Morton Thiokol's recommendation that any launch should only proceed if the O-ring seal temperature was at least fifty-three degrees. Kilminster supported the position of his engineers.

NASA's response was highly critical of this recommendation. One member of NASA's team, George Hardy, was reported to be "appalled at that recommendation." Larry Mulloy, chief of solid rockets at the Marshall Space Flight Center, also strongly opposed Morton Thiokol's position. He objected to what he considered to be a substantive revision of the Launch Commit Criteria at what was almost literally the last minute before a launch. It is reported that Mulloy complained in exasperation, "My God, Thiokol, when do you want me to launch? Next April?"[9] Confronted by this withering criticism, Kilminster asked for a five-minute caucus with his engineers, putting the NASA side of the teleconference "on hold."

In his testimony before the Rogers Commission that later investigated the *Challenger* explosion, Boisjoly described the caucus as follows: Jerry Mason (senior vice president of Wasatch Operations at Morton Thiokol) insisted that a "management decision" was necessary. Boisjoly and Thompson attempted to reargue their position, but stopped when they perceived that no one else was really listening to them anymore. Jerry Mason, who was reported to have said, "Am I the only one who wants to fly?," then instructed Bob Lund to "take off your engineering hat and put on your management hat." Following a brief discussion, the four Morton Thiokol managers at that discussion then voted unanimously to recommend *Challenger's* launch.

Organizational Features of NASA and Morton Thiokol

Some critics of NASA charge that its lack of mission and its vulnerability to bottom-line pressure contributed to shortcuts on safety. To these critics, it should be pointed out that space exploration is inherently risky. Even in its early glory days, NASA was plagued with failures. In 1959, seven of its seventeen rocket launches misfired. In 1967, in what was supposed to have been a routine test, a flash fire erupted in an *Apollo* command module, burning to death the three astronauts strapped in their seats. Even then, some critics claim, NASA was motivated by more pragmatic interests:

> Despite "official" stringent safety standards, the agency was more concerned with meeting deadlines than with safety issues. NASA used this tragedy to its best advantage. Invoking the memory of the dead, they stressed the importance of getting on with the program because that's what the astronauts would have wanted. In spite of this setback, Kennedy's challenge to land a man on the moon was met.[10]

Increasingly, decisions at NASA were made from a management and a political perspective, as well as from a scientific or engineering perspective. Interestingly, a similar conflict in organizational perspective could be found at Morton Thiokol.

Morton Thiokol, a company formed when Morton Salt Company acquired Thiokol, was an organization that displayed features of two different, somewhat contrasting corporate cultures.[11] Morton, the parent company, endeavored to create an organizational structure that promoted candid, direct communication through the corporate hierarchy. It sought to implement an "open-door" policy through actions such as giving its workers the home telephone numbers of all its management.

Thiokol was also a hierarchical company, but it contrasted with Morton in the ways in which it funneled communication through its layers. The Wasatch division, responsible for manufacturing the solid rocket boosters for the space shuttle, has been described as an autocratic organization. In this division, employee complaints were not particularly encouraged or welcomed. In such a setting, it would be hazardous for any employee to do an end run around his or her boss in order to communicate a complaint higher up in the organization. According to business ethicist Patricia Werhane, who is speaking about the Wasatch division:

> This rigid hierarchy led to difficulties. There was a lack of communication and with that an absence of trust between managers and engineers so a subsequent isolation of managers from proper reading of the data, and, as a result, isolation of NASA not from information, but from varying analyses of the information. The lingering effects of the old Thiokol culture demanded unquestioned loyalty from engineers such as McDonald or Boisjoly.[12]

In the end, it was individual persons who made critically important decisions that led to the January 28, 1986, launch of the *Challenger* shuttle. The responsibility for that decision belongs to them. But their decision making was shaped by long-standing traditions in the policies and cultures of organizations. If the organizational patterns of decision making had been different, it is possible that the individuals in question would have reached a different decision about whether to launch. . . .

NOTES

1. As recorded by the *New York Times*, 29 January 1986, A1.

2. Robert Marx, Charles Stubbart, Virginia Traub, and Michael Cavanaugh. "The NASA Space Shuttle Disaster: A Case Study," *Journal of Management Case Studies* 3 (winter 1987): 316–318.

3. Russell Boisjoly, Ellen Foster Curtis, and Eugene Mellican, "Roger Boisjoly and the *Challenger* Disaster: The Ethical Dimensions," *Journal of Business Ethics* 8 (1989): 223.

4. *Report of the Presidential Commission on the Space Shuttle Challenger Accident* (Washington, D.C., June 1986).

5. Unless otherwise indicated, the following account of Roger Boisjoly's experience concerning the O-ring and Morton Thiokol is taken from Boisjoly, Curtis, and Mellican, "Roger Boisjoly and the *Challenger* Disaster," 217–230.

6. Roger M. Boisjoly, Applied Mechanics Memorandum to Robert K. Lund, Vice President, Engineering, Wasatch Division, Morton Thiokol, 31 July 1985, quoted in Boisjoly, Curtis, and Mellican, "Roger Boisjoly, Curtis, and Mellican, "Roger Boisjoly and the *Challenger* Disaster," 220.

7. Ibid., 220.

8. Charles E. Harris, Jr., Michael S. Pritchard, and Michael J. Rabins, *Engineering Ethics* (Belmont, CA: Wadsworth, 1995): 1.

9. Malcolm McConnell, *Challenger, a Major Malfunction: A True Story of Politics, Greed, and the Wrong Stuff* (Garden City, N.J.: Doubleday, 1987).

10. Marx, Stubbart, Traub, and Cavanaugh, "The NASA Space Shuttle Disaster," 308.

11. As Pat Werhane observes in her article on the *Challenger*, it is appropriate now to speak of Morton Thiokol in the past tense because in 1989 Morton divested itself of the rocket booster divisions of Thiokol. Patricia H. Werhane, "Engineers and Management: The Challenge of the *Challenger* Incident," *Journal of Business Ethics* 10 (1991): 605–616.

12. Ibid., 611.

Exercises and Notes

MORE PROFESSIONAL CODES

Pick one or two professional fields that interest you, fields you are studying, maybe, or that you plan to enter. Then ask what are the "internal goods" of those fields—those basic aims that determine the ethical and professional standards of anyone in the field. Use them to put together what *you* think would be a useful code of ethics for that profession. What kinds of virtues will you include? How will you defend your proposed code against skeptics? How can you institutionalize your code—that is, what kinds of supporting practices will your code need to be effective, to make a difference?

Now look up the professional code(s) already proposed for the field you have chosen, and compare it (them) with yours. Have you overlooked some things? Have *they* overlooked some things? What might account for the differences?

A Code for Students

Since the appropriate virtues of doctors, teachers, airline pilots, and all the rest arise out of their *roles*—out of the practice they are engaged in—isn't the same thing true of students? You too are engaged in a practice with a certain nature, needs, and so on. It too should imply certain virtues.

Lay out the general values you think apply to student life. Explain *why* you think these values apply. Then specify them by addressing the particular kinds of problems that arise in student life. Brainstorm a list of problems and issues (plagiarism? alcohol issues? community service?) and try to say something clear and reasonable about them. Try out your proposed code on your friends. Make changes if needed and try again.

Your school may already have a code of conduct for students. Find a copy and compare it with yours. What are the similarities and differences? What do you think accounts for them? Are your codes addressed to different sorts of problems? Find out who wrote the official one (students? faculty? administrators?). Does it show? How?

The text also suggests that any such codes have a variety of limits. What are the limits of yours? What kinds of supporting structures (enforcement procedures? record-keeping?) does such a code invite or require?

Your Company's Ethics Statement

Suppose you are setting up a new business. Make it your dream company. Describe it: who works for you, what your company does, where it operates, its size and budget, its impacts both good and bad on the community and the land.

Now sketch an ethics code or values statement for your company. What are the key virtues for you and your employees? What are your social responsibilities? How will you promote your code, enforce it, make it real? How can you invite and honor employee (and other stakeholder) participation in formulating the code in the first place? How will whistleblowing issues be dealt with?

Who are your investors—your stockholders—and what are their interests? Don't assume that their interest is just in the biggest profits. "Socially responsible" investment houses, designed for investors for whom profit is *not* the only consideration, are now a multi-hundred-billion-dollar business.

Likewise, who are your *stake*holders? What are *their* interests? Expect a variety of stakeholders and a variety of interests.

Notes and Further Readings

Full texts of the Hippocratic Oath and the AMA Principles of Medical Ethics can found at the end of Tom Beauchamp and James Childress, *Principles of Biomedical Ethics* (Oxford University Press, many editions). Also included are various codes for nurses, the preamble to the World Health Organization's constitution, model Patients' Bills of Rights, and others. The Society of Professional Journalists' code can be found at <www.spj.org/ethics>. For other codes, including the American Bar Association's Model Rules and codes for social workers, codes for engineers, and so on, see the Appendix to Joan Callahan, *Ethical Issues in Professional Life* (Oxford University Press, 1988)— a thorough introduction to the issues raised in this chapter and many others besides. On the argument over lawyers' neutrality, see Alan Goldman, *The Moral Foundations of Professional Ethics* (Rowman and Littlefield, 1980).

All cited corporate codes of ethics may be found in Patrick Murphy, ed., *Eighty Exemplary Ethical Codes for Business* (University of Notre Dame, 1998). On the formulation and uses of such codes, see also Lisa Newton, "The Many Faces of the Corporate Code," in *The Corporate Code of Ethics: The Perspective of the Humanities* (Fairfield University, 1992). On the history of the Dalkon Shield, see Morton Mintz, *At Any Cost* (Pantheon, 1985). On the Pinto case, see W. Michael Hoffman, "The Ford Pinto," in Thomas Donaldson and Al Gini, eds., *Case Studies in Business Ethics* (Prentice-Hall, 1996). On GE's ethical difficulties, see Nanette Byrnes, "The Smoke at General Electric," in the Donaldson and Gini collection. For other classic cases of ethical difficulties in business, look through the Donaldson and Gini collection and/or Lisa Newton and David Schmidt's *Wake-up Calls*, from which the reading in this chapter comes.

On Johnson and Johnson's response to the Tylenol poisonings, see Carl Cannon, "Tylenol's Rebound," in Donaldson and Gini. James Liebig, *Business Ethics: Profiles in Civic Virtue* (Fulcrum Publishing, 1990) profiles two dozen contemporary business leaders, "virtuous managers" who have "exhibited a concern for people and our common life that is integrated with their pursuit of business success." Some corporate ethical "success stories" can also be found at the end of the Donaldson and Gini volume. Useful suggestions for the structural reform of large corporations can be found in Christopher Stone's *Where the Law Ends: The Social Control of Corporate Behavior* (Harper and Row, 1975).

For a detailed discussion of the social responsibility of corporations and the stakeholder/stockholder debate, see John Boatwright, *Ethics and the Conduct of Business* (Prentice-Hall, 1997). Boatwright's is one of a number of philosophers' anthologies in business ethics that discuss a wide range of issues, including whistleblowing, affirmative action, ethical issues in advertising, conflicts of interests, and so on. For some intriguing cross-cultural perspectives, see Sally Stewart and Gabriel Donleavy, *Whose Business Values? Some Asian and Cross-Cultural Perspectives* (Hong Kong University Press, 1995).

For texts of further philosophical treatments of ethics in business and the professions, and a wide variety of useful links, go to the "Ethics Updates" website at <ethics.acusd.edu> and select "Business and Professional Ethics." Another useful site is <ethics.ubc.ca/resources>, the Center for Applied Ethics at the University of British Columbia: look under "World Wide Web Resources" and select "Business Ethics" or "Professional Ethics." A number of specific business and professional codes of ethics may be found here as well.

For more on the *Challenger* disaster, including live testimony by Roger Boisjoly and others on the flawed decision to launch, see the ABC News video "From Disaster to Recovery: The Challenger Explosion and the Rebirth of America's Space Program" (from ABC's "Great TV News Stories" series, 1989).

CHAPTER 19

○

Poverty and Welfare

BACKGROUND

A Very Brief History of Welfare

The "welfare state" as we know it is a twentieth-century development. Assistance to the poor, though, is as old as human civilization itself. Families have always relied on each other for help. Tribal peoples did (and do) rely on their tribes. The ancient city-states gave pensions to widows and the disabled. Athens even provided free public drama—considered to be a fundamental need of all Athenian citizens—paid for by the rich. Feudal people fell back on their clans and their feudal lord, who was expected to provide some minimal security in exchange for his serfs' more or less forced labor. Priest and church provided salvation—once again paid for by those who could.

As capitalism replaced feudalism, European and early American communities set up almshouses for local orphans and the handicapped, gave the able-bodied poor low-grade employment (threatening jail or the stocks otherwise), and apprenticed out destitute children. This was paid for by local communities, which is one reason almost no one cared for the needs of destitute strangers. The dominant Christian tradition did suggest that there was an obligation to help the poor "fare well"—at least a tiny bit better. The main problem motivating the ruling class, though, was not concern for poverty but annoyance with begging. Provision was grudging. Conditions in the almshouses were often, as one writer put it, "unbelievably deplorable."

But the Industrial Revolution began to overpower the almshouse system by the mid-1800s. Poverty and social stress in the new cities were vast and growing. Many of the new poor were without the family, clan, or community fallbacks that softened poverty in the past.

Religious groups began responding by setting up private social welfare services. At the same time, public opinion began to shift against the unrestrained capitalism that produced the "robber barons," child labor, and eighty-hour or longer work weeks. A new and radical idea began to grow on people: that *government* might both regulate industry and take upon itself to provide social welfare services. Limited government funding of health, housing, and slum clearance began around 1900. Worker protection and child labor laws came into effect around the same time.

Even so, it took the Great Depression to force a massive change in the American response to poverty. After a period of high-flying general prosperity, the stock market crashed in October of 1929. Three years later the number of jobless Americans had jumped from three million to fifteen million. It became clear that people could fall into poverty through no fault of their own, and sometimes only the government had the resources to help.

President Franklin Roosevelt responded with a range of programs—the "New Deal," he called it. Social Security was established to provide for the aged and disabled. Public assistance programs, such as Aid to Families with Dependent Children (AFDC) were started. Work programs such as the Civilian Conservation Corps were set up for the able-bodied poor. Governments began to sponsor adoption and foster care programs.

World War II and a period of economic growth followed. But government involvement in poverty and social welfare programs expanded again in the 1960s. Poverty was found to be much more extensive than previously thought. Nearly a quarter of the U.S. population turned out to be impoverished. The Physician Task Force on Hunger found severe hunger and malnutrition throughout the country. President Johnson responded in 1964 by declaring what he called a "War on Poverty." Head Start, Medicare, and Medicaid were created and other programs were greatly enlarged.

By 1977 the Physician Task Force found hunger vastly reduced. The official poverty level decreased from 22 percent of the population in 1960 to 11 percent in 1972. In the meantime, though, there were a sucession of other crises: the Vietnam War, the environmental and energy crises, and so on. These led to growing budget deficits and economic strains. Taxpayers felt the pressure, and resentment grew against poor people who were perceived to be living off the hard work of others rather than making their own contribution.

Coupled with Americans' seemingly innate suspicion of bureaucracy, this growing pessimism led to a series of changes and reductions in social welfare programs in the eighties and nineties. Presidents Reagan and Bush oversaw the first large-scale reduction in social welfare programs in American history. Many programs were eliminated or consolidated into other programs that were in turn drastically reduced or transferred to the less than tender mercies of the states. Rates of poverty and malnutrition began inching up again.

Change continued under President Clinton and the mostly Republican Congresses with which he dealt. A series of reforms in 1996 largely ended welfare as an entitlement. Work requirements are now common, and application processes have been deliberately made more involved and slow. Total benefit-year limits have been imposed as well. Federal laws limit a person to five years total on welfare, with a maximum of two years at any one time. States can and sometimes do set much lower limits. AFDC is now called

"Temporary Assistance for Needy Families"—TANF—with the emphasis very much on "temporary."

Current Statistics

Some thirty-five to forty million Americans now officially live in poverty, about 14 percent of the total population. Many others teeter on the brink, vulnerable to the next economic downturn. About 75 percent receive federal aid in some form, and the range of programs is wide: there are unemployment compensation, Medicaid, housing assistance, food stamps, TANF, child nutrition programs, and others still. About 25 percent of the poor receive no federal assistance at all.

About ten million people are now on TANF, a little less than 4 percent of the total population, down from a peak of fourteen million in 1994. The new welfare laws are part of the reason for the decline. So is the continued health of the economy. About half the people who have left the welfare rolls since the 1996 reforms have jobs; the other half do not. Some find the requirements too stringent and make other arrangements. (And many requirements are intended to be stringent enough to have just this effect.) Some fall through the bureaucratic cracks. Others are condemned to homelessness and hunger. Of those who get jobs, some are real success stories. Others find only minimum-wage or part-time work and remain below the poverty level. Most experts agree that it is too early to say what the overall effects of the new laws will be, though already another set of changes is being urged.

SHARED VALUES

Welfare is another one of those moral debates where we often let our disagreements overshadow our agreements. In speaking of values it's therefore useful to start with the obvious—with certain basic shared values. Once again they may surprise us.

The Need to Respond

One shared value is: the need to respond. The bottom line is that our moral traditions do not allow us to abandon other people to abject poverty or hunger or death. It offends our own humanity and our society's decency if we allow anyone to fall that low—even, normally, if we think that their condition is in some way their "fault." Provision may be grudging, meager, and it may come with a good dose of moralizing, but we are required to do *something*.

This does not necessarily mean that we must support governmental welfare programs as they currently exist, or maybe any governmental welfare programs at all. Conservatives tend to favor private charitable provision instead, which has the added virtue in their eyes of being voluntary. Many other forms of provision are also possible.

But the first point, again, is that even conservatives favor *some* form of help. We are not really debating about whether to help at all. We are only (though it's a big "only") debating about *how*.

Responding Effectively

Well, how? Another obvious shared value is: the need to respond *effectively*.

It's clear that poverty is a major waste, not just for poor people but for all of society. On the other hand, it is not so clear how to respond in a way that isn't wasteful itself, or perhaps even self-defeating. Much of the welfare debate is therefore really about practical effectiveness. When we seem to be debating about the morality of welfare itself, we're often in fact debating about the best way to really make a difference.

Programs like Head Start have been a clear success, keeping poor children from entering school disadvantaged from the start. Social Security and Medicare have largely lifted the elderly out of poverty, though they also are costly. Cost capping may be necessary too. But other programs have unintended negative effects. Some welfare programs may unwittingly perpetuate poverty, discouraging people from seeking work and rewarding dependence and lack of initiative. Some utilitarians, more persuaded of the dangers and costs of some welfare programs, therefore argue even for strong measures (sometimes cutting off benefits even if it will harm the innocent, for example) in the name of the long-run social good (discouraging people from having children they cannot support, for example).

But do such policies really work either? We tend to follow our prejudices on these questions rather than looking at the evidence. More reasonable from a utilitarian point of view would be to conclude that we need a lot more experimenting and research to figure out exactly which programs in what contexts have the most benefits, and which are useless or worse. Presumably there are some of both. Once again this seems to be a difficult but not impossible question to answer.

Rights Pro and Con

The pro-welfare side argues that simple justice—basic respect for human dignity—requires that no one be abandoned to poverty and misery. No one must be allowed to fall beneath a level at which dignity itself is compromised. The argument concludes that we all have a *right* to at least the minimum necessary to a human life—not just mere survival but some degree of happiness, self-expression, and the opportunity to make a contribution.

The other side argues that once such "welfare rights" are introduced, someone else's freedom may have to be infringed. For instance, a national medical care system might guarantee basic medical care as a right to all citizens, but it might also require infringing the freedom of doctors to practice where and how they see fit. Likewise, spending tax money on welfare programs infringes taxpayers' rights to use their money as they see fit.

Here rights seem to collide with other rights. Yet it is worth noting that rights in both cases are *limited*. Maybe there is a way to map out the domains of welfare rights and other rights that gives both a fair place.

The pro-welfare case, for its part, does not claim that everyone must be made equal, or even that welfare provisions be particularly generous. The claim is only for a decent minimum. Meanwhile, taxpayers' rights are not absolute either. Most of us are willing to require people to contribute money to the government to provide services that not every taxpayer actually favors. Many people oppose the military establishment, for example, but pacifists who resist paying for it don't get much favorable press. We all have to pay for the courts even if we never get inside one. We all pay for the roads even if we don't drive.

The real question seems to be: is welfare, or some limited form of it, more like an "extra" good than a right—something that should not have to be supported by the unwilling—or is it, like a legal system or the roads, a basic enough civil or moral requirement that taxpayers can justly be required to pay for it even if not all of them support it? This is a hard question, to be sure, but answering it does not seem utterly impossible. Try to answer it yourself. Is a kind of middle ground imaginable?

The Work Ethic

Finally, we all value making a contribution, and we largely share the conviction that all of us who can make a contribution have a responsibility to do so. Broadly speaking, this is the *work ethic*—one form of an ethic of virtue applied to work. Pull your own weight, we say.

America inherited a fairly harsh work ethic from its European originators. With the rise of industrialism came a new class of ambitious and hard-driving people who valued individualism and ambition and who insisted that they were masters of their own fate. Those who have the advantages of wealth, income, and social power, they said, have *earned* them. Those who don't, haven't. So the poor deserve pity, maybe, but not much help. Let them pull themselves up by their own bootstraps. They can "make it" too if they just try.

We still hold many of these values, at least in a muted form. For some of the poor, we want to say, poverty really is their fault, a predictable consequence of choices and attitudes for which they are responsible. *More* of us surely could make it—at least, pull our own weight—if we really tried. And it's certainly true that we all ought to be encouraged to do so when we can.

On the other hand, for many others poverty has to do with accidents or crime or larger social and economic forces far beyond their control. Even the best workers lose their jobs when a factory closes or moves overseas. Many of the homeless are women fleeing domestic violence. Many are children (21% of all American children, and 42% of black children, live in poverty) who just inherit the consequences of others' bad luck or poor choices. And it's not at all so clear that anyone can make it if they just try hard enough. Chance rules all of our lives, from being in the right place at the right time, or vice versa, to the very major chance of our family of birth. As the saying goes, if you're born on third base don't imagine that you've hit a triple.

Once again it does not seem impossible to respond intelligently to both (all) points. Linking welfare payments with work requirements (for those who *can* work) is controversial all around, for example, but it does seem to be in the spirit of our shared work ethic. Maybe what we really need is to make that linkage more imaginative and flexible. Promoting more public jobs, for instance, like child care or library or ecological work—jobs also, hopefully, open to others besides those on welfare, so that the work is not stigmatized and so that jobs like these are done widely and done well. This kind of work is vital to our communities, and it is not being done, while good people remain idle. Why not make one opportunity out of two problems?

UNDERSTANDING POVERTY

We would certainly make more progress on the *real* issues if we had a better understanding of the causes of poverty. What causes poverty, anyway? Why are we facing this problem in the first place?

Causes of Poverty

For some people it is difficult to get a job. Why?

Some lack the necessary skill and/or motivation. People with little experience of work and no family history of work-based discipline find it hard to adjust to the demands of the work place. Unable to keep a job or save money, unpersuaded of the value of education and unattracted by or afraid of it, they slide into poverty, or don't rise above it, and the next generation follows in the same tracks—perpetuating a cycle that sociologists call the "culture of poverty."

Then again, often jobs are not available, even to the well qualified. Businesses are downsizing, jobs are shifting overseas, and old trades are vanishing, stranding workers in mid-life or in fading communities where minimum-wage service work is the only option, if they're lucky.

Even when people do find work, it may be poorly paid. Lifting yourself out of poverty may be nearly impossible working at the minimum wage, especially if you have extra costs (medical needs, say; very few minimum-wage jobs have health insurance) or a family. This is one of the main reasons that liberals favor raising the minimum wage—though the downside of that, business-people argue, is that the total number of jobs may decrease. It is also one of the main reasons that liberals as well as some businesspeople favor national health care programs.

Discrimination doesn't help either. Women still get only something like seventy-five cents on the dollar compared with men doing comparable work, which is one reason half of all female-headed households in America live in poverty, surely an astonishing statistic. And black, Hispanic, and Native American households, also bearing a historical burden of discrimination, are more than twice as likely to live in poverty as white families.

Talk to people in poverty and you will learn of yet other causes. Vietnam veterans, still shellshocked or too alienated to rejoin the workaday world, make up half or more of the homeless men in some cities. A wave of reforms in the 1980s "deinstitutionalized" mentally ill but essentially harmless people, and large numbers ended up poor or on the streets. In the shelters you meet everyone from children fleeing abusive homes to modern transients who, like the old hobos, have taken to the road on purpose and prefer to be there.

All of these populations have different needs, and there are no easy answers. Policies that serve some well may miss or even worsen things for others. It's no surprise that the nature of poverty has *changed* in America with the advent of modern welfare programs, and keeps changing as the programs as well as social and economic conditions change. But it's also no surprise that poverty hasn't gone away.

Reframing the Problem

Understanding the problem of poverty as a collection of more specific problems also opens up the possibility of some creative responses. Specific programs, for example, for specific populations. Ways to break the cycle of poverty by giving the children a "head start." More initiatives to keep jobs in local communities. Quicker community intervention in cases of domestic violence.

We might also try *shifting* our understanding of the entire problem in the ways suggested in Chapter 12. I want to make just one proposal along these lines.

Poverty looks to us like a lack of money—a natural view in a capitalistic society where money is everything. But looking at poverty worldwide suggests a different and maybe usefully provocative understanding.

People in some other countries may have far less money than poor people in America, for example, but they may still have access to all of their society's goods: education, travel, a deep sense of community and security. Tribal, nonmobile societies where families or small groups live in common do not abandon any members to destitution or homelessness. Life may be precarious, but its precariousness is shared by all—and therefore, except in some major disaster, no one goes hungry.

Most fundamentally, then, mightn't we conclude that poverty is a matter of disempowerment and exclusion? Lacking money isn't the root problem everywhere, for societies may *em*power and *in*clude in more than one way. Money is the problem *here* because here money is the way to power and inclusion.

Recognizing this in turn may suggest some interesting integrative possibilities for reframing the problem of poverty as we know it. In particular, there are other solutions besides distributing more money. Mightn't there be other and better ways to empower and include people in America too, ways that might both respond to the needs of the poor and also avoid the "handouts" that so aggravate conservatives?

There are some modern social democracies in which poverty barely exists. In Norway, for example, health care, transportation, housing, and food are subsidized and available to all. Of course, taxes are also steep. Forty percent of Sweden's gross national product is spent on social welfare—27 percent in Germany—compared with only 15 percent in the United States, the lowest of any industrialized country except Japan (12%).

What's really important, though, is not the amount of money spent on social welfare, but *what* it's spent on. It's not spent on so-called "handouts" to people who have already fallen into poverty. Norway spends it on social-support measures that are intended to *prevent poverty* (as exclusion, disempowerment) *from even arising in the first place*. Good medical care for all; good education; good transportation and housing. As one writer describes the system: the approach "is not an individualistic, Band-Aid approach but rather a universal, preventive one, a policy consistent with a value system based on care and absolute security." Notice that such a system has immense advantages not just for those who would otherwise be poor, but for everyone. Medical care for *all*; education. . . .

The Transportation Trap

One concrete example may bring this back home. In the homeless shelters where my students and I work, we encounter many people trapped by a simple lack of decent transportation. They cannot get a well-paying job partly because they have no car, and they can't buy a car because they can't get a well-paying job. Jobs are far too distant from the place they live for bicycling or walking, and public transportation barely exists. They're stuck in a low-paying and economically depressed part of town. So they spend their days at a succession of minimum-wage downtown jobs within walking distance of the shelter. No way out.

What do they need? Not handouts—what they really need is a decent mass transit system. And the *rest* of us would benefit from such a system too. Many of us might be able to get around without cars, easing our lives and air pollution too. That seems to be Norway's approach: the aim is to provide the "infrastructure" that gives people options so that even people with very little money are not disempowered, while further empowering and benefiting everyone else too.

Why not here? Even die-hard conservatives who oppose more government spending on anything would be unlikely to oppose *shifting* the money currently spent on welfare programs into "infrastructure" programs that visibly and directly benefit everyone—and help those who otherwise would have been poor to get to work. It needn't cost more. What we need to change, once again, is our thinking.

"So How Did I Get Here?"

ROSEMARY BRAY

Here are a few interesting facts. The majority of welfare recipients are white. Fewer than 5 percent are black ghetto residents. Statistically, the typical welfare recipient is a white child. The average number of children of a mother on TANF (formerly AFDC) is slightly lower, by most counts, than the national average for all women. And the vast majority of people on welfare stay for only a few months and do not return.

If these facts are surprising, it is because we have internalized certain stereotypes of welfare recipients offered to us by the media and in political campaigns. But what does it mean that this is how we have learned to think about welfare?

Rosemary Bray wrote this essay as a new national debate over welfare was getting under way, the debate that culminated in the 1996 revisions in welfare programs discussed in the first section of this chapter. Dismayed by what she calls the "code words" and undertones in this argument, Bray suggests that race and gender issues—bluntly, racism and sexism—run deep. "The punitive energy behind these actions and proposals," she writes, "goes beyond the desire to decrease welfare costs; it cuts to the heart of the nation's racial and sexual hysteria. . . . If citizens were really aware of who receives welfare in America, however inadequate it is, would most of these things be happening?" She thinks not. What about you?

Read her story also for an account of what it actually is like to grow up in poverty, and on welfare. "What did it take to live?" she asks.

The answers may surprise you. It may also surprise you that, as Bray puts it, "the investment made in our lives by the State of Illinois came to fruition." But then remember, as she also points out, that this is the norm rather than the exception. Again that raises her basic question: why don't we know this already? Or, to put it another way: what does the welfare debate as we know it say about *us*?

MY MOTHER CAME TO CHICAGO in 1947 with a fourth-grade education, cut short by working in the Mississipi fields. She pressed shirts in a laundry for a while and later waited tables in a restaurant, where she met my father. Mercurial and independent, with a sixth-grade education, my Arkansas-born father worked at whatever came to hand. He owned a lunch wagon for a time and prepared food for hours in our kitchen on the nights before he took the wagon out. Sometimes he hauled junk and sold it in the open-air markets of Maxwell Street on Sunday mornings. Eight years after they met—seven years after they married—I was born. My father made her quit her job; her work, he told her, was taking care of me. By the time I was 4, I had a sister, a brother and another brother on the way. My parents, like most other American couples of the 1950s, had their own American dream—a husband who worked, a wife who stayed home, a family of smiling children. But as was true for so many African-American couples, their American dream was an illusion.

The house on the corner of Berkeley Avenue and 45th Street is long gone. The other houses still stand, but today the neighborhood is an emptier, bleaker place. When we moved there, it was a street of old limestones with beveled glass windows, all falling into vague disrepair. Home was a four-room apartment on the first floor, in what must have been the public rooms of a formerly grand house. The rent was $110 a month. All of us kids slept in the big front room. Because I was the oldest, I had a bed of my own, near a big plate-glass window.

My mother and father had been married for several years before she realized he was a gambler who would never stay away from the track. By the time we moved to Berkeley Avenue, Daddy was spending more time gambling, and bringing home less and less money and more and more anger. Mama's simplest requests were met with rage. They fought once for hours when she asked for money to buy a tube of lipstick. It didn't help that I always seemed to need a doctor. I had allergies and bronchitis so severe that I nearly died one Sunday after church when I was about 3.

It was around this time that my mother decided to sign up for A.F.D.C. She explained to the caseworker that Daddy wasn't home much, and when he was he didn't have any money. Daddy was furious; Mama was adamant. "There were times when we hardly had a loaf of bread in here," she told me years later. "It was close. I wasn't going to let you all go hungry."

Going on welfare closed a door between my parents that never re-opened. She joined the ranks of unskilled women who were forced to turn to the state for the security their men could not provide. In the sterile relationship between herself and the State of Illinois, Mama found

Reprinted by permission of Rosemary Bray. "So How Did I Get Here?" *New York Times Magazine*, 1993. Copyright © 1993. All rights reserved.

an autonomy denied her by my father. It was she who could decide, at last, some part of her own fate and ours. A.F.D.C. relegated marginally productive men like my father to the ranks of failed patriarchs who no longer controlled the destiny of their families. Like so many of his peers, he could no longer afford the luxury of a woman who did as she was told because her economic life depended on it. Daddy became one of the shadow men who walked out back doors as caseworkers came in through the front. Why did he acquiesce? For all his anger, for all his frightening brutality, he loved us, so much that he swallowed his pride and periodically ceased to exist so that we might survive.

In 1960, the year my mother went on public aid, the poverty threshold for a family of five in the United States was $3,560 and the monthly payment to a family of five from the State of Illinois was $182.56, a total of $2,190.72 a year. Once the $110 rent was paid, Mama was left with $72.56 a month to take care of all the other expenses. By any standard, we were poor. All our lives were proscribed by the narrow line between not quite and just enough.

What did it take to live?

It took the kindness of friends as well as strangers, the charity of churches, low expectations, deprivation and patience. I can't begin to count the hours spent in long lines, long waits, long walks in pursuit of basic things. A visit to a local clinic (one housing doctors, a dentist and pharmacy in an incredibly crowded series of rooms) invariably took the better part of a day; I never saw the same doctor twice.

It took, as well, a turning of our collective backs on the letter of a law that required reporting even a small and important miracle like a present of $5.

All families have their secrets, but I remember the weight of an extra burden. In a world where caseworkers were empowered to probe into every nook and cranny of our lives, silence became defense. Even now, there are things I will not publicly discuss because I cannot shake the fear that we might be hounded by the state, eager to prosecute us for the crime of survival.

All my memories of our years on A.F.D.C. are seasoned with unease. It's painful to remember how much every penny counted, how even a gap of 25 cents could make a difference in any given week. Few people understand how precarious life is from welfare check to welfare check, how the word "extra" has no meaning. Late mail, a bureaucratic mix-up . . . and a carefully planned method of survival lies in tatters.

What made our lives work as well as they did was my mother's genius at making do—worn into her by a childhood of rural poverty—along with her vivid imagination. She worked at home endlessly, shopped ruthlessly, bargained, cajoled, charmed. Her food store of choice was the one that stocked pork and beans, creamed corn, sardines, Vienna sausages and potted meat all at 10 cents a can. Clothing was the stuff of rummage sales, trips to Goodwill and bargain basements, where thin cotton and polyester reigned supreme. Our shoes came from a discount store that sold two pairs for $5.

It was an uphill climb, but there was no time for reflection; we were too busy with our everyday lives. Yet I remember how much it pained me to know that Mama, who recruited a neighbor to help her teach me how to read when I was 3, found herself left behind by her eldest daughter, then by each of us in turn. Her biggest worry was that we would grow up uneducated, so Mama enrolled us in parochial school.

When one caseworker angrily questioned how she could afford to send four children to St. Ambrose School, my mother, who emphatically declared "My kids need an education," told her it was none of her business. (In fact, the school had a volume discount of sorts; the price of tuition dropped with each child you sent. I still don't know quite how she managed it.) She organized our lives around church and school, including Mass every morning at 7:45. My brother was an altar boy; I laid out the vestments each afternoon for the next day's Mass. She volunteered as a chaperone for every class trip, sat with us as we did homework she did not understand herself. She and my father reminded us again and again and again that every book, every test, every page of homework was in fact a ticket out and away from the life we lived.

My life on welfare ended on June 4, 1976—a month after my 21st birthday, two weeks after I graduated from Yale. My father, eaten up with cancer and rage, lived just long enough to know the oldest two of us had graduated from college and were on our own. Before the decade ended, all of us had left the welfare rolls. The eldest of my brothers worked at the post office, assumed support of my mother (who also went to work, as a companion to an elderly women) and earned his master's degree at night. My sister married and got a job at a bank. My baby brother parked cars and found a wife. Mama's biggest job was done at last: the investment made in our lives by the State of Illinois had come to fruition. Five people on welfare for 18 years had become five working, taxpaying adults. Three of us went to college, two of us finished; one of us has an advanced degree; all of us can take care of ourselves.

Ours was a best-case phenomenon, based on the synergy of church and state, the government and the private sector and the thousand points of light that we called friends and neighbors. But there was something more: What fueled our dreams and fired our belief that our lives could change for the better was the promise of the civil rights movement and the war on poverty—for millions of African-Americans the defining events of the 1960s. Caught up in the heady atmosphere of imminent change, our world was filled not only with issues and ideas but with amazing images of black people engaged in the struggle for long-denied rights and freedoms.

We knew other people lived differently than we did, we knew we didn't have much, but we didn't mind, because we knew it wouldn't be long. My mother borrowed a phrase I had read to her once from Dick Gregory's autobiography: Not poor, just broke. She would repeat it often, as often as she sang hymns in the kitchen. She loved to sing a spiritual Mahalia Jackson had made famous: "Move On Up a Little Higher." Like so many others, Mama was singing about earth as well as heaven.

These are the things I remember every time I read another article outlining America's welfare crisis. The rage I feel about the welfare debate comes from listening to a host of lies, distortions and exaggerations—and taking them personally.

I am no fool. I know of few women—on welfare or off—with my mother's grace and courage and stamina. I know not all women on welfare are cut from the same cloth. Some are lazy; some are ground down. Some are too young; many are without husbands. A few have made welfare fraud a lucrative career; a great many more have pushed the rules on outside income to their very limits.

I also know that none of these things justify our making welfare a test of character and worthiness, rather than an acknowledgment of need. Near-sainthood should not be a requirement for financial and medical assistance.

But all manner of sociologists and policy gurus continue to equate issues that simply aren't equivalent—welfare, race, rates of poverty, crime, marriage and childbirth—and to reach conclusions that serve to demonize the poor. More than one social arbiter would have us believe that we have all been mistaken for the last 30 years—that the efforts to relieve the most severe effects of poverty have not only failed but have served instead to increase and expand the ranks of the poor. In keeping women, children and men from starvation, we are told, we have also kept them from self-sufficiency. In our zeal to do good, we have undermined the work ethic, the family and thus, by association, the country itself.

So how did I get here?

Despite attempts to misconstrue and discredit the social programs and policies that changed—even saved—my life, certain facts remain. Poverty was reduced by 39 percent between 1960 and 1990, according to the Census Bureau, from 22.2 percent to 13.5 percent of the nation's population. That is far too many poor people, but the rate is considerably lower than it might have been if we had thrown up our hands and reminded ourselves that the poor will always be with us. Of black women considered "highly dependent," that is, on welfare for more than seven years, 81 percent of their daughters grow up to live productive lives off the welfare rolls, a 1992 Congressional report states; the 19 percent who become second-generation welfare recipients can hardly be said to constitute an epidemic of welfare dependency. The vast majority of African-Americans are now working or middle class, an achievement that occurred in the past 30 years, most specifically between 1960 and 1973, the years of expansion in the very same social programs that it is so popular now to savage. Those were the same years in which I changed from girl to woman, learned to read and think, graduated from high school and college, came to be a working woman, a taxpayer, a citizen.

In spite of all the successes we know of, in spite of the reality that the typical welfare recipient is a white woman with young children, ideologues have continued to fashion from whole cloth the specter of the mythical black welfare mother, complete with a prodigious reproductive capacity and a galling laziness, accompanied by the uncaring and equally lazy black man in her life who will not work, will not marry her and will not support his family.

Why has this myth been promoted by some of the best (and the worst) people in government, academia, journalism and industry? One explanation may be that the constant presence of poverty frustrates even the best-intentioned among us. It may also be because the myth allows for denial about who the poor in American really are and for denial about the depth and intransigence of racism regardless of economic status. And because getting tough on welfare is for some a first-class career move; what better way to win a position in the next administration than to trash those people least able to respond? And, finally, because it serves to assure white Americans that lazy black people aren't getting away with anything.

Many of these prescriptions for saving America from the welfare plague not only reflect an insistent, if sometimes unconscious, racism but rest on the bedrock of patriarchy. They are rooted in the fantasy of a male presence as a path to social and economic salvation and in its corollary—the image of woman as passive chattel, constitutionally so afflicted by her condition that the only recourse is to transfer her care from the hands of the state to the hands of a man with a job. The largely ineffectual plans to create jobs for men in communities ravaged by the disinvestment, the state-sponsored dragnets for men who cannot or will not support their children, the exhortations for women on welfare to find themselves a man and get married, all are the institutional expressions of the same worn cultural illusion—that women and children without a man are fundamentally damaged goods. Men are such a boon, the reasoning goes, because they make more money than women do.

Were we truly serious about an end to poverty among women and children, we would take the logical next step. We would figure out how to make sure women who did a dollar's worth of work got a dollar's worth of pay. We would make sure that women could go to work with their minds at ease, knowing their children were well cared for. What women on welfare need, in large measure, are the things key to the life of every adult woman: economic security and autonomy. Women need the skills and the legitimate opportunity to earn a living for ourselves as well as for people who may rely on us; we need the freedom to make choices to improve our own lives and the lives of those dear to us.

"The real problem is not welfare," says Kathryn Edin, a professor of sociology at Rutgers University and a scholar in residence at the Russell Sage Foundation. "The real problem is the nature of low-wage work and lack of support for these workers—most of whom happen to be women raising their children alone." Completing a five-year study of single mothers— some low-wage workers, some welfare recipients—Edin is quantifying what common sense and bitter experience have told millions of women who rotate off and on the welfare rolls: Women, particularly unskilled women with children, get the worst jobs available, with the least amount of health care, and are the most frequently laid off. "The workplace is not oriented toward people who have family responsibilities," she says. "Most jobs are set up assuming that someone else is minding the kids and doesn't need assistance." . . .

In the heated atmosphere of the welfare debate, the larger society is encouraged to believe that women on welfare have so violated the social contract that they have forfeited all rights common to those of us lucky enough not to be poor. In no area is this attitude more clearly demonstrated than in issues of sexuality and childbearing. Consider the following: A *Philadelphia Inquirier* editorial of Dec. 12, 1990, urges the use of Norplant contraceptive inserts for welfare recipients—in spite of repeated warnings from women's health groups of its dangerous side effects—in the belief that the drug "could be invaluable in breaking the cycle of inner-city poverty." (The newspaper apologized for the editorial after it met widespread criticism, both within and outside the paper.) A California judge orders a woman on welfare, convicted of abusing two of her four children, to use Norplant; the judge's decision was appealed. The Washington state legislature considers approving cash payments of up to $10,000 for women on welfare who agree to be sterilized. These and other proposals, all centering on women's reproductive capacities, were advanced in spite of evidence that welfare recipients have fewer children than those not on welfare.

The punitive energy behind these and so many other Draconian actions and proposals goes beyond the desire to decrease welfare costs; it cuts to the heart of the nation's racial and sexual hysteria. Generated neither by law nor by fully informed public debate, these actions amount to social control over "those people on welfare"—a control many Americans feel they have bought and paid for every April 15. The question is obvious: If citizens were really aware of who receives welfare in America, however inadequate it is, if they acknowledged that white women and children were welfare's primary beneficiaries, would most of these things be happening?

Welfare has become a code word now. One that enables white Americans to mask their sometimes malignant, sometimes benign racism behind false concerns about the suffering ghetto poor and their negative impact on the rest of us. It has become the vehicle many so-called tough thinkers use to undermine compassionate policy and engineer the reduction of social programs.

So how did I get here?

I kept my drawers up and my dress down, to quote my mother. I didn't end up pregnant because I had better things to do. I knew I did because my uneducated, Southern-born parents told me so. . . . Most important, my family and I had every reason to believe that I had better things to do and that when I got older I would be able to do them. I had a mission, a calling, work to do that only I could do. And that is knowledge transmitted not just by parents, or school, or churches. It is a palpable thing, available by osmosis from the culture of the neighborhood and the world at large.

Add to this formula a whopping dose of dumb luck. It was my sixth-grade teacher, Sister Maria Sarto, who identified in me the first signs of a stifling boredom and told my mother that I needed a tougher, more challenging curriculum than her school could provide. It was she who then tracked down the private Francis W. Parker School, which agreed to give me a scholarship if I passed the admissions test.

Had I been born a few years earlier, or a decade later, I might now be living on welfare in the Robert Taylor Homes or working as a hospital nurse's aide for $6.67 an hour. People who think such things could never have happened to me haven't met enough poor people to know better. The avenue of escape can be very narrow indeed. The hope and energy of the 1960s—fueled not only by a growing economy but by all the passions of a great national quest—is long gone. The sense of possibility I knew has been replaced with the popular cultural currency that money and those who have it are everything and those without are nothing.

Much has been made of the culture of the underclass, the culture of poverty, as though they were the free-floating illnesses of the African-American poor, rendering them immune to other influences: the widespread American culture of greed, for example, or of cynicism. It is a thinly veiled continuation of the endless projection of "dis-ease" onto black life, a convenient way to sidestep a more painful debate about the loss of meaning in American life that has made our entire nation depressed and dispirited. The malaise that has overtaken our country is hardly confined to African-Americans or the poor, and if both groups should disappear tomorrow, our nation would still find itself in crisis. To talk of the black "underclass threat" to the public sphere, to demonize the poor among us and thus by association all of us—ultimately this does more damage to the body politic than a dozen welfare queens.

When I walk down the streets of my Harlem neighborhood, I see women like my mother, hustling, struggling, walking their children to school and walking them back home. And I also see women who have lost both energy and faith, talking loud, hanging out. I see the shadow men of a new generation, floating by with a few dollars and a toy, then drifting away to the shelters they call home. And I see, a dozen times a day, the little girls my sister and I used to be, the little boys my brothers once were.

Even the grudging, inadequate public help I once had is fading fast for them. The time and patience they will need to re-create themselves is vanishing under pressure for the big, quick fix and the crushing load of blame being heaped upon them. In the big cities and the small towns of America, we have let theory, ideology and mythology about welfare and poverty overtake these children and their parents.

Exercises and Notes

WHAT IS "WELFARE," ANYWAY?

One sticking point in the welfare debate is that the term "welfare" is used in different ways. Sometimes it is even reduced to just one or two out of several dozen major social-support programs—AFDC (TANF, now, but many people don't realize it has changed), and/or maybe food stamps. Among others, remember, are Unemployment Compensation, Medicaid, Supplemental Social Security for the disabled and the elderly poor, housing assistance, and infant supply and nutrition programs.

These programs are all "means tested": that is, to receive benefits a person must demonstrate a certain level of financial and other need. Other "entitlement" programs that are *not* means tested include the more familiar kind of Social Security, military and civil service retirement funds, Veteran's Administration medical care, student loan programs (yup, you're on welfare too), and still others.

Means-tested programs together account for 12 percent of the federal budget. Total entitlement spending accounts for roughly 60 percent.

"Welfare" could be interpreted more broadly still. The Preamble to the United States Constitution lists "providing for the general welfare" as one of the rationales for the Constitution itself. The government of the uniting states was empowered to build roads, raise an army, and support schools (many of the founders believed that public education, free and open to all, was a cornerstone of democracy). All of these measures helped the new nation's people "fare well."

As the U. S. government has grown over the past two centuries, more and more of its activities have been aimed at promoting the "welfare" of at least *some* group of citizens. Farm subsidies help farmers fare well. Medical school subsidies benefit doctors. Low grazing and timber-cutting fees benefit ranchers and timber companies. Assorted tax breaks and subsidies benefit corporations—so much so that in the recent congressional debates, some prominent critics of "welfare" (for poor people) felt obliged to come out against "corporate welfare" too. Suddenly the issue was all over the media. Just those corporate tax breaks, critics point out, cost the Treasury more money than all means-tested "welfare" programs put together.

So how would *you* define "welfare"? What is the most useful way to understand that term? Most people in national polls oppose something called welfare, but when asked whether they favor most of the individual programs that make it up, they overwhelmingly say yes. Is it possible, then, that simply clarifying what we mean by "welfare" could open up some unexpected common ground?

Get the Facts

Chapter 8 points out that in many moral debates more attention to the facts would be a good idea. The welfare debate is surely one of them. Here are some things you might check out.

What social support programs are available, and to whom, in your area? When cash is involved, how much is paid? In TANF programs or their equivalents, for instance, do benefits increase with the recipients' number of children? If so, find out how much more money a parent gets per month for a second, third, or fourth child. How does it compare with the additional monthly costs of diapers, baby food, medical care, and so on?

How do you qualify for welfare? How do you get *dis*qualified? How adequate is nongovernmental aid for the poor and homeless? Welfare policies and even the basic facts of poverty are always in flux. Look for the most up-to-date information. Local social-service workers, administrators of soup kitchens and shelters for the homeless, and human-services departments at your school should be good sources of information. For current U. S. government data, try <www.census.gov/hhes/www/poverty>.

And finally, and hardest: talk to poor people themselves. Work in a homeless shelter or soup kitchen. I have found that many nonpoor people with the strongest views about welfare (both pro *and* con) have little or no experience of the life of the poor. This is easy to remedy, though, and you can help out while you learn besides—recall Chapter 15.

Keep on Thinking

Some standard objections to welfare programs are fairly specific and not so hard to fix once you seriously try to multiply options. For example, many people are offended by the use of food stamps to buy morally disapproved items like cigarettes and alcohol. Supposing that this *is* a widespread problem (which is not so clear, as hard data are not easy to come by and it is always tempting to fly by the stereotypes), is it so hard to resolve?

My classes have thought of a number of possible solutions. For example, the government could give away food directly, rather than giving away money or food stamps to buy food. This happens already at state-sponsored soup kitchens and in some states with baby food and supplies. Can you think of other options?

To rethink the problem more fundamentally—to begin to "reframe" it— consider the Norwegian strategy mentioned in this chapter: providing the infrastructure, like medical care, afforable housing, and transportation, that makes a passably decent life cheap enough that even people with very little money are not disempowered—and meanwhile everyone else is cared for too. What would such strategies look like applied in America? Brainstorm—and remember to lower your critical weapons for a while, to really explore and invent before you begin to look for problems.

Even the wildest of the problem-shifting strategies—taking the seeming problem as an *opportunity*—might get a grip here, opening up the problem in still another unexpected way.

When new technologies put people out of work, we usually regard it as a disaster—as indeed it is, when everything depends on having a job and a living wage. But could this sort of "technological unemployment" also be an *opportunity*? After all, looked at another way, it is a marvelous thing that now we can produce the same things with far less work. Maybe it should be a cause for celebration!

Of course the question is: what are the displaced workers going to do? But why should they lose their jobs completely while everyone else has to work the same number of hours as they did before? If we really thought of technological unemployment as an opportunity, we'd try to *cut the work week all around*. Call it "spreading around the burden" if you like—which might be reasonable enough just in the name of fairness—but we might also think of it as "spreading around the new free time."

After all, there's nothing sacred about a forty-hour work week. Work weeks in the nineteenth century were double that, seventy or eighty hours. Cutting the work week to thirty hours was proposed by President Roosevelt in 1932 as a response to the unemployment caused by the Depression (opposition from big business forced him to pull it back). Thirty-five-hour or less work weeks are standard in Europe (along with four to six weeks paid vacation), and European workers are not less competitive than Americans— quite the contrary. People seem to be more productive with a shorter work week.

Would workers have to take a pay cut? No, not if the productivity gains that have fueled past wage increases were used to scale back work time instead, holding wages steady.

What would people do with their new free time? Well, whatever they chose. Maybe something quite wonderful. People could even be encouraged to propose worthy projects for support, using money currently spent to prop up the unemployed. Philosopher Frithjof Bergmann has proposed such a system, and writes:

> The image of the currently unemployed is formed from the waiting lines in hiring halls, and from the daily pilgrimage to the local bar with its game of pool. But those stepping off the economic escalator in the future [could do] it with a purpose, with a definite conception of something that they want to do. They would be off on their own projects, alone or with a group, growing a new kind of plant, designing fabulous mechanical contraptions, sawing, hammering, or nailing, learning anything from Chinese poetry to the neurology of frogs, and teaching all of that—they would cure and build and think. . . .

"Sabbaticals" for everyone—like (some) college teachers get now, one year in seven for regeneration and some individual project. Why not? It might cost nothing more than we are already spending, and it would be vastly better for all of us.

It should be clear, anyway, that there are some creative options! Much more must be done to fill them out, but a number of thinkers, like Bergmann, are hard at work doing just that. In any case, we are not stuck with "the" welfare debate in the form we encounter it today. Even here—especially here—there is a lot of room for imagination.

Notes and Further Reading

For portrayals of life in poverty around the contemporary United States, see Alex Kotlowitz, *There Are No Children Here* (Doubleday, 1991); Elliot Liebow, *Tell Them Who I Am: The Lives of Homeless Women* (Free Press, 1993); and the works of Jonathon Kozol, especially his *Savage Inequalities* (HarperPerennial, 1992).

A history of welfare programs from a liberal point of view, up through the changes of the 1980s and 1990s, is Michael Katz, *In the Shadow of the Poorhouse: A Social History of Welfare in America* (Basic Books, 1986, revised 1996). For a parallel account from a conservative point of view, see Marvin Olasky, *The Tragedy of American Compassion* (Regnery Gateway, 1992). On video, see PBS's film series "America's War on Poverty" (1995). On Americans' willingness to support most welfare measures if they are described without the term "welfare," see Charles Noble, *Welfare as We Knew It: A Political History of the Welfare State* (Oxford University Press, 1997), page 12.

On social support systems in Norway, see Katharine van Wormer, "A Society without Poverty," *Social Work* 39 (1994): 324–327. Frithjof Bergmann is cited from his *On Being Free* (Notre Dame University Press, 1977), pages 226 to 227. On the way in which productivity gains might be translated into shorter work weeks and lowered unemployment, see Juliet Schor, *The Overworked American* (Basic Books, 1992).

For one exemplary kind of direct social/religious action in reponse to homelessness, think of Habitat for Humanity. See for example the many works of Habitat's founder, Millard Fuller, such as *Love in the Mortar Joints* (Habitat for Humanity, 1980).

Those interested in applying ethical theory specifically to the welfare question should start with two intriguing books by Robert Goodin, *Protecting the Vulnerable* (University of Chicago, 1985) and *Reasons for Welfare* (Princeton University Press, 1988). The titles speak for themselves. For texts of some philosophical treatments, a bibliography for others, and a wide variety of useful links, go to Lawrence Hinman's "Ethics Updates" website at <ethics.acusd.edu> and select "Poverty and Welfare."

VII

THE EXPANDING CIRCLE

CHAPTER 20

◯

Animals

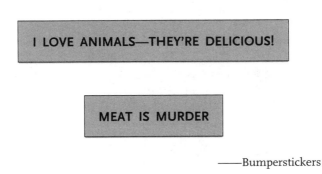

I LOVE ANIMALS—THEY'RE DELICIOUS!

MEAT IS MURDER

———Bumperstickers

WHY SHOULD WE CARE ABOUT ANIMALS?

Animal Lives

Most of us have some idea what it takes to produce the meat on our tables and to test the drugs and chemicals whose safety we count upon. It isn't a pretty picture.

Animals of all sorts are tightly confined, against all of their natural instincts, often for their entire lives. Every element of their environment is manipulated to produce the most meat (or eggs, or milk . . .) in the shortest time, or to be sure not to interfere with whatever product or drug test is being conducted. By natural standards their lives are usually extremely short as well. And they come to their deaths with at least some sense of what is happening—in slaughterhouses with hundreds of others, the smell of death in the air, often with other animals killed in front of their eyes.

You may know how veal is produced. At birth the calves are immediately separated from their mothers. They are tightly penned to prevent them from developing muscles (it toughens the meat). They are restricted to a liquid diet when all their urges tell them to begin chewing grass. That diet among other things deprives them of iron (which would also develop muscle and color the meat) so that they become so desperate for it that they may spend hours gnawing on the bars of their pens or any nails in sight. Then they are killed, at

4 months or less, unless they have died already, as 10 to 15 percent regularly do, from the sheer stress and frustration of their lives.

Veal is a delightful meat. But the cost to the animals for our pleasure and a few corporations' profit is so immense that many people, even people otherwise comfortable with our treatment of animals, have stopped eating it. It has become a moral issue.

Animal advocates argue that veal production is only slightly more horrible than what is done routinely with *all* the familiar meat animals. Commercially raised chickens, to take just one other case, may spend their whole lives in cages too small for them even to turn around, much less spread their wings or fly, or in huge sheds holding tens of thousands of birds, so large that all social structure breaks down and the birds have to be "debeaked" (have their beaks cut off) so that they do not kill each other in their fury and confusion.

When egg production in a multiple-thousand-bird unit falls off too much, the whole bunch is just shipped off to slaughter. Americans eat about five *billion* chickens per year. You can see them regularly being transported on the highway. I pass trucks roaring along the freeway with hundreds of chickens in cages, fully exposed to the driving rain and winds at 70 miles per hour, battered and bewildered. Chickens naturally have about a seven-year life span. When raised for slaughter they live about seven *weeks*.

Hundreds of thousands of cats, dogs, monkeys, and many other kinds of animals, meanwhile, are used in laboratory tests to be sure that drugs and household products marketed to humans are safe and have the effects promised for them. Dripping new chemicals into the eyes of rabbits is an especially good way of testing them for possible skin irritation to humans. Of course the rabbits have to be strapped into holding frames for weeks on end, and their eyes pried open as they struggle for some relief. Until recently a standard way to test new drugs for safety was to determine the dose that would kill half of a group of test animals, often with profound agony on the way.

There are still other issues as well. Animals are kept in zoos and aquariums. We hunt and fish for them, cherished and traditional activities both. We have rodeos and other contests involving animals. Rats are produced by the million for laboratory use. Many introductory psychology students can remember training "their" rat, usually a cute and winning creature despite rats' bad name, but disposed of at the end of the term in the same way one might sell back one's textbook. There are also at least a hundred million pet animals in America—dogs, cats, racoons, ferrets, snakes, and a host of others.

In short, animals pervade our lives, for better or worse, for them and for us. But with their presence, increasingly, come moral questions.

Moral Arguments: Suffering

For utilitarians, naturally, the key issue is pleasure and pain. All too often, the way we treat and use animals makes them *suffer*. They often die in fear and pain, yes, but still worse is the frustration of nearly all their natural instincts while they are *alive*. Death must sometimes be only a relief—not that that excuses it.

There are those who deny that animals suffer at all. Animals are just machines, they say. This kind of thinking even led early scientists to cut up animals while they were still alive (now called "vivisection.") This kind of thinking may still serve as a kind of offhand self-justification for people who would prefer not to think at all about the effects of their actions on animals. But it is very seldom advanced seriously anymore, and it is not hard to see why.

We know that animals suffer in the same way we know that our friends or children suffer—from their expressions both verbal and physical. Screaming, trembling, trying to get away, trying to find comfort—all of these are a universal language of pain and need, beyond words.

We also know that monkeys and dogs and pigs and many other animals have nervous systems just like ours. Indeed their bodies are so similar in general that some of their organs can be transplanted into our bodies— another growing threat to animals, actually. That no other animals but humans are conscious of pain and pleasure is too unbelievable a stretch.

On the other hand, it is a serious question how *much* animals suffer, and how to measure and weigh their suffering compared with ours. Certainly it differs. You or I would be incredibly frustrated if we couldn't move around or had to spend our whole short lives in one small building. But we are curious, long-lived, large-brained creatures whose nature is to move around and explore. Do chickens feel the same way? How do we know? What about fish in a fish tank? Do they get bored? What about cats, who as pets often live a life of indolence and ease? Even if they never go outside, isn't that likely to be a happier life for them than having to scrounge food all the time wherever they can find it?

Also, of course, by the very same kind of argument advanced above— from parallel nervous systems to parallel feelings—it also seems to follow that animals with less developed nervous systems probably suffer less and have less rich experience than most normal humans do. Pigs or monkeys may suffer as we do, but what about a rat or a shrimp? Maybe we are inappropriately projecting our feelings onto animals whose mental life barely exists.

These are important questions. They suggest that the whole matter is more complicated than it might seem at first. On the other hand, none of them deny that animal suffering exists, and that when it exists it matters. How to balance everything out will get tricky, and will probably take some guesswork, but (say utilitarians) that's nothing new. Ethics takes guesswork even when the question concerns only, say, two people. What *is* new is the insistence that animal suffering *counts*. That alone may make a radical difference in how we treat them.

Moral Arguments: "Speciesism"

Many people think that animal suffering does not count simply because, to put it baldly, *they're animals*. They're not *us*.

Kant would agree. According to him only rational beings can be ends in themselves, for only such a being can understand himself or herself as one being among others following "laws" that apply equally to all. To put it more broadly: only beings such as ourselves can recognize the legitimate expectations of others (remember our definition of moral values). Bears or chickens cannot understand or respect my rights, so it follows that they can have no rights that bind me. They are just not part of the moral story.

Pro-animal philosophers in the rights tradition respond to these arguments in several ways.

First, at least *some* animals *can* recognize the legitimate expectations of others, including ourselves. Most animals similar to ourselves, including all pets and most food animals, live in social relationships with us. Mutual trust and joint expectations are part of the story. Think of a rider and horse who train together, or family dogs with young children, or even the cat who keeps still in the mornings until someone gets up but then has every right to meow for her food bowl (thank you, Ketzi). This may create special obligations toward those animals who do live in community with us, such as horses and pets, though it does not extend to those who don't.

Second, restricting moral standing to "rational" beings in Kant's sense just does not work. Young human children are surely ends-in-themselves, for instance, and so are humans who are mentally impaired, through birth or brain damage or age. They do not cease to count just because they do not understand themselves as one among others under the moral law. Morality goes farther than that.

"But young children and the mentally impaired are still *human*," the skeptic responds. They are indeed. Still, they do not have the capacities that Kant demands for an end in itself. And certain other animals *do*. To draw a moral line between the whole human species on the one hand and every other species on the other, regardless of the actual capacities of specific members of those species, therefore begins to look arbitrary. How can species alone carry that kind of weight?

Philosophers and animal activists have given a label to what they see as arbitrary preference for our own species over all others. They call it "speciesism," on the model of terms like "sexism" and "racism." To the racist it seems justified, for example, to mistreat or even enslave people of another race just because they belong to another race. The bottom line is: "They're not *us*." Not white; not male; not civilized; and so on. But we recognize the injustice and blindness of this. It is only a self-congratulatory prejudice. If one race doesn't recognize its commonalities with others, that is part of the *problem*, not somehow an excuse to keep on mistreating them.

And so, say the animals' defenders, the same goes for species. Sure "they're animals"—but then, really, so are we.

The Expanding Circle

It's hard to resist the conclusion that at least *some* things must change in our relation to other animals. Just taking account of them, paying attention, giving their suffering even a little weight, already calls into question much of our habitual use of them. At the very least, the offhand treatment of animals must end: the treatment of veal calves or chickens, for example, as if they were nothing but pieces of meat or egg-laying machines even while they're alive; the automatic use of animals to test any new product, however unnecessary and however much pain the animals must suffer.

Morality is becoming more inclusive, says the philosopher Peter Singer. Historically, it was an accomplishment even for ethics to include all humans— to not exclude women or nonwhites or noncitizens, as it so often did in the past. The circle of moral concern keeps growing: from certain small groups of familiar humans, to larger groups of humans, to all humans as a whole. Now, Singer says, we are beginning to take the next step: moving beyond species in turn.

Of course, any place that this "expanding circle" rubs up against old assumptions and habits, the new moral concerns will be uncomfortable to many, or even offensive, and will look simply silly to some, beneath notice. There was a time not so long ago when women's rights were considered silly and beneath notice too, and before them the rights of nonwhite peoples. Maybe this is just where ethics takes some backbone: it asks us to at least be willing to consider such questions even when others consider them silly or impolite. Values change, after all—maybe this is one place where we still need to learn and grow.

WHAT CAN WE DO?

What would it mean in practice to take animals more seriously? Can it be done?

Moral Vegetarianism

If humans literally could not live without veal, or chicken or beef or fish, then we would have some serious trade-offs to make. Our lives would be bought at the price of animals' suffering, and we would simply have to face that fact.

Even so, of course, we would have no reason not to *consider* animals' suffering and reduce it as much as we could. We'd be obliged to raise them in decent conditions, to eat only those animals who suffer confinement the least (or perhaps those that, like fish, need not be confined at all), and to eat as little meat as possible.

But the fact is that we *can* live without meat. Indeed, nonmeat or low-meat diets may well be healthier. The two leading killers in America, cancer and heart disease, are both linked directly to high-meat diets. People who eat neither meat nor dairy products have the highest life expectancy of any Americans. And, vegetarians report, their meals taste just as delightful and varied, if not more so, than the traditional meat meals.

Reducing or eliminating meat eating has other advantages as well. Meat production is spectacularly inefficient in economic terms. Only 5 to 10 percent of the protein fed to meat animals is regained by eating the meat at the end. It is ecologically inefficient as well. Vast amounts of water, for one thing, are used up or polluted.

In short, then, on the vegetarian argument, we have the opportunity not merely to reduce the suffering of animals raised for meat but actually to eliminate it, by making a lifestyle change that is also healthier for us and probably, once you're used to it, even more pleasant. A vegetarian world could also be cleaner and less hungry. Why would we not do it?

Objections to Vegetarianism

"But cabbages suffer too," critics object. Plants have feelings too. Maybe we cannot eat anything without causing suffering some way or other.

Some Buddhists make this argument. They argue that all things have souls, and that life pretty much *is* a round of suffering. But Buddhists would never conclude that we should therefore go on being completely heedless of our effects upon animals, as if, since suffering is inevitable, it doesn't really matter how much suffering we cause. Their view, by contrast, is that since suffering is inevitable, we must be as careful as we can be *all the time*.

Besides, even if plants have feelings too, on any reasonable scale the reaction of a cabbage to being picked hardly compares with the four-month torture of a veal calf. Maybe utilitarians are wrong to suppose that pleasure and pain can ever be measured precisely, but you hardly need precision to make a judgment like this.

Still, several more genuine objections to vegetarianism may be implicit in this one. One of these is: perhaps giving up meat, *all* meat, is a bit of an overreaction to the arguments advanced above.

Undeniably some animals suffer in completely unnecessary ways. On the other hand, not all animals suffer that much, or, maybe, at all. Chickens who spend their lives pecking around the farmyard with their flock; fish who live out their life cycle free and entirely apart from humans until a hook puts a quick end to it—here, anyway, there may not be much loss to the animal, and there is (or may be, depending on health considerations) a clear gain to the human who eats them.

Of course, this is not the normal case. Most people buy meat in supermarkets that comes from factory farms. That kind of meat may well be morally suspect. Still, it does not follow that all meat is suspect in the same way. So maybe the best response to the misery of animal lives (according to utilitarianism, anyway) is to promote more humane conditions in factory farms, rather than to give up meat entirely?

Ecological concerns also come up. Though meat production tends to be an ecological disaster, vegetarian diets are not ecologically benign either. Many little animals of the fields die when grains are harvested. Racoons and hedgehogs and others would quickly eat their way through the squash or the tomatoes and must be fenced out or shot. Vegetables and fruit are sensitive to growing season and are often shipped cross-country in trucks, which pollutes and increases the demand for fossil fuels—the same fuels that are often used to produce fertilizers and power the farmers' tractors. Some hunters therefore seriously argue that shooting and eating a local elk, say, is far more ecological than eating vegetarian!

Of course, once again, this is no defense for eating hamburger that may also have been shipped across the continent from a slaughterhouse that pollutes the local rivers and brings you meat from cows that were fed grain produced in the same harvests just mentioned. But these arguments do have a deep and serious point. They reveal that moral eating is a complex matter. We have obligations to ourselves and other people; to the animals; and to the earth; and how all of these balance out, case to case, isn't always clear.

Maybe the most morally responsible way of eating even varies with location. In the Arctic, it might mean eating seal, as the Inuit have done since time out of mind. In the tropics, maybe the occasional fish is quite enough. And for *us*?

Animal Testing

About the use of animals in product and drug testing there is a more two-sided debate. Diseases would run rampant among humans, according to the defenders of animal testing, were it not for clinical drug trials using animals. Advertisements in support of animal testing always seem to find some adorable kids who, the ad claims, would be dead today if animals had not died in their place. Here at least we may be willing to step up and say: animal suffering is worth it.

On the other hand, we have serious doubts about the morality of tests for yet another new toilet-bowl cleaner or shampoo that leave dozens of animals blinded or in agony. There are too many stories of unbelievably callous treatment of animals over whom the researchers have absolute power. Even some former poster children for animal testing have reversed themselves in adulthood and spoken up for animal rights. It's not *always* "worth it."

Maybe there are some drugs or products that are desperately needed and must be tested on whole organisms. In that case utilitarianism, at least, would allow a test, in whatever way would cause the least overall suffering. If animals would suffer less or would not be seriously put out by confinement, then animal testing in that case might be the right thing to do.

On the other hand, if a human suffered less or was not seriously put out by whatever side effects a drug or product might have, then *we* are the ones who ought to put them to the test on ourselves. The hardest test of our consistency in this regard would be if we were willing to test a drug on ourselves where the chief or only benefit would be to other animals. Would it be "worth it" then—when *we* suffer and *they* gain (more)? In that case and only that case, by the "judge like cases alike" principle, are we really entitled to test a drug on other animals where the chief or only benefit would be to us.

Sometimes, after all, our greater brain power means that we suffer *less*. We can understand the purposes of such tests, whereas most animals are only aware of the confinement and the pain. Other times they may suffer more because their senses are more acute (sounds that we don't even notice may be painful to dogs, for example). Some careful—and nonspeciesist—consideration is necessary to really minimize suffering and maximize benefits all around. Once again things get complicated.

Meanwhile, some other strategies would be useful here too. Multiplying options, for one. One result of the usual dismissal of animals is that until very recently we have't seriously tried to develop alternatives to animal testing. Animals were cheap and available, and for the most part were completely unprotected, so we used them.

Computer models, though, can take the place of animal trials for many drugs, not only avoiding animal suffering but giving much cheaper and quicker results. Animal tissue can be grown in laboratory dishes, without nerves or a nervous system, so chemicals can be tested without causing any suffering at all. (Human tissue can be used, too, if the drug or product is meant for human use; so there are no dangers that a drug harmless to animals may be disastrous for humans, as some have been.) "Cruelty-free" products, developed without any animal testing, are now widely available. Computer simulations and plastic models take the place of animals raised and killed for dissection. And the list goes on. . . .

Zoos, Fur, Hunting, . . .

You get the picture. Maybe it is best to leave the remaining questions about animals for your consideration on your own. Again it may turn out that the answers are more complicated than any simple "yes" or "no." The most crucial point is that, once animals are given even a little moral consideration, the answers will almost certainly turn out to be quite different than they now seem to us.

"Animal Rescue"

LORRI BAUSTON

Many animals live horrible lives for the sake, sometimes, of pretty trivial advantages for (some) humans. On the other hand, it is also true that many animals—our pets—often live wonderful lives. They are genuine co-inhabitants of a moral universe, whom we know by first names and who live in complex relationships of trust and exchange with us. We even have laws that protect pet animals from mistreatment of the sort routinely meted out to animals raised for food, who may be every bit as (or more) intelligent as dogs and cats but who are specifically exempted from the animal-cruelty laws because, well, we like to eat them.

In short, we seem to have a radically divided view of animals in practice. Some are friends and companions. Others are just objects, not worth a second glance or any care at all.

Normally we are not aware of any conflict. These two ways of seeing animals do not come into contact. But what if they did?

The following reading makes this question vivid. Here is a couple who pick up animals from discard piles at slaughterhouses and take them home, heal them, and make them treasured pets and life companions. They are also committed "vegans"—people who eat no animal flesh and use no products that depend on animal exploitation (e.g. milk, leather, fur).

Two radically different ways of viewing animals couldn't be more sharply contrasted. Is there any way that they can be reconciled? *Should* they be reconciled? Maybe it's really true that the factory method of treating animals is unbelievably cruel and blind . . . or maybe Bauston's "animal rescue" is purely sentimentalized and a form of projection. Or maybe something else. What do you think?

IN 1986, GENE AND I decided we wanted to do something to help farm animals, but we didn't know what or how we would do it. So we started visiting factory farms, stockyards, and slaughterhouses to educate ourselves, and that's when we started rescuing animals like Hilda.

We were investigating a stockyard in Pennsylvania when we found her. Gene and I were walking though the auction pens and discovered the stockyard deadpile in the back of one of the buildings. Mounds of dead and decaying animals were thrown on a cement pad. Cows with ropes tied

Copyright © 1998 by Michael Tobias and Kate Solisti-Mattelon, from the book *Kinship With the Animals* (Beyond Words Publishing, Hillsboro, Oregon).

tightly around their necks. Pigs with large wounds. Goats with twisted legs. The insistent buzzing of the maggots and nauseating smell wrenched my stomach, as did the lingering questions. How long had they suffered? How many days of agony and terror did they endure before dying alone and in pain?

Gene took out the camera, and we walked closer to the pile. The camera clicked, and one of the animals on the pile lifted her head. Gene and I stared at each other, both not wanting to believe what we had just seen. I knelt down next to the animal, and Hilda looked back at me. She was just inches away from a rotting carcass, and flies and maggots were crawling over her body. I held her head in my hands whispering "poor baby, poor baby" to calm her and keep myself from screaming.

Gene ran to get the van, and within ten minutes we were rushing to the nearest veterinarian. Hilda had collapsed because of the brutal transportation conditions. She was not suffering any other injuries or diseases. We learned that Hilda had been loaded onto a truck with hundreds of other sheep. Despite humid, near-one-hundred-degree temperatures, the sheep were severely overcrowded, a standard livestock marketing strategy to get more dollars per load, even when some sheep will die from the stress. Hilda was part of the meat industry's "economic loss" calculations. The meat, poultry, and dairy industries even have a name for animals like Hilda. They call them "downers."

We took Hilda home, and then we knew what we could do to help farm animals. We started a shelter for victims of "food animal" production so that we could care for Hilda and other suffering farm animals, and we started exposing the atrocities of the food-animal industry.

As we continued our investigations, Gene and I learned that Hilda's story was not unique. Every year thousands of animals used for "food" production are abused and neglected because animal suffering is considered part of "normal animal agricultural practices." Blatant animal cruelties, like severe confinement, overcrowding, and abandonment, are deliberately practiced to increase profits, despite the tremendous cost to animals.

We have found day-old chicks discarded in outdoor dumpsters because they do not grow fast enough to be profitable for meat consumption. We have seen emaciated diary cows dragged to slaughter with chains when they were too sick or weak to walk because they can still be sold for human consumption. We have heard turkeys screaming in terror while they were hung upside down fully conscious and bled to death because poultry are exempt from slaughter-stunning requirements.

People often ask us how we cope with seeing so much suffering and death. Whenever I'm asked that question, I find myself thinking about what inspires me and gives me hope, and I think about a pig I have dearly loved, a pig named Hope.

Hope had been dumped at a livestock market because she had a crippled leg and was no longer "marketable." Hope was just a baby, barely two months old. I remember how frightened she was and how she frantically crawled away when we approached her. Hope had never known a kind touch. Humans had only kicked, dragged, and abandoned her. Gene and I spoke gently to her and wrapped a blanket around her shivering body. She let out one small grunt as we picked her up and then nestled into my arms like she had always known me.

For seven years, Hope was a part of our lives. We cared for all her special needs, and she filled our hearts with love. Hope touched many other people, too. Over the years she taught thousands of Farm Sanctuary visitors that farm animals are just as capable of suffering from isolation, fear, and neglect as a dog or cat or you and me.

I am comforted knowing that Hope reached so many people, especially now that she is no longer with us. Hope passed away at our shelter, surrounded by those who loved her. After two years, I still find myself glancing in the direction of her favorite corner. I will never forget how she rolled over for belly rubs at the touch of my hand, or her distinct thank-you grunt when I placed her food bowl in front of her. Most of all, though, I will always remember how her life inspired us to continue the fight for farm-animal rights.

You might easily lose hope when you've been to a slaughterhouse or factory farm and witnessed so much cruelty. I will never forget the first time I went to an egg factory and saw the horror of modern-day egg production. To produce eggs, four to five hens are crammed into a cage about the size of a folded newspaper. The cages are stacked by the thousands in row after row. Between 80,000 and 100,000 are housed in a single, windowless warehouse. Feed, water, and manure disposal is completely automated, so just a handful of workers oversee the entire production. There is no individual care or attention. The birds endure this misery for two to three years, unable to stretch their wings, walk, or even lie down comfortably.

After months of intensive confinement, the birds lose most of their feathers, because their bodies are constantly rubbing against the bare wire cages. With little feather protection their skin eventually becomes coverd with painful bruises and sores. When the hens become too sick or injured to produce eggs at peak production levels, they are literally thrown out of the cage and left on the floor to die slowly from starvation.

We found Lily on the floor of an egg factory, waiting for death to end her nightmare. She was standing in a corner, trying desperately to keep from falling on a mound of feces and decaying feathers and bones. Lily had given up all hope. Her entire body was hunched over, and her head drooped close to the ground. She was covered with sores, and her left eye was swollen shut. I reached out and gently lifted her into my hands.

For two weeks Lily received intensive rehabilitative care. Lily was too weak to walk, and throughout the day I would hold her up to help her regain strength in her legs. She also had bruising over 75 percent of her body, and four times a day we wrapped heating pads around her to reduce the swelling. Since Lily was severely emaciated, she could only eat small amounts of liquid food through a dropper every few hours. On more than one occasion, I wondered if we were doing the right thing, or if we were just prolonging her suffering.

It is the shelter question whenever an animal is near death—but then one morning I had the answer. I opened the door to Lily's rehab pen, and she walked over to me and looked up. I immediately sat down to get as close as I could to "chicken height," and Lily climbed onto my lap. I reached down, and this time, I was the one trembling as I stroked her chin. Lily gave me her love in a way that I could understand, just like a dog talking with his or her tail or a cat purring soothingly.

Rescuing an animal like Lily always carries me through those times when we cannot save a suffering aninal, like the time Gene and I visited a California slaughterhouse in the Chino Valley south of Los Angeles. This area has the highest concentration of dairy cows in the world, which means it has one of the highest concentrations of beef production, too. Dairy cows are not being retired to Farm Sanctuary; they are slaughtered and ground for hamburger. The majority of hamburger sold in the United States comes from dairy cows, not rain forests.

We stood near the unloading area, watching the cows come in one by one. Gene was videotaping the scene, and my job was taking photos. Some of the cows were "downers." According to California dairy industry reports, one in four dairy cows becomes a downer due to illnesses and diseases caused by excessive milk production. Dairy cows are forced to produce ten times more milk than they would in nature, and the problem is getting worse with the use of rBGH (bovine growth hormone) and genetic manipulation.

They put all the downers into one killing pen, and then a worker came around and shot a cow in the head. It was a slow process. Several minutes would pass between each killing, and the ones that were alive had to just lie there and watch. There was one cow who looked a lot like Maya, a cow at our New York shelter. She was shaking from fear, and I wanted so badly to put my arms around her and comfort her. Later, when I was in the car, it was so unbearable. I kept thinking of Maya and how much she loves life. Well, actually, how much she loves my husband, Gene.

Maya adores Gene and is actually jealous of me. She pushes me out of the way whenever Gene and I are in the barn, and since she's an 1,800-pound woman, she's even knocked me down a few times. Of course, Gene has to be careful too. When Maya goes into heat, she tries to mount him. In the bovine family, the females take charge of the mating situation. She'll stand there and gaze adoringly at Gene, softly mooing to him, and then turn around and give me the evil eye.

I thought of Maya and her likes and dislikes, her unique personality, and I thought of that poor trembling cow who wanted to live as much as Maya, or you and me. Farm animals are living, feeling animals; they are not "breakfast," "lunch," and "dinner." Americans have drawn an imaginary line and classified some animals as "pets" and some animals as "dinner." Our society is horrified (and rightly so) when we hear of other cultures eating dogs and cats, and most people would never be intentionally cruel to a dog or cat. I have to hope that they would never be intentionally cruel to a cow or chicken either. People who love animals called "pets" would not eat animals called "dinner" if they would only look into the eyes of a suffering farm animal.

Gene and I were making a cross-crountry trip with seveal turkeys during one of our annual Thanksgiving "Adopt-a-Turkey" projects. Every year, we encourage people to save a turkey rather than serve a turkey for the holiday season. We adopt turkeys into safe, loving vegetarian homes, and the media is invited to report on our unique way of celebrating Thanksgiving.

We were going through Colorado (which is a major beef-producing state) when I spotted her along the interstate. A young Angus calf was just a few feet from whizzing cars. We pulled over, threw on our boots, and started toward her. She was extremely frightened and started running away from us. An injured leg prevented her from moving very fast, and we had her within a few minutes. Our new "baby" weighed about 150 pounds, and as we struggled to get her into the van, we heard angry shouting and saw a man running toward us.

We soon learned that Jessie had jumped out of a trailer while it was traveling sixty miles an hour. When I realized what she had done to escape her fate, I felt like an angry mother cow, ready to tear her horns into anyone who tried to take her calf away. Finding it difficult to keep calm, I explained to the owner that we were anti-cruelty agents and would be willing to take this calf off his hands because, of course, he couldn't take her to the auction now. To my surprise, the owner agreed. I was gearing up for a major battle, since injured and sick animals are legally sold at auction all the time. To this day, I don't know if he agreed because he was in shock or because he saw a raging cow in my eyes or because maybe, just maybe, he got a dose of vegan kinship.

The next feat was getting Jessie through the California border, because she needed to be treated at a specialty veterinary clinic in northern California. We drove all night with her and four turkeys through a torturous snowstorm, and just as it was getting daylight, we came to the California border—and the California agriculture checkpoint. Now, every turkey mother knows that daylight is the time when turkeys wake up and start chirping, and we knew we didn't have much time. We turned up the radio and inched cautiously toward the checker. He asked us if we had any apples or oranges. I smiled sweetly and replied "no" and drove on with the biggest grin I've ever worn. Jessie survived and is now a big healthy cow. I've never considered myself a religious person or one who thinks "everything happens for a reason." Still, I can't help wondering if she knew we were behind her when she jumped out of the trailer—at least I'd like to think so.

As a vegan, I have experienced so many incredible things, so many special bonds with farm animals. We all know that people bond with so-called companion animals. Most people have loved and cared for a dog or cat and have experienced many moments of profound understanding and love. I know that whenever I'm feeling blue, my dog friend Suzy can always tell and will come and sit by my side in sympathy. She will look up at me with such a forlorn expression, such concern, that I have to smile.

At Farm Sanctuary, we share special bonds with our farm-animal friends too. Most of the time, it's the little communications that we experience every day, but sometimes we are reminded with a powerful vegan kinship message. Diane, our California shelter coordinator, told me of one of these "precious moments" when she injured her arm while she was in the cattle barn. She was in too much pain to even move and just sat on the barn floor and cried. Though they were not in the barn at the time, within minutes two of the cattle, Joni and Henry, suddenly appeared. Cattle have a distinct "distress moo," and both cried loudly when they saw Diane on the ground. They approached her cautiously, reaching out their noses. Their urgent mooing turned to soft, comforting moos. For more than twenty minutes, they stood carefully around her, gently licking her face, until Diane could move again.

If you let yourself be touched, animals will touch you, and farm animals are animals. A cow or turkey or pig or chicken is just as capable of feeling joy and sorrow, or pain and comfort, as a dog or cat. Like many people, I am fortunate to have the love and companionship of dogs and cats, animals who are truly a part of my family. But unlike many people, I have also known the love and friendship of cows and pigs and turkeys and chickens—farm animals that suffered horribly at factory farms, slaughterhouses, and stockyards. . . .

I often find myself glancing out the window to the sheep barn. Hilda is there, quietly grazing the pasture. Sometimes I wonder what she remembers of that horrible trip to the stockyard. Hilda has remained shy of humans, even after all these years. It is a rare treat when she approaches you and an even greater privilege when she allows you to scratch her chin.

It took us a while to resign ourselves to this and to one embarrassing moment with Hilda—embarrassing for us, that is, not for Hilda. It happened about a year after Hilda's rescue. I was working in the barn when Gene came running up to me, smiling ear-to-ear. "She likes me! Hilda likes me!" he proclaimed, grinning like a proud father. "She's following me everywhere I go. She won't leave my side." I couldn't believe it, and feeling a twinge of jealousy, I'm not sure if I wanted to believe it. But as Gene walked into the sheep pasture, there was the evidence. Hilda trotted up to him and even leaned up against him. Gene walked toward me and Hilda stayed by his side.

Hours went by, and still Hilda stayed with Gene, following him while he was painting, following him into the barn, following him to the compost pile. True to his nature, Gene kindly remarked that perhaps she had chosen him over me because I was the one who trimmed her hooves. But after several hours of adoration, even Gene started to wonder about this sudden display of affection. Then it hit us, and that day we officially turned from "city slickers" into "farmers." Hilda wasn't in love, Hilda was in heat. Now, after hearing about Maya's story too, you're probably wondering just how charming can one human be? But then you probably haven't met Gene, so how can I, or Maya, or Hilda, possibly explain? We all share a special vegan kinship with him, and there is nothing more I can say.

Exercises and Notes

CRITICAL REACTIONS

Here are some critical student reactions to this chapter. Use them to help you work out your own responses. Some of them raise sharp challenges to what the chapter presents. What do you think of those challenges? Does this chapter have a bias? What is it?

> All of your readings and most of your arguments are pro-animal. You even told us in class you are a vegetarian. Where's the other side, Mr. You-Have-to-Look-At-All-Sides? Maybe the pro-meat (or pro-animal-use) case is one of your blind spots? Aren't there *any* moral arguments for factory farming, for example? Where are they?

> My vegetarian friends really puzzle me. They're always campaigning against meat and making people feel guilty about eating at McDonald's, but here they are wearing leather shoes and belts and probably squashing bugs with their cars and maybe even feeding their cat tunafish or turkey innards or whatever kind of meat goes into catfood. I don't get it. Don't you have to be consistent about this? To me the only consistent ones are the vegans, who don't even eat dairy products because the eggs and milk are still products of "misery." OK, but I think what they eat is pretty miserable too. So if you don't eat meat or dairy or wear leather or fur and if you only grow your vegetables yourself and share them with whatever deer or hedgehog comes along and wants to chow down, then maybe I want to talk to you. The rest, they need to sort out their lives a little better first.

Why don't you come right out and say that most of the meat-eaters in this class are hypocrites? Because that's what they are. I saw a film one day about people eating cats and dogs in China. I guess they are a great delicacy there. I saw a little girl led up to a cage of cats by her parents and happily pick out the cat she wanted to eat for supper, which promptly got boiled and skinned alive. It was like we go to lobster tanks in seafood restaurants and pick out our lobster. Everyone watching was groaning and several people got sick and had to leave. Well, where do they think hamburgers come from? Pigs and cows are just as intelligent and have just as many feelings, if not more, than cats and dogs. In the slaughterhouses they get hung upside down and have their necks cut and bleed to death. It's about like being boiled and skinned alive I guess. We just don't pay attention—we don't *want* to pay attention. You said in Chapter 7 that there are times when we should hold firm and not compromise. This is one of them. No compromise with animal torture! I'm ready to march—you bet.

KEEP ON THINKING

There are many more aspects to the debate about animals and ethics, and also, surely, many more possible responses to the moral problems that come up. Keep using your problem-solving tools.

Can "what if . . . ?" thinking, for example, help us here? Try EXAGGERATION. Vegetarians question whether we should eat meat at all. Perhaps we could exaggerate in the other direction.

What if . . . we eat *nothing but* meat?

Some native peoples do: traditional Inuit (Eskimo), for example, who live so far north that nothing really grows. Fish, seals, and whales form their entire diet. What shall we say of them? Should they move? But moving would destroy their culture: other values would suffer more. Importing nonmeat foods would also damage the culture, making them economically dependent. It may be better to conclude that for them, at least, eating meat is acceptable.

The other side of this thought is that meat eating may be much more questionable when there *are* alternatives. Almost all of the rest of us do have alternatives. So perhaps "ethical eating" is different depending on where one lives?

Try ESCAPE. Meat as we know it comes from animals. So:

What if . . . meat does not come from animals?

Again, of course, at first the idea seems crazy. But keep thinking. . . . Scientists can now take a single cell from an animal body and create tissue cultures—test-tubes of animal tissue, but without bodies or brains—on which to test drugs. Might they do the same for meat, that is, grow hunks of animal muscle tissue without body or brain? Certain science fiction writers have imagined this already: it could be a way of having meat without animals, and therefore without animal suffering.

This may or may not be a good idea. (If it strikes you as ghoulish, a good question would be: why does it *not* strike you as ghoulish to eat the flesh of an actual animal?) In any case, the point is: it's an idea. Something new. There may be completely unexpected ways out of the problems that now face us.

What about REVERSAL? Here some "normal" feature of a situation is turned exactly on its head. We eat animals, so . . .

What if . . . animals eat *us?*

A few animals do eat us, or would if they could. It strikes some people as "only fair" that therefore we eat them. The problem is that the animals who eat us are not the animals we eat, like cows and chickens, who tend to be friendly and who in nature mostly eat plants or insects. We don't even favor animals who typically eat each other (except for fish). So maybe it is acceptable to eat animals, but not the ones we currently eat?

Or maybe the idea is that if we are to eat animals, we need to allow ourselves to be eaten in return in some way? After death, many of the Plains Indian tribes put out corpses in special places where the wolves and the vultures would pick the bones clean. Is that the idea—some appropriate ceremonial return of our own flesh to the flesh of the living world? How might we do something of the sort now? (And if *this* strikes you as ghoulish, the question may be the same as above: why is it not ghoulish for us to eat other animals en masse and randomly throw out the remains to the dogs and the worms?)

Here's another REVERSAL. Vegetarians sometimes complain that the lives and deaths of the animals we eat are normally completely out of view. Children often are shocked to discover what meat actually is when they finally put two and two together. So . . .

What if . . . the lives and deaths of the animals we eat are completely *in* view?

The "facts of meat" would not be hidden; we would not try to disguise the costs to animals with cute ads about fish leaping into tuna cans and chickens living it up in factory farms. Perhaps people might even be expected to kill some of the animals they themselves eat. This is not impossible: hunters do it all the time. But it does change the picture. It makes us think about meat eating in another way, and that, once again, is the point.

Keep at it. What other thoughts might arise from using DeBono's "provocations"? What about reframing and problem-shifting?

The Vampires Come

In the reading in Chapter 10 Colin McGinn asks us to imagine a species of vampire doing to us essentially what we do to other animals we use for food. Elaborate this into a challenge you can take up as a class. Suppose that vampires or some species of alien have taken over Earth and are preparing to factory-farm humans for meat and use us to test drugs and other products. Could we—and *how* could we—persuade them to stop?

Just such a scenario has been the premise of science-fiction movies from time to time: for example, "Z," a TV miniseries from the eighties. You might take one of these as a starting point for your scenario. In all of the science-fiction versions of which I am aware, though, the aliens lose in the end, usually through some fluke, as in "War of the Worlds," the original of this theme, where they are killed off by the common cold. Beware of the Hollywod cliché that humans will somehow win out in the end, and of the Wild West version in which we finally just fight them off. No: for us only moral arguments will do.

Suppose the human race has one last appeal before the aliens put their plan into effect. *You* must convince them to stop. Teams of students should prepare arguments that can be presented to the aliens (also role-played by students from the class) in a grand hearing. This exercise works especially well if *animals* also show up. The animals need not be anti-human—though you can understand why they might be—but they should make sure that humans judge like cases alike. If the humans really want aliens to take human suffering seriously as a moral counterargument to their plan, for example, humans need to clean up their own act as well. Or is there some way to show that humans are distinct from the other animals in ways that make them more akin to the aliens, so that, maybe, the aliens really should eat animals too?

Notes and Further Readings

A useful descriptive overview of the animal rights struggle, both in theory and in practice, is Harold Guither, *Animal Rights: History and Scope of a Radical Social Movement* (Southern Illinois University Press, 1998). Classic philosophical defenses of animals are Peter Singer's *Animal Liberation* (Avon, 1975) and Tom Regan's *The Case for Animal Rights* (University of California Press, 1983). Singer is a thoroughgoing utilitarian; Regan takes a rights perspective. For some discussion of the tension between these two ethical approaches, see my book *Toward Better Problems* (Temple University Press, 1992), Chapter 4. In practice, however, especially in the context of a society in which animals are routinely given no moral consideration at all, their common insistence on taking animals seriously is their most important contribution.

A variety of other views, both pro and con, can be found in Andrew Harnack, ed., *Animal Rights: Opposing Viewpoints* (Greenhaven Press, 1996) and Harlan Miller and William H. Williams, eds., *Ethics and Animals* (Humana Press, 1983). For alternative philosophical pro-animal views, see Mary Midgley,

Animals and Why They Matter (University of Georgia Press, 1984); Vicki Hearne, *Adam's Task* (Knopf, 1986); and Carol Adams, *The Sexual Politics of Meat* (Continuum, 1990). On the Web, go to Lawrence Hinman's "Ethics Updates" website at <ethics.acusd.edu> and select "Animal Rights." Another useful site is <ethics.ubc.ca>, the Center for Applied Ethics at the University of British Columbia.

For a classic popular defense of animals, see John Robbins, *Diet for a New America* (H.J. Kramer, 1987). True to his title, Robbins includes recipes, as does Peter Singer in *Animal Liberation*—surely a first in philosophy texts! For more information on vegetarianism (its various forms, menu planning, vitamins, vegetarianism and children, etc.), start with the Vegetarian Resource Group's web site at <www.vrg.org>.

CHAPTER 21

◆

Environmental Ethics

WAKE-UP CALLS

One day in Cleveland in 1968, someone threw a cigarette into the Cuyahoga River, and the river burst into flames. Enough oil and other pollutants had been dumped into the waters to set off an inferno. The fire department came with its pumpers and sprayed down the river.

It wasn't just one river. By the late 1960s, Lake Erie—a whole, vast Great Lake—was dead. Too much junk was in the water for life to survive. Other lakes seemed to be close behind. Suds from phosphated dish detergents ran thick in the streams. DDT showed up in unhatched bird eggs. Even the bald eagle seemed headed for extinction. Offshore oil wells blew out on a regular basis.

Junk dumped into the air was coming back to haunt us too. Toxic air had been around for a long time, locally, but suddenly whole cities were blanketed. The word "smog" was coined for the first time. People were beginning to die from it, had to stay inside, and in places like Los Angeles the sun disappeared for weeks at a time behind rolling brown clouds, mostly because of what chugged out of the tailpipes of our cars.

Responses

We'd been used to thinking of nature as an endless source of raw materials and an infinite disposal site for our trash. Now, all of a sudden, our junk was floating back onto the beaches and clogging our lungs, the landfills were starting to fill up with no replacements in sight, and raw materials too—oil and coal and even wood and water—were becoming scarce. We began to learn that nature has limits, and that "what goes around comes around."

And we began to respond. The early 1970s saw the passage of Air and Water Quality Acts that began the clean-up of the worst and most obvious pollutants. Other landmark environmental legislation followed, such as the Endangered Species Act. The Environmental Protection Agency (EPA) was established. Environmental impact assessments were required of all major projects. DDT was banned in industrialized countries. Catalytic converters, unleaded gas, and more efficient engines cut down on air pollution from cars. Phosphates were removed from detergents.

There was, and is, widespread agreement on these and other responses. It's worth keeping in mind that most of our landmark environmental legislation was passed by a heavily Democratic Congress and signed by a Republican president, Richard Nixon. There is common ground here. Even now something like three-quarters of the American population tells pollsters that environmental quality is so important that cost considerations should never stand in the way. EPA is now a cabinet-level agency, right up there with Justice and Defense.

The Challenges Now

There have been successes. Air and water are now markedly cleaner. Lake Erie lives again. Many of the worst toxins and pesticides are controlled, at least in theory. Some species have pulled back from the brink of extinction, including such American icons as the brown pelican, the buffalo, and the bald eagle too. We've learned to recycle, cut down on wasteful packaging, even carpool.

Yet major threats remain. Rain forest burning continues, taking with it kinds of plants and animals we will never know. Right here at home, ancient forests are still being clear-cut for toilet tissue and newspaper and plywood. Half a trillion tons of topsoil have been allowed to wash or blow away. Habitat destruction threatens fully one-quarter of America's twenty thousand native plants.

Whaling continues, both legal and illegal, and the larger species of whales, like blue whales and the rights, whether hunted or not, are so depleted as to be on the brink of extinction. Offshore oil wells still blow out. Supertankers still run aground. And the oil that is not spilled in one massive goo eventually finds a million smaller routes into the soil and air and water.

Other worries are more subtle or long-term or global, like ozone depletion and global warming. Many of the pollutants that now especially concern us are minute toxins—even tiny amounts can disrupt whole ecological systems. Researchers estimate that up to 70 percent of all cancers are caused by chemical and other pollutants, including artifically elevated radioactivity, products of bombs or nuclear wastes, some of which will take a million years to reach safe levels. And wastes of all sorts continue to pile up.

In short, serious challenges still lie in front of us. Environmental issues may even be the most major ethical concern of the twenty-first century. Environmental awareness and responsibility are more crucial than they've ever been.

BEYOND ANTHROPOCENTRISM?

For many people, "environmental ethics" means just what we've so far discussed: cutting back on pollution, reducing waste, saving endangered species.

And if we were to ask *why* we should do any of these things, the likely answer would be: because they are good for *us*. After all, we need to keep air and water clean so *we* can breathe and drink in good health. We need to save other species because there's no telling what good they will someday be—to us. Save the rain forests—maybe we will find the cure to cancer there.

Less familiar human values are also often at stake with the environment. Human justice often requires environmental respect, for example. Much environmental damage is also damage to other human communities. Rain forest destruction displaces whole forest communities. Whole native cultures are being driven into extinction. Strip mining, drift-netting, toxic-waste dumping—all of these immediately and profoundly affect *people* too. Nuclear wastes are bad for our own children, as is using up all of a scarce resource, so that future generations will have to scrounge or do without.

So environmental ethics in this sense may well call for radical changes. We may need to cut way back on ozone depleters and auto driving and the many kinds of waste we now just take for granted. If it's really true in nature that what goes around comes around, we need to be a lot more careful about what goes around!

Values Beyond the Human

Still, the reasons for these changes, so far, may not be radical at all. The ultimate appeal is still to *human* values: human goods, fairness and justice, and so on. Taking care of nature, even taking very good care of nature, may just be a way of taking care of ourselves.

Could it be that there are also *other* reasons to care about nature? Mightn't we be beginning to recognize that nature also has some claim in its own right?

People are taking that step. In the last decade, for instance, many people have begun to say that endangered species have a right to exist just for themselves. *Not* just for us. Spotted owl, blue whale, even certain endangered bats and tiny, out-of-the-way fish—these are co-travelers with us through the eons. In religious terms, they are just as much a part of creation as we are. It is wrong to drive them off the earth just for some small convenience to ourselves, or perhaps solely out of thoughtlessness. They have as much right to be here as we do. So perhaps do wild rivers and forests and mountains—they have a right to remain in their natural states.

Most environmental philosophers therefore conclude that purely human values are only part of the story. It's the height of arrogance, they say, to reduce nature's value to its usefulness or pleasingness to *us*. There's more to the world than that.

Human needs are *part* of the story, yes. These philosophers are not arguing that we humans should simply sacrifice ourselves to nature. No—the aim is to achieve some sort of balance. But it does follow that sometimes human interests take second place. Wild places have moral claims, for example, even if a nice subdivision would make more people happier. Endangered species have moral claims even if property rights have to be limited. *The world is bigger than we are,* say environmental philosophers—morally as well as physically.

Alternatives to Anthropocentrism

Most contemporary environmental philosophers therefore seek a way to speak for that bigger world—to speak for other animals, not just individually but as species as well, and wild animals as well as domestic ones; and beyond them, possibly, even rivers and mountains and the whole Earth itself. Remember again the "expanding circle". Environmental ethics seeks to stretch the circle wide indeed.

The traditional, human-centered view philosophers call *anthropocentrism.* Alternative views are therefore "non-anthropocentric." More specifically, *biocentric* theories extend moral consideration to all living things, not only ourselves and all other animals but also trees and plants. Usually the argument is that all living things, even if not "aware," at least strive toward something, have a "good of their own," which can also be taken as a good by others. The whole world of life is a world of striving, self-maintenance, reproduction, and change, and for biocentrism this is where value really arises.

The Swiss doctor and humanitarian Albert Schweitzer put biocentrism well:

> The great fault of all ethics hitherto has been that they believed themselves to have to deal only with the relations of man to man. In reality, however, the question is what is his attitude to the world and all life that comes within his reach. A man is ethical only when life, as such, is sacred to him, and when he devotes himself helpfully to all life that is in need of help. . . .

Schweitzer acknowledges human ethics too, as a special case of the larger *life* ethic. "The ethic of the relation of man to man is not something apart by itself; it is only a particular relation which results from the universal one. . . ."

Another and still wider kind of theory has also been proposed—for even biocentrism in turn may leave out too much. What about rivers and mountains? What about families of animals—species—considered as a whole? For that matter, what about whole ecosystems, systems that include many different kinds of creatures and elements? Ecology is supposed to be a holistic science—surely moral value should attach to whole natural systems too, and not just to certain of their parts!

Ecocentrism therefore attributes moral value to whole ecosystems, in their own rights, including their nonliving elements (soils, streams, . . .) too. The early twentieth-century forester and essayist Aldo Leopold formulated what he called the "land ethic" in his book *A Sand County Almanac*. "A thing is right," he declared, "if it promotes the beauty, integrity, and stability of an ecosystem." Value for Leopold lies in nature as a whole. Moral judgment is finally from the standpoint of the *system*.

INTEGRATING ENVIRONMENTAL VALUES

At the same time too, other and less theoretical approaches are also being explored. Some environmental philosophers, your author included, believe that with environmental values it finally becomes clearest that *no* one single theory can encompass all moral values. Not when we add in everything from individual animals to ecosystems to the Earth itself.

To put it another way: maybe *all* of these things have value, but values of different sorts. Maybe there is no way—and no need—to put them all together in a single tight theory that allows us to prioritize them when they conflict and understand them all as variations of a single theme.

Faced with environmental issues, at least, one vital strategy is to try to *integrate* values. We need to find a way to honor *all* the values at stake: we may need to seek win/win solutions, common ground, and all the rest. Do you think it is possible?

"Owl Versus Man"

The usual answer is: no. Environmental values are supposed to be invariably at odds with human values.

A few years ago, for example, *Time* magazine published a striking cover article called "Owl Versus Man" about the standoff between timber interests and endangered spotted owls in the Pacific Northwest. They pictured it as a classic polarized debate. Environmentalists want to preserve the remaining old-growth forests—the few remaining forests never logged—and their resident endangered species like the spotted owl. Timber companies want the wood, and logging communities want their jobs—to hold on to their community and way of life.

What one side wins, we're told, the other must lose. Each side therefore feels compelled to put down the other, so environmentalists are pictured as almost *anti*-human, insensitive to human needs, while the "other side" is sometimes painted as no more than short-sighted, narrow-minded vandals.

Really?

You're at the end of this book: you know by now that the real story is likely to be more complicated. There are probably many more possibilities and

∞

Olam, 2274 CE

Imagine that your class is a human starship crew crash-landed on an unknown planet called Olam. You have no way to leave for a *long* time. You quickly discover that most of Olam is quite temperate and there are many suitable places for human habitation or other use (mining, agriculture, etc.), though of course all of them are currently occupied by Olamian ecosystems and species.

Olam has an enormous number of species. The exact number or even its order of magnitude cannot be guessed even by your best scientists. Tiny single-celled beings make up the bulk of its inhabitants, as measured by biomass. These beings live just about everywhere, from high in the atmosphere to the intestines of some of the animals to deep in some rocks. Next most common are the beetle-like species, of which there are at least several million. Other species range from the microscopic (1 millimeter or less, like the single-celled beings just mentioned) through the enormous (there are several huge four-legged land species, up to 3 meters tall and 7 meters long, and sea creatures up to 30 meters).

There are intelligent species on Olam too. Among them are sea organisms of different sorts, like a tentacled blobby creature with complex feelings (it changes colors with different emotions) and a seemingly high capacity for problem-solving. Some of your scientists have established contact with several species of large finned sea creatures with brains up to six times the size of human brains. They produce complex sound patterns, and it appears that some of these "songs" (100 million "bytes" in length—about like *The Odyssey*—sung in half an hour) are transmitted all the way around the planet through the oceans. Your scientists have held "jam sessions" with these animals using electric guitars and microphones lowered into the Olamian oceans. However, you have not been able to master their language, nor they yours, if indeed there *is* any way you might translate their "songs" at all.

There are two- and four-legged social species that show advanced social behaviors (love, fidelity, complex interaction patterns). Some of your crew members, perhaps out of homesickness, have adopted them as pets. (Actually, many of your survey crews have adopted Olamian "pets," everything from some flying and swimming creatures to large predators to snaky reptile-like tubular creatures. It all seems to work out quite well.) There are some vaguely humanoid animals that have a rudimentary language and also very tight social groupings. These creatures seems to be too disturbingly similar to yourselves to be made into pets, or perhaps they wouldn't tolerate it, but they have been fairly friendly and are certainly smart.

There are also vast communities of smaller organisms, sometimes containing millions of individual members, which appear to work together as a single unit. Indeed your scientists disagree about which is the real "organism":

the individual insect-like creatures, or their whole "hives." At any rate, it appears that on Olam intelligence can exist on several levels at once. Some scientists even speculate that *all* life on Olam works together as a single unit, maintaining the optimal atmospheric and other conditions for life itself.

Again, this is only a small sampling of Olamian species. Some of these species consume each other for food. Many other species eat the plants, trees, or even the rocks. Humans could survive and thrive on a diet of either Olamian plants, animals, or both. Certain Olamian animals could also live on humans.

As you take stock of your situation, you ask ourselves how you should relate to Olam. Are there moral limits to what you should do here? Should you take into account only your own good, or do the goods of some of Olam's species or ecosystems or perhaps the planet itself also have a claim on you? As you continue to talk, you find yourselves divided into five basic views:

A: Might makes right. We should take and use anything and everything on Olam. No moral considerations apply. Tough luck to the other species; lucky for us they're here to use. God probably planned it this way from the start so they'd all be here when we crash-landed.

B: Only we humans count morally—morality only came to Olam with us, as it were—but we need to take a little care not to ruin the planet for ourselves and our children. So we need to keep our consumption and exploitation somewhat within bounds, but of course only where necessary to serve our own future happiness. It also wouldn't hurt to try to understand Olam a little better. If it's anything like Earth, it's an incredibly complex place with a lot of hidden surprises.

C: We do need to take some care for Olam and its species in their own right. Maybe we're the most important species here but the other species have some valid claims too. They are ancient, beautiful, mysterious: this planet is bigger than us, even though, now that we're here, we're at the moral center.

D: We are only one species among all the others. Rightly understood, all species are at their own "centers." Nothing special about us—or rather, something special about all. Thus, we should seek to become part of Olam's larger community of life. We should seek to establish only limited colonies, and only where we will cause the least harm. We should also try harder to make contact with the intelligent life forms on Olam.

E: We have no right to be here at all. We are alien invaders in a world that is complete without us and does not want us. We should write a statement explaining what we are doing, in case anyone ever finds the wreckage of our starship, and then commit mass suicide (of course in an ecologically responsible way).

Which view strikes you as the most reasonable? Why? How would you defend your view against the others?

opportunities here than we suspect. Let's bring a few of our integrative and problem-solving tools to bear and see how the problem looks then.

Surely both sides, in the first place, are speaking for something important. Preserving ancient species and their old-growth forest habitat is essential for its own sake: we respect their antiquity. Their beauty and even their sheer difference have value as an expression of life's richness. Their possible contribution to environmental health is important too, not least because we barely understand how Earth's ecosystems really work.

On the other hand, we also care about preserving people's jobs and the communities that depend on the timber economy. People should be able to live with the forests and survive economically. We care about the quality of life that timber products make possible. We care about the health of local and global economies and the quality of life that depends upon it. We don't want a world in which no tree is ever cut down either.

At the very least, then, we might split the difference. Suppose we maintain at least some forests untouched while allowing selective logging elsewhere. This kind of thing has happened already. Here in North Carolina the Nature Conservancy and Georgia-Pacific Lumber Company jointly manage a 21,000-acre forest owned by Georgia-Pacific. Over six thousand of the most ecologically prime areas are off-limits to logging, plus buffer zones along streams and rivers, and the Conservancy has half-say in how the remainder is managed. Cut trees are hauled out by helicopter rather than roads.

Win/win solutions are possible too. The companies want timber—but it could come from many different places. Environmentalists are usually concerned with certain *specific* places, for their beauty or their value as habitat, stream sources, and so on. This suggests that both sides could sometimes "win" if land were *traded*—if more ecologically or aesthetically vital land were preserved by trading less vital land for it. Precisely this policy was adopted by the Clinton Interior Department and (although criticized by some on both sides) has managed to somewhat defuse the "timber wars" in recent years.

Creative Common Ground

It is also possible to go farther. Conflict certainly makes for good press, as in headlines like "Owl Versus Man." Both sides sometimes play it up to keep themselves flush. But there is actually more common ground than conflict.

Both environmentalists and logging communities obviously depend on *preserving the forests*. At the very least, then, they both depend on avoiding timbering methods so savage that neither a viable ecology nor a sustainable timber harvest are possible after they are used. We need to find other ways to use the woods.

We could be creative here. If we could create jobs based on owl-watching tourism, for instance, as has been done so successfully with whales, then owl interests and human interests would converge rather than diverge. The forests would survive—they might even expand—and existing communities could find a new way to make a living within them, just as former fishermen have done as whale watching has taken off. Old fishing boats now make their owners much more money taking children out to see whales than going out to fish. Likewise, some rain forest peoples and scientists have created skyways through the thick forest canopies and promoted "ecotourism." The forest lives on, and so do the local communities.

We do need to cut and use some trees. But what we really need is a *sustainable* timber industry, using wood in a more intensive, craft-based way rather than shipping massive amounts of raw wood abroad or pulping it for plywood, as is currently done. Imagine forest communities once again developing furniture shops and specialty wood crafts—living *with* the forests, rather than "off" them while they last. The wood stays at home, and every tree, every log, invites a great deal more labor than it takes merely to cut it down. That kind of logging, unlike the present practice, would have a future: better for loggers *and* the forests.

There is a rain forest parallel here too: it turns out that it is far more profitable for local peoples to use the rain forests on a sustainable basis for rubber-tapping and harvesting of medicinal and other plants than to give it over to be cut down (once) for timber.

Conflict remains, of course. A tourism-based economy and sustainable timbering practices would not be as good for the timber companies' short-run bottom lines. The companies are already fighting back, blaming environmentalists for the economic hardships in logging communities. Still, while it may be in the interests of those timber companies to vacuum up the forests and move on, it is *not* in the interests of either environmentalists, owls, *or* loggers' communities. There are other ways out of this bind.

Conclusions

In short: don't assume that what nature "wins" *we* (humans) must lose. Good practical compromises can often be found, for one thing, but the possibilities also go much deeper.

Do we necesssarily "win" when we get to use more natural resources or consume more land for malls or subdivisions? No—that's far too narrowly *commercial* a picture of human values. We do care about comfortable living, of course, but we also care about many other things, like keeping awe and respect alive in the face of nature, or just having natural and wild places to go to to see the stars and let the children discover the tanagers and the turtles. These are genuine values too. Each time the bulldozers take down a new woods in our neighborhood there is heartbreak all around, and lost opportunities for many who will never know what they are missing.

In that sense, titles like "Owl Versus Man" sell "man"—humans—terribly short. Our interests, our values, are not just economic. The integrative vision is one that is better for us *and* nature—for us as *part* of nature. Tensions no doubt remain—as in any family, short-term interests sometimes pull apart—but the idea that "we" live irrevocably at odds with "nature" is really part of the problem. It's time to look first for the commonalities, the ways in which the "web of life" is *one*.

Violet Woodsorrel Oxalis,
"It's a Little Wild Out There"

It may be a long time before we can decide which ethical theory finally expresses environmental values in the best way. After all, *human* ethics have been around for a long time, and the best ethical theory is still not clear. Environmental ethics is barely in its infancy.

Is it possible, then, that environmental questions invite us to an ethics in a completely different key? Maybe the key task, especially for us now, is to begin to *feel* ourselves part of a larger living whole, to really know in our bones that "the world is bigger than we are."

Many philosophers and environmental activists therefore look first to changing everyday life rather than to the philosophical challenges just outlined. Violet Woodsorrel Oxalis, environmental philosopher and educator, is one of these. In this rather quirky interview conducted especially for this book, she presents environmental ethics as a challege to *pay attention* to nature—even in the most elementary ways.

Notice how consistently Oxalis challenges many of the interviewer's assumptions. Does she challenge yours too? Could it be that environmental ethics in this key is much more difficult, but also much more inviting, than the usual ethics of principles and rules?

Q: What *is* an environmental ethic, anyway?

VWO: Some people say: a new system of moral rules and principles. And maybe we will have such a thing, some day. But right now, for me, it is much simpler—so simple it's often overlooked entirely in the rush to an official "ethic." Above all, it's a way of paying attention. Just that. It's a profound and constant kind of awareness.

Q: I suppose the natural questions is: awareness of *what*?

VWO: Well, if you have to ask the question, that's part of the problem. What I mean is: awareness of the larger world, the world beyond the purely human world, not in some abstract way but concretely, sensually as it were, right now in your own body.

Q: Sounds abstract to me. How do you "sense" the "larger world"?

VWO: Just listen—right now, right here. There are birds singing all around us. *Chick-a-dee-dee-dee*: like the chickadee, named for her call. At my school the crows sit up in the tops of the firs and comment on the students and professors busily passing by. The mockingbirds imitate the carillon, even people's voices. The birds are holding up their end, so to speak. There's a whole world of meaning out there, which we usually miss completely. There's one place to start.

Q: Listening to the birds?

VWO: Like I said, it's a start. But everywhere the world is rich like that. Were you out last night? There was the almost-full moon; warm breeze carrying a hint of rain; cicadas, Great Horned Owl in the distance. Fireflies, jeweling the wet grass, mingling with the stars.

Q: Very poetic. All of that is nice, I agree, but . . .

VWO: But what?

Q: But . . . we're usually told that it doesn't really matter. Not ethically anyway. It's just a pleasant diversion. Faintly silly when brought up in serious contexts.

VWO: Who tells you this?

Q: It's just in the air. You hear it from pulpits and pundits and in all those books about the glories of civilization and even in the ads on TV.

VWO: Where of course what really matters is just what we can *buy*. As if *that* weren't faintly silly.

Q: But people are looking for some kind of argument. People say "Why should I care about nature?"—in the deeper way you are talking about—and environmental ethics is supposed to be an answer.

VWO: Do you require an argument to love your children? Not that you couldn't talk about ethical rules and principles later. You can and should. But love doesn't *start* there.

Q: So it's love of nature that you're after. It's an emotional thing.

VWO: Love is no single emotion. It ranges from desire to fascination; a sense of depth and complexity and infinite promise; a feeling of mystery and wonder and belonging all at once . . .

Q: Still—where's the ethics?

VWO: To put it ethically, we could say something like: love gives us a sense of respect, even awe, in the presence of another. In nature, it gives us that same respect and awe in the presence of non-human beings.

Q: Like whales? People get it if you're talking about whales.

VWO: Whales, sure. Some whales have brains many times bigger than ours, and communciate across whole oceans, all the way around the globe, bouncing their "songs" off the ocean floor as they go. It's a little wild out there.

Q: It's fairly easy to project to whales, though. We like big brains, even if we haven't got the biggest.

VWO: So here we have to stretch. Buddhists say that we live in a universe *every* part of which is alive, every part of which is—I don't know, "deep," "wild," it's hard to find the right word. Take anything—take butterflies. Not much brain, eh? Yet some butterflies migrate, every year, up to four thousand miles, from all over North America, to winter at one or two spots on the California coast, following what nature writer John Hay calls "nature's great headings," invisible to us. We couldn't do it. They flutter up into the headwinds and float four thousand miles and drop out of the sky by the hundred millions to breed at the exact same place, year after year, a place they have never seen before and will never see again.

Q: OK, but it's got to stop somewhere. Trees, rocks . . . you can't really believe that there's something going on with rocks.

VWO: Rocks are moving all over the place, sliding around as tectonic plates, thrown around by volcanoes, disassembled and transformed by lichen and streams and geologists and god knows what. There are even bacteria in rocks, three miles below the Earth's surface, where some scientists now think life itself may have started.

Q: But they're still just rocks. Not like us . . .

VWO: Who said they must be like us? Like with the butterflies or the mockingbirds or even really the whales, there are all kinds of expression in the world, going on right over our heads, that we have no clue about. The whole *point* is that they're not like us. We're not the measure of all things.

Q: Sorry, I'm stuck on this. The rock is just, well, *there.*

VWO: Sheer "thereness" can be a kind of expression too—even in us. I've known rocks like that. I've been honored to know rocks like that.

Q: OK, OK, but it's a stretch. Like you said.

VWO: Choose your own examples. The real point is: we live in a world that is vastly more intricate and interconnected than we know or maybe ever will know.

Q: That does strike a chord with me. "A world intricate and interconnected . . ."

VWO: Which is why paying attention is so important. That's how we find out. That's how the wonder grows on us.

Q: So what follows from this? What does all this mean for what we do? How do we change our lives?

VWO: Paying attention is itself a way of changing our lives. Not the only necessary change, but maybe the most fundamental one.

Q: All by itself?

VWO: Think of love again. When you love someone, the most fundamental thing you do is to *cherish* them. It's a way of seeing, a way of appreciating them as whoever they are. What needs to change is *you*. Indeed love may utterly transform you. But you may not "do" anything different at all, apart from just letting the loved ones be who they are.

Q: It will take a lot, now, to "let nature be."

VWO: Yup.

Q: I guess you want me to fill this in myself. OK. Obviously, for starters, we need to leave some land to itself. And some wild animals. Cut pollution. Stop allowing roads to go everywhere. How about this too: make less noise. Stop spreading light everywhere. We're so proud of that, lighting the whole world up. Driving away the dark. But I heard somewhere that the great sea turtles, the ones who come ashore only in a few places and a few nights a year to lay eggs, get disoriented by all our of lights—they can't find the moon anymore—and go the wrong direction. So there are beaches now where lights are not allowed around full moon, when the turtles come ashore.

VWO: Yes. It's a new kind of attitude, almost a kind of *etiquette*. We need to impose less on nature. We need to stop assuming that nothing else is going on out there, so we can just move in and do what we want. Sometimes we're the ones who need to get out of the way.

Q: Usually we picture environmentalism in terms of recycling, carpooling, no more aerosol cans, stuff like that. We're in a crisis, after all.

VWO: More burdens. Sigh.

Q: They *are* burdens, aren't they?

VWO: One reason so many native peoples could not fathom Christianity was that the missionaries kept insisting that Heaven is somewhere else. Whereas it was quite clear to them that they already lived in a perfect world. Heaven is *right here*. That's what we cannot see. I would say that *that* is the real—the deepest—environmental "crisis."

Q: I guess you're saying that if we thought defending Heaven were our task, it wouldn't feel like just a bunch of new burdens.

VWO: Absolutely. And *then* we will have some practical ideas about what to change, too. Maybe we will build new kinds of houses, for example, open to the winds and the outdoors—or new kinds of neighborhoods, open to other creatures and the darkness and the sweep of the land. No outdoor lights, for example.

Q: Carl Sagan wrote somewhere how ironic it is that at the very moment we discovered how vast the universe really is, we blotted it all out with so much light at night.

VWO: There's a nice idea for a holiday, too. Turn Out the Lights Night. See the stars again. Not just for the sea turtles but for *us*, eh?

Q: It's interesting you are talking about holidays. We started out talking about environmental ethics as a set of rules. But now it is a kind of celebration.

VWO: That's the spirit!

Q: The fundamentalists won't like this. Nature holidays to them are a form of paganism.

VWO: Actually, most of the holidays we already celebrate will do quite nicely.

Q: Better explain that. Christmas?

VWO: Theologically, Christmas is the birth of the Savior; the promise of salvation. OK. What's happening in the world at that time? The days are getting shorter as the sun sinks to the south. It's getting colder and darker. It feels as though the world is dying. And then, it's Winter Solstice, the sun stops going south. It's only the barest hint, just a slight lengthening of the days again, it's still cold and dark mostly, nothing is growing, but—what? Now we know that life will return.

Q: The promise of salvation! The New Year, at the Solstice, as a kind of . . . newborn baby. Savior.

VWO: And so on that darkest night of the year we light candles. For Hannukah and Kwaanza too: liberation and rededication festivals. Now we know that the light will come back. Life will be renewed. We all can celebrate that. I think we all *must* celebrate that.

Q: Then in the Spring . . .

VWO: . . . the promise of salvation is fulfilled. Right here in this world, life *has* returned. The days are lengthening and warming. The flowers are out. All ancient peoples celebrated this time, long before Christianity. The archetypal meaning is: Resurrection! But of Earth herself. . . .

Q: The fundamentalists will go through the roof.

VWO: These are times that all humans have honored since the beginning of agricultural civilization. Their meaning—and yes, their sacredness—does not belong to any particular religion. They belong to *Earth*. They are common to all of us, part of the great cycles of light and dark, life and death.

Q: . . . Death too?

VWO: Midpoint between Fall Equinox and Winter Solstice is the time the Celts called "Samhain." For Catholics, All Saints' Day; in many Catholic countries, also, All Souls' Day, the Day of the Dead, called "All Hallow's Day" in medieval times. In Mexico people have picnics in cemeteries, honor the ancestors. And the night before—All Hallows' Eve—became . . .

Q: Halloween!

VWO: It was not invented by the candy companies. Late Fall is naturally the time of death. Leaves fall, plants shrivel up. Death is part of life, as life is shortly to spring from death in the great circle of the seasons.

Q: You really think we can recover all this?

VWO: Why not? The psychological or archetypal meanings haven't changed at all. We're still so sensitive to the cycle of light and dark that people even talk about "Seasonal Affective Disorder." But that just means: people get depressed in the late Fall because everything is so dark and dreary. They need some *light*. A Christmas tree or a menorah will do just fine.

Q: All I can say is that it sounds like a lot more fun than the usual doom-and-gloom environmentalism.

VWO: There *are* great dangers in massively assaulting Earth as we have done. There have been heartbreaking losses too. There is much we need to change. Still, once again, to see only the losses and dangers is to miss all the wonders that surround us. It's as bad as the other extreme view, that Earth is just a backdrop for the drama of human life. Both are blind to all that is happening, right out the door. I can't say it enough: it's time to *stop, look, and listen*. . . .

Exercises and Notes

GIVING VOICE TO NEW VALUES

When we say that a river or a tree or an endangered species has value for its own sake, we are not speaking of goods (pleasures or happiness), or virtues, or even rights (though the language of "respect" comes naturally, it is not a matter of fairness or rights but more like a kind of religious awe). Here it may be that we are glimpsing a new, fourth family of values.

How shall we describe these new values? How do you *feel* in the presence of animal eyes, alien yet kin too; or of summer thunderstorms in the woods; or of the ocean at dawn? How do we invoke and keep alive the sense that the world, morally speaking, is "bigger than we are"? How can we speak and think in order to remember nature's awesomeness and preciousness when we are not right in the presence of it, or when others need reminding or have no clue?

As a philosophical challenge this will take some time to answer. But it is also a practical challenge, and often a pressing one. It's one thing to appreciate a forest when you are right in the middle of it, after all, and quite another thing to try to somehow convey its value to politicians and builders and lawyers at a public hearing on some development question. This is a real practical question. How do you bridge the gap?

So: practice writing a letter to your senator about some natural area you know and love. How do you convey its value in a few paragraphs? Practice telling your friend the same thing. Don't overlook less familiar means of expression, like poetry or "nature writing." Remember again Edward Abbey's attempt to do just this in the reading in Chapter 3. Or: are there other kinds of lyrical or religious expression you'd want to use? And are there other (possibly still more creative and unexpected) means of expression yet?

Also: can you understand some of the more radical forms of environmental action in this light too? Environmental activists sometimes use costume, ritual, and dance, as well as chaining themselves to polluting pipes or living in trees to keep them from being cut down or interposing themselves in little boats between whales and whale hunters. Aren't they trying to convey nature's values in symbolic ways? Sometimes they may speak directly to us, too: there are groups of people who attempt to speak for other life forms by speaking *as* those lifeforms (and there are ritual forms for doing so, such as the "Council of All Beings"). What else might *you* suggest?

ANALYZING THE "EXPANDING CIRCLE"

Notice that taking animals seriously, as discussed in the last chapter, already carries us beyond anthropocentrism. It's not just *humans* that count, but (at least some) other animals too. And this step already has environmental implications. If the well-being of tigers and condors and salmon needs to be considered in our moral decisions, we need to take care for their habitat too.

On the other hand, this kind of argument still begins with the traditional anthropocentric families of values and ethical theories and then "extends" them to make them more inclusive. Of course there is some power in calling on familiar norms in this way. If the good is happiness (pleasure, avoiding suffering), as utilitarians claim, for example, then it is hard to deny ethical consideration to any creatures that can feel pleasure or suffer pain, to whatever degree they can.

Even at its most radical, though, this kind of argument leaves out too much, according to many environmental philosophers. An ethics that stops at the boundaries of the animal kingdom cannot be the whole story either. Whales get in, yes, but trees and rivers and ecosystems don't. So environmental ethics urges us to *keep going*.

Do you think biocentrism or ecocentrism do better? Or do you think some other sort of theory (or something other than a theory) is necessary? And can you translate your theory or other approach back into real-life terms for your friends and neighbors?

Apply your favorite theory to some practical questions: endangered species; global warming; local development issues (if you're not sure what they are, find out); costs of pollution versus costs of cleaning it up; how we build houses and other buildings; and so on.

To get you going on some of the farther-out questions, here's a case in point (from the environmental ethicist Holmes Rolston, one of the founders of the field):

> Do your Christmas festivities, lasting about ten days, justify cutting a wild Colorado blue spruce, which if left uncut would have a lifespan of 150 years? Should real people use artificial Christmas trees, in addition to wearing fake furs? About thirty million trees are used in the U. S. each year, with ninety million seedlings replanted. Does it matter whether the trees are farmed or wild? Does a family gain more than the tree loses? What would the Christmas spirit be like in a family that thought too much of a blue spruce to sacrifice it for their festivities?

What does your theory say about these questions? Don't slight the last question—it might even be the key to the others.

KEEP ON THINKING

Use your other tools too. How about multiplying options and reframing problems?

Take the quandary of the modern grocery checkout: "paper or plastic"? It *is*, in part, an ethical question: a question of our impact on Earth and on future human generations. It's also a debatable question. Even some ecologists advise using plastic bags, because they can be used longer and take less and cleaner energy to produce. Plastic bags save trees. On the other hand, thousands of tons of nonbiodegradable plastic wastes are an environmental disaster too. Which is the "lesser of two evils"?

We could stop with that question, and try to answer it by multiplying options. Maybe we could invent lighter bags, or perfect biodegradable plastic ones, or. . . .

But: must we pick one or the other "evil"? Suppose that we step back a little and reframe the problem itself. Why do we need to use disposable bags in the first place? Surely the best answer is to *reuse* bags: cloth bags, super-strong paper bags, backpacks, and so on. We do not need to choose the lesser of two evils. (Recall the box in Chapter 12: "Don't Settle for Too Little.") Try to pick *no* evils: try, if you can, to *change the problem*.

The best answer to the littering question is to avoid creating the potential litter in the first place. My Chinese students tell me that it's common in China for people to carry around their own chopsticks, rather than requiring new ones every time they eat out. Japanese carry around their own cups. Why couldn't we?

Could the problem of litter even contain the seeds of its own solution? The story goes that when Henry Ford was setting up the first assembly lines to build the Model T, his suppliers got very specific requests about how to build the boxes in which they sent their bolts or cushions. A certain kind of wood had to be used, cut to certain sizes, with holes drilled just in certain places. Puzzled, but anxious for Ford's business, they complied. It turned out that once the boxes were unpacked at the assembly line, they were taken apart and used for the Model T's floorboards. They were already cut and drilled in just the right ways!

In short, Ford took two problems—procuring floorboards, and getting rid of unwanted boxes—and turned them into one solution. Instead of becoming litter, the excess box material became an *opportunity*. Reuse was planned into the very design of things. Some thinkers now call this "precycling": it is still, sadly enough, a cutting-edge idea. Rather than raising the question of *recycling* only after a thing has been used, we ought to raise it before the thing is even made.

The last chapter explored some creative new options to deal with litter—biodegradable fast-food wrappers, redesigning "junk" into kids' construction sets, and so on. Good options, as far as they go. Now you can see that there is another set of questions to be raised as well, opening up possibilities that might eliminate the litter problem almost entirely before it even occurs. Imagine buying food in containers that you could then use as plates and glasses (or just *eat*), or milk or juice containers that you could refill at the store, or automotive frames that can be updated in pieces rather than junked as a whole. Or . . . ?

In similar ways, environmentalists argue that there are good alternatives to most of our environmentally destructive practices. For another example, electric air conditioners are massive energy hogs and therefore contribute to global warming (through coal- or oil-burning power plant emissions) and the nuclear waste problem (from nuclear power plants, which have other dangers as well). But there are other ways to beat the heat: building houses open to the breezes, for example, or partly earth sheltered, as many houses in the south used to be. The supposed problem might also be reframed. Maybe we should just get used to the heat again, or take siestas rather than insisting on working all day in wool suits; and so on.

There is an enormous literature on this kind of thing. For a start, look at Jim Mollison's *Permaculture: A Practical Guide for a Sustainable Future* (Island Press, several editions)—a wonderful all-purpose practical compendium of new (and also often quite old) ways of living, building, growing food, and getting around that return us to a life in balance with the earth.

You could make a contribution, even a career, of exploring and applying some of these ideas. For now, pick a current environmental problem and do a little research with the aim of widening our options in an environmentally more intelligent way.

NOTES AND FURTHER READING

For up-to-date information on the global environmental situation, see the Worldwatch papers, such as the *Vital Signs* annual series, published by the Worldwatch Institute, 1776 Massachusetts Avenue N.W., Washington, DC 20036. On the Web, try the Environmental News Network at <www.enn.com>, and (a general resource) Envirolink Library at <www.envirolink.org>.

For a general "next step" into the philosophical themes raised here, see my collection *An Invitation to Environmental Philosophy* (Oxford University Press, 1999); don't overlook its extensive annotated bibliography, "Going On." Good academic anthologies in environmental ethics include Susan Armstrong and Richard Botzler, eds., *Environmental Ethics: Divergence and Convergence* (McGraw-Hill) and Christine Pierce and Donald Vandeveer, eds., *People, Penguins, and Plastic Trees* (Wadsworth). Many of the themes introduced here, especially the varieties of theories in environmental ethics as well as ecofeminist and other critiques, are covered in detail in these texts. For an ethics-oriented history of environmentalism in modern times, see Roderick Nash, *The Rights of Nature* (University of Wisconsin Press, 1989). On religious expressions of environmental ethics, see Roger Gottlieb's collection *This Sacred Earth* (Routledge, 1996) and David Kinsley, *Ecology and Religion* (Prentice-Hall, 1995). See also the "Ethics Updates" website at <ethics.acusd.edu>; select "Environmental Ethics."

Albert Schweitzer is cited from his *Out of My Life and Thought* (Holt, Rinehart, and Winston, 1949), pages 158 to 159. Holmes Rolston is cited from his *Environmental Ethics: Duties to and Values in the Natural World* (Temple University Press, 1988), page 122.

Time's "Owl Versus Man" cover appeared on 25 June 1990. For background on the integrative approach to "Owls Versus Man" suggested in this chapter, see the accompanying article (which, remarkably, is not at all as polarized as the cover suggests); and John B. Judis, "Ancient Forests, Lost Jobs," *In These Times* 14:31 (August 1–14, 1990). A thorough study concluding that environmentalism and economic welfare are *not* at odds—that in fact they go together—is Stephen Meyer, *Environmentalism and Economic Prosperity* (MIT Project on Environmental Politics and Policy, 1992).

Notes for Teachers
The Toolbox in the Classroom

This appendix offers comments and suggestions for philosopher-teachers planning a course using this book as primary text. I describe my own uses of this material and offer some more pedagogically oriented notes and further readings. I am concerned especially with the teacher for whom the interactive classroom presupposed by this book is not yet entirely familiar or comfortable. For you I hope, as the preface said, that this book helps to make it truly *inviting!* All instructors, though, should find at least a few useful ideas here. Let me add again that I would very much appreciate hearing any of *your* suggestions and exercises or projects that prove useful with this material. (E-mail me at <weston@elon.edu>.)

GENERAL ISSUES

A Note on Philosophical Starting Points

Philosophers and others trained in ethics will recognize that some of the starting points of this book vary, sometimes sharply, from those standard in the field. It's been clear since the beginning of this book that I see ethics as a reconstructive and practical enterprise, open-ended and evolving, rather than a contest of theories or an attempt to discover at last the real truth about how we should live.

Many philosophers prefer to concentrate on ethics' unique intellectual challenges—on theory building and conceptual analysis—following a model of ethics essentially laid down by the English philosopher Henry Sidgwick in the late nineteenth century. And this *professional* model of ethics, as it were, may be entirely appropriate in upper-level classes, in courses mostly for majors or minors or where some specialization is useful and appropriate. But for lower-level, introductory, general-curriculum ethics courses, in which very few if any students intend to become specialists in ethics, it seems to me that we are missing an opportunity to do them much more good.

Students in such classes, like most people, come to ethics to learn how to *live*. This is a far broader matter—not merely an intellectual challenge, but a challenge to the imagination and to the heart too. It may be that by concentrating on certain intellectual challenges unique to ethics, we have slighted the practical (and creative, and imaginative) skills that are vital to ethics but *not* unique to it. So part of the aim of this book is to rejoin ethics to life skills, to put ethics into what I see as its rightful place.

Philosophers will recognize that this approach to ethics traces back to the American pragmatists, John Dewey in particular, and has affinities as well with a number of pragmatist, feminist, and other critical views of ethics that are now developing rapidly in the midst of the current and vast philosophical debate about the very foundations of ethics. But I don't defend my starting points in this book itself (though it's been difficult to resist!) nor even critique the usual ones. A textbook is just not the place for methodological debates. Interested or provoked readers might consult my book *Toward Better Problems* (Temple University Press, 1992) for a development and defense of some of my assumptions. Some other representatives of the ongoing philosophical debate are noted at the end of Chapter 6.

My aim in this *Toolbox* is different. It's a remarkable thing, I think, that despite all of the current challenges to "ethics as usual," it remains virtually impossible to teach *practical* ethics without plowing the same old theoretical furrows. No available textbooks present ethics primarily in another key. My main aim, then, has been to write just such a book—to make it possible to teach ethics on the view laid out in this book's preface: as a collection of practical skills that enable us "to make a constructive difference, in word and in deed, in problematic ethical situations." And that is quite enough for one book!

Finally, though, I do admit that I hope *A 21st Century Ethical Toolbox* will be read as a contribution, albeit oblique, to the current philosophical debate about the foundations of ethics too. Every approach to ethics must be judged partly by how it looks in action: by what kinds of tools it brings back to practice; by how constructively and invitingly it enables us to contribute to improving our common life. Could not each then be judged partly by what kinds of introductory texts and courses it makes possible, by what an introduction to ethics *that* way leaves students able to *do?* Proof is partly in the pudding. I am proud to offer this book as one relevant kind of pudding.

Course Design Using Toolbox

The book is designed to serve as the chief or even sole textbook in an ethics course, though it can be supplemented in a variety of ways too, and could well serve as a supplement itself. Some may wish to supplement it with a standard text, like a collection of readings from traditional ethical theories, or a collection of professional articles on "applied" themes, or a text that combines both. Others may supplement it in quite different ways: say, with books that go into depth on a single issue raised here more briefly. Some colleagues have used it successfully with Peter Singer's *Animal Liberation*, for example; others have used Ram Dass and Paul Gorman's *How Can I Help?* (extending Chapter 15) or Paul Ignatieff's *The Needs of Strangers* (extending Chapter 19) or Colin McGinn's brisk little essay *Moral Literacy*, which takes provocative positions on a number of the issues discussed here. (You'll recall that I have drawn upon McGinn several times myself.) Others have coupled it with popular and provocative books such as Daniel Quinn's *Ishmael*.

I assign roughly one chapter from the Toolbox sections per class (I have 100-minute classes twice a week) and one chapter from the Issues sections per week (two classes). This schedule presupposes that students read and understand the chapters mostly on their own. In class I may spend five or ten minutes reviewing the readings, just to remind people of the main points, but I rely on the students to raise questions or issues if there are sticking points in the chapters. (A useful way to do this, by the way, is to pass out index cards as class is beginning each day and ask for questions or points of unclarity in the day's reading. Organize these at a later short break and respond to them right away.)

I don't lecture. I've already shot my bolt in the book, as it were. Class is almost entirely application and practice. Suggestions for in-class applications and practice, chapter by chapter, follow below—they are the main part of this appendix.

Please note that there are many substantive new points in the "Exercises and Notes" sections. I find it wise to assign them along with the text sections, even if the exercises aren't always assigned as writing projects or classwork.

Colleagues have assigned the chapters of *Toolbox* in a variety of diferent orders. Some prefer to move back and forth between tools and "applied" chapters. Others begin with chapters 1 and 2 and then go to 13, 14, and 15 for more general orientation before going back into specific tools. You might also begin with 8, 9, and 10. Some instructors omit specific tools, or leave the relevant chapters as background reading (for example, to emphasize some more traditional dimensions of ethics, you might concentrate on chapters 4, 5, 6, and 10 in the Toolbox proper).

In any case, the chapters of this book are mostly independent enough of each other that alternative arrangements are natural and easy. Some chapters make a natural sequence (especially Parts II [Chapters 3–7] and IV [Chapters 11, 12]), but apart from this, the chapters can be readily reordered to suit your needs and preferences. All of the Issues chapters are independent of each other too, with at most an occasional cross-reference. In many courses, I expect, not all of the Issues chapters will be covered anyway. I usually leave this choice partly up to the students.

Indeed, sometimes part of students' work for the course is to help prepare and present one of the "applied" topics in the "Issues" part of the course. They pick topics early on and then work in topic groups periodically in the first half of the course too—practicing problem-solving skills, for example, with regard to "their" topic. It helps to give the in-class tool practice some focus and direction, and student-led discussions always enliven the applied topics. Some of the suggestions later on in this appendix come right from my students.

I also very strongly suggest setting up a class service project, as discussed in Chapter 15. My students almost always report that working in the homeless shelter was among the most significant aspect of the course for them; for some it actually changes their lives. This kind of work is not hard to set up—quite the contrary, most service organizations are dying for help, are more than happy to help coordinate a hefty group of volunteers (a class of thirty-five can basically staff a small shelter for a term), and often take public education to be part of their mission. Make the phone call!

Over the years I have graded my course in a variety of ways. Half of the grade has sometimes depended on journals—student notebooks with notes *and their own thoughts* (that's a crucial part) on all the chapters and class discussions. Group work, attendance, and service work made up the rest of the grade. Other times I have graded mainly on short weekly papers, mostly assignments directly from the "Exercises" that conclude each chapter. Currently I keep tabs on students' reading with short weekly quizzes. Completing the service work, short weekly projects, and a term paper—all checkoffs, not letter graded—gives students a progressively better final grade. In any case, there are a lot of options. If you assign papers, remind students of the specific paper guidelines in Chapter 13's box.

APPROACHING THE TOOLBOX CHAPTERS

What I offer now is essentially an outline of my teaching methods for each chapter, a kind of walk through my course with running commentary and suggestions.

Chapter 1. Ethics as a Learning Experience

My strategy in most of the text chapters is to focus on just one or a few practical topics, so that the "applications" stay somewhat consistent through the chapter. I try to do this in each day's class as well. Thus, for Chapter 1, I take up the theme of the C. P. Ellis story: racism, and how we find our way beyond it, both individually and as a society. How does learning like his happen? Take some time in class with the questions that introduce the story. How did Ellis manage to change so much? Why do other people in similar circumstances *not* learn and change?

Ask the same questions about society as a whole. How did our society manage to change so much from, say, the fifties to the seventies, in regard to race issues? What are the remaining sources of racism now? The PBS documentary series "Eyes on the Prize," widely available in most college and public libraries, is a good source of provocative scenes and events from the civil rights movement. For a shorter single film try "A Time for Justice" (Montgomery, Alabama: Teaching Tolerance, 1992).

The end of the third exercise suggests an interview project. I have tried this several times with great success.

Finally, a bit of a heretical note about relativism. Relativism is mentioned only briefly in the main text, and I often prefer to say no more about it. It's striking, for example, that although the spectre of relativism seems to loom extremely large for some ethics instructors (and most textbook writers), it simply *doesn't come up* the minute a real issue or a real person, like C. P. Ellis, comes on the scene. (Nobody says: "Oh well, maybe racism was right for him. . . .") Despite the veneer of relativism, most of us come with strong moral opinions. Dogmatism is the much more real danger.

Sure, students express relativistic sentiments from time to time ("Who am I to say?," etc.). I think that philosophers read too much of a theory—Relativism with a capital R—into them. There are other and perhaps better interpretations. Maybe when students say things like "Who am I to judge?," they are just trying to give others some space, and asking for space themselves in a context where they are unsure of themselves. After all, college is a time of radical change and experiment for many people: things are in flux; they justly want room to move. Maybe they want some freedom from the moral deliverances of others, time to work things out for themselves. This is not unreasonable—and it has nothing to do with the philosophical debate about relativism. I don't think it's wise to take a few relativistic-sounding expressions as "on the way to relativism," as it were, and then try to lay out the whole capital-R theory and defeat it. It may actually *make* them relativists, for one thing; if they're persuaded by this that philosophical relativism is the only way to defend the personal space they geuninely do need, then it *will* be a problem.

Besides, even if they really are (philosophical) relativists from the beginning, it strikes me as unwise pedagogy to think that we must begin a course by "defeating" something students are supposed to believe so strongly. Much wiser and more effective would be to take them where they are and build from there. How inviting is ethics likely to be if it sets itself up from the start as an assault upon their convictions?

So my advice is to just tolerate the occasional "who is to say?" rhetoric without wheeling out the heavy artillery. Just point out that we do in fact have more to think about and say. Send the harder-core relativists to the box in Chapter 1. You'll have a lot more space for the real work of ethics.

Chapter 2. Ethics and Religion

Modern philosophical ethics tends to avoid religious themes and terms. However wise this may be as an expression of secularism and pluralism, it does make it harder to speak to many of our students, whose ethical frames of reference are often insistently religious and sometimes sectarian. I think we need to take them more seriously. The aim of this chapter is to suggest a path toward the sort of ethics familiar to philosophers that lies *through* religion rather than opposed to it.

Invite in your college chaplain for a dialogue on these matters with you and the class. Maybe we are blessed with an especially ecumenically minded and humane college chaplain, but I can report that in my classes these discussions have always been helpful. Most college chaplains deal with a religiously diverse community: they *have* to be at least somewhat ecumenical. In most places they also have to make their peace with the prevailing secularism.

The second exercise invites us to read the Bible, though perhaps in a different spirit than usual. This can be a fascinating project in an open college classroom. A few examples are suggested in the text. Another I find useful is the story of Judah and Tamar in *Genesis* 38. Sometimes I hand out a copy of that chapter and we read it right in class. It is a wild tale of sudden unexplained death, betrayal, seduction, and adultery, which concludes with the pardon and full acceptance of the female adulterer (Tamar) and no question even being raised about the male adulterer (Judah). In fact, Tamar is specifically listed as one of the ancestors of King David and therefore of Jesus Himself. Judah founds one of the twelve tribes of Israel and later gives his name to one of the two Jewish kingdoms. So the story seems to go rather light on adultery and seduction, to say the least. It is also complicated by certain sexual customs practiced by the Hebrews of the time, in particular the expectation that if a husband dies, it is the obligation of his next youngest brother to impregnate his widow—in particular, to sire a son—who counts as the dead man's son for the sake of inheritance.

In this story, Onan, the second son, does in fact follow his dead brother (killed by God for an unspecified reason) to the widow's bed, but deliberately does not get her pregnant. God kills him too, for a reason that seems unclear. Was it that he disobeyed his father? Was it his selfishness—for if his dead brother had no heirs then the father's property would pass to Onan and *his* descendants? Or something else? It is not so clear. Yet this story, like the story of Sodom, was made the basis for a very strong prohibition in the Christian tradition. Challenge the students to figure out what exactly, on this view, was the sin of Onan (hint: they can look up "onanism" in the dictionary) and then to ask whether the actual story can be made to bear such weight.

One way or another, anyway, keep religious themes and language alive through your course. For example, in Chapter 3 I sometimes use a section of "Humanae Vitae" as an exercise in paying attention to values. Students tend to dislike the Pope's argument, and sometimes are therefore disinclined to pay enough attention to get it right, but for just that reason it's a useful exercise—and (arguably) the Pope has a rather more compelling point than it might seem at first. Note other places where religious themes and challenges come up in this text: for example, the second exercise in Chapter 10.

Chapter 3. Paying Attention to Values

Take current issues out of newspapers; dig values out and spell them out just as the chapter does. Try to be fairly specific. For example, if a value like "responsibility" is mentioned, ask *whose* responsibility and *for what?*

I organize this work by dividing the class or group into small groups each of which is assigned one such issue (make up a handout of newspaper article clippings or short explanations). Each group's assignment is to identify *one* value at stake in the situation and write a description of it, in a few words, on the board (use one section of the board for each issue) or on a flipchart, in, say, three minutes (the first one is easy).

Then each issue passes to the next group (number the groups and issues: issue 1 now goes to group 2, etc.), with the same assignment and, say, five minutes. Repeat for as much time as you have, allowing a few more minutes each time around if needed.

My students generally do not believe that more than two or three values can be drawn out of such issues. They are surprised when the groups are still going strong on the fourth or fifth round. Sometimes in later rounds a number of values of the same general sort come out together: it's striking to see connections between quite different issues emerge. By the end, you have a board full of different values all drawn out of situations that we are used to just quickly passing over. Next time we ask more of ourselves.

Students who are completely stumped by Edward Abbey's essay in this chapter might find Chapter 21 helpful. Or might not. I deliberately chose a quirky piece calling on unfamiliar values for this reading—it helps to stretch people's minds a little. The idea of valuing something precisely because it is *in*human (hostile to us, painful, or so ancient as to not even take notice of us) will strike students as novel and maybe odd—but at least provocative, I hope.

Take children's stories seriously too. "Even in an age of computer games and electronic toys," writes William Bennett, "there is still resonant power in the phrase *Once upon a time . . .*" He goes on:

> And so what we choose to read to our children matters a great deal. Legends, folktales, sacred stories, biographies, and poems can introduce the youngest children to the virtues; they can clarify notions of right and wrong for young people; and they can serve as powerful reminders of [humanity's] best ideals all the way through adulthood. More than one great man or woman at a critical instant has recalled a simple fable, a familiar verse, a childhood hero.

Bennett suggests that stories can inspire and intrigue us at all ages, not just the early years. But adult stories become more complex and subtle, less clear, as Chapter 2 suggests. There are many other stories from cultures around the world that appeal to us for precisely this reason. They concern how to live, they are concerned for virtue broadly speaking, but they are sometimes very subtle indeed. Indeed in some traditions, like Zen, the very impenetrability of the story is part of the point! A good collection of Zen stories is *Zen Buddhism: An Introduction with Stories* (Peter Pauper Press, 1959). For Sufi teaching stories, see Idries Shah, *Tales of the Dervishes* (Penguin/Arkana, 1993). For Hasidic stories, see Martin Buber's *Tales of the Hasidim* (Schocken, 1947). The list of stories that moral philosophers have either written themselves or found philosophically provocative is long, but a few accessible and provocative short pieces are: the plays of Jean-Paul Sartre and Albert Camus (for an unfamiliar but fascinating example, try Camus's "The Just Assassins"); Tolstoy's "The Death of Ivan Ilych"; Wilde's "The Portrait of Dorian Grey"; Susan Glaspell, "A Jury of Her Peers," in *A Jury of Her Peers* (E. Benn, 1927); Ursula K. Leguin, "May's Lion," from *Buffalo Gals and Other Animal Presences* (Penguin, 1990); Arturo Vivante, "The Soft Core," in *The Tales of Arturo Vivante* (Sheep Meadow Press, 1990); Farley Mowat, "The Trapped Whale," in Jane McIntyre, *Mind in the Waters* (Scribner's/Sierra Club, 1974); and Stanislaw Lem, "Non Serviam," in *A Perfect Vacuum* (Harcourt Brace Jovanovich, 1983). Of course this is the barest list. Many nonfiction stories are also useful and inspiring in this way. I have taught ethics with Studs Terkel's *Working* (Pantheon, 1974), for example, as a main text. Look at movies as well: start with the kinds you know and like, but try some wild and different kinds as well.

Chapter 4. Families of Moral Values

The key word is: practice, practice, practice. Take current issues out of the newspaper again, or return to those you discussed when practicing paying attention to values. Start in class with the first exercise and then move to the second.

I am not entirely happy with the goods/rights/virtue distinction used in this chapter. Though "virtue" is a fairly specific and definite term, this is not true of either of the others, and this tends to be confusing to students. "Goods" sounds very inclusive (all moral values are in some sense "good"), while "rights" tends to be read too narrowly, just as "rights-to" or claim rights. I adopt this language nonetheless because it is philosophically standard, but be warned that it will take some persistent explaining and reminding to students to keep it straight.

Sometimes, if I have time, I run a version of the role play described below as a suggestion for teaching Chapter 19 (Poverty and Welfare), except that rather than designing an entire welfare system I ask students to, say, devise a set of rules for distributing a scarce drug that saves you from an excruciating death from a disease that, as far as we know, randomly hits a certain percentage of the population. (See the notes for Chapter 19 if this interests you.) Debrief the role play with special attention to the different families of values that come up. Map the debate if you have time.

Chapter 5. Some Traditional Ethical Theories

For this chapter I usually arrange for brief classroom visits by J. S. Mill, Immanuel Kant, and Aristotle (they can be contacted at your local costume store or theater department). The enterprise of theory needs some explaining in varied ways; it always helps to personify them.

Theoretical thinking as such may not be familiar to many students. Don't assume that the point of the whole enterprise is clear. You may have to go into detail about what a theory is and what it does. (This may raise some useful questions for you too!) Some philosophers define philosophical ethics itself in terms of ethical theory, so theory itself never arises as a question *within* ethics—but it is nonetheless a real question (in my view, anyway), and worth explicitly answering for ourselves as professionals too.

Compared with the usual treatment of theory in ethics texts, this chapter (coupled with Chapter 6, of course) is quite short and, I hope, sweet. This reflects my own teaching practice, in which the traditional ethical theories and the usual forms of contention about them are introduced in the usual elaborate ways only in the *second* ethics course, as explained above. For instructors who wish to do more theory, of course, supplementation is natural and easy. There are literally dozens of theory-oriented anthologies and monographs to choose from. Theodore Denise et al., *Great Traditions in Ethics* (Wadsworth, many editions) presents a number of traditional theorists (and some less traditional contemporary and ancient figures) in their own words with helpful arrangement and commentary. For other possible texts, see the notes to this chapter.

Chapter 6. When Values Clash: Theoretical Approaches

Students who have difficulty with the idea of theory can often get through Chapter 5 reasonably well. There the theories still look mostly like summations of different sets of values, and have not yet come into contact with each other. When they do, though, in Chapter 6, it will sometimes be puzzling to students. What is going on? Why should the theories contend with each other? Here, if not in Chapter 5, some of these methodological questions need answers.

The subject here is among the most controversial topics in ethical philosophy. There are many more subtle and complex arguments than could possibly be considered in this chapter. On the other hand, this is true for *all* of the topics in this book. I have tried to keep this one in perspective.

It may be helpful to emphasize the controversy up front. These are debatable tools. Different teachers will have different views of their usefulness as a whole, as well as commitments to different theories and different ways of resolving their conflicts. Open the question to class consideration, just as with any "applied" debate. Consider the debate between theories; the debate about how to *use* theories (e.g. one theory across the board? or keep all theories in play . . . ?); and indeed about *whether* to use theories at all. Challenge my rather skeptical conclusions at the end of the chapter.

Chapter 7. When Values Clash: Integrative Approaches

In presenting the theories in Chapter 6, both in class and in this book, I try to leave space for a largely nontheoretical approach to conflicts of values as well. Regardless of what you think of the usefulness of theories, sometimes an entirely different set of approaches is needed.

  Integrative methods will be less familiar to many ethical philosophers, at least in the context of ethical debates. I'm sure they're *quite* familiar, though maybe not so explicit, in our everyday lives. I used to feel tempted to spend some class time justifying them. I don't anymore, and I don't recommend it— I think it just succeeds in making them seem fishy. The justifications were more for myself, I finally concluded, or for colleagues I imagined looking over my shoulder. Few students have this kind of resistance. Indeed it's the other way around: they resist *theory*.

  Since the culture does not support them, though, at least in ethics, integrative skills may be hard to put into practice. They need practice. Spend some time on the exercises. Start with the first. Better yet, assign it in advance. Though it sounds easy, in my experience it is very hard for most students to pull off. Typically they end up, despite the instructions, describing moral debates in an "I think . . ."/"They think . . ." kind of way. It takes some work to get to "*We* think. . . ." Then move to the second exercise.

  Note that many of these strategies are useful on the practical level even if you wholeheartedly subscribe to a theoretical approach too. A fuller toolbox of conflict-resolution skills is still helpful. Fisher and Ury, for example, make no claims about the disutility of theory: they only elaborate another and very powerful—but often overlooked—set of tools in addition.

  The notes for Chapter 17, below, offer an attitude survey on matters relating to abortion. The survey tends to reveal a surprisingly large common ground on this issue (see the discussion below). It's a useful accompaniment to the Rosenblatt reading in this chapter, and sometimes I use it here instead of waiting until Chapter 17.

Chapter 8. Finding the Facts

These are more familiar themes, though not so often considered in ethics courses. Obviously there is time only to touch on a few main points: chiefly, that taking some care to identify and seek out the relevant facts is a key to intelligent ethical thinking. A handout of sample ethical arguments, drawn from the newspaper or widely available critical-thinking texts, is useful to analyze inferences. Don't overlook the first and second exercises, though— these are usually where I spend most of class time. Just to identify the relevant factual questions, and to consider how we might begin to answer them, is the most essential step of all. Most people are unused to taking care here unless they've already studied critical thinking. Model a more open-minded approach.

Chapter 9. Watching Words

Practice identifying loaded language in various statements, perhaps first in statements students disagree with, and then in more congenial statements, including their own (have some class discussions on controversial topics, and videotape them for this and other purposes). Most textbooks in informal logic have a section on loaded language, and exercises to practice identifying and avoiding it. The habit of analyzing ethical arguments on their merits and putting them fairly, even if we don't agree with them, comes as a shock to many students, but for precisely that reason it is crucial.

Practice definition. I usually have my students in groups by this point in the term, assigned to specific issues from the Issues part of the text (or others), and so I ask each group to work out a definition of a key term in "their" debate: "welfare" or "poverty," for example, or "genetic engineering," or "environmental ethics." Each group proposes an initial definition on the blackboard after fifteen minutes or so; then we discuss each, allowing me to bring in the tools in this chapter and to suggest further issues and refinements; then they return to group work to refine their definition. Be prepared for the kinds of issues that might, and should, come up. On the definition of "welfare," for example, see the first exercise in Chapter 19.

Chapter 9's box is difficult for most students. I often just ask students to look it over but reassure them that we will take up its issues later, when we consider the abortion issue and/or ethics and other animals.

Chapter 10. Judging Like Cases Alike

The best way to practice these skills, to make them vivid and compelling, is to put students directly into situations where challenges of these sorts are unavoidable. For example, I often run a simulation based directly on McGinn's little vampire story in the reading for this chapter. This simulation is described in Chapter 21's exercises, but I often use it along with Chaper 10 to make the more general point.

You could easily imagine others too. The moral psychologist Lawrence Kohlberg used to speak of "moral musical chairs" as a concrete way of cashing out the requirements of a Kantian universalism in practice. A moral act is one that you must be able to consistently will (or, in broader and more modern terms, embrace or approve of) from the points of view or "chair" of each affected party. For any moral issue students can readily identify many of the necessary chairs, and then they can even label them and quite literally move between them, speaking from each in turn. You can play "moral musical chairs" in class.

Chapters 11 and 12. Tools for Creativity in Ethics

These tools are less familiar to many ethical philosophers, but I hope the text makes their usefulness clear enough. Remember that, at least on the assumptions of this book, our task is not just or even mainly to teach students the history and theory-testing methods of ethics, but to give them the real-world skills to make a constructive difference in practice. There is no gainsaying creativity skills there.

Some persistent philosophical prejudices need to be noted and at least bracketed. For example, as I note in Chapter 11, it seems to be tempting to some philosophers to redescribe the famous "Heinz dilemma" or other examples to cut off each new option if someone brings it up, so that finally Heinz must "just choose." If your purpose is solely to illustrate the clash of different ethical theories, this may seem to be a natural move. Trying to come up with new options may indeed seem to confuse things, even to miss the point. Traditional philosophers get impatient. Research subjects in Kohlberg's research were actually labeled "immature" if they did too much of this. They were not looking at the problem the way the researchers wanted them to see it. Could it just be, though, that they saw it more accurately than the researchers—as a *false* dilemma, not a true one?

From a practical point of view, anyway, it remains the case that a great many of our apparent dilemmas have more options than at first it seems. Even a few problem-solving skills therefore can go a long way. We need the encouragement to look for other options, to avoid locking ourselves into unpromising problems. We do our students a disservice by slighting these skills, and a double disservice if we present ethics in such a way that students are tempted to reduce every issue to a dilemma. Consider that even the Heinz dilemma as originally posed is not really a dilemma, as the text argues—and that's what it was invented to be! Why ever suppose that real life would be simpler?

These tools typically do not need much explaining. The real challenge is to induce people to *use* them. It's one of those peculiar occasions when people can master a skill completely in a classroom context and then utterly fail to put it to use in the simplest case that smacks of "real life." So you have to make the link.

If there is time, begin by organizing into three- to five-person problem-solving teams. Make each team's first challenge to devise a team name or slogan ("Brainstormers"; "We eat problems for breakfast"; etc.). This is fun, it builds group spirit, and it opens up the kind of mutual appreciation and whimsy helpful to creative thinking generally. Then start on "novel function practice" and other warm-ups. The first exercise starts on purpose with nonethical problems. You might spend half a class or more on this before shifting to moral problems. Note that exactly the same tools apply in exactly the same way; then move into the second exercise. A follow-up writing exercise is to ask students to come up on their own with a completely new idea on one of these or other ethical topics.

For some points at which even our currently most tangled and "stuck" problems might still be open to creative new measures, instructors might find it useful to look ahead to the issues chapters with particular attention to the sections in the Exercises and Notes called "Keep on Thinking." And there is more in the issues chapters themselves!

You may be tempted to combine these chapters to save time. I don't advise it. The skills in each are different, for one thing, but most important is that they are all underrated and certainly underused. Spend enough time on them that students *remember* them and begin to discover just how powerful they can be. If you're unsure about them yourself, check out some of the references in the Notes sections at the end of these two chapters.

Chapter 13. Picking the Right Tools

This is a summary chapter, in a way, and can be left as a reference reading for students if you like. It may be useful to assign some sort of paper at this point in the course. Students can go right to the box on "Writing an Ethics Paper" for help, and will soon find themselves back in the chapter as a whole. Almost the first task is to decide what the goals of their paper will be, and this chapter outlines four alternatives and sets some directions to take with each.

Some students are surprised by this chapter because (I think) they expect that there must be some method for using the toolbox as a whole to arrive at a more or less definitive moral judgment about what is right and wrong in some situation or issue. What this chapter offers instead is a varied set of tools and goals. Stress that this is how it should be! People come to ethics with many different kinds of needs or problems. Closure is only one of these. The toolbox aims to be inclusive enough to help with all of them.

Chapter 14. Dialogue: Learning by Talking

Again, practice is key. Work through the exercises' dysfunctional dialogues in class. Be especially alert to missed opportunities: to questions that could be taken as real questions, for example, and not just as mere rhetorical questions. Highlight any movement toward creative thinking.

Don't allow students to simply rewrite the disagreements in these dialogues in a way that preserves the disagreement but merely makes it "nice." It's not enough if people just don't insult each other any more. My students, at least, are sometimes too easily satisfied if tensions are kept submerged or merely politely sidestepped. No: they need to *confront* those tensions, but in a constructive way.

For more dialogues to work on, videotape some talk shows on current issues, and pick some excerpts short enough to view a number of times. For an example of an intense, often angry or despairing but also constructive dialogue on an enormously difficult problem—race relations—look at Lee Mun Wah's film "The Color of Fear" (Stir Fry Productions, <www.stirfryseminars.com>). You may find the topic itself a useful one to raise with your students, but the film also appeals as a model of dialogue under the most trying conditions.

As a follow-up to the points about "silencing" at the end of this chapter's box, ask students to recall some occasions in their own experience when dialogue failed. Consider *why* it failed. Recall the various kinds of nonparticipation, resistance, advantage and disadvantage outlined in the box. Were any of these factors at play? What could have been done about them? What could be done about them next time?

If you're very brave, consider your own class or group in this regard. Who typically speaks and who doesn't? Why? Consider having a day when only certain people can speak: only people who have not spoken before; or only women (say, on the subject of abortion); or only those who admit to being confused about the whole topic; or . . . ? What changes? Or try a "talking stick." Again: what changes?

Chapter 15. Service: Learning by Helping

I usually assign this chapter as we are about to begin service work (usually out of sequence, as we begin working in the shelters early in the term). It does not necessarily need a lot of additional explanation. Some helpful meditative exercises can be found in Dass and Gorman's *How Can I Help?*, pages 81 to 82 and 102 to 103.

On service learning, useful references for teachers are Janet Eyler and Dwight Giles, *Where's the Learning in Service-Learning?* (Jossey-Bass, 1999) and Robert Sigmon and colleagues, *Journey to Service-Learning* (Council of Independent Colleges, 1996).

APPROACHING THE APPLICATION CHAPTERS

These chapters are a fair bit longer than the typical chapter from the Toolbox proper. Often I spend more time on them in class, sometimes with additional readings. There may not be time to cover all of them, so you and/or the class may have to pick and choose.

As noted in the preface, these chapters have a dual task. Like a normal discussion of a given issue, they lay out some background, summarize the values and other matters in controversy, and so on. However, they also have the task of explicitly applying and therefore illustrating and carrying farther various tools from our toolbox—especially the less familiar tools that are seldom used but that can genuinely transform the debate. Each chapter brings forward at least one of these.

You may need to highlight this for your students, at least at first. Despite all of the build-up in the Toolbox proper, I find that a few students still expect that we will have knock-down and drag-out debates when we get to specific issues. At least they expect a survey of contending "positions" on the issues and a cafeteria of arguments for each. I find that it helps to emphasize again that we are really looking for the creative possibilities, the areas of common ground and shared values, ways in which we might more beyond the debate to make some *progress*. (By the way, I also find it useful to be sure that if I bring in any guest speakers, they understand this approach too.)

Chapter 16. Sexuality

Sexuality is not often treated as an "applied ethics" topic, since there is no easily identified and specific controversy that comes readily to mind ("premarital sex" is pretty much a settled question, though I always have some students committed to chastity until marriage; you probably do too). On the other hand, few topics are more on students' minds. In my experience as a college instructor, I would say that students' sexual explorations are sometimes almost as important as anything else they learn at college. Yet we give these relationships very little attention. I think ethics has something deeply important to say about them, and that, for starters, just *talking* about these things is vital symbolically. Sex does not lie outside of ethics—not at all. I find that many students really appreciate taking up this topic in this way.

Others on your campus are probably struggling to get across something of the same message. Consider inviting in someone from the counseling office or Student Life. Make some connections. By this time in their college careers your students have probably heard a lot (not necessarily enough) about date rape, but usually in isolation from any larger and more open-ended ethical issues, such as how we talk (and, even more importantly, *don't* talk) about sex, gender-role expectations, socialized ideas about what sex is, and so on. Date rape is one of the most lethal expressions of these attitudes, but they take many other, everyday forms as well.

Chapter 17. Abortion

This chapter essentially argues for the broad outlines of a moderate position on the abortion question. I do this because it seems to me that such a view flows directly from the toolbox in this case—acknowledging that both sides are partly right, and looking for creative options and ways to reframe the problem. Besides, the abortion issue is *so* painful and "stuck" that I believe it is worth approaching in a different way from the very start, as emphatically and as positively as possible. The first exercise, I hope, helps to counterbalance whatever tension this "advocacy style" may have created for students used to the more neutral presentation in the usual textbooks.

The survey on the next two pages is used by the Common Ground Network for Life and Choice. If you use it, have the class fill it out *before* you assign this chapter (or try it on some other group), since (I hope) reading this chapter might affect how they answer it.

To tabulate the results, divide the answer sheets into three groups: pro-life, pro-choice, and uncertain. Then calculate the average answer for each question for each group. (At my school I have the class answer on opscan sheets and the computer center can produce the averages quickly and easily.) Now compare the averages. Take it that differences of 1.0 or less between the averages are not significant differences. Differences of more than 1.0 show some serious divergence. Ask how many of the twenty-five questions show a significant difference between pro-life and pro-choice groups.

Network organizers find that there is generally much less difference than we are led to believe—and that's among activists on the issue. Using this survey over a number of years, I have seldom had a class differ significantly on more than five questions, usually the same ones. So what about your class, or whatever group you surveyed? Where are the disagreements? How do they compare with the agreements? Go through the questions one by one. They'll be surprised.

Now continue: it is not merely that our agreements are more numerous than our disagreements. We can also use those agreements as starting points for "common ground" problem-solving: that is, for integrating values. Look at the questions on which your class or group agrees. Number 3, perhaps: that reducing the number of abortions is a worthwhile goal? Number 2? What would that suggest? Number 7? Then start working on alternatives! Number 8? Once again you have an agenda—quite likely a *shared* agenda.

Network organizers sometimes use this survey to open their dialogue sessions, and ask people to answer it twice: once for themselves, and once giving the answers they think the "other side" would give. It emerges that both sides think the other side is much more extreme than they really are. Once again it's a useful basis for reframing the problem in the way proposed in this chapter. This usually leads to quite a bit of surprise and discussion too.

Chapter 18. Business and Professional Ethics

Invite in representatives of various business and professional fields to discuss ethical problems in their work. Make up a panel. I have also had very good luck drawing upon people from my school's Career Services office. The second exercise makes an especially good in-class project.

Student groups on this topic often use parts of movies or other videos, looking at ethical tight spots in a number of professions: "The Rainmaker," "Quiz Show," various films highlighting journalists, doctors or nurses, teachers ("Dead Poets' Society"), and others. Don't overlook documentaries either, such as the *Challenger* video cited in the notes to this chapter.

Abortion Attitudes: Survey

Are you: Pro-Life ———
           Pro-Choice ———
           Uncertain ———

Answer each of the following questions on a scale of 1–5, where 1 means *strongly agree* and 5 means *strongly disagree*.

1. Economic constraints make it very difficult for some women to carry their pregnancies to term, or to imagine being able to raise their children.
   1   2   3   4   5

2. Adoption can be a positive choice for structuring family life.
   1   2   3   4   5

3. Reducing the number of abortions is a worthwhile goal.
   1   2   3   4   5

4. Abortion is an appropriate method of birth control.
   1   2   3   4   5

5. To preserve their independence and freedom women sometimes need to have abortions.
   1   2   3   4   5

6. There are acceptable alternatives to abortion currently available.
   1   2   3   4   5

7. Alternatives to abortion should be encouraged.
   1   2   3   4   5

8. In order to reduce the number of abortions, it is important to improve the economic status of women.
   1   2   3   4   5

9. It is inevitable that some of society's problems can only be solved by using violent means.
   1   2   3   4   5

10. Recreational sex without relational commitment is acceptable.
    1   2   3   4   5

11. Women and men are equal in rights, value, and human dignity.
    1   2   3   4   5

12. Motherhood is one desirable full-time career for women.
    1   2   3   4   5

13. The future of children ought to be a major concern of U.S. public and private policy.
    1   2   3   4   5

14. Women and men are equally capable and both should be encouraged to take part in public decision-making roles.

     1   2   3   4   5

15. Spirituality is an important dimension of being human.

     1   2   3   4   5

16. Abortion is an acceptable option for terminating a pregnancy.

     1   2   3   4   5

17. The natural order of things dictates that males are the dominant gender in societal structures.

     1   2   3   4   5

18. Belonging to an organized religious group is an important aspect of full human development.

     1   2   3   4   5

19. In most circumstances a collaborative decision-making process is preferable to having one clearly designated authority figure.

     1   2   3   4   5

20. We cannot always live up to our ideals, because the world of everyday circumstances makes this impossible.

     1   2   3   4   5

21. Fidelity to one sexual partner is preferable to multiple sexual relationship.

     1   2   3   4   5

22. Abortion is a violent procedure for terminating a pregnancy.

     1   2   3   4   5

23. I feel certain about when human life begins.

     1   2   3   4   5

24. It is very difficult to establish a law or rule that can be applied universally and justly in all circumstances.

     1   2   3   4   5

25. Marriage is the proper context for sexual intercourse.

     1   2   3   4   5

Chapter 19. Poverty and Welfare

One reason I take my students into the homeless shelters is that poverty and welfare are usually the subjects they know least about, or at least the subjects where people fly mostly by stereotype. Working in a shelter, meeting people and hearing their stories, even for just a few nights, can make an immense difference. Students get out into the "real world," learn things they could never learn in a classroom, and help out too. They also often have some internal resistance to overcome, which is useful to think about too. Even if you don't require your class to help out, take them on a shelter tour anyway. Some will come back to help, and all will learn something. If nothing else it will demystify the place.

You probably have students in your class who are or have been on welfare. They may or may not want to talk about it. At least be sensitive in your discussion (and remind the class) that this is not just "someone else's" problem. It also may be worth stressing to students that by some criteria they too—even many of the wealthiest—are "on welfare." Discussions will raise strong feelings on all sides: this might be a good time to review the dialogue rules again.

For visitors, draw on local expertise: human services workers, or activists for the homeless, who are sometimes homeless themselves. This will be awkward, but that's exactly the point.

For an in-class exercise, try the following simulation. Try to design a welfare system that you can all live under. Appoint certain groups (by random lot, say, to make it fair) to represent rich people, poor people, middle-class taxpayers, and social-service administrators. Each group should try to speak for its interests, but each group should be realistic too. They can't have everything they want. They should seek a system that all can agree to.

You can deepen and vary this exercise in various ways. A Rawlsian variant: instead of assigning people to known interest groups, ask the students to imagine that they have entered a special kind of moral space in which they *don't know* whether they are rich or poor—they don't know whether they will be supporting the system they are designing, or supported by it. What kind of system will they design then?

You could add another level of impartiality too, also a Rawlsian point. Even if the simulators do not know whether they are rich or poor, they may still come to this choice knowing "who they are" in the sense that they know their age, gender, race, general level of motivation and ability, hopes and fears, and so on. So a young well-educated white male, for example, might feel confident that he could easily work his way out of poverty, and therefore might be tempted to opt for a minimal welfare system that expected people to go out and make it on their own. He might not feel the same way if he could just as easily find "himself" an older person or a minority group member or someone who has never had the opportunity of good schools or family support. More systematic barriers and prejudices might have to be recognized.

So make a list of various people (gender, race, education levels, family support, life situation), representing a good cross-section of the population, and then ask students to imagine that they are designing a welfare system *in which they will potentially play any one of these roles*. They might be a billionaire or a sports superstar or a rich right-wing heiress, but they might also be a middle-aged single mother of three young children or a survivor of an abusive childhood or a physically challenged war veteran or . . . ? What kind of system will they design then?

You can make this more vivid by ending this exercise by assigning roles (I use numbered playing cards) and figuring out how each person will fare under the system they designed.

This simulation is my own variation of an exercise developed by Peter Williams of SUNY-Stony Brook. For another way of modeling the Rawlsian "original position" in the classroom, see James Moulder, "Playing with Justice," *Teaching Philosophy* 10 (1987): 339–344. I am grateful to my colleague Nim Batchelor for this reference.

Chapter 20. Animals

This is one topic that students initially often do not see the point of. There are large measures of avoidance, guilt, and unfamiliarity in the usual responses. Expect this and be patient. Make it a useful teaching moment.

Colin McGinn's challenge to "speciesism" in Chapter 10 has already raised moral questions about our treatment of other animals—though this reading was primarily introduced to illustrate a more general theme. You might want to return to it here for further provocation on the specific topic of ethics and animals, as in the third exercise.

Bring in some vegetarian food (sometimes I cook right in class) or a real-life vegetarian. Sometimes my college's health program sponsors a vegetarian cafeteria in conjunction with health classes—maybe they'll cook for you!

Chapter 21. Environmental Ethics

One way or the other, provoke students to go beyond the usual anthropocentric kind of thinking that takes environmental concern as a kind of species self-interest. You might explicitly pose the question how far such self-interest will take us toward an adequate environmental ethic. It may take us farther than it seems at first, especially when the interests of future human generations are factored in. But does it take us far enough? Most environmental ethicists would say no, and the chapter tries to explain why. Bring in a little poetry; ask students to speak of their own experiences in nature. Make the reasons vivid.

Sometimes I run a "Council of All Beings," a session in which certain students role-play other creatures, who speak to the remaining humans. They offer gifts: "I, lion, give you my roar, the voice to speak out and be heard." "I, lichen, work slowly, very slowly. Time is my friend. I give you patience. . . ." And they speak directly to the humans about how human actions affect them and their chances of survival. This is an evolving form of ritual among certain ecological activists: see John Seed et al., *Thinking Like a Mountain: Toward a Council of All Beings* (New Society Publishers, 1988), or <www.forests.org/ric/deep-eco/>.

The box on "Olam" offers a simulation exercise that is a provocative follow-up to this chapter. Have students divide themselves into groups corresponding to the five possible responses outlined. Each group should prepare to present its case (some groups may need subgroups), after which you can try in discussion to reach some sort of consensus. My classes often end up roughly in the middle.

When they're done, ask them how their proposed Olamian ethic compares with the way we've treated our own Earth. Likely it will be much more ecologically minded and respectful. This is an interesting result already. It's a little as if (as one of my students put it) Olam offers us a "second chance"—a chance to do right what we did so wrong on Earth. But then: why couldn't we begin to do better *now*?

There also is a further twist. Olam actually *is* Earth! Every animal on or feature of Olam is actually an animal on or feature of Earth (whales, octopi, bacteria; the "Gaia Hypothesis," . . .). Sometimes when I have my students do this exercise I play whale songs in the background—they sound truly alien indeed—so this is the time to reveal what they really are. Even the abruptness of our own arrival on Olam is mirrored, more or less, by our evolutionary history here on Earth.

Now ask: what does it mean that the class has (probably!) settled on an ethic for Olam that is so radically out of joint with the kind of ethic we have lived by on our own planet, which actually *is* Olam except for a few details? Does the question of our relation to this earth now seem a little different?

The "expanding circle" theme is also a useful and intriguing note on which to end the course as a whole. It leaves ethics open-ended and intriguing, not fixed or final. In this way the course and book circle back to their beginnings: the need for open minds. Environmental values in particular have changed dramatically just in the last twenty years. That's a pretty good reminder that ethically, as well as every other way, there is always more to learn!

Ask your students how they expect values will continue to change through their lifetimes. Encourage them to help *make* change too. And wish them well.

Index

Page ranges in boldface indicate readings by indexed named writers.